THE

PUBLICATIONS

OF THE

SURTEES SOCIETY

VOL. CXCI

Printed in Great Britain by
Northumberland Press Limited
Gateshead

THE

PUBLICATIONS

OF THE

SURTEES SOCIETY

ESTABLISHED IN THE YEAR

M.DCCC.XXXIV

VOL. CXCI

FOR THE YEARS MCMLXXVI & MCMLXXVII

LOWTHER FAMILY ESTATE BOOKS 1617–1675

EDITED BY

C. B. PHILLIPS

PRINTED FOR THE SOCIETY BY
NORTHUMBERLAND PRESS LIMITED
GATESHEAD
1979

CONTENTS

ACKNOWLEDGEMENTS

The first Viscount Lonsdale recognised A1/4 as *A booke considerable to be kept*. Three centuries later his heir, the Seventh Earl of Lonsdale, has given permission for it, and the other manuscripts, to be printed.

I must thank the Trustees of the Curwen Archives Trust whose generous subvention made possible the printing of this volume.

Bruce Jones, the Cumbria County Archivist, and responsible for the Earl of Lonsdale's muniments, has been an enormous encouragement and help in preparing the present text. For their assistance in construing Sir John's Latin phrases in his Autobiography I am particularly grateful to Dr. J. H. Denton and Dr. A. K. Bowman, my colleagues at Manchester University. Dr. D. R. Hainsworth, of the University of Adelaide, shared his knowledge of the Whitehaven branch of the family with me.

A special tribute is due to Mrs. Hilda Graham who typed almost all the manuscript in draft and final versions with great skill and dedication; my thanks too to Miss E. M. Dychoff. Mr. A. J. Piper, the Secretary of the Surtees Society, and the General Editor have saved me from many mistakes.

Mr. and Mrs. O. R. Bagot, of Levens Hall near Kendal, and the Dean and Chapter of Carlisle kindly made their manuscripts available to me. I am grateful to the staff of the Public Record Office, London, for help with a number of searches there.

The opinions expressed in the introduction, and in the footnotes to the text, are my responsibility, and so are any errors that there may be.

Manchester,
September 1978.

INTRODUCTION

The manuscripts printed here are remarkable not only for what they tell us about the Lowther family, but also for what they tell us about the north as a whole, especially Cumbria and Yorkshire. Of their authors we learn the least about Sir John Lowther of Lowther, knight, who died in 1637. His autobiography (Appendix I) chronicles the rise of a young man lacking wealth or influence. Apart from a flirtation with Buckingham, Lowther continued to value his independence from great patrons, and while a member of the Council of the North from 1626 was never a creature of its most powerful president, Wentworth (p. 229). Careful planning, hardwork and ability underlay Lowther's success, although in the autobiography he undervalues the advantage which his position as heir to a major gentry family gave him. His self-effacing comments on his own progress serve really to magnify rather than to play down his achievements. Through all his life the quality of determination, even ruthlessness, which first enabled him as a young man to outwit his uncles (pp. 210, 220) and latterly led him not to settle any land on his youngest son, William, was probably his greatest asset. His autobiography is of great incidental value when he explains the intrigues which racked his family, and how careful conveyancing in family settlements overcame these; and also for its unique, if highly personal view, of Cumbrian politics in the early seventeenth century. Undoubtedly the most interesting pages are the year by year "diaries" of his son, Sir John Lowther of Lowther, 1st baronet, head of the family from 1637 to 1675[1] (below, pp. 58–74, 152–198 and Appendix III). God and the common law were the twin foundations of his life, and flavour his writings; rarely are the depths of his feelings exposed, as in his tribute to his first wife (p. 62). But precedent did not rule his work as a farmer: he was an early contriver of water meadows, and an advocate of contour ploughing (pp. 234, 241; 239). Improvement and profit were not his only considerations as an estate owner for, amongst other reasons, he planted trees in order to enjoy their beauty (p. 239). Against these pages the more prosaic rentals, accounts and memoranda seem unimportant, even boring! But these were the realities of the Lowther achievement, and the measure, in acres or cash, of two remarkable men.

THE MANUSCRIPTS

The two manuscripts which comprise the bulk of this volume are part of the archives of the Earl of Lonsdale, now in the Cumbria County Record

---

1. Sir John (d. 1637) and Sir John (d. 1675) are referred to in this edition as Sir J.L.(1) and Sir J.L.(2) respectively.

Office, Carlisle; and referred to by their office call numbers, A1/4 and A1/4a.[2] They are paper books bound in the seventeenth century in parchment. They were therefore described by their owners and writers as *the Longe white booke of rents* (A1/4), and *the longe vellume rent booke* (A1/4a).[3] A1/4 is the work of both Sir J.L.(1) and Sir J.L.(2); A1/4a is the work of Sir J.L.(2). A1/4 measures 15 × 49 cm, with a seventeenth-century parchment cover over a fly sheet made from an illuminated medieval manuscript. There is now no trace of the initial letter A by which Sir J.L.(2) identified it in 1657.[4] A label stitched to the spine is in the hand of William Armitage, steward at Lowther from 1738 to 1766, and reads: *Accounts and purchases 1604 to 1655*; there is a later label in the hand of Mr. Barnes, the estate archivist between the wars. A1/4a measures 17 × 45·5 cm, with a seventeenth-century parchment cover initialled by Sir J.L.(2): *J.L.*; there are two parchment ties. Armitage's label reads: *1656–1675 Accounts*; there is no label of later date. Both books were foliated by their authors, except for a few pages at the beginning and end of each book.

None of the material in this volume has been printed before. The Historical Manuscripts Commission Report of 1893 on the Earl's records does not mention these books.[5] A1/4 was clearly known to the estate archivist *c*. 1935, and some unacknowledged references to it are made in the Lowther genealogies of Canon C. M. Lowther Bouch.[6] A1/4a appears to have languished from the mid-eighteenth century until the present editor and Mr. B. C. Jones, the Cumbria County Archivist, identified it in the muniment room at Lowther in 1969.

CONTENT OF THE MANUSCRIPTS

The format here adopted preserves for the reader the essential integrity of these two books: the formal and repetitive material is mostly calendared; the important text, which outlines and explains the growing wealth of the Lowther family in the seventeenth century, is transcribed in full. The material in Appendices I–III is also transcribed in full, and comprises additions by Sir J.L.(1) and Sir J.L.(2) to the sixteenth-century manuscript books of Sir Richard Lowther. A1/4 and A1/4a provided for their authors a compact record of their estates: current rents and receipts, with the essential evidence for the amounts due, and major expenditure on land and the family, all conveniently set out together.

Sir J.L.(1) inherited A1/4 from his father and, like him, used it to record

---

2. For office call numbers see p. xxii, where the manuscripts comprising the appendices are also described.
3. A1/1, ff273v, 285v; on F280v A1/4a is called: *the booke of Memorandums*, see pp. 239, 255, 248 below. In Appendix II A1/4 is called *my great booke*.
4. A1/4a, f227r (p. 152 below).
5. *Thirteenth Report, Appendix VII*.
6. Cf. *CWs*. XLII, p. 75 with A1/4, f93r (p. 40 below); on pp. 72–3 of this article he appears to refer to A1/1, f276v (p. 243 below). Cf. also *CW2*. XLIV, p. 102, with A1/4, f106r (p. 64 below).

the general fines of his customary tenants and subsequent customary
incidents (pp. 11–14). But he also followed his grandfather, Sir Richard
Lowther's habits, displayed in A1/1, and entered valuations and surveys
of his estate for 1617. These records evolved into rentals, and eventually
from 1625 Sir J.L.(1) made a rental for each year, beginning at Martinmas,
and he also began to record receipts of the rents due. New purchases in
a year were noted at the end of a rental. To amplify these annual rentals
Sir J.L.(1) had detailed rentals of his major properties copied into the book,
especially as new properties were purchased, or the rents revised (e.g.
Egleston, 1629, p. 35). Accounts of the crops and stock farmed on the
demesne were also entered in the book. Pleased with his swelling rent roll,
Sir J.L.(1) periodically added up his expenditure on land and the amount
of his personal estate, and worked out the gratifying increase from account
to account. Towards the end of his life these calculations became so frequent
that they amounted to a year-by-year listing of major purchases.

After his father's death Sir J.L.(2) continued to use A1/4, but he
elaborated the recording of the receipts in the annual rentals and from 1656,
in A1/4a, allocated separate pages for rents due and for monies received.
He kept a year by year "diary" of lands purchased, major sums lent on
mortgage, and family payments and important family events, more regularly
written than the autobiography (Appendix I) which his father had infre-
quently compiled. Sir J.L.(2) also kept a second "diary" in parallel, in
which he concentrated on agricultural change at Lowther, and improvements
to and rebuilding of his manor houses (Appendix III). Both "diaries" not
only record, but also explain why, decisions were taken. From the start
Sir J.L.(2) kept a separate book for recording both general and particular
customary fines, and as A1/4 filled up, he turned to other books, especially
to A1/1, to record his summaries of demesne farming (p. 24, n. 96. cf. p. 146).
Otherwise A1/4a is similar in content to A1/4.

Besides these books both father and son were careful to preserve their
family muniments: the endorsements on the documents by both men show
that they read them. As new manors were purchased, both required the
handing over of relevant documents. It was probably Sir J.L.(2) who carried
this interest in such records further and began to abstract the deeds of
properties purchased in the *booke of evidences*; later he required his mortgage
broker in London to make similar abstracts from deeds deposited as security
for money lent (p. xxiii below). Very few of the notebooks of the estate and
manorial officers survive: only three books from Sir J.L.(2)'s time (A1/5,
A1/10 and A1/11, below p. xxii), despite the clear indications of such books
in the receipt entries of the rentals. The receipt entries themselves are an
unusually detailed record of rent payments, throwing light on the conditions
of the tenants, the impact of taxation, and the difficulties in realising the
paper income of a rent roll. Likewise, while A1/4 and A1/4a tell us much
about Sir J.L.(2)'s financial interests, only one of the more detailed debt
books which both men kept survives (A1/9, below p. xxii); certainly A1/4
and A1/4a mention only some of Lowther's financial transactions.

The cross-references to and from entries in A1/4 and A1/4a (e.g. p. 33),
Sir J.L.(2)'s index to A1/4 (pp. 1–4), the references from A1/4 and A1/4a

to the *booke of evidences*, to the debt books and to the fine books, show how central A1/4 and A1/4a were to the Lowther's estate administration, and also how central they are now to understanding the minds which brought about the growth of their estates and capital. To have provided only extracts from A1/4 and A1/4a would have made this edition incomplete and left the reader guessing at omissions; to transcribe every word was unnecessary. The solution is a calendar and transcript.

Most of the annual rentals and the detailed rentals, both customary and leasehold, of individual properties have been calendared, Annual rentals have been transcribed at ten year intervals from 1617, and also the rental for Sir J.L.(2)'s last year beginning Martinmas 1674. The periodical estimates of total wealth have been transcribed, except for the rather bare calculations which Sir J.L.(2) made in his closing years. The annual "diaries" have been transcribed in full. All the records of the customary tenants and of demesne farming have been calendared in sufficient detail to point to their richness.

The voluminous deeds, abstracts, letters and other records of the Lowther archive have helped the editor to elucidate the text, especially that of Appendix I, and so footnote references have been supplied to the more important of such muniments; such references are not normally given for properties held only on mortgage.

THE LOWTHER FAMILY

The achievement of the two Lowthers whose books are here printed needs to be measured against a longer perspective than their own lives. Sir J.L.(2) may have been the thirtieth knight in an ancient family, but that family was financially weak in 1617; later the succession in the male line was to change twice, but there was always another branch of the family to carry on the family name as the outline pedigree shows.[7]

In the later sixteenth century Sir Richard Lowther's involvement in national politics through the Border situation cost him much and gained little reward. More seriously, his relationship with his eldest son was bad; the two quarrelled to an extent which endangered the survival of the family. The achievements of Sir J.L.(1) when he succeeded in 1617 were twofold: firstly, he restored and increased the family's prosperity; secondly, he produced three able sons, whose careers must now be briefly followed in turn.

Sir J.L.(2), the eldest son, inherited all his father's lands and estates except that in the manor of St. Bees; his life can be followed in this volume. His eldest son John died before him, a relief to his father who worried about his lifestyle (pp. 171, 179). Sir J.L.(2)'s grandson was created Viscount Lonsdale, but his two sons died without male heirs, and that title with them. Sir J.L.(2)'s baronetcy, and the Lowther estates, passed to the descendants of his son Richard, and after the extinction of the Whitehaven branch in 1755 the joint wealth of the two branches warranted the creation of the Earldom of Lonsdale. When the Earl died in 1802 his estate passed to the

---

7. There are brief accounts of Sir Richard Lowther, and of John, Viscount Londsdale, in *D.N.B*; detailed pedigree: Appendix IV.

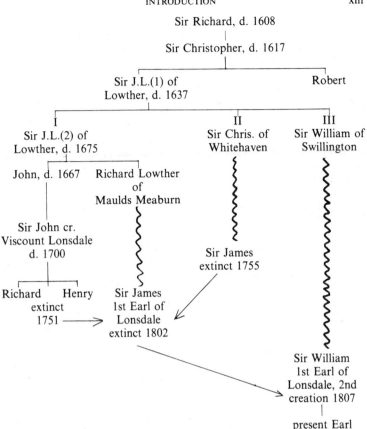

descendants of Sir J.L.(1)'s third son, William of Swillington.[8] So for the long-term welfare of the family all Sir J.L.(1)'s sons were important. Sir Christopher of Whitehaven died in 1644, and after a long minority his remarkable son Sir John (d. 1705) greatly enhanced the considerable estates which Sir Christopher had inherited with his wife and from his father.[9] Sir William Lowther of Swillington founded the third branch, chiefly on the profits of trade, and sometimes in partnership with Sir J.L.(2).

There were other branches of the family, as Appendix IV shows, but none of their estates passed back to the main line of the family; indeed, most of these branches died out in the male line or descended into obscurity. Yet other younger sons, while successful in their own lifetimes, left no descendants.

---

8. Based on G.E.C., *Complete Peerage, sub* Lonsdale.
9. See Hainsworth.

Sir J.L.(1) may therefore be regarded as the most remarkable member of the family. His life can be summarised as follows: born 1581/82, died 1637; married on 2 February 1601/2 Ellinor, daughter of William Fleming of Rydal Hall (Westmorland) esquire. Educated at the Inner Temple 1599–1609, when called to the bar. Escheator of Cumberland and Westmorland 1610, justice of the peace 1616, member of Parliament for Westmorland 1623–1628, knighted 1626 and then made a member of the Council of the North, deputy-lieutenant of Westmorland 1627.

His initial estate was the manor of Meaburne, worth £72 per annum; he raised £1,850 capital on this by enfranchising the tenants and selling wood. He estimated that his income from the law in his early days never exceeded £150 a year (pp. 27, 212). He inherited a gross income of £710 from his father in 1617, less £220 in annuities. These were the foundations on which he funded an increasing fortune in both personal and real estate. His appointment to the Council of the North raised his legal income to something like £300 a year (pp. 32, 40, 44–50), and by this time (1626) he had virtually doubled his landed estates (pp. 25–7). Otherwise we know little of the details of Lowther's fund raising, except the profits sometimes made from demesne farming. Mortgages and, after 1630, the trading ventures of his sons Christopher and William, provided most of his income. One such venture involved £2,300 capital in a ship sailing from Hull to Hamburg (p. 40). The following table showing income and capital growth sets out the results of these efforts: Sir J.L.(1) added estates worth over £1,200 a year to the family's inheritance, and left his eldest son a personal estate of £2,700.[10]

Sir J.L.(2) followed very much in his father's footsteps. He was born in 1605 and died in 1675; he married in 1626 Mary daughter of Sir Richard Fletcher of Hutton-in-the-Forest (Cumberland), and in 1652 Elizabeth, widow of Woolley Leigh esquire of Norfolk. Lowther was admitted to the Inner Temple in 1621 and called to the bar in 1630. He was a justice of the peace, deputy lieutenant, member of Parliament in 1627–28 and 1660 for Westmorland, and sheriff of Cumberland in 1661.[11] His financial beginnings were carefully recorded by his father (pp. 4–6), and by himself (pp. 51–5). His jointure estate was initially worth £188 a year, but he sold £58 of this. From 1630 he practised law in York with his father and earned as much as £250 a year (p. 40); it is not clear that he practised after inheriting the estate, although he held legal offices.[12] Between 1629 and the death of his father he purchased further property worth £319 a year, and had amassed a personal estate of £2,600. This augured well, and Sir J.L.(2) proved himself able to match his father's abilities.

---

10. P. 59 below. At 8% and allowing for the war, this was almost enough to pay his father's legacies without the aid of the estates assigned to finance them. His father's other debts were mortgages from which Sir J.L.(2) benefited.

11. The Cliffords and their descendants were hereditary sheriffs of Westmorland.

12. Steward for the King, the Bishop of Carlisle and the Earl of Annandale; Recorder of Kendal (below, p. 83; A1/4, f115v) and Recorder of Appleby (WMB Appleby).

Income, capital growth and accumulation 1617–1675

p. ef.	date	*landed income p.a.* £		*from "diary" entries* *land purchased*		*family expen- diture*	*stock* £	*increase of stock, over expenditure, from last account* £
16	1623	824					5,320	
18	1624	935					6,117	
22	1625						5,700	
27	1627			12,455 (1617–1627)		1,000	6,000	
28	1628			3,617			4,000	1,617
37	1633	1,846		6,090			6,300	8,390
39	1634/35			2,548			5,800	2,048
40	1635/36			1,300			5,000	2,400
	1636/37	2,024		2,075				
				28,085		1,000		
59	Residue of Sir J.L.(1)'s stock, all debts & legacies paid:						£2,700	
	Sir J.L.(2)'s personal estate:						2,600	
							5,300	
					legacies, Civil War losses			
10	1653	2,500*		6,752	7,750	7,650	11,800	28,652
	reversion	250	(Mother)					
		2,750						
111	1659			11,313		1,850	20,507	21,870
148	1664	3,983*		9,837		11,690	28,565	28,222
	reversion	500	(Yanwath & Son)					
		4,483		27,902		21,190		
149	1668	4,837*		7,174		2,600	investment capital only[1]	
	reversion	250	(Yanwath)				20,000 at 6%[2]	
		5,087					24,000 at 5%	
150	1672[3]	5,201*		1,173		3,300	40,000 at 6%	
							48,000 at 5%	
				36,249		27,090		

Includes a sum for casual profits from customary tenants.
. The nature of the entries in the MSS change at this point.
. These totals are alternatives, as Lowther seems to have used both rates of interest.
. There is no clear statement of income, by Lowther, after this date, nor of personal estate. No probate inventory is known.

Sir J.L.(2)'s years at Lowther began with a dispute over his father's will and settlements, primarily about the gift of St. Bees to Sir Christopher Lowther of Whitehaven, but also involving a disagreement with his mother over her jointure and share of the personal estate (pp. 58–9). These early divisions persisted: as far as these books tell us Sir J.L.(2) had very little contact with Sir Christopher, and after his death in 1644 was not a trustee of young Sir John Lowther. Subsequently only two financial transactions involving Sir John of Whitehaven are recorded by Sir J.L.(2), compared with his considerable involvement with his brother Sir William. However, Sir J.L.(2)'s stepdaughter did marry Sir John of Whitehaven. There are traces of the same dispute in Sir J.L.(2)'s comments on his mother's will (p. 161). But if these divisions persisted, they were never exploited; if there was little co-operation, there was also little rivalry. Sir J.L.(2) worked well with his brother William (see his comment on p. 184) and his uncle Robert in a number of financial matters. Moneylending and mortgages were Lowther's main interests besides his estates, but he did invest in trade—some £3,700 with son Christopher and more with his brother Sir William (p. 151)—and he also developed an interest in the Yorkshire alum industry.

Like his father Sir J.L.(2) founded two more branches of the family out of his estate, which in land totalled over £5,000 per annum and in personal estate was in excess of £50,000 at his death. Richard Lowther, his only surviving son by his first marriage, was given lands with the manor of Meaburn as a seat; Ralph, the eldest son of the second marriage, received the Yorkshire estates of Marton and Tolsby.

THE LOWTHER FAMILY IN SEVENTEENTH-CENTURY CUMBRIA

In 1600 the Lowthers were one of a number of important gentry families in Cumbria. By 1700 Viscount Lonsdale, and Sir John Lowther of Whitehaven, individually, probably exceeded the wealth of any other local family. They also closely rivalled the Howard Earls of Carlisle and Sir Christopher Musgrave in national politics and affairs at London.[13] But this London influence was largely the work of the Viscount, Sir J.L.(2)'s grandson, and Sir John of Whitehaven; Sir J.L.(2)'s main interests were in Westmorland and his estates.

The economic pre-eminence of the Lowthers of Lowther began with Sir J.L.(1), and most of his land purchases were in Cumbria (£18,000 out of £28,000 capital), so that the wealth of the family was largely invested in Cumbria. Indeed Sir J.L.(1) points (p. 230) with pride, to the local economic stimulus which their efforts at Whitehaven gave the west coast. Nevertheless, by 1642, with £1,094 of the Lowther landed inheritance of £2,511 coming from outside Cumbria, the geography of their economic interests was widening. When Sir J.L.(2) died roughly half of the income from estates of inheritance came from outside Cumbria. In Yorkshire, Marton and Wensleydale were the main centres of accretion.[14] Furthermore, while we know little about Sir J.L.(1)'s moneylending activities in detail, Sir J.L.(2)

13. See *D.N.B.*, *sub nomine*.
14. See Map II and pp. 37, 40.

began to lend money outside Cumbria in the sixteen-fifties in partnership with his brother William. From 1660 this trend accelerated as the London scrivener George Perryer handled more of Lowther's money. With the purchase of estates and the lending of money outside Cumbria the Lowthers might be considered an economic drain on the region, the more so as Sir J.L.(2)'s daughters all took their marriage portions and social connections into Yorkshire.

But of course the lands acquired outside Cumbria produced their own income to fund such enterprises, while Sir J.L.(2) continued to buy suitable land in Cumbria and certainly to lend money there. Between 1650 and his death, over £12,000 lent in Cumbria is recorded in the "diary" alone; in 1674 his estates of inheritance closely centred on Lowther were worth £2,396 a year[15]; other Cumbrian estates were situated in the lower valley of the Lune, and at Thwaites. In addition, the rebuilding at Lowther, and the agricultural improvement of his estates, the full cost of which is not given in these books, brought further work and prosperity to the area. More importantly, Sir J.L.(1) was chiefly a Cumbrian resident, and Sir J.L.(2) spent even more time in the region, and, as his comment at his second marriage indicates, appreciated his Cumbrian, northern lifestyle (p. 68). Thus the controlling influence of the Lowther fortune between 1617 and 1675 remained in Westmorland.

This introduction serves only to point to the variety of the family's economic interests; it cannot do justice to other Cumbrian families with similar interests nor can it analyse or assess in full the significance of the material presented. But the manuscripts which follow contain, and largely explain, the decisions which brought about the growth of the Lowther family estates and wealth between 1617 and 1675.

---

15. See Map I, which omits Asby, Plumpton and Threlkeld.

EDITORIAL CONVENTIONS

The overriding aim of the editor has been to do as little violence to the originals as possible.

TYPE FACES
The text is presented in roman, and the calendar in italics; text quoted in footnotes is also in italic type.

ORIGINAL HANDS IN THE TEXT
The manuscripts were written by many hands, with minor exceptions only those of Sir J.L.(1) and Sir J.L.(2) have been identified in the present volume; other hands are described as unknown. Changes of hand are noted. Changes in style of the same hand, and in inks used by the same hand, are also noted where significant.

CONTRACTIONS
Contractions have been expanded silently save in a few cases where it seems desirable to indicate the letters supplied by putting them in italic.

PUNCTUATION AND SPELLING
Original punctuation and spelling have been retained. Stops and capital letters to end and begin sentences have been inserted to make the sense clear where it is otherwise in doubt. All place and personal names have been capitalised. Where *i* has been used for *j j* is given in transcript, and *ii* for *y* has been rendered as y. *ye* and *the* are both used in the MSS, but have been standardised to the in this edition; *Li* has been printed as £. Spelling and abbreviation in the manuscript are inconsistent, noticeably so for: besides, particular, Thrimby and ancestor.

ALTERATIONS TO THE MANUSCRIPT
All these books were used as working manuscripts, and therefore much altered; further comments were sometimes added, or matter deleted, by the authors at a later date. Most alterations are, however, nearly contemporary with the original form. In this edition words or letters which have been altered or deleted so as now to be illegible or nonsensical are indicated in transcript thus: (*erasure*). Words which have been deleted but remain legible are transcribed *in situ* within brackets thus: ⟨Lowther⟩; figures which have been altered so that the original is still legible are usually indicated by

footnote. Major insertions into, and subsequent additions to, the text are identified by footnotes; words which have been interlined are indicated thus: (*interlined*: Lowther), the first bracket coming after the word preceding the interlineation, the final bracket indicating the end of the interlineation.

ARRANGEMENT OF THE TEXT

Where a page of text is divided into parallel columns of words, the columns are here printed sequentially rather than in parallel, unless the layout of the text dictates the preservation of the parallel columns (as the 1647 rental does, pp. 77–84 below). The three rentals transcribed from A1/4a comprise rents due (verso in text; l.h. page here) and monies received (recto in text; r.h. page here) on facing pages of this edition (beginning on pp. 88–9, on pp. 112–13 and on pp. 130–31 below). Otherwise the basic layout of the text has been maintained so far as practicable, but the original lines and spacing have been compressed as much as the text permits.

DATING

In transcript *May 65* has been rendered May [16]65 to differentiate dates and figures; dates in the year before 25 March have been left as they are. In the introduction and calendar however, the year is taken to begin on 1 January: dates before 25 March are referred to thus: 1 February 1624/25.

CALENDARED RENTALS OF INDIVIDUAL ESTATES

The number of tenants given is the number of names in the rental, this figure may be swollen when the same person holds more than one tenancy.

PLACE NAMES

In the calendar the spelling of place names has been standardised, where possible, with the forms in the Cumbrian volumes of the English Place Name Society (see p. xx below), or, for other areas, with *Bartholomew's Gazetteer*. In transcript the original spelling has been retained, but initial letters have been capitalised.

CROSS REFERENCES TO DEEDS AND PERSONS IN FOOTNOTES

When the purchase of a manor, or purchase of the first part of a manor, is recorded, a footnote refers to deeds and other significant archive material, including abstracts from the *booke of evidences*. Subsequent transactions for that manor, rentals, or surveys, are cross referenced to that note. Most manorial deeds were kept in Lowther in boxes named by manor, footnote references here give manor name, box number (roman) and bundle number (arabic) thus: Helton B[ox].I.[bundle]6, is Helton B.I.6.

Persons are identified in footnotes only where such identification adds to the context. Where the text is not explicit, references to members of the Lowther family, who often have the same Christian names, are given by their number on the detailed pedigree (Appendix IV) thus: P.2.

BOOKS

All books cited are published at London, unless otherwise indicated.

ABBREVIATIONS

GENERAL

B.	[Manor] Box
col.	Column [of text]
C.R.O.	Cumbria County Record Office, Carlisle
C.R.O.K.	Cumbria County Record Office, Kendal
CW2	*Transactions of the Cumberland and Westmorland Antiquarian and Archaeological Society*, new series
CWPRS	That society's parish register section
D.C.C.	Dean and Chapter of Carlisle
D.N.B.	*Dictionary of National Biography*
E.P.N.S.	English Place Name Society. Their Cumbrian volumes are: *The Place Names of Cumberland*, (3 vols) ed. A. M. Armstrong *et al.*, (E.P.N.S., XX, XXI, XXII, 1950–52); *The Place Names of Westmorland*, (2 vols) ed. A. H. Smith, (E.P.N.S., XLII, XLIII, 1967)
E.D.D.	*English Dialect Dictionary*, ed. Joseph Simpson
Hainsworth	*The Commercial Papers of Sir Christopher Lowther 1611–1614*, ed. D. R. Hainsworth. Surtees Society Publications, CLXXXIX, 1977
H.M.C.	Historical Manuscripts Commission
l.h.	left hand
Levens Hall MSS	Manuscripts of Mr. & Mrs. O. R. Bagot, Levens Hall, nr. Kendal
MS(S)	Manuscript(s)
N&B	J. Nicolson & R. Burn, *The History and Antiquities of the Counties of Westmorland and Cumberland*, (2 vols; 1777)
Nightingale, *Ejected*	B. Nightingale, *The Ejected of 1662 in Cumberland and Westmorland. Their Predecessors and Successors*, (2 vols, continuous pagination; Manchester, 1911)
O.E.D.	*Oxford English Dictionary*
P. PP.	Number or numbers of the pedigree, Appendix IV
p. pp.	page(s)
Phillips, Thesis	C. B. Phillips, "The Gentry in Cumberland and Westmorland, 1600–1665", (unpublished University of Lancaster Ph.D. thesis, 1973)

P.R.O.	The Public Record Office, London
r.h.	right hand
Sir J.L.(1); Sir J.L.(2)	Sir John Lowther of Lowther, knt. died 1637; Sir John Lowther of Lowther, Bt., died 1675
Surtees Soc. vol. LXVIII	*Selections from the Household Books of Lord William Howard of Naworth Castle*, [ed. G. Ornsby] Surtees Society Publications, LXVIII, 1878
V.C.H. Yorks N.R.	*The Victoria History of the County of York: North Riding*, ed. W. Page, (2 vols; 1914, 1923; index vol. 1925)

RECORD OFFICE MANUSCRIPT CALL NUMBERS

THE PUBLIC RECORD OFFICE, London
Chancery:

C2	Chancery Proceedings, Series I
	Chancery Proceedings, Six Clerk's Series, before 1714:
C5	Bridges' Division
C6	Collins' Division
C8	Mitford's Division
C10	Whittington's Division
C78	Decree Rolls
C54	Close Rolls

Court of Wards:

Wards 9	*Miscellanea*: Account Books

Exchequer:

E112	Exchequer court, bills and answers

Prerogative Court of Canterbury:

PROB 11	Registers of Wills (These records were recently transferred from Somerset House)

State Paper Office:

SP.14	State Papers, Domestic, James I

THE CUMBRIA COUNTY RECORD OFFICES, Carlisle and Kendal

D/Lons/L, D/Lons/W	Earl of Lonsdale's MSS, Lowther and Whitehaven offices, respectively
D/MH	Documents collected by Mr. Mounsey-Heysham
WD/Ry	Manuscripts of the Fleming family of Rydal Hall
WMB	Borough records

LIST OF LOWTHER MANUSCRIPT BOOKS CITED

All call numbers begin D/Lons/L

A1/1	Estate and general memoranda book, 1557–1673, mainly of Sir Richard Lowther
A1/2	Eighteenth-century transcript of A1/1, ff.270–285
A1/3	Account book 1569–1608, 1634
A1/4	Books of accounts, memoranda and rentals, 1604–1656/7
A1/4a	Continuation of A1/4, 1657–1675
A1/5	Steward's account book 1626, 1638–1674
A1/6	Estate and family memoranda book of Sir Richard Lowther, 1558–*c*. 1670 (a book of evidence)
A1/7	Estate accounts and general memoranda book 1558–1635, 1650. Much copied from A1/1
A1/8	Book intended for Sir J.L.(2)'s general fines, 1637; includes notes re customary tenants
A1/9	Sir J.L.(1)'s law notes, *c*. 1612; used as Sir J.L.(2)'s debt book 1661–1675
A1/10	Receipt book of the bailiff of the manor of Thwaites 1651–1662
A1/11	Steward's pocket book (William Atkinson) 1668–1691

un-numbered:

Note book of Sir William Lowther of Swillington (cr. Earl of Lonsdale 1807); genealogical notes
Sheriff's memoranda book 1660–1661
Fine book 1648–1698
Book Z: book of evidence, Barony of Burgh accounts
Book of evidence 1668–1675

THE BOOKS OF EVIDENCE

Three books of this period now extant fulfilled this function, each book with a different use.

A1/6 was begun as a book of evidence by Sir Richard Lowther in 1573, and then later used to record abstracts of deeds of lands purchased by Sir J.L.(1). It is not clear that Sir. J.L.(1) made these abstracts, and certainly some and possibly all were written by Sir J.L.(2). The latest acquisition for which there is an abstract is Kirkby Lonsdale, taken as security in 1667, but these entries did not fill the book although no further abstracts were entered.

Book Z, so called from an initial letter on its parchment front cover, is a copy by a John Lowther of the 1573 evidences listed for Sir Richard Lowther in A1/6; some other material from A1/6 is also copied. An imitation of the sixteenth century hand is used for the 1573 list. The abstracts of lands purchased by Sir J.L.(1) and Sir J.L.(2) are copied in a different, neat, uniform hand, annotated by Sir J.L.(2). Book Z thus contains all the abstracts in A1/6, and one or two other deeds. It also contains abstracts of deeds held for security with properties mortgaged after 1667, and these are not in A1/6. Sir J.L.(2) also frequently annotated these abstracts.

The 1668–1675 Book—the title is from Mr. Barnes' label—does not overlap at all in content with A1/6, but does contain some material found in Book Z. It includes abstracts of deeds and copy indentures of mortgaged properties dated between 1668 and 1675, and abstracts of deeds and other documents relating to Nether Worsall which was purchased in 1666 after an earlier mortgage (p. 178); most are not in Book Z.

Sir J.L.(2) makes only three references to these books. In 1654 he refers to abstracts of the Short Wood property in *the booke of the Evidences in the White velum cover* (p. 171). Both A1/6 and Book Z contain such abstracts and fit the description; the 1668–1675 Book clearly is not that referred to. Why would Lowther need two such books, and why get a John Lowther to copy A1/6? Was this an educational exercise for John the first Viscount Lonsdale, or do Sir J.L.(2)'s initials: *J.L.* on the first page indicate that he was the copyist as well as the owner of the book? Certainly the copying into Book Z of abstracts in the same order as those written in A1/6 suggests a post-1667 date for at least some of the copies in Book Z, and perhaps therefore an exercise for the first Viscount. If the date of Book Z is post-1667, then A1/6 is the book referred to in 1654.

The second reference is in 1672 to *the Greate Booke of evidences* (p. 194), a title which only Book Z merits, on both grounds of its size and its comprehensive content. The abstracts in Book Z include those of mortgaged properties for which Thomas Massam acted as Sir J.L.(2)'s broker, but none for which George Perryer acted as broker—except for two instances when Massam and Perryer acted together. Book Z might be Massam's book. But the amount of annotation by Sir J.L.(2), the presence of Sir J.L.(2)'s initials and the presence of abstracts of deeds back to the 1573 list, as well as of abstracts from transactions with which Massam was not concerned, suggests that this was Lowther's book rather than Massam's.

The third reference to these important books was made in 1675 in connection with the mortgage of the manor of Drayton Bassett, arranged by George Perryer (p. 198). The entry mentions that *securities mentioned in the booke of the severall securities were left in Mr Peryers custodie in the chest*. Drayton Bassett is only mentioned in the 1668–1675 Book. The abstracts for another transaction managed by Perryer, written in the book, are endorsed thus: *These writings are together in a black box in my custody 21 July 1668. George Perryer*. Sir J.L.(2)'s annotations are legion, and the abstracts include some for a mortgage handled by Thomas Massam as broker.

Clearly then Sir J.L.(2) used all three of these books and one of his brokers, Perryer, at least read the abstracts. The importance of the deeds abstracted in them derives firstly from the fact that not all the originals are now known, and secondly that the abstracts show the important role of the mortage as a preliminary to purchase in the acquisition of land by both Sir J.L.(1) and Sir J.L.(2). Footnote references in the present text to these abstracts are made to A1/6 rather than to Book Z, where entries are common to both books.

TABLE OF FEAST DAYS

The feasts most frequently used for dating are given here in the order of the Lowther rent year which from 1625 began at Martinmas. Feasts marked * are not used in the rentals, but are used elsewhere in the books.

Feast	Abbreviations, etc.	Date
Martinmas	M., Mar., Mart., Martimas	11 November
St. Andrew		30 November
*St. Thomas	St. Tho.	21 December
*Christmas	Xmas., Christen., Nativitie	25 December
Candlemas	K., Kand., Kandles., Cannd., Cand	2 February
Annunciation	Ann., Ladie Day	25 March
*St. George		23 April
*May Day		1 May
Whitsun	Whis., Whitsuntide., Penticoste	7th Sunday after Easter
Midsummer Day	Mid. Som., Midsor	24 June
St. James	St. Ja. tide	25 July
Lammas Day	Lam	1 August
*St. Matthew		21 September
Michaelmas	Mi., Mich.	29 September

SIR JOHN LOWTHER (d. 1637)'s GREAT BOOK

D/Lons/L, A1/4[1]

Unknown hand]

Accounts and jottings of Sir Christopher Lowther, 1604.	1r
The like, 1603.	1v
The like, 1603; includes accounts of cloth and lace purchased by Edward Cooke, the last of March [1604] at Coventry.	2r
A list of wages paid [n.d., c. 1603].	2v

Hand of Sir J.L.(2)]

An Alphabeticall table for most of the ⟨most⟩ materiall things in the booke

A   Admittances of Tennants in Lowther upon casual changes by death or Alienacion: fol:34a.

Accompt of profit per stockinge fol: 68b.

B   Bampton parsonage fol.45. a

Bampton rentall Mart [16]41.fol:50a and 95b

Boones services of the tenants f5

C   Sir Henry Curwens estate as valued fol.8b

Consideracion of improvement of estate and what spent and saved fol.13b made good for the time vide fol.42b vide fol 54a. vide fol 93 resolution upon it.

Crosby fines paid upon there purchase fol.32a.

Fines upon changes fol.40.

Crosby rental 1628 as paid fol.49

Courts the perquisits fol.57b

Cattle bought vide fol. 58b et 81 fol 62b fol64b

   1630 fol 35 ab

Corne sowne fol 60 a

Clifton rentall 1648—fol 127a

Clifton services foll ibidem

D   (blank)

E   Egleston Abbey purchases fol 67a

A rentall of Egleston foll 72[2]a b.

---

1. Parchment flysheet endorsed by the 1st Viscount Lonsdale: *A booke considerable to be kept; begininge in the tyme of Sir Christopher Lowther and continewed by Sir John Lowther his son and by Sir John Lowther Bart the grandson.* When Sir J.L.(2) took over this book he called it his Long White Book of Rents.
2. Altered to 72 from 42.

2v *cont.*   Estate reall and personall fol 65b my fathers estate fol 13b.
 F   Fines paid by the severall tenants of Lowther Hackthrop and Helton to Sir Chr Lowther 1608 fol et 17 foll. 28
    Fee farme rents paid out of the severall lordships fol.82

3r [*Unknown hand*] *List of receipts from the Annunciation 1603.*

3v [*Unknown hand*] Item Received of my mother at the Annunciation in the yeare of our Lord 1609   £V

[*Hand of Sir J.L.(2)*] *The index, continued from f2v.*
 G   (*Blank*)
 H   Hackthropp rental 1654 fol.41a
    Household stuffe delivered 1632 f82b
    Household stuffe bought by my father at my grandfathers death fo.42.b.
    Helton generall fine paid to my father Sir Jo Lowther fol 29b
    Helton casuall fines upon admittance f. (*blank*)
    Helton in question but cleared by a fine leavyed by mee quo vide.
    Hirdship at Buckholme fol.61.a, and for 1649 vide fol.70.b.
    Horse grasses the particular rates in New Parke fol.78.
      Stocke of horses fol.95.a.
    Helton rentall purchased of Mr Sandford, f: 130a[3]
    Helton boone plowes as cast for our old part fol 39a
 I   Inventory of my Grandfather Sir Chr Lowthers goods fol:25.a
 K   Kentmyre price 12b
    Knipe admittance of tenants, fol.40a
    Knipe rentall 1630 fol.49.b
 L   Lowther note of services due per the tenants fol.5to
    Lowther demesne surveyed and the particulars measured fol.7.b
    Lowther generall fines assessed by my father upon my grandfathers death fol.28.b
    And the rentall fol. ibidem 28.b: for 1654 fol:44:a
    Lowther and Hackthropp yearely value 1654 foll 7a[4]
    Lowther parsonage the vallue yearely fol 39 the further page beeing twice 39:
 M   Maske rentall as purchased 143a
    Meaburne purchases fol 14:b
    Mirkmire bought fol.42.b.
    Marton purchase as 92 b
    Marton Rentall as purchased fol: 96.b
    Marriage the time and estate settled thereupon f.102b
    Marton Rentall 1648 fol.130.b
    Marton goods in the house of myne foll.131:a
    Melkintropp rentall for 1654 foll 40 b
 N   Newton fines assessed by my father Sir John Low. at my grandfathers death fol.27.b

3. The whole of this line inserted in another ink by Sir J.L.(2).
4. The two entries here relating to 1654 are later insertions in the hand of Sir J.L.(2).

Newton rentall Mart [16]47 fol.127.b   3v *cont.*
Nuntropp rentall 1654 fol 60:b.

Unknown hand] *Receipts, from the feast of St. Philip and St. James, 1604.*   ▮4r
Hand of Sir J.L.(2)] *The index continued from f3v.*   4v

O   (*Blank*)
P   Parson holme in m*y* fathers possession and valued fol 13a vide fol.41.b
     Penrith land fol 41b
     Purchases 1627 by my father fol.66.b 1633 fol 91a
     Purchases by me upon and after my fathers death fol.102.b
     Plumpton purchas foll 108a
     Plumpton rentall as paid for the parke (*erasure*) fol 10a and of
     Plumpton Heade and fogage as given into mee foll 11b.
Q   Parsonage of Lowther, the value and particulers foll 39b
     Preston Greate and Astley, the particulers fol 140 141
R   Reagill grange measures fol.8.a the purchase fol.45.a
     A rentall of Lowther Hackthropp Meaburne, Helton Newton demesne
     at my fathers entry to his estate 7b
     Rentalls as lett and valued 1618; 1619 fol 12a 13a 16a 1621 fol 42,
     1623 fol 43a 1624 b. 1625 fol 61a, 1628 a. Generall rentall fol.71 ab.
     a generall rental fol. 91a fol 97a fol 100 b at my fathers death
     fol 100 b
     Rentalls generall after my fathers death death 1638 fol.112a f.114 b
     for 1641 fol.118.b. for 1643 a. for 1646 fol. 123a for 1647 fol. 124.b.
     for 1648 fol. 128.b.
     Rents paid out of all our lands fol. 82.a.
     Rosgill Rentall as purchased 1655 foll 37a[5]
S   Sleddall purchased fol.12.b. 82a.
     Stock of good*s* 1621 fol.15a, 1617.27a stocke of sheep and cattle fol 43a.
     Sleddall rentall fol:47. for 1647 vide fol. 128.b.
     Shap Tyth rent as purchases [*sic*] fol 47b
     Sleddall fines paid there fol.56.b.
     Sheep stock vide fol 58a fol 76a
     Servant wages 1629 fol.69. for 1649. fol. 70.b
     Saint Bees fol.73a.
     Services paid by the Tennants and their diett f:5.
     Cowper tenement in Sledall purchased by mee f 108b[6]
     Strickland parva services first foll of 39.b.
     Strickland parva the rentall as purchased fol ibidem.
T   Thrimby admittances and harriot paid fol.39.a.
     Threlkeld purchases 1624 fol.44.a [*recte* 41].
     Thirmby Rentall fol.46.b.
     Thwaites as valued f 91a
     Thorpe in Surrey rentall fol.145.a

---

5. This entry an insertion [in the hand of Sir J.L.(2)].
6. A like insertion.

4v *cont.*   Thrimby Grange Perticuler and boons f.47.a
    U   (*Blank*)
    W   Wenesladaile purchase of Mr Moore fol.95.b.
         Wenesladale rentall 1638.fol.113.b. for 1640 fol.116:a. for 1647. fol.
         126:a.
    Y   Yeanewith rentall as delivered by my Cousen Dudley Martinmas 1655
    33 fol 33b.[7]

5r [*Unknown hand*] *A receipt for 40 todd of wool, £58, St. Matthew's day* [*21
    September*] *1604.*

5v [*Hand of Sir J.L.(1)*] *A note of the services performed by the tenants of Lowther,
    Hackthorpe and Helton, listed for each manor; includes the manor of Whale.
    * [*Continued with annotations in the hand of Sir J.L.(2).*]

6r [*Unknown hand*] *Note of receipts since St. George's day* [*23 April*] *1605.*

    [*Hand of Sir J.L.(1)*] (*The note of provisions for John Lowther in 1629 is divided
    in the text into two parallel columns, the r.h.col. reads on from the l.h.col. For
    ease of arrangement the columns are here given consecutively, l.h. first.*)

A Remembrance how my sonne John Lowther was provided when he did
goe to Hackthropp howse to begin for himself at Martinmasse 1629.[8]

Look my	
wifes book	
he had 6 horses	£18
360 shepe	90
140 more shepe	35
8 oxen	35
3 kine	7
Plate of his owne and his sonnes	15
Money in his purse	30
The Easg[9] K and L	60
Rent dew from me and Giles[10] for Hackthropp Sleddale Shapp and Threlkeld	105
Linnin and other things for his house, ⟨besideș⟩ clothes and Bootes	35
Total £430	
Lent by me in money to buy him seede	20
Hay straw and fogge to make his crops above	20
6 Oxen to plow with	27
Househould stuffe and necessaries of myne left him to use at Hackthropp untill I call for them which I intend not as yet	20

Borrowed £87
(*erasures*)

---

7. *33b* altered, *33* written in l.h. margin.
8. Compare this with Sir J.L.(2)'s comments, below p. 51 *et seq.*
9. Very difficult to read, so this is uncertain!
10. i.e. Giles Moore, Sir J.L.(1)'s steward.

Given him 22 shepe Bear[11] Swine meall pultrie—[12] etc.   7[13]   6r *cont.*

total stock	£524
use theirof for a year	42
his land at present	190

Total	232

(*r.h.col.*) His forecast by my direction to rayse upon this besides maintenance is or may be as followeth

wooll and draught shepe	£40
graseing and brede of cattle to be bought with this stock	40
Agistment at Sleddale	15
Corne (*interlined*: more then) to pay for his crop makeing and his yeres expence and wages (*erasure*)	40
Davie,[14] to salve his sheep, and buy trifles	(*blank*)
Threlkeld rent at present £50 hereafter 60	50

totall like to increase	185

out of which deducting for their expence in money though they
thinke they will live of lesse: 55
then[15] may then stick by addited of this remanet of   £100
be made up   530
and their totall expence will be upon themselves there   131
which I doubt will not serve though they be reasonable,

(*The page is still divided into two columns, but all that follows is written in the*   6v
l.h.col. R.h.col. blank.)
Moreover besides this I gott him of my mother in law[16] the some of £100
gratis.

The rent of his lands and use of his stock beinge about £238. All this is spent as appeared upon a short view of an accompt 6 Jan 1630 and his owne stock that was £430 is now lessened to £350 wherein £25 is allowed for his Milnes, so spent this yere of his stock £80 and of his land and use of stock as above in all £318. And yet he and his wife were carefull to doe their best and this is the fruet if the housekepeing there were sett upon, when I would have kept them all but clothes and payed them Threlkeld rent Sleddale Shapp tythe and left them the use of all their stock

Jo Lowther

Soe are they worse by £150 at least then they needed have been this year whitch God grant they amend.

---

11. i.e. Beer.
12. Indecipherable.
13. Altered from £2.
14. Uncertain reading.
15. Sense difficult to construe.
16. Agnes Fleming of Rydal.

Whitsuntide 1632

6r *cont.*   John gave me an accompt that his stock (Cowpland Parke Sheriff Parke, Sleddale Milne Wallers grounds, and this years cropp at his comeing to my house at Lowther ageine was all his detts payed, and his rent of £50 of Threlkeld ⟨rent⟩ was not yet due till K [Candlemas] 1632) is now as I esteem it £600 his detts beinge £207 payed and soe will be Kandlemasse 1632. His quick goods being only 82 catle 500 shepe 5 horses and mares detts £60 in price £50 the rest being in Corne, househould stuff agistement and his Cropp.

7r   [*Unknown hand*] *Notes of receipts since St. George's day 1606.*
[*Unknown hand*] *Valuation of lands at Lowther and Hackthorpe, of uncertain date.*[17]

[*Hand of Sir J.L.(1), n.d. 1617*]

7v   A particuler of my demesnes when I entered to my lands as I estemed it

Lowther demens above [the house]		Belowe the house	
abated £4[18] Highfield	£34	Dowland £20 ab*ated*	£1[19]
abated £2 Grenarigs and			
Brackeba*nk*	£34	Milnefield £10	£1
Mathew close			
bought £4 Burtrybanke and		Tow Flats £22	£4
abated £4 the hay closes	£26		
		Buckholme £16	£8
Owlde Parke	£28	Eskla Moore £10	
abated £2 Rowland field	£24	Tow Skellane £16	£6
abated till I			
walled Whale Inge	£10	Warren £2	
New Parke	£30	Orchards and Garden £3	
to abate £2 Rents and Court	£25	The Milne £12	£2
£39 fallen[20] Boones Moulture			
Malt			

Hackthropp demein from the howse to the water, followeing the hedge to the Gill 110[21] acres Wealth[22]	£55	Rents heriots and boones their £10 Wood to fell yearly their and at Lowther £10	
Above that hedge to the high way with the 8 grasses in the pasture £35		Casualties there £20	
	£130		

---

17. Sir J.L.(2) subsequently headed this valuation: *The perticuler value of Lowther and Hackthropp*, and noted the total: *10 br 1654 Som £540.*
18. The notes at the margin are subsequent annotations [by Sir J.L.(1)].
19. The abatements at this margin are subsequent annotations [by Sir J.L.(1)].
20. If this figure is the total of abatements of Lowther rents, it is apparently an error for £40. The total value for Lowther, not given in MS, is £322.
21. This figure altered from 100.
22. i.e. Worth.

7v *cont.*

Helton rents declaro £9-10s   Casualties   £12[23]
Tythes about 40s But
note the demein grounds lately   leased[24]   £16
                       £37[25]

Newton rents £24-7s-5d   Casualties   £16-3
Milne £8 ferme £8   £6   Court   40s
Note 53s 4d in lease   for lives worth £30 per annum[26]
                 £58

Penrith in lease to my Uncle Gerard   £11[27]
   The Schoole rent payed
                 £11

[28]Meaborne In demein   £64   Rents   £40
   £40—west of line—   Milne   £20
   £24 on the east side   Court   40s
   Coles 40s
                 £128
£693[29]   Total   £693

7v *cont.*

[*he end of the valuation is followed by a long inserted note, written by Sir J.L.(1)*
around the list of acreages which followed the valuation when the page was first
written]

So the whole estate I had from my auncestors save that I got upon sale
of Meaborne fines these abatements deducted and my purchases was but
in revenew at rack £570[30] per annum out of which I payed yearly £250
charges upon me besides owne charges.

[31]The Quantitie of my Grounde as we did measure it 12 February 1617 by
the Acre accountting seven yeards to the peartch not precisely cast to the
oddes

Highfield with the Head close (*interlined*: bought in by me)   109 acres
Grenerigs and Brakenbe   192 acres
BurtrieBanke and tow hay closes   45 acres
Owlde Parke with the tow hay closes   110 acres

---

23. Annotations here [by Sir J.L.(2)] are unclear.
24. Added [by Sir J.L.(1)]: *by my Grandfather.*
25. Marginal note [by Sir J.L.(2)]: *£2.* Probably a note of the £2-10-0d error in the addition for Helton.
26. Note [by Sir J.L.(1)]: *Given in tayle by my Grandfather first by me turned but I bettered this by purchase of Sewborwens since.*
27. Barely legible note [by Sir J.L.(1)]: *Note Mutch is in lease, other in fee ferme. Sowlde by tenant in tayle. J. Low.*
28. Marginal note [by Sir J.L.(1)]: *Ther was in all but £70 when I entered, the rest I purchased.*
29. The total rounded up from £692-10-5d. Include the £2-10-0d error under Helton, total £695-0-5d.
30. Deducting the abatements and purchases as annotated above gives a total of £595, deduct a further £11 for Penrith in lease, total £584. See below p. 25 for another total.
31. Marginal note [by Sir J.L.(1)]: *7 yards by the Poole.*

7v *cont.*	New Parke with Crag Close	115 acres
	Rowland field	52 acres
	Low Skeland 14 high 12	
	whereof the parsons about 4	22 acres
	Flatt 14 acres Milnefield 15 and adde	29 acres

8r [*Unknown hand*] *Odd receipts dated 1617.*
   [*Hand of Sir J.L.(1)*] *Survey of that part of Reagill Grange purchased in 1624 from Mr. Wharton*[32]. *Gives field names with measurements in acres, roods and pecks, total 159 acres 2 roods, cost £538.*

8v [*Unknown hand*] *A particular of Sir Henry Curwen's estates at Workington, Harrington and Stainburn, giving rents of properties and estimates of casual profits, total £801-3-4d.*[33] *With notes by Sir J.L.(1).*

9r [*Hand of Sir J.L.(1)*] *List of [demesne] grounds in hand May 1617–May 1618, giving names and values of properties, totalling £243. The list concludes:* What is possible to retourne to me towards this besides my house keping and wages whitch my wife payeth and I governe

Woolle and draught shepe—aboute	£60
Catle sowlde and stock as good	£120
Cropps will be made besides the ground	£85[34]
provision for next yeare Corne to sell but to pay my wages	£20[35]

9v *Notes of the expenses of a trip to London, and of sales of crops, 1618.*

10r–v [*Unknown hand*] *Rental of Plumpton*[36] *as gathered for the bailiff there, due Martinmas 1653. List of 70 tenants' names, with their rents, totalling for the half year £60-10-9d. With notes, in the hand of Sir J.L.(2), of additional payments due, and of money allowed to the bailiff for collecting the rent.*

11r–v [*Hand of Sir J.L.(1)*] *Leasehold rental of lands leased out by Sir J.L.(1), 1618.*

11v [*Unknown hand*] *Rental of Plumpton Park at £121-6-9d. [a year] having been increased to that figure by an Exchequer Decree, followed by rentals for Plumpton Head and Ednell. Copy signature of the Earl of Annandale, with notes by Sir J.L.(2).*

12r [*Hand of Sir J.L.(1)*] *Rental of all Sir J.L.(1)'s estates arranged under the days on which they fell due, compiled 25 March 1619. Gives names of properties and amounts due.*

---

32. Deed: Reagill B.8.
33. There are errors in the addition in the Ms.
34. Altered in a different ink, so to read from £60.
35. This entry altered in a different ink.
36. For Plumpton see p. 69. Ednell is probably Edenhall.

Notes by Sir J.L.(1) of his purchases: land of John Hodgson; the manor of   12v
Kentmere;[37] *customary lands belonging to John Addison;*[38] *and the estates*
of Mr. Salkeld [of Corby] at Wet Sleddale, Knipe, Bampton, and Michelmyre
(with enclosures).[39] *[n.d.]*

List of properties remaining in hand, 25 March 1619, with note of value of   3r
each property, listed separately for the manors of Lowther and Meaburne.
Valuation of stock, of crops, animals and household goods, 25 March 1619.

Notes of expenses, 1619 and 1620, followed by calculation of wealth: 13v
1 Jan 1620

My revenew in lands I estimate to be ritchly worth per annum	£850
My personall estate in detts and stock is at this (*interlined:* time)	
reckened unto £3700 whereof as yet unprofitable aboute £700 with	
my househowlde stuff the rest yields per annum	£300
My practise at the law to sett it at the least, it hathe bene double,	
treble	£50

In yearly revenew	£1200
I apportion for my payments forth in annuities and other things	£200
to spend in house and otherwayes	£400
to dispose to Increase my estate and prefer for my children yearly	£600

whereof tow years will now prefer Men in mariage or theiraboutes, at which
time I shall be If I live 41 years of age, then If I can howlde out that
proportion as is likely common in possibilitie upon thee cesser of annuities
by death[40] whitch may adde, as my parte dothe Increase that £600 per annum
will (if God prosper all being bestowed in land at £6-13s4d per centum whitch
is 15 years purchase) purchase and buy at least £2000 by year Inheritance
in 24 years, whitch if I live will be the year of my age 65, but in stricture
it is £2333-6s-8d whitch computation I hope is not offensive to God but a
fore seeing (*MS damaged:*) providence whitch shall make me be (*MS
damaged:* more) temperate in all for this is too (*MS damaged:* mutch).

List of rents and other dues payable to Sir J.L.(1) 1620–21, arranged under   14r–v
feast days when due; gives name of each property and amount due.

Note of Sir J.L.(1)'s purchases in 1621: [customary] lands worth per annum
£9-10-0 at Lowther and Meaburne for £130; and Mr. Salkeld [of Corby]'s
rents at Sleagill and Meaburne for £80.[41]

---

37. Copy deed: Kendal Barony B.III.4 abstracted in part in A1/6, f46. Lowther
    found the manor troublesome, and sold it by 1622, see below p 25, and P.R.O.,
    C2 Jas I/S16/56; C2 Jas 1/S10/26.
38. Perhaps in Reagill, see Reagill B.11.
39. Deeds: Rosgill B.1 and Bampton B.I.16; see p. 25 below. Abstracts: A1/6,
    ff76, 77. Further purchases from Salkeld family below, and p. 36. For the
    circumstances of this purchase, Phillips, Thesis, p. 181 and *CW2*, 66, pp. 190–200.
40. Marginal note by Sir J.L.(1): *The Ladie Lowther my mother in law is since dead*
    1622 by whome I pay out less £100 per annum. P.II.3.
41. Deed: Reagill B.10.

15r   *Rental of grounds in Sir J.L.(1)'s hand, 1621; gives names and value of properties, and notes of stock.*

15v   [*Hand of Sir J.L.(2)*] I (*interlined:* Sir J.L.Baronet) had the first of 10ber 1653, in lands of Inheritance with the mortgage of Clifton beeinge as much upon it as it is really worth   £2400
Casualties of fines estimated at the least unto   0100

  Soe the totall revenew of Inheritance is   2500

  besides my mothers Joynture of £250 per annum
In leases for years at this present beinge now worth per annum (as they cost me,) as appeareth by the rentall for this yeare in this booke one year being only expired, soe worth per annum the years   1000
My wives Joynture for our joynt lives besides all sesses declaro per annum but covenanted by her joynture to be £800 per annum   600

  Soe totall revenew in lands and leases is   £4100

Notat that my Leases of (*interlined:* neare) £1000 per annum cost mee £6000; and one yeare is spent soe worth bether then £5000
My personall estate then in debts by the alphabett letters in my debt booke[42] aboute   5700
In rent arrers of Wensladale Marton and elsewhere above   1300
In payne with my Brother Will   2000
In payne at Hamber[43] et arr*ears*   0700
In debts for fines as appers by the finebookes arrer and dew[44]   0340
In stock, viz in Catle 140 worth   0400
In sheepe of all sorts about 750 worth   0200
In horses 20 viz Coachhorses Geldings and Mares and 2 foles worth at least   0660
In plate   0200
In househould stuff ⟨£400⟩ £500   0500
Cropp of Corne and hay worth   0300

Soe the totall personall estate is besides leases, (worth ⟨besides⟩ £5000)   11800

by which estimate may bee seene the increase of my estate reall and personall from this tyme; and what considerable somes I disburse or receive besides my revenew—after this tyme; vide for that foll 108b.[45]

---

42. Does not survive; A1/9 is debt book of 1661–1675.
43. i.e. Hamburg.
44. A fine book for 1648–1698 survives.
45. Below, p. 69.

'nknown hand. This is the first page of a series of records of general fines and 17r[46] admittances of customary tenants by Sir Christopher Lowther on all his manors. The heading for the entries, and one example of the record of the fine and admittance for each manor, is transcribed. There is a summary on page 00 below.]

The Fynes and Rents of tenants admitted in Lowther Hackthropp, Whayle, Helton and Newton Anno Domini 1608 by Sir Christopher Lowther knight and lands lord there of.

Gressum	John Wilkinson alias Chragg rent is	ixs.
in all	paying his gods pennye is admitted tenaunte	
is £6	and is to pay at the next Saint John day 40s.	
	for one part of his fyne and that day twelmunth	
	other 40s. for another part and the next Candlemasse	
	after other 40s for the last part of the payment.	

Tenaunts admitted in Hackthropp Anno Domini 1608 et (*interlined:* decimo) 18v quarto die Aprilis by Sir Christopher Lowther Knight and lands lord there of

Gressum		
is £7-10s.	Christopher Chappelhow rent	9s
	is admitted tenaunt and is to pay	
	at the next Saint John day 50s and	
	the next saint John day after 50s Anno	
	1609 and Candlemasse next after 50s	
	the said Christopher Chappelhowe haith	
	his gods pennye and so is tenaunt of	
	Sir Christopher Lowther knight.	

Tenaunts admitted in Whayle Anno Domini: 1608 et decimo sexto die 19v Aprilis by Sir Christopher Lowther knight and land lord there of.

Formula for this manor similar to those already used.

Tenaunts admitted in Helton Anno Domini: 1608 et octo decimo die 20v Fabruary by Sir Christopher Lowther knight and lands lord there of.

Formula similar to those already used.

Tenaunts admitted In Newton Anno Domini: 1607 [*sic*] and quarto die 22r Fabruary by Sir Christopher Lowther knight and lands lord there of.

GRessum	John Dawson rent	4s.
is £3-6-8d.	is admitted tenaunt and is to pay at	
	the next Saint John Day 33s4d. and	
	next Saint John Day after 33s4d.	

---

46. There is no folio 16. The sewing of the book indicates that there was an error made when numbering the folios, rather than that a folio has been lost; but see below, p. 69.

22r *cont.*   *The following is a summary of these fines and admissions:*

Manor	No. of tenancies	No. of tenancies whose entries are incomplete	Total fines due from completed entries**
Lowther	27	1	£191- 2-8d.
Hackthorpe	15	2	127
Whale	15	—	114-16-8d.
Helton	30	7	195- 6-8d.
Newton	38	—	272- 3-4d.***
	125	10	900- 9-4d.

Notes: **   *Arithmetical errors in the MS have been corrected.*
***   *Does not include £3-6-8d. noted as abated from one fine.*

24r   (*Blank*)

24v   [*Hand of Sir J.L.(1)*] *Priced list of household goods, plate, crops, farm gear purchased from his sister by Sir J.L.(1) at the time of his father's death; similar list of goods owned by Sir J.L.(1) before his father's death. Total £458-16-10d.*

25r   [*Hand of Sir J.L.(1)*] My father died the 2 of August 1617 at Lowther, before whitch some fower dayes I made his will[47] and gave all his goods whatsoever away to my Brothers and sister and woulde not have anie one pennie myselfe bycause I knew their estate did requier it and need it, and the money he gave them was to be payed as I showlde appoint and as their necessitie did require. Which I ordered as followeth first his unkinde ladie their step-mother did cleyme a third whitch we compounded for goods and money payed her (*interlined*: worth) £134. I had just detts dew to me for want of £20 by year (*interlined:* whitch) my father covenanted to make me in demein at Meaborne more than it was £800 and odde Whitch I woulde not demaund to hinder my Brothers, and the rest of his estate I thus ordered His Inventorie was £1376-17s-4d My mother[48] had forth of it £134-13-4 then remeined £1242-4s unto which I added in fines and Rents not dew to them halfe for teime past—£66-10s then remeined £1308-14s

his Knowen dettes were £262-6s-5d and £27 was likewise deducted £27 for over appraisement and things given my sister soe remained £1019-7-7d

Whitch I ordered thus five hundred pounds to my sister to my Brother Richard £160. To Willyam Robert and Lancelot everie one £100 the rest to remein in my sisters hands for seven years to pay all other dettes which may arise, and then to pay the remanet equally to my Brothers, and if more

---

47. No text of this will is known, and there are no extant references in probate act books of the prerogative courts of York or Canterbury, and no act books for the Archdeaconry of Richmond or Diocese of Carlisle.
48. P.II.3. Mother = Stepmother.

fall to be in detts then they to give bond to pay their portions of it back 25r *cont.*
for their £100 apiece as she for her £500. The 27 day of August 1617.
Jo. Lowther

(*Blank*)   25v

Notes of stock [animals] in hand, indicating how and where acquired, September   26r
1617; notes of subsequent sales and purchases[49]*, either through named*
persons, or throughout the north of England at these places: Preston, Gisburn,
Richmond, Penrith, Wensleydale, Ripon and Appleby.

(*Blank*)   26v

Stock sales, [n.d., 1617–1619. Format as f26r above]   27r
Places: Richmond, Appleby.

(*ff 27v–33r comprise entries extending over the reverse and obverse of con-*
secutive folios. They record customary fines paid to Sir J.L.(1) when he
succeeded his father in 1617. Apart from headings for each manor, the entries
comprise a series of columns, listing the name of the tenant, his annual
customary rent, the fine levied, the columns for recording payment in three
instalments, with additional columns for noting arrearages. A summary table
of these fines is given on p. 14 below.)

and of Sir J.L.(1), transcript of heading:] Fines assessed by me John Lowther   27v–28r
upon my tenants of Newton upon Change of Lord after my fathers death
for their allowance to be tenants during our Jointe lives. *The columns, in*
an unknown hand, provide for the fine to be paid in instalments on 24 June
1618, 1619, 1620.

and of Sir J.L.(1), begins in margin:] Lowther and Whale 8 February 1617.   28v–29r
Fines assessed by me John Lowther (*interlined in another hand:* sonne of
Sir Christopher) upon my tenants of Lowther and Whale upon Change of
Lord after my fathers death for their allowances to be tenants during our
Jointe lives, wherein I used but one woord, what I woulde have, and they
submitted and were pleased wherefore I abated them halfe a years rent.
The columns, in an unknown hand, provide for payment of fines at Michaelmas
1618, 1619, 1620.

Lowther and Whale continued; Hackthorpe.   29v–30r

Fines assessed by me Jo Lowther of Helton Flecham upon change of Lord   29v–31r
for my allowance of them to be tenants to me as they were to (*MS. damaged*)
though Hewett, Withewath[50] and the milne lately built was in my grandfathers occupation in demein and he tenant in tayle.
Columns written and arranged as for Lowther.

---

49. Prices are given for each transaction, but not for each item, i.e., 5 cows £10.
50. Widewath Mill in Askham (E.P.N.S., XLIII, p. 201); Mill records: Helton B.I.13,
    20, 23. See p. 245.

31v–33r[51] [*Unknown hand*] The fines of the tenants of Crosbie which did not purchase themselves of me as they agreed to paie them unto me after my purchase from Mr Thomas Pickering to admitt them my tennants dueringe our Joynt lives.[52] *Instalments payable at Lamas 1620, 1621, 1622.*

Summary of general customary fines due after death of Sir Christopher Lowther

Manor	No. of tenancies	No. of tenancies whose entries are incomplete	Total fines due from completed tenancies
Newton	43	—	£295 14 8d
Lowther and Whale	40	—	327 1 8
Lowther and Hackthorpe	3	—	24 13 4
Hackthorpe	16	—	133 7 8
Helton	35	5	236 10 4[53]
	137		£1017 7 8
Crosby Ravensworth	70	5[54]	250 16 5
	207	10	£1268 4 1

33v [*Unknown hand*] *Rental of one year's customary rent of Yanwath and Eamont Bridge [n.d., 1655][55]; list of 29 tenants' names, with customary rent, total £14-14-9d.*

34r–35v [*Hand of Sir J.L.(1)*] *Manors of Lowther, Whayle and Hackthorpe: abstracts of manorial court transactions. (Continued on f36v.)*
   i) *Licences for the sale by customary tenants of their customary estates; admittances of customary tenants, after either sale by, or death of, previous tenant. Includes names of parties, annual rents, services and fines due, and details of properties.*
   ii) *Notes of heriots, and arrangements for the wardship of minor customary tenants.[56]*

36r   *Manor of Newton: abstracts of manorial court records. Licences and admittances. (As ff34r–35v.)*

---

51. No folio 32; sewing indicates an error in numbering.
52. For purchase see P.R.O., C5/42/78. Agreements over tenantright: P.R.O., C2 Jas I/C30/16 (1621) and P.R.O., C78/1205, No. 7 (1639); Sir J.L.(2) comments below p. 58; see also pp. 59, 61.
53. £1 noted as abated not included in this total.
54. One incomplete as the tenant was a minor: fine due at his majority.
55. See the index at f4v (p. 4) above for this date. The manor was purchased in 1654 (below, p. 71).
56. Similar records temp. Sir J.L.(2) are in A1/8, for all manors; this also contains customary rentals for the manors, see also fine book 1648–1698, and p. 45 n. 24 below.

Records of the manorial courts of Lowther, Whayle and Hackthorpe. (Con-   36v
tinued from f35v.)

[Unknown hand] Rental of the manor of Rosgill: names of 39 tenants, annual   37r
customary rents, total £14-12-4d. With [in hand of Sir J.L.(2)] list of boon
carriages [of coal] and notes of free rents. [n.d., c. 1655].[57]

[Unknown hand] List of boon carriages and hens due from tenants of Rosgill.   37v

[Hand of Sir J.L.(1)] Manor of Helton, abstracts of manorial court records.   38r–39r
Admittances. (As for Lowther, f34r.)

[Hand of Sir J.L.(2) for heading only, rest in another hand; heading:] A note   39r cont.
of the Boone plowghes at Helton as they were to joyne together to make
10 plowges 1654.
List of [tenants'] names with value of their boons in £-s-d, divided into ten
groups, each group to find one draught [team].

[Hand of Sir J.L.(2)] Copy estimate of the value of Lowther Parsonage, by Rev.   39v
Christopher Teasdale, 1656, which gives the value of individual tithes and glebe
properties; total £85. With a note, by Sir J.L.(2), of how Mr. Smith the
incumbent, let it for £92 in 1658.[58]

[Hand of Sir J.L.(1)] Manor of Crosby Ravensworth, abstract of manorial court   40r
records. Admittances. (As for Lowther, f34r.)

Manor of Thwaites, abstract of manorial court records. Admittances. Manor   39ᵇr[59]
of Thrimby, the like. (Both as for Lowther, f34r above.) Followed by three
notes by Sir J.L.(2) in his hand, the last two initialled, concerning heriots
at Thrimby, 1655–1659.

[Unknown hand] Note of the boon services of Little Strickland, gives name of   39ᵇv
19 tenants, and amount due, £1-4-2d.

[Change of hand, unknown hand] A rental of Little Strickland as rented when
it was purchased from Richard Crakenthorp, gent. Gives names of 22 tenants
and their customary rents, total £6-7-0d; with a note of free rents totalling
10s-4d. to be paid out of the above. A marginal note [suggests that the free rents
are part] of a rent of £1 payable to the Castle of Kendal, part of the Marquis
fee.[60]

[Hand of Sir J.L.(1)] Manor of Knipe, abstracts of records of the manorial court.   40ᵇr–v
Admittances temp. Sir J.L.(1). (As for Lowther, f34r.)

[Unknown hand] Rental of Melkinthorpe, 1654, which is noted as all being   40ᵇv
heriotable. Gives names of 6 tenants, and annual customary rent. [With
alterations and notes in the hand of Sir J.L.(2).][61]

57. For Sir J.L.(2)'s purchase of the manor in 1655 see below p. 72.
58. See below, p. 74.
59. The next two folios are numbered 39 and 40, and then the folios are numbered
    from 41 consecutively, so there are two folios 39 and 40. See f4v (p. 2), *sub*
    Lowther parsonage.
60. For the Marquis fee, see *N&B* I, p. 40.
61. Purchased then, see below, p. 71.

41r [*Hand of Sir J.L.(1)*] *Note of a fine payable by Thomas Todhunter of Threlkeld, n.d.*

42r [*Unknown hand*] *Rental of the half-year's customary rent of Hackthorpe, due Candlemas 1654. Gives names of 19 tenants, with customary rents, total £4-0-3¼d.*[62]

> *Rental of the half-year's customary rent of Hackthorpe, due at Lammas 1654. As above, but only 18 names, total £3-19-0¼d.*

41v [*Hand of Sir J.L.(1); transcript of heading*] Groundes and other profitts of inheritance not rented as yet this 24 November 1621.

> *Lists separate [demesne] properties in hand, also casual fines and boon rents, at Lowther, Knipe, Bampton, Sleddale, Sleagill, Helton, Maulds Meaburne, Crosby Ravensworth and Penrith. Total £362-13-4d.*

42r [*Heading: hand of Sir J.L.(1)*] Rents of tenants groundes letten and other certein yearly revenewes this year the 24th of November 1621: et 22.
Here follows a list of properties, with their rents, arranged under the feast days when due. The document concludes:
Tottall letten and not as I estimate it is
£922 8s 8d.   out of which deducte for stocke
  098 0 0   and for my annuities; remeins
  824 8 8   in good landes securely estated
as I thinke, charged to my uncles my brothers and mother in law with £224 per annum.

> *Note of mortgage of £60 from Mr Roger Otway; and of £65 for Kirkby Thore demesne paid by Henry Lough and mortgaged from Mr Thomas Wharton, to whom Lowther subsequently sold the mortgage.*

42v [*Hand of Sir J.L.(1)*]   Aprill 1623

	£
Groundes and other profits unletten as appears upon the next leaf	334-1-8
Groundes leased, with morgages, and Annuities, and my rents of tenants due amount unto	693-3-7
whereof not inheritance absolute near 220 (*erasure*)	⟨53⟩
And to adde Penrith Lands now in leas to my Uncle Sir Gerard Lowther	17
	1044-5-3
Out of which deduct not inheritance	0220
Remenieth lands and inheritance	0824-5-3

And besides this £824-5s-3d in land I have in stock and Margages and detts above £5320 and alle my detts payed whereof remote or

---

62. This total figure has been altered. The word *heriotable* [in the hand of Sir J.L.(2)] has been added at the end of the rental's heading.

desperate I esteme at the moste £150. Unprofitable as house-   42v *cont.*
howld stuffe and long to come £500. The rest will make me as
it hath done in Revenew and meintein the stock   450

                                                                      ―――――
                                                                      1274-5-3
In all by my accompt in yearly revenews whereunto I may adde
my practise by the law whitch in these deceying times is fallen
under £80 but was £120. But I will weive it for a time to perfect
my sonnes Breading, to satisfie allsoe myself in my desier to
know, and to advantage me in other things least in attending
it I loose as mutch or more otherwise

I am to payout onely to my uncle Heugh—£20 by year
My uncle Sir Gerard if I please £17 my brothers for £80
Helton rent to wrangle for[63] or   125
loose halfe £8 (*interlined:* my mothers[64] annuitie ceased)   ―――――
Which being deducted remeins clear   1149-5-3
Out of whitch eleven hundred fortie nine pounds deduct for
expenses lossess in the makeing it, in and governing of it;
my yearly charge and other things   449-5-3
By Good Husbandrie with Gods help we may save and adde
to our estate and preferment of our children yearly 700.

Properties at Michelmyre, Meaburne and Thrimby mill purchased in 1623;
with a note of the purchase price and [estimated] annual value of each piece.

[*Heading:*]   April 1623   43r
Groundes and other profits in my occupation this year not rented of
inheritance: wherein I abate by the cheapness of the times.[65]

List of profits and properties at Lowther total £279-1-8d and at Meaburne
£56. Also note of stock of horses, cattle and sheep, and of purchases thereof
at Milnthorpe and Kendal.

[*Heading:*]Rents of my tenants and groundes letten and other yearly profits   43v
of Continewance 1623.

List of properties with their rents due at the following feast days: Whitsun
1623, Lammas 1624,[66] Michaelmas 1623, Martinmas 1623, Candlemas
1623-[1624] and the Annunciation 1624.

―――

63. This complicated lawsuit is P.R.O., E112/129/72; copy pleadings: Helton B.I.19.
    In 1511 the Lowthers acquired a part of Helton (p. 214 below), and leased two
    more parts from Mount Grace Priory in 1523 for 99 years at £6-13-4 (A1/3,
    list of outpayments. 1605-6). The crown granted a new lease and the assignees
    sued Sir J.L.(1). His successful defence was a matter of law involving the
    manorial status of the land, and the probity of the Mount Grace lease. Sir
    J.L.(1) retained the land and paid nothing for it. Sir J.L.(2) bought the last
    part of Helton in 1654 (p. 70).
64. i.e. stepmother, P.II.3.
65. The final clause is a subsequent insertion by Sir J.L.(1).
66. Presumably an error for 1623.

0

43r *cont.* With a note of the purchase of Thrimby town rent and leasehold properties additional properties purchased [since April 1623,[67] of estimated] annual value £101-10-8d.

44r [*Unknown hand*] Rental of the half year's rent at Lowther, due Whitsun 1654. List of 42 tenants' names, with customary rents, total £9-16-1¼d.

44v–45r [*Hand of Sir J.L.(1)*] Rental of all Sir J.L.'s lands of inheritance, mortgages, leases, annuities and fees, Martinmas 1623 to Annunciation 1624.

45r Note of properties purchased 1624–25, with their annual value, purchase price, and name of vendor. Places mentioned are: premises in manors of Hackthorpe, Lowther, Meaburn and Sleddale; Bampton Manor and tithe cost £1750[68]; lease of Newby Manor for one life, cost £150; part of Shap tithe, and Hallgarth cost £228-14-8d[69]; and Threlkeld Manor cost £2,700.[70]

45v–46r Rental for all Sir J.L.(1)'s estates, year ending Martinmas 1624. Divided into lands let out, and lands kept in hand, and concluded by a calculation of Lowther's wealth

Total income from lands let out		£793-9-6	
Deduct: Mortgages	132-11-0		
Leases & Annuities	195-17-9	328 8 9	£465-0-9d.

The total of demesne lands, and other profits, in hand is £484-10-0,[71] whereof £8-10-0 is deducted as a lease,

Total	476-0-0
	941-0-9[72]

The rental concludes

Totall in finable rents demein rents demeins not rented and other caseuall profits *of* Inheritance	930-0-9[73]
out of whitch deducting £13 for stock of shepe let with Sleddale demein[74]	13

67. For this date see f42v.
68. Deeds: Bampton B.I.21; see below, p. 25. Further purchase, see below, p. 162
69. Deeds: Shap B.I.11; see pp. 20, 26, 175 below. Abstracts: A1/6, ff124v–125r. Further purchases: below, pp. 59, 152. Extracts from Cartulary of Shap Abbey: A1/1, ff379v–385r (see G. R. C. Davis, *Medieval Cartularies of Great Britain* (1958), p. 101), and see below p. 219.
70. Purchase and sale, see pp. 26, 51; deed: Threlkeld B.7. Tenant-right, below, p. 52.
71. *Recte* £478-10-0d.
72. *Recte* £935-0-9d.
73. This figure is presumably the sum of £465-0-9d. for lands of inheritance let out, and £476 for land of inheritance in hand. This later figure should be £470, the correct total here should, then, be £935-0-9d.
74. A marginal note deducts a further £12 at this point for twice counting Underbanke, and over-valuing wood sales. This deduction is not incorporated in the calculation.

Inheritance Remeineth Clear with some small rents payed out of it in all under the £9[75]	917-0-9	46r *cont.*

Whereof I want the possession of Penrith *for* my Uncles lief	⟨16[76]⟩
Barneskeugh banke for 17 yeres	3
Shappe tythe for thre yeres	10
And I pay out in annuities	100
And Helton halfe if not all in daunger[77]	5[78]

I have clear in lands	783[79]

In personall estate and morgages this 23 of October 1624 all detts payed or allowed £6117-0-6

Whereof at the most desperate £300 $\left.\begin{array}{l}\text{clear}\\5000\end{array}\right\}$

remote—£300 unprofitable ⟨500⟩ 800 may yield	400

	[1183]
Whereof allowinge for expenses losses decey and repreation[80]	583

We may yet spare to add to our estate by year	600

(The page is divided into two columns: l.h.col.:) Rental of Sir J.L.(1)'s tenants 46v
in the manor of Thrimby, 1625. Gives names of 28 tenants and their yearly customary rents, total £10-4-6d.

(r.h.col.:) Rental of Sir J.L.(1)'s tenants in the manor of Knipe, 1623. Gives names of 37 tenants, with yearly customary rents due, total £7-3-9, with details of rents and premises sold by Lowther.
Both columns have been annotated by Sir J.L.(2).

(Page divided, l.h.col.) [Hand of Sir J.L.(1). Heading:] A rentall of my lands in 47r
Sleddale purchased likewise of Mr Salkeld Martinmasse 1623[81]
Weete Sleddale
Tenements parcell of the demesne as I proved in a Decret in Chancerie
against Noble and Jackson this vacation *Here follow the names of 10 tenants,*
with their rents.   Auntienter tenants[82]

---

75. The £9 is not deducted.
76. A later marginal note dates the death of his uncle Sir Gerard Lowther as 14 October [1624], P.II.5. The £16 was then struck out.
77. There is a later marginal note that Thrimby rent is twice valued as both land and stock. For Helton see p. 17.
78. This figure is obscured. £5 makes the addition correct!
79. This whole line has been much altered, probably after the death of Sir Gerard Lowther.
80. i.e. repairs.
81. The *likewise* refers to the lands mentioned on f46v, which were also purchased from Mr. Salkeld of Corby; see p. 9. For the decree see Rosgill B.1.
82. Presumably those tenants whose customary estate Lowther accepted. The sum total rent in the MS for both categories of tenants is £9.12.2, but this is altered. Correct figure £9-8-0d.

47r *cont.*   *Here follow the names of 17 tenants with rents total £4-7-4d.: concludes with*
a note of additional names and rents of uncertain date.
[r.h.col., hand of Sir J.L.(2). Heading:]
A particular of Thrimby Grange as valued and let before 1660.
Lists of properties, with [annual] rents, total £32; noted as leased to named
tenants for £30 in 1663. List of the number of days boon mowing due, total
50 days. Further list of the boon days due for mowing, shearing, ploughing,
leading coals and harrowing, with value of payments due; total £1-2-4d.

47v–48v *[Unknown hand] The tithe rents for Shap, half of which is due to John Lowther*
of Lowther, esquire [Sir J.L.(1)] by purchase from Mr. Randall Washington.
[n.d., c. 1624]. Total rents £18-12-9d. Lists names of 102 tenants at Mardale,
Swindale, Naddale, Shap, Shap outsides, Hardendale, Tailbert and Rayside,
Sleddale, and Wasdale Foot. Noted [in hand of Sir J.L.(1)] that £9-6-4½d.
is due to Sir J.L.(1), plus £7 for the rent of a close called Hallgarth.[83]

48v *[Hand of Sir J.L.(1)] Note of the seven year running fines paid at Crosby*
Ravensworth Candlemas 1624 [–25]. List of names of 14 tenants, with
amounts paid.

49r *[Heading of rental, and total, in hand of Sir J.L.(1), rental in an unknown hand:]*
Rental of Crosby Ravensworth as the rent was to be collected at Whitsun
1628.
List of 96 tenants' with customary rent due, total £24-3-9d.

49v *[Unknown hand] Rental of Knipe, Whitsun 1630. List of names of 53 tenants,*
with customary rent due, and boons due. [The nature and purpose of this rent
is not clear.]

50r[84] *[Unknown hand] A rental of Bampton as paid at Martinmas 1641, (continued*
on f50v).
(This page is divided; l.h.col.:) List of 66 tenants' names with old rents, i.e.
customary rents, (continued in r.h.col.)

(r.h.col.) List of 33 tenants' names with free rents due, total, half year, 12s.-4½d.

50v *List of boon days at Bampton, with name of tenants and amount due,*
[total 15s-0½d].
List of tenants who pay 'Mategeld', with amount due, [total 9s-9d]. Rental
concludes with a calculation [in hand of Sir J.L.(2)] of the half-yearly income
as: free rent Martinmas 13-10d, Whitsun 12-6d; old rent £6-4-6d; boons 15s-0d.

51r *(Blank.)*

52v *[Hand of Sir J.L.(1)] Arrears of rent, March 1624 [–25]. A cumulative list of*
arrears, giving the date each one became due, the name of the property or,
in the case of a mortgagor, the person's name, and the amount outstanding;
annotations indicate payment. The rents in arrears were due between Whitsun
1622 and Candlemas 1624[–25].

---

83. See above, p. 18.
84. Before the seventeenth-century numeration of the folios, three folios were cut
out at this point. They were the counterparts of ff41, 42, 43.

Notes of arrears due from sales of corn, cattle, and from agistment, due   52r
1624. Name of debtors and amounts owed, with annotations indicating
payment.

Rental of all Sir J.L.(1)'s estates for the year 1625.   52v–53v
List of properties, with rents due, arranged by rent days. For each rent
day mortgages and leases are listed separately.

(The page is divided into two columns. The entries were written at two   54r
separate times. The top of the l.h.col., calendared below as entry 1, and the
r.h.col., transcribed below as entry 2, were written first, and the content of
these two columns relate to each other. Later, a final entry, transcribed below
as entry 3, was written at the bottom of the l.h.col.)

(l.h.col., entry 1:) List of demesne lands in hand, 1625, with values, total £470.
Additional properties valued at £48 are added, total £518.

(r.h.col., entry 2) [Hand of Sir J.L.(1)]

	£	s	d
It appeareth under my accompt[85] of Catle this year that I raysed of these groundes and my stock upon them the stock not lessened	769-10- 6		

My groundes and winter provision upon them I did accompt to be worth	410		
The use of £2000 stock	160		
Wages and charges aboute them	60		

	£	s	d
totall charge	630		
soe gained clear	139-10- 6		

Whereof Giles Moore my servant upon his accompt by the
bargein of grounds and stock he did take of me gained by
his peins   105- 7- 8

And I geined above all charges and househowlde kept and
use received   34- 2-10

Saveing £6-13-4d not reckoned in the Catle which I
delivered to John L my sonne to make up my remenet to
249 Catle

This year also my other personall stock is thus altered as
appears by my last years accompt in this booke 4 Octoberis
1624

it was all debts payed 23 Octoberis 1624   6117- 0- 6[86]

I have since bought[87] Bampton whitch cost	1750
Newbic whitch cost	150
Harrisons tenement in Sleddale	70

---

85. p. 23, below.
86. For this figure see f46r (p. 19) above.
87. For these purchases, see p. 18.

54r *cont.* John Willans ground Meaborne   20
And I have as yet in personal stock debts and Morgages
all detts payed   5700
and somewhat oddes as doth appear in my newly made debt
booke[88] 24 Octoberis 1625 soe in this year I amended in my   7690
state in lands
Bought and in stock remeining
                                                                                            _____
                                                                                            1572-19- 6[89]

Of whitch £1572-19-6 I had for Composition of my Uncle
Willyam[90] and his sonne Richard for my Uncle Sir Gerards[91]
lands   200
For lands sowlde at Penrith to Bartram, Whelpdale and
Stephenson[92]   130
And received in bonds for Newbie fines   100
                                                                                            _____

Soe added onely by my care and husbandrie and govern-
ment all charges Borne   1142-19- 6

And (*interlined:* of) the other £330[93] I may allsoe accompt
£300 to be geined by me for without my mutch labour and
art I had forgotten noe pennie of it.

(*l.h.column: entry 3*)   Another order set Martinmasse 1625
My demeins of Lowther Hackthropp and Sleddale being
worth by year I have thus disposed   400
Gyles Moore my servant hath Oulde Parke Grenerigs
Highfield Burtrebanke and Rowland field and £750 in
stock in farme and he payeth £182—Use of stock is   56
John Lowther my sone and my servant W Ion hathe the
wintering theirof and all the rest and £1400[94] in stock ⟨use⟩
and he findes himself his mother and Brothers and house
keeping and showld pay me £150. Use of his stock is   112
he hath alsoe Boones hens Mowlta Mallt and fewell   20
                              Total charge is   588
                                                                                            _____
Giles returneth me   182
John Lowther   150
                              _____   _____
                              total received   332
                                                                                            _____

88. Does not survive.
89. A line and numbers under these figures has been erased.
90. William Lowther of Ingleton, Yorks. P.II.8. See p. 35 below.
91. Sir Gerard Lowther, chief justice of the Common Pleas in Ireland (d. 1624).
    P.II.5.
92. Residents of Penrith, see *Penrith P.R.* (CWPRS).
93. Altered from £300.
94. Figure altered.

Spent clearly	256	54r *cont.*
I have to pay (*interlined:* and disburse)		
annuities	100	
Rents aboute	10	
Sewets in law aboute	50	
My owne necessaries and Jernying expenses	100	
totall to disburse	516	
to maintain whitch I have in		
landes aboute Inheritance	1000	
£6000 stock 1000 unprofitable may yeald me by year	400	
The practise of law at	80	
totall to receive	1480	
soe may remain clear	964	

List of fines due to the Lord of the manor of Crosby Ravensworth, gives tenants' names and amounts outstanding. Begins 1 March 1624[–25], with subsequent entries to Whitsun 1625. Annotations indicate payment. 54v

The like, for the manors of Lowther and Hackthorpe. 55r

The like, for the manor of Newton Reigny. 55v

The like, for Lowther's moiety of the manor of Helton. 56r

The like, for Lowther's tenants in, or manors of, Sleagill, Sleddale, Thrimby and Thwaites. 56v

The like, for Lowther's tenants in the manor of Knipe, and for the manor of Bampton. 57r

Arrears of perquisites of [manorial] courts, 1 March 1624 [–25] for the manors mentioned above, ff54–57, and the manor of Meaburne. 57v

Variety of hands, including Sir J.L.(1)] (Arranged as f26r (p. 13) above.) Accounts of buying and selling cattle, sheep and horses, 1624–1625, places: Darneton,[95] Witton, Penrith, Ireby, Richmond, Northallerton, Kendal, Burnley, Padiham, Blackburn, Milnthorpe, Sleagill, Middleton, Barton, Clifton, Ingleforth, Kirbie [sic], Carlisle, Bampton, Helton, Askham, Appleby, Rosley, Garstang, Ravenglass, Settle. 58r–59r

List of people with numbers [of animals grazed or stints allocated?] who agisted cattle on Lowther's [demesne] land, 1625; with amount due from each, and annotations indicating payment. 59v

---

95. Darlington?

60r   *Account, in bushels and pecks, of corn sown and reaped on Sir J.L.(1)'s demesne in 1624, and corn sown in 1625. Gives amounts sown and reaped for named fields of the demesne, with notes of some purchases. Crops are: oats, bigg, peas, beans and wheat; with notes of malted grains.*[96]

60v   *(Page divided into two columns, l.h.col.:) List of persons to whom cattle were let out for draught use, n.d.*

      (r.h.col.:) Notes of sales of wood, n.d.
    [Across both columns; unknown hand:] A particular of the moiety of the manor of Nunthorpe in Cleveland, Yorkshire, June 1652. Abstract of leases comprising tenants' names, term of lease, number of parcels held, acreage and annual rent. Total acreage 403 acres 3 roods 14 pecks, plus 4 cottages. Total annual rent £151-0-7d, less £5 a year payable to the curate as wages.[97] *With a contemporary note [in the hand of Sir J.L.(2)] of the subsequent purchase of the tithe wool, estimated to be worth £1 a year.*

61r   *[Hand of Sir J.L.(1)] Notes of arrearages of rent which at Martinmas 1623 had not been assigned to Gyles [Moore, Lowther's steward].*
    Note of the assignment of the hirdwick of Lowther's Low Grounds to Hugh Newton, specifying conditions of appointment.

61v–62r   *Rental of all Sir J.L.(1)'s estates for the year beginning Martinmas 1625, ending Michaelmas 1626. (Arranged as f52v (p. 21) above.)*

62v   *[Unknown hand:] List of cattle bought and sold [n.d., but refers to cattle bought off his father]: (arranged as f26r (p. 13) above). With concluding calculations [in the hand of Sir J.L.(1)]. Places: Darneton,*[98] *Richmond, Ingleforth, Appleby, Rosley, Penrith, Kendal, Northallerton, Carlisle, Broughton fair.*

63r   *[Hand of Sir J.L.(1)] Statement of account, between Sir J.L.(1) and his steward Giles Moore, of demesne farming, n.d.*

63v–64r   *[Unknown hand] List of cattle bought and sold, n.d. (arranged as f26r (p. 13) above). With concluding calculation [in hand of Sir J.L.(1)]. Places: Knipe, Sleagill, Richmond, Northallerton, Kendal, Penrith. Ingleforth, Kirbie [sic], Appleby, Rosley, Thirsk, Hornby, Settle, Carlisle, Lancaster, Dalton, Kirby Moore, Kirkby Stephen, Meaburne, Preston, Ireby, Garstang, Thrimby.*

64v–65r   *[Hand of Sir J.L.(1)] Cattle accounts 1626–1628; sheep, horse and corn accounts, 1627–1628, (arranged, respectively, as f26r (p. 13) and f60r above). Places: Penrith, Appleby, Rosley, Lancaster, Kirbie [sic], Kendal, Shap, Northallerton, Preston, Clitheroe, Garstang, Arkengarthdale, Thwaites.*

65v–66r   *Rental of all Sir J.L.(1)'s estates for the year beginning Martinmas 1626, (arranged as f52v (p. 21) above).*

---

96. There are grain accounts for many more years in A1/1 (1557–1607, 1654–1673), A1/6 (1558, 1575, 1603–4) and A1/5.
97. For this purchase see below, p. 70.
98. Darlington?

10 Julii 1627   vide f71 f72

A remembrance how my estate hathe bene Improoved by me since my mariage which was Kandlemasse 1601, when I entered, my revenue at Meaborne was in rent £47 milne £13 a tenement £10 in all   £70

1617
Lowther Hackthroppe Newton Helton   490
                                        ———
     totall left me   560

Note that this whitch was charged with annuities of £220 by year and that I had nothing but Meaborne until 1617 when in July my father died.

I bowht in land in Meaborne; of my fee farmers and tenants and Reagill Grainge lands to the (*interlined* yearly) valew of   150

this with the building my house fenecing and other charges their cost cost me   £2500
for they made me pay deer at first

I have yet of the Manor of Crosbie £25 rent and odde besides service, peats and common wherein I was mutch troubled for want of them at Meaborne before, and are now worth yearly besides generall fine   40

This standeth me in £1200 wherein I considered the hope of benefitt by Comons etc and some command their before whitch I had not left for me a place in the church at church for Meaborne unlesse I showld have sewed for it whitch I loved (*erasure*) not. Besides ould Pickering potted my wifes peats in my absence but he etc [sic].

I have left of Kentmyre[99] a bad Milne unsold whitch I intended for corne milne worth declaro but yearly   (*erasure*)

This I geived and more and somewhat may yet be thought upon for that Mannour as I have sett downe for John

I bought of Mr. Salkeld Sleddale Sleagill land and rent etc in Knipe and Bampton worth by year   £70

This cost me in all   £1450
whereof I have sowlde some part but bought of the tenants of Sleddale as great in yearly valew.

Bampton[1] Mannour all yet remeining (and the tythes all but £30 per annum sowlde) is now worth by year   £90

It standeth in and is worth well with the owlde rent   £1300

---

99. For Kentmere see p. 9.
1. For the purchase of Bampton, and Shap and Threlkeld here listed, see p. 18.

66v cont. I bought in Mathews close in Grenerigs, a part of Hilton tythe whitch he had. Thrimbie Ing before whitch I had no water in summer. Weata. Three crofts at Lowther and a litle at Hackthropp and I walled and am now building houses whitch bettereth the yearly rent. Inclosed heads.[2]   £30

This cost me and will stand me in extraordinarie at the least £1500, besides annuitie to my uncle Lancelot bought in which cost   £180

Some land in Thrimbie and Strickland I allsoe bought whitch in owlde rent   £1

This cost me about £35.

I bought in Sewborweins Demein whitch was granted out in tayle to Jo. Lowther worth by year above   £35
and was letten at £36 to Tom Harrison[3]

This cost me but aboute £350 by reason of some tytle made.

I Bought with my sonnes portion and £700 by me disbursed out of promise the Mannor of Threlkeld woorth by year with casualties £120

This cost me but I purposed to sell the woods least the tenants showlde consume them   £2700

I Bought the Lordshipp of Thwaytes[4] whitch is woorth by year besides my stock with the money I bestowed on the milne   £66

That cost in readie money with the milne repayred   £990

I Bought Hall garth in Shapp and the tythes of Shappe as hay etc whereby I freed Sleddale whitch was in daunger woorth   £16

This cost me about £250[5] whitch may be improved as Thornethwayte in kinde etc and Sleddale freed and Hardendale.

£618-6-0[6]

Soe have I doubled the revenew left me and £50 by year at least more, in a short time and have in stock leases and morgages at this day all debts payed aboute £6,000 and a good part of my purchase is owlde rent the

---

2. *Inclosed heads* a contemporary addition. For Lancelot's annuity see p. 220 below.
3. *to Tom Harrison* a contemporary addition, change of ink; see pp. 222–3, 223, n. 81.
4. Bought from John Thwaites of Ewanrigg (Unerigge), esqr., and the trustees of his father's settlement, for £895, paid 15 June 1627 (D/Lons/W, Thwaits B., 1/4, 5). Sale and mortgage of manor below, pp. 175–82. Customary rental in A1/8; A1/10 is the bailiff's account book, 1651–1662.
5. Altered from £200.
6. Altered from £648.

benefitt whereof is to my heirs in generall fines and I have prefered my 66v *cont.*
daughter with £1000

total disbursed £13405[7]

Remaneth in stock 6000.

It appears by this accompt on the other side,[8] that I have bettered my 67r
estate in purchases, and in stock yet remeineing since I entered[9] near
£20,000 and all my receits of that I entred unto was not near halfe soe much
(*interlined:* if I spent nothing but layde up all) and these disbursements being
all extraordinarie beyond our meintenance, and our children, and familie.
If it be demanded or objected that it cowlde not rise out of this fortune,
and anie Competent fashion meinteined, without some other means as great
gettings by the law etc.

Trewth is, my fees at Law never amounted to £150 per annum. But by
providence and sparing of litles and putting all to the advantage, and with
care and peins (*interlined:* and good bargeins) I meinteined our fashion with
the best of our neighbours and our children, and saved yearly a good part
and bargeined with it, with the best discretion I cowlde, yet in all, studied
still to do it, with love and good reports of those with whome I delt, and
these titles multiplied and the first observable begining was my sale in
feeferme of Meaborne whitch was £1500 near in 1500 payments at long
dayes,[10] to whitch I allsoe sowlde woodde for near £350, and soe mutch
for land in Penrith, whitch is but in all £2200 and this is all I had out of
aniething[11] left me extraordinarie above the revenew, to adde to my estate,
the rest all I saved and geined whitch is near £18,000. Whitch God give
me grace to dispose and use as I aught to his honor and the comfort and
creditt of me (*interlined:* and) my familie.

July 1627   Jo. Lowther

Since this upon the 14th of May 1628 when I and my sonne John
(*interlined:* by my means he beinge at the Temple London) were Knights
for the Countie of Westmerland at the parliament, I purchased Eglestone
Abbey and the Rectories of Startfoarth and Arkilgarthdale[12] of Sir H
Compton Knight for whitch I have payed and am to pay this year thre
thousand five hundred and fortie seven poundes whitch is worth declaroe
to (*interlined:* be) letten £224 by year besides £300 poundes worth of wood
groweing upon it and a faire scite for a house, with great convenience of
stone Wrought, Marble, and lyme to build with, when anie shall be
disposed, wherewith I am tyred.

---

7. Total of purchases £12455, plus £1000 portion, equals £13455.
8. f66v.
9. i.e. at the death of Sir Christopher Lowther his father, 1617.
10. See also p. 212, fee-farm deeds (enfranchisements): Maulds Meaburn B.6, 7.
11. Smudged.
12. In Yorkshire, *V.C.H. Yorks N.R.*, I, pp. 39, 113, 137; deed: Detached Estates
    Box, see also Yorkshire Estates Box. Abstracts: A1/6, ff84v–86v. At least part
    of Arkengarthdale tithe was paid in lead ore (see p. 128 below, and H.M.C. *Report
    no. 76/41*).

67r *cont.*   My stock nevertheless with this Martinmasse rent is as yett all detts being payed ⟨is⟩ fower thousand poundes with my morgages and leases. Soe in this year and hallfe besides my charge at Parliament and housebuilding whitch will not yet in (*interlined:* a) year be finished,[13] I have geined and saved above all charges above £1500.

£70   I bought allsoe Thirnbie Grange tenants and tythe whitch I had forgott whitch cost me £70 and I am to have eyther the tenants or Cowpeland Parke. But it is two years in reversion at least soe it is worth £100 being £7 per annum.   1 Novembris 1628

£70   20 Novembers 1629 I have bought unto since all the tenents of the grange (*interlined:* of Thirnbie) being £3-3-0d. rent and Cowpland Parke, the tythe of them, Cregill Myer which cost me £75 more. But I want the Parke for oulde Rich Salkelds[14] lief.

£100   And I bought John Hodsons tenement in Meaborne for whitch I gave Allan Bellingham[15] and him—£100.
John Lowther   1 Decembris 1629

---

13. For Sir J.L.(1)'s building at Lowther see pp. 233–4.
14. For him see below, p. 52.
15. Either brother or younger son of Sir James Bellingham of Levens, whose manor of Gaythorn included land in Meaburne (Levens Hall MSS, B.VI. 26; D/Lons/L, Meaburn B.29).

(Rental of all Sir J.L.(1)'s estates, ff67v–68r. This page is divided into two 67v
columns, r.h.col. blank) [hand of Sir J.L.(1)]
A rentall of my lands morgages and leases which are let at
rents this year from Martinmasse 1627 till Martinmasse 1628

	£	s	d
Martinmas			
Giles Moore for part of my demeins Rents and stock to			
I him letten	500		
Martinmasse finable granted Gyles			
Newton Reyney	10	12	3
Thwaytes finable	10	17	2
Threlkeld let my B[rother] Fletcher	*(blank)*		
Lowther Towne besides L. Atkinsons tenement granted me	10	13	8
I 3s Knipe rent de claro	3	9	
Sleddale towne	4	9	5
Crosbie towne to Giles	12	1	10ob
q to me which Giles hathe not		3	6
Sleagill		17	6
Bampton let to H Cliburne	*(blank)*		
Newbie amongest leases	*(blank)*		
Thirnbie purchased of L. Salkeld		6	2
	53	6	11[16]
demeins and fee fermes. Penrith	2	14	
Meaborne towne	18	06	11
Milne ther	8	10	
q My sonne Kirby[17]	46	15	
James Fletchers ferme	27	15	
Crosbie services	3		
Newton Milne	3	16	8
I Kentmyre Milne		3	
Lowther Milne	5	10	
I Meaborne kilne decayed		10	
Bampton Demeins etc.	40		
I Thwaites services & hens	6		
I Milne their hereafter	5	15	
Meaborne oxe field £5			
Morgages Clifton groundes	12	10	
I Atkinsons tenement	5		
Rob Powleys tenements	20		
Thirnbie grange rent		12	7

16. *Recte* £53-10-6½d.
17. This entry interlined, it is for the rent of Crosby demesne. For Kirby see P.IV.5.

		£	s	d
67v *cont.*	Leases Crosbie Demein	10		
	My Cousen Barwys fee	2		
	Thirnbie Milne	1	18	
	Denisons tenement	6	8	
	Newbie rent and Milne	5	11	1
	Milne their	1	5	
	Low close at Thirnbie	2	0	
	Ch Jacques low field	5		
	Kandlemasse. Hackthropp finable	3	18	11
	Hilton Towne	7	17	7
	Gyles Moore demeins & stock	245		
	Demeins. Threlkeld	96	13	4
	Hallgarth let to Giles	6		
	Sewborwens	30		
	Penrith Copiehoulde	4		
	Jo Addisons tenement	3	10	
	[18]Thirnbie tythe	(*blank*)		
68r	(*l.h.col.*)			
	Morgages. Blencogoe	16		
	Thirnbie Banke Closes	2		
	Leases. Chappelhowes tenement	2		
	Lewes Grounds		8	6
	Shappe tythe	14	10	8
	Annunciation 1628. Jo Addison's tenement	3	10	
	Milnefield	5	10	
	Newton Multure	7	15	
	Wharton Crofts	3		
	James Fletchers Ferme	27	15	
I	Lanc*elot* Wilkinsons tenement	2		
	My sonne Kirbie for grange	19		
	[19]Eglestone since purchased	(*blank*)		
	Whisundy finable. Newton	10	12	3
	Lowther towne besides Atkinsons	10	13	8
q	Knipe rent	3	6	
	Sleddale towne	4	9	5
	Crosbie towne	12	1	[20]0ob
	Sleagill	0	17	6
	Thirnbie		6	2
	Bampton and Threlkeld lett	(*blank*)		

18. This is a doubtful reading.
19. An insertion in a different ink.
20. Figure illegible.

		£	s	d	
Demeins and feefermes. Penrith		2	14	0	68r *cont.*
q	Meaborne towne	17	13	4	
	Milne their	8	10		
	Crosbie services	3			
I	Kentmyre Milne		3		
	Lowther Milne		5	10	
I	Meaborne kilne		10		
	Murreys rent		5		
	Milnefield		5	10	
	Bampton demeins etc.		40		
	Shapp hay tythes to John	9	6	4	
I	Newton Milne obli*gatione*	3	16	8	
	Thirnbie tythe rent & grounds[21]	*(blank)*			
Morgages. Clifton Groundes		12	10		
	Lanc*elot* Atkinsons tenement	*(blank)*			
	Thirnbie grange rent	2			
Leases. Crosbie Demein		10			
	Thirnbie Milne	1			
	Newbie towne & Milne	6	16		

Thus farre Gyles hathe letten out[22]

(r.h.col. begins opposite here)

Lamasse Finable. Hackthropp		3	18	11
	Hilton towne	7	17	7
	Thwaytes Saint James [day]	12	6	8
Demeins. Hilton tythe		17		
	Thwaytes Milne	5	15	
Leases. Shappe Tythes Jack*son*		14	10	
	+Mr. Washingtons tythes	⟨15⟩		
	+Mr. Laytons tythes	⟨20⟩		
	+Mr. Edenes annuities	⟨3	6	8⟩
Mich. Wharton Crofts X		3		
	+My fee of stewardshipp[23]	8		
	+My brother Flemings fee[24]	3	6	8

Gil*es* Moore out of those rents demeins & stock to him letten

	425	6	8

21. This entry an interlineation.
22. The total of rents to this point is £715-8-10d.
23. See p. 226 for Stewardship of the Richmond fee, for which see *N&B*, I, p. 34.
24. A retainer paid by John Fleming of Rydal, esquire.

		£	s	d
68r *cont.*	Fees at Yorke per annum	200		
	Egleston purchased Mich	110		
	worth by year £230			
	+Coles at Meaborne ovene	1	14	1
		851	2	11[25]

Demeins and profits not in lease nor rented in this year
(*Heading covers both columns*)

	£	s	d
Howse, Parke, Whayle Ing and all below the howse at Lowther but Milne and Milnefield	70		
Some Boones and springs of wood Fines of all my tenants besides Threlkeld being about £150 per annum	80		
Demeins at Meaborne the which my sonne Kirbie had besides the £12 which els were doubled	60		
hews Boons, Bodhole[26] and besides rents before	18		
More, halfe rent of Milne and Reaslack to come in	25		
Atkinsons tenement	5		
Threlkeld is underletten by agrement at mariage,	20		
Hackthropp and Sleddale	10		
Barneskeugh Banke and Whartons howse and garths not yet comed in to me	5	10	

(*r.h.col.*) [*Receipts*]

	£	s	d
Hilton towne 21 Octo[27]	6		
Thwaytes	11	14	7
Hilton tythe	14		
Mr. Washingtons tythe	15		
Mr. Laytons rent	20		
Mr. Edens annuitie qr	3	6	8
rec Jo Fletcher all—[28]	2		
by Will Ion in 2 fine	4	13	4
Giles accompt before Christe	6	10	
Jo Jackson Feb 17	15		
More of L 27	7	10	
Hackthropp rent	3	18	11
Whartons croft	3		
My fee of stewardship	8		
My brother Flemings fee	3	6	8
Hilton tythe more	1	13	4
Coles at Meaborne	1	14	7
Eglestone rent paid	110		
York	200		

---

25. *Recte* £851-2-3d.
26. Boddle: a coin, *E.D.D.*
27. Date a later note by Sir J.L.(1).
28. Undecipherable.

	£	s	d	
Giles	425	6	8	68r *cont.*

[29]

| wrong placed bothe   [total] | 854 | 8 | 1 |
| Jo Fletcherss and Jo Jacksons rents | | | |

68v

(*Page divided into two columns, l.h.col.*) [*unknown hand*]
Separate agistment accounts for horses and cattle, 1628, (arranged as f59v
(*p. 23*) *above*).

(*r.h.col.*) [*hand of Sir J.L.(1)*]
In accompt made at Mich 1628 a little before the time because
I goe to Yorke of my husbandrie of my demeins this year
1627 and 28.

I spent in grasse and medow at Lowther and Meaborne	£110[30]
Use of stock	024
Stock of Catle	398
totall charge	532

I kept horse which stoude to	16
shepe grasse for house	3
house for travaylers	4
Bredd calves worth	10
54 catle soulde [*or*] deade and	162- 1 [-0]
95 remeins beside calves	270
darie	020
Oxen for teame	20
Agistment	26
totall in all was	531 -[1- 0

Cattle sheep and horse accounts 1628–1629 (arranged as f26r (p. 13) above).   69r–69v
Places: Kirbie [sic], Penrith, Preston, Appleby.

(*Page divided into two columns, l.h.col.*) *List of Sir J.L.(1)'s horses, divided*   69v cont.
into types, with value of each type. Agistment accounts for cattle and horses,
(*arranged as f59v (p. 23) above*).
(*r.h.col.*) *List of servants wages 1629, gives 20 servants' names, offices held*
and wages. With a cross-reference [in the hand of Sir J.L.(2) to his list of
1649] to f70v.[31]

Rental of all Sir J.L.(1)'s estates for the year beginning Martinmas 1628.   70r
(*The rental follows the arrangement of that for 1627 (ff67v–68r) which is*
transcribed on pp. 29–33 above; that is, rents due are entered in the l.h.col.
of each page, and receipts in the r.h.col. of each page (although in the earlier
rentals few receipts are recorded). Rents are grouped together under the rent-

---

29. *Recte* £862-14-9d.
30. Altered from £100.
31. More servants' wages are in A1/5.

70r *cont.*   *days when due; each day shows customary rents, demesne rents, mortgages,*
            and leases separately. Under leases are included not only leases but also fees.)
            Concludes, (in the r.h.col. of f70v), with a list of demesnes and profits in hand.

70v *cont.*   *(Bottom of r.h.col.) [hand of Sir J.L.(2)] A note of servants' wages paid by*
            Sir J.L.(2) in 1649, to be compared with that given on f69v, paid by
            Sir J.L.(1).[32]

71r *[Hand of Sir J.L.(1), transcript of heading;]*
            Vide[33] A valeuation of my *(interlined:* Rents and) demeins whitch are not
      f66   particulerly mentioned how they are leased in the rentall before
      f72   according to whitch vallewes I have sometimes let moste of them,
      f67   and doe valew the rest not heartofore letten, made the 20th of
            November 1628.
            List of properties, grouped together in manors, for the manors of Thwaites,
            Threlkeld, Newton Reigney, Lowther, Hackthorpe, Helton, Bampton,
            Sleddale, Knipe, Sleagill, Crosby Ravensworth, Meaburn, Egleston; lands at
            Penrith; and Shap tithe.

71v   *Breakdown of the income of Lowther's estates, 24 December 1628, arranged*
            under feast days and type of income:

	Finable	Demesne	Mortgages	Leases	Total
Mart 1628	53- 8-11	241-17-7	34-10-0	22- 2-9	351-19- 3
Kand					
1628/29	11-16- 6	139-13-4	—	33-19-2	185- 9- 0
Ann 1629	—	159-14-0	—	—	159-14- 0
Whit 1629	42- 8- 9	97- 5-4	14-10-0	17-11-0	171-15- 1
Lam 1629	24- 3- 2	22-15-0	—	53- 6-8	100- 4-10
Mich 1629	—	9- 0-0	—	211- 6-8	220- 6- 8

| Total | 131-17- 4[34] | 670- 5-3 | 49- 0-0 | 338- 6-3 | [1189- 2-10] |

            Add: *Gyles Moore, steward, pays for £500 stock, some*
                     demesnes in hand, and £750 of the rents above, the
                     sum of £420 per annum.   420- 0-0
                                                                  _____
                                                                  1599-18-6[35]
            Demesnes, boons and fines not leased out   294- 0-0
            Reaslack (£20) Wharton Croft and Barneskeugh not
            in possession   26- 0-0
            Lands let to Giles and Brother Fletcher[36] *underlet by* 40- 0-0
                                                                  _____
                        Total yearly revenue: 1959-18-6

---

32. Marginal cross-references in the hand of Sir J.L.(2). More servants wages are
    given in A1/5.
33. In l.h. margin.
34. £44 more finable rent from Bampton and Threlkeld is leased with the demesnes.
35. *Recte* £1609.2.10. This £10 error is carried throughout this calculation, so the
    final total should be £1747.2.10.
36. i.e. Sir Richard Fletcher of Hutton, father of Mary Lady Lowther, P.IV.2.

	£ s d	
Deduct: *Annuities paid by good will to brothers £60, quit*		71v *cont.*
rents (besides Egleston[37]) £12, and not in possession		
and underlet £66: total	132- 0-0	

Clear total for my son and me	1827-18-6	
Short leases £82: fees and annuities for my life and		
others £240. Total:	322- 0-0	

Total	1505-18-6	
Add: *lands not yet in*	132- 0-0	
Other debts, household stuff and stock, all debts paid	100- 0-0	

Clear total to remain to wife & children	1737-18-6	

Hand of Sir J.L.(1), transcript of heading:]   72r
A rentall of Eglestone as I have let it and fermed out for 21 years from the
Annunciation of our Ladie 1629 wherein I have lett it almoste £30 by year
under the former rent that I may be well paid.
*Details of each lease give names of properties and tenants, total rent £234.1.8d
net of £8 payable to curate of Arkengarthdale.*
*List [by Sir J.L.(1)] of all his manors, with, where appropriate, names of
vendors, and annual values, n.d.; total of £1410[38] including Egleston.*

Hand of Sir J.L.(2)] A rental of Egleston Abbey, Lady Day 1650. Gives tenants'   72v
*names, half-yearly and yearly rents; total annual rent £209-11-8d. The rental
is followed by detailed notes, up to 1654, of deductions from this rental for
properties sold, and additions to the rental for properties, including the Abbey
House, repaired; with notes of the cost of repairs.*

Hand of Sir J.L.(1), transcript of heading:] 16 aprilis 1630 I purchased Saint   73r
Bees that part that my Uncle Willyam and my Cousen Richard had by
an imperfect conveyance from my Uncle Sir Gerard whose heir I was and
released to them for £200 and now I gave £2450 for it halfe at the fine
passing the other halfe at 6 monthes, now in trewth I as heir had right
but to part, but especially to that part not divided My Uncle Sir Gerard[39]
surviveing and noe perfect estate made by nyther him nor my Cousen
Wibergh to sever the Jointure of that undevided.[40] The whitch part I have
thus leased the same week I bought it.
*Here follows a rental of the Lowther moiety of the manor of St. Bees, a list
of properties with names of tenants, terms of lease, annual rent and, occasionally, some notes about covenants and other terms of the leases. Total annual
rent £231-14-10d., less rent due to the King and the Bishop of Chester,
£45-4-9d., and £6 to the Curate in part of his wages.*

---

37. Egleston is not, apparently, included in this calculation, see end of f72r.
38. *Recte* £1423.
39. Sir Gerard Lowther (d. 1624) and William Lowther of Ingleton and his son
    Richard. See above, p. 22; for further purchases, see below, p. 38.
40. This is a reference to a complex legal problem which was disputed for the rest
    of the century between the Lowthers and the Wyberghs. Abstracts of deeds:
    A1/6, ff83r–84r. The deeds are in D/Lons/W.

73v–74r   *Rental of all Sir J.L.'s estates for the year beginning Martinmas 1629, written up to Whitsun 1630, (arranged as f70r (p. 33) above).*

74v   *Notes of rent payments in arrears, 1628 to July 1631, with annotations indicating payment.*

75r–75v   *Cattle account for year beginning Martinmas 1629, (arranged as f26r (p. 13) above).*

76r   *Account of horses agisted, 1630, (arranged as f59v (p. 23) above). Account of Sir J.L.(1)'s sheep and horses, 1630–1631.*

76v–77v   [*Rental in unknown hand, receipts noted in hand of Sir J.L.(1):*] *Rental of all Sir J.L.(1)'s estates for the year beginning Martinmas 1630, (arranged as f70r (p. 33) above).*

78r   (*Page divided into two columns, l.h.col.:*) *Agistment account for horses, 1631, (arranged as f59v (p. 23) above). Account of purchases and sales, horses, 1631, (arranged as f26r (p. 13) above). Place: Penrith*

78v–79r   *The like account, sheep and cattle, 1631. Place: Clitheroe*

79v–81v   [*Rental in an unknown hand, receipts noted in hand of Sir J.L.(1):*] *Rental of all Sir J.L.(1)'s estates for the year beginning Martinmas 1631, (arranged as f70 (p. 33) above).*

82r   [*Hand of Sir J.L.(1)*] *List of rents and annuities paid out of the estate, 1632.*

82v–84r   [*Part in hand of Sir J.L.(1), part in unknown hand*] (*arranged in columns across the open pages*). *A list of household furnishings delivered at Lowther, 5 June 1632 to John Lowther [Sir J.L.(2)] and his wife to be kept [as heirlooms]. The quantities of each item are listed, arranged under the various rooms at Lowther [Hall], with a few items referred to in rooms at Hackthorpe Hall.*

84v–85r   (*Blank.*)

85v–87v   [*Unknown hand, possibly that of Frances Lowther, daughter of Sir J.L.(1)*]. *Rental of all Sir J.L.(1)'s estates for the year beginning Martinmas 1632, (arranged as f70r (p. 33) above).*

87v–89v   [*Unknown hand*]. *Rental of all Sir J.L.(1)'s estates for the year beginning Martinmas 1633, (arranged as f70r (p. 33) above).*

89v–90v   [*Hand of Sir J.L.(1)*]. *Rental of all Sir J.L.(1)'s estates for the year beginning Martinmas 1634, (arranged as f70r (p. 33) above).*

91r   29 October 1633

[Value p.a.]   [Purchase price]

+   Since my last accompt of my purchases folios 66 and 67 72 and
£2   73 I have purchased £4 rent charge out of Thirnbie Grange and
sould £2 to Sir Harry Bellingham of it. Cost   £35

+   I have allsoe purchased Thirnbie rent (*interlined:* and mannour)
5.0   of the same Tho Salkeld[41] being £4[42]   230

41. Thomas Salkeld of Corby, see above, p. 9.
42. Subsequent note by Sir J.L.(1): *ouldrent Besides* (erasure) *Websters to be had.*

91r *cont.*

I allsoe have purchased Thirnbie Grange below the way whitch, in manie, purchases and leases, as the every[43] owners were necessitated, troubled me much and cost[44]   400

I have allsoe purchased Assbie Upper Grange of Mr Myles Scafe[45] whitch cost me   730

I have allsoe this year 1633 purchased of Mr. Thomas Layton Merton[46] in Cleveland in Yorkshire it must cost me when I have payed all   2070

I allsoe purchased Saint Bees whitch cost me   2450
and as appears before Hodshons tenement[47]

Thirnbie Grange rent Milne and other parcells   175
   and at that accompt made 1 November 1628 I had as appears
   f67 in clear stock with Martinmasse rent £4000 and have now
   £6,300
   Soe Increased in five years 1 November 1633   2300
   Besides my purchases whitch added togither their is Increased
   this 5 yeres   8390
   whitch devided in 5 is yearly £1676-12-4d [*sic*]

Looke the 7th lefe[48] what estate I entered unto whitch (*interlined:* accompted and) racked to the uttermoste was but £570 by year and with my purchases added at Meaburne Lowther Newton and when my father died it was £693 by year as is in the seventh lefe valewed at my entrie, more than it is now valewed unto with £100 bestowed in Walling upon it and £1000 in building and now as hereunder (*interlined:* my inheritance) ⟨it⟩ is valewed, it is   £1846
                                                       per annum

---

3 febs 1633 Richard Gibsons[49] tenement in Knipe repurchased of 5s 5d ould rent cost   11
Tolesbie of Mr Andertons[50] cost me July 1634   1000

29 October 1634 I esteme Thwaytes worth by year   070
   St Bees £200 Threlkeld 120 Newton £80   400
   Lowther and Hackthropp £450 Hilton and Bampton 130   580

---

43. Doubtful reading; *duing?*
44. Subsequent insert by Sir J.L.(1): *and since this upon accompt new—£200 more.*
45. This Scaife family distinct from the Scaifes of Winton: deeds of property: Detached Estates B.14.
46. See *V.C.H., Yorks N.R.*, II, p. 265; see also pp. 39, 53** below. Abstracts: A1/6, ff86v–87r. Further purchases below, pp. 53**, 64, 74, 172.
47. Above, p. 28.
48. i.e. f7, see p. 6 above.
49. Deed: Bampton B.I.13.
50. In Yorkshire, see *V.C.H., Yorks N.R.*, II, p. 267. Abstracts: A1/6, ff86v–87r. Further purchases below, pp. 68, 184.

91r *cont.*   Sleddale 54 Knipe 12 Shappe 17 Slegill 3 Thirnbe 44[51]   130
           Meaburne £224 Crosbie 40 Asbie 46   310
           Eglestone 224 Marton 132   356

           These are inheritance besides lease and mortgages   1945[52]
           The woods and generall fines ⟨and perquisites of Courts⟩ being
not valewed, but an easie estimate made of my casuall fines
whitch tenantright fines I dislike as an occasion of mutch trouble,
and uncerteintee, for if they will not pay a reasonable fine, if
we goe to sewet for it we loose more than we get. Theirfore I
advise that it be studied how to selle a legall certeintie of that
revenew, by sale or decease and [*apparently unfinished*].
[*Same hand, change of ink or pen*]
In June 1634 I purchased George Andersons lands in Tolesbie
of him and his father and mother worth yearly £66 for whitch
I payed £1000[53]

December 1634,[54] my clear estate is 7460 for that my purchase
accounted this year increase—2160 as may appear above. But
(*interlined: sale of*) Threlkeld and Penrith is £400 theirof.

91v   [*Unknown hand*] *Account of Cattle sheep and horses, 29 October 1633 (arranged as f26r (p. 13) above). Places: Rosley, Penrith, Ireby, Garstang, Ravenglass, Appleby, [North]Allerton, Carlisle, Broughton, Kirby [sic].*

92r   (*Page divided into two cols; l.h.col:*) *List of animals to be wintered in 1634.*

           Agistment account of horses 5 May–8 July 1634 (arranged as f59v (p. 23) above).

           (*r.h.col.:*) *Valuation of [Sir J.L.(1)'s] horses, 15 November 1634, gives number of each type of horse, and value.*

92v   [*Hand of Sir J.L.(1)*] (*there is a single column for figures at the r.h. margin*)
           vide folio 91   £
           16 January 1634 I purchased My Cousen Wibergh his part of
Coles in Saint Bees[55] except in his owne demeins, all his tenants
and tenements about £6-13-4d owlde rent, and his Saltpannes and
Coles in Henrie Davies groundes worth £88 per annum ⟨for⟩   88
whitch cost me in surrender of a lease and money £1037 soe the
totall inheritance is now   2000
And my stock now is only £6500
I must kepe Giles Moores lands I fear for £600 but as yet but
£500 worth by year 40

51. In this line all the figures are inserted above the line.
52. *Recte* £1969.
53. Mentioned above on this folio.
54. For a valuation of his estate 1 May 1634 see Appendix II.
55. For the commercial effects of this purchase see Hainsworth, p. 64. For St. Bees
     see above, p. 35.

8 Febrewary 1634 I gave my sonne my estate in Crosbie demein
whitch I had for two lives whitch I had rented at £20 by year,
and the arreres of the same rent of £8 per annum for 5 yeres,
whitch goeth in the purchases and £36 payed in rents beforehand,
and £35 payed towards the purchase. (*erasure*) My lease was
valewed in part of the price for the lands I sowld in Penrith after
the estate made at his mariage whitch were lesse than nothing
for I payed 28s odde for soccage rent 13s 4d bondage rent £6 schoole
rent and sume purpresture rent,[56] soe I payed out more than
received, and it never worth to me that [which] appears in this
rent booke 20s declaro, whitch he should have had after my death,
and this above theirfore, is not only to be taken as satisfaction
but in addition of my love. Whitch with the rest God grant be
soe taken, that I may be Inj*oin*ed to give away greater matters.
29 October 1633 my stock clear   £6,300
I have since payed as appears for Gibsens tenement—£11 Tolesbie
£1000, Giles land—£500. Coles salltpannes and tenants at Saint
Bees—£1037 in all £2548.[57] And have yet in stock with the
Annunciation rent besides £220 or rather £350 given my sonne
(*interlined:* John) my my [*sic*] lease of Crosbie demein—£5800 all
detts payed and allowed for. For this year (*interlined*: and halfe)

with the addition of Threlkeld and Perrith £400 increased	£2048[58]
Deduct back the	400
Cleared out of Revenew and peins	1648
Besides the £220 above in all	1868

This 12th of Febrewarie 1634[59]

June 1635 I purchased Mr Wildews[60] Mannour and Lands of
Marton and tythe hay of that parish for £2200, if the Inclosure
procede to pay £200 more worth by year cleare now   146
In this my sonne John Joineth and I pay £200 more than he yet
allow him halfe profit, and Intend to leave it all to him and more
if he doe deserve it. [*Change of ink and pen.*] Januarie 1635 we lett
it upon the division whitch I brought to passe, by a decree at
York by consent, up*on* the Inclosure of the moore their for £150
for 10 yers and it will be then better.

21 February 1635 since this purchase stock rests clere detts payed
£6600 with the Ladie dayes rent next. Soe increased this year with
the purchase of Mr. Wildews land my part £1300 as doth appear
in my dett booke, £2100. But their is their (*interlined:*, and [in]

---

56. A late use of the term, see John Reeves, *History of the English Law*, ed. W. F. Finlayson (3 vols; 1869), I, p. 208.
57. For these purchases see p. 37 and above.
58. Figure 4 altered.
59. For a further calculation see "A note of my father's stock 22 June 1635", total £6,482.19.9d., by Sir Christopher Lowther of Whitehaven in Hainsworth, pp. 177–78.
60. See J.L.(2)'s comment, below, p. 53**; for Marton see p. 37.

92v *cont.* the owlde stock,) desperate by my sonnes adventure (*interlined*: and)
£1000, and unprofitable £600. Soe rests £5000 whereof the use in
stock yealds yearly at 8 per Centum £400 and my sonnes Intend
to double it in trade and I have besides (*interlined*: what) my sonne

John (*interlined*: hath in) lands	£1900[61]
and I have in fees payed me at York at	260
Totall revenew lands Stock and fees	2560
Whereof we doe not now expend the	560

[*Change of pen and ink.*]
August 1636 I and my sonne purchased Wensledale the tow Allens

parts viz Mathews and Edwards whitch cost £2505[62]	175

But John sowlde Threlkeld[63] demein and Milne £70 per annum
and the purchase rented at £175 odd soe we have added to our

revenew when payed for	105

Soe 8 Sept 1636 our lands of inheritance are £2300 besides my
sonnes particular purchases beinge—[64]

93r   20 February 1636

We have now as appears on the otherside £2,300 per annum of Inheritance.
Whereof if I leave John my eldest £2000 and Christopher £300 I have
besides putt £5,500 into my sonnes hands for them and their sister and yet
will remein if I live one year a convenient stock to advance theim that
deserve. I haveing withdrawn the land I Intended from my sonne William[65]
whoe would perforce marie against my desire, my reasons everie way tried,
and contrarie ⟨to⟩ his promise under his hand to me (*interlined*: unto) whitch
I may aide £300 per annum, that I have at York and in fees elsewhere by
my owne dayly peins. Soe as we may conclude we have in revenew amongst
us our stocks considered £3000 per annum (though their be fear we have
lost £2,300 in an Hambergh shipp goeing from Hull to ⟨Leeds⟩ (*interlined*:
Hamburgh never heard of ship men nor goods[66]) of whitch £1000 is the
moste we all spend and John getteth before me near £250 per annum by
practise. Soe as if my sonnes in Marchandiseing our goods with anie success
we may spare £2500 per annum for their advancements. Whitch if Imployed
at 8 per centum or in their trade may produce at least in 9 yeres, if we
live togither if God soe please £30000. Whitch if bestowed in land will then

---

61. Figures obscured by alterations.
62. In Yorkshire, see *Three Seventeenth Century Yorkshire Surveys*, ed. T. S. Willan
    and E. W. Crossley (Yorks. Arch. Soc., Record Series, CIV, 1941), pp. vii–xxv,
    1–81. For the purchase see pp. 42**, 53 below. Deeds and abstracts: A1/6, ff113r–
    119v; Detached Estates B.25; Yorkshire Estates Box. Wensleydale coal account
    1639 in A1/5. Further purchases below, pp. 42**, 53, 60, 70, 74, 156, 157, 177**, 182.
63. See also below p. 53; for Threlkeld see above, p. 18.
64. Illegible.
65. Cf. below, p. 230–1.
66. Interlineation difficult to read. Sir Christopher Lowther's papers tell us that this
    ship probably sailed on 2 November 1636 and that the cargo was valued at
    £2,352.9.10d. Hainsworth, p. 196.

93r *cont.*

buy £2000 per annum, and if bestowed in land as precedeth with the procede
will buy above £1500. And if I die I leave theim the means to make
that good. Whitch in nine yeres further being but 18 may be as the first
(*interlined*: is accompted) £90000. Whitch would purchase £6,000 per annum.
(*erasure*) But if Imployed in land above £4000. Whitch were too mutch to
desire and then my Eldest sonne would not be 50 yeres of age. Soe as this
Considered we may prayse God that sets soe faire hopes in wordlely[67]
ceirteintie before us, and kepe us from base and covely desires, and not
to toyle ourselves beyond reason and discretion, and if we fall short of this
mutch ⟨as⟩ (*interlined*: though) my forward young sonnes presumed to
thinke to doe better) yet have. we great cause to prayse God that hath sett
us before all our neighbours in our ranck in these tow Counties, yet to live
mearly Idle untill weaknes or Infirmities inforce us we may not without
offence. But I now groweing aged 55 years Infirmed with an hernia in my
left stone and in that side of my brain, must think of ease, and to take
up from publick Imployment while all hathe succeded well haveing now
noe desires left me, but of rest, findeing it damageing for me that must
lead, soe to carie my self as to please and kepe my station and securitie,
though I be as circumspect as I think anie man can be.

And yet if I give over all, studie without use is follie. Husbanderie sutes not
my yeres nor state, and though the example be good the trouble is great
(*interlined*: profit little) and to sequester from friends and Countrie by
whome I have continuall trouble is hard to doe, hazards sume, and stands
not with conscience as some say whitch is to be regarded, wherfore we will
with what care and moderation that we can kepe us in our way, therein
giveing content to all that we can, and (*erasure*) after a short time, leave
of all that doth displease us in our course whitch we are not necessitated
unto, and everie one according to our years and occasions studie to put
things in (*interlined*: sutch) a certeintie as we may, for we that would
increase welth must otherwise increas trouble, care, envie and daunger,
and in the end, part with all without great care, or desire, what becomes
of it when we die, those whome we are bounde to provide for haveing a
Competancie, and perhaps may be forced before we die to part with it,
with losse, and perhaps grief, or shame, soe as I care not for honar, whitch
now in England is tituler and the shaddow of what was, and without power,
nor for pleasure as an enemie to health, nor for wealth, whitch is not got
nor kept without danger (*interlined*: and) am resolved, in a faire prudent
way to husband our fortunes, and direct my children and their children,
with some benificence, yet reserveing the mein and myne owne honor in
that. Whitch is now noe longer to be kept, then I have to give, as all examples
shcw me.   Jo Lowther

67. i.e. worldly.

94v   *Sheep account, November 1635 to 29 July 1637 (arranged as f59v (p. 23) above).*

95r   *Cattle and horse accounts, 1636 (arranged as f59v (p. 23) above). With some sales (arranged as f26r (p. 13) above) at: Appleby, Rosley, Penrith.*

95v   [*Hand of Sir J.L.(1)*]
        vide folios 91:92:93:22 July 1637   £-s

        The purchase and Inheritance folio 93 appears   2,300
        Since June 1637 purchased of Mr Roger Moore his lands in
        Wensladale called Symonstone and lyeing in the Midle of our late
        purchase formerly parcell for the some of £1600 besides use being
        worth per annum   0,100[68]

95v–96r [*Change of hand, unknown hand*] *Half year's* [*customary*] *rental of Bampton, Martinmas 1653. Gives names of 63 tenants with, for some, their place of residence, and rent due, total £6-3-9d.*

96r   *Rental of the free rents due at Martinmas* [*1653 for Bampton*]. *List of names of 30 tenants, with rent due, total 13s-9d.*

96v   [*Hand of Sir J.L.(1), transcript of heading*] A note of the rents of Marton and Tolesbie as it was when I purchased them and as is now anno domini 1635.

        Rental giving tenants' names, details of leases in being, with estimate of value when each lease expires.

        Total now   *£126-17-0d*
        Improved in 2 years   10-0-0
        Improved in 7 years   15-0-0
                                    ─────────
                                     25-0-0
                                    ─────────

        Rental of Tolesbie, tenants' names and total rent £66.

        [*Change of ink and pen*] Mr. Wildews Mannour of Marton
        purchased June 1635 for £2400 if division hould otherwise £2200
        rented at my purchase declaro[69]   £146

        August 1636 we purchased Wensledale of the 2 Mr. Allens rented
        at our purchase £175 but is better then £180 present will be £200   £180
        It cost us £2505
        June 1637 we purchased Symonstone lyeing in the Midle of our
        purchase formerly made in Wensladale for £1700 pounds worth
        with a morgage   £110[70]

---

68. Compare this with the entry on f96v below, for Wensleydale see above, p. 40.
69. See above, p. 39.
70. Compare this with the entry on f95v above; for Wensleydale see p. 40.

(Blank.)   97r

Rental of all Sir J.L.(1)'s estates for the year beginning Martinmas 1635,   97v
with notes of receipts. (Written and arranged as in f70r (p. 33) above.)

Rent arrears from Martinmas 1629 [to 1636?].   99r
[Partially in hand of Sir J.L.(1), with annotations indicating payment.]

(The page is divided into two columns, l.h.col.) [Unknown hand] List of   99v
properties and rents beginning Martinmas, n.d. [1636].

(right hand column) [Hand of Sir J.L.(1)] List of properties with monies.
The left-hand column appears to be a rental, the right-hand column notes of
receipts begun for the year 1636–37, but left incomplete at the death of
Sir J.L.(1).

and of Sir J.L.(1)] List of properties with monies, purpose not clear.   100r
and of Sir J.L.(2)] List of Sir J.L.(2)'s horses, June 1641.

A rental of all Sir J.L.(1)'s estates for the year beginning Martinmas 1636,   100v–101v
with notes of receipts. (Written and arranged as above f70r (p. 33) above)

(l.h.col.) [unknown hand]

Martinmas 1636	£. s. d.
×| Lowther finable	11- 4- 2
× Knipe finable	3-10- 9
× Sleadell finable	4-10-11
× Thrimby	1-10- 6
× Thrimby of Tho Salkeld[71]	2 ⟨2- 6⟩
× Sleagill	0-17- 6
× Crosby[72] towne	12- 1- 9
× Lewes and Winnster	0- 8- 2
Newton	10-12- 9
× Threlkeld *(ink blot)*	15-12- 6
⅄ Sainte Bees finable	6-17- 6[73]
× Thwaites and Walke Mill	10- 5- 0^ob
× Bampton finable	6- 4- 7
£85-16-1[½]	

John my sonne is to pay me for all these and their fines	82[74]
hereafter at Saint Andrews Day Midso and Kandlemasse	

Demaines	
× Marton and Tolsby rent Yorkshire[75]	131 0 0
× Lowther Mill	5 0 0

---

71. For this property see p. 36.
72. Crosby partially obscured by blot; i.e. Crosby Ravensworth.
73. These figures heavily altered.
74. Figures and note in hand of Sir J.L.(1); deed of the lease Lowther B.II.5, Sir
    J.L.(2)'s rental for the lease on the end leaf of A1/8.
75. The letter "k" in Yorkshire is interlined.

		£.	s.	d.
100v *cont.*	Bampton free rent	0	13	6
	× Bampton demains	34	10	0
	× Meaburne Towne	19	4	1
	× Meaburne Mill	8	0	0
	× Crosby services	3	0	0
	× Cowper tenant right refused	0	1	8
	× ⟨Knipe Boones⟩ ⟨Whitson⟩[76]	0	4	3
	× Eglleston and mill	100-	15-	10
	× Newton mill	4-	5-	0
	× St. Bees pecke mill ⟨Coles⟩	3		
	× Coles and Salt pans purchased	13	10	0
	× Preston tythes	22	10	0
	× St. Bees tythes	20	0	0
	× Hensingham tythes	17	0	0
	Hassap meadowes	0	15	0
	× Thwaites Mill	5	15	0
	× Carriges and hens theire	3	7	4
	Towne tearme [at Thwaites]	0	13	4
	⟨× halfe Oxe close	3	0	0⟩[77]
	Lan*celot* Garnett Whar[ton] Croft	1	0	0
	My Coles at 6d per tune	30	0	0
	× Bartriebancke	9	0	0
	× Highfield	23	0	0
	× Skellans and Sheepe	7-	10-	0
	× Wensledale	80	0	0

Morgages
× Clifton towne per tenants[78]　　　　　　30　0　0

Leases (*the r.h.col. of text ends opposite here except for*
　　　　a note opposite the Thrimby Grange entry below)

× Divident at York　　　　　　　　　　30　0　0

Candelmas

John is to have these rents and fines
and other lands paying at this day £82[79]

× Hackthorpe finable	4	3	2ob	
× Hilton towne	7	17	7	

　　　　　　　　12-9-ob[80]

---

76. The words *Knipe Boones* were struck out, and annotated *Whitsonday*, presumably an instruction to the copyist to enter the boons under Whitsunday in the next rental. The annotation was deleted then by the copyist.
77. This entire entry struck out.
78. Dubious reading.
79. The whole of this entry an annotation [in the hand of Sir J.L.(1)].
80. i.e. £12-0-9½d.

Demesnes	£.	s.	d.	100v *cont.*
⟨Tythe fish Saint Bees	00	15	00[81]⟩	
Estretes besides Crosbie and Saint Bees	8			
× John Brian	3	15	0	
× Sewbourwens	30	0	0	
×|Haberkeld field and Little Haber	⟨0	14	6[82]⟩	
× Turne bancke and Lowfield at Meaburne	8	10	0	
× Cringleings	4	5	0	
Brayton and Ensides	8	[?]	6[83]	
× Arkendale tyth	32	0	0	
Hassap	0	13	0	
× Pecke Millne	3	0	0	
× Milnefield	5	0	0	
× Mr Tankard for Edge close Habber closes	7	8	4	
× Weaty Lanclot Walker	2	10	0	
Thirmeby Grange	16	5	10[84]	
× Oxe close Haberkeld Little Haber and Risselmyre	9	0	0[85]	
× Thirmby mill for yeares[86]	2	0	0	
Coles and saltpans	13	10	0	
× Tyth fish	0	15	0	
Giles more rent	22	8	0	

r.h.col.) [*Hand of Sir J.L.(1)*]

	£.	s.	d.
Clifton towne rent allewd	30	0	0
Bartriebanke rent paid A	9	0	0
Meaburne Milne	8	0	0
Threlkeld rent ff	15	12	6
Bampton demein ff	34	10	
Highfield rent at	23	01	
Wensledale paid me	50		
Crosbie towne 2s 6d sould Rooke 3s4d Dudley 5s for gathering	00	10	10
Paid in to ff thereof	11	10	3
Services	3		
Lewes and Winster	4	8	2
Crosbie services	3		
Meaburne towne with allowed	19	4	1
Lowther ff allowance paid	11	0	10
Sleddale besides Johns A	3	12	11
Newton with Kings rent	10	02	
Bampton rent A	6	4	5

81. The whole of this line, an insertion [by Sir J.L.(1)], has been struck out.
82. The figures in this line struck out.
83. The whole of this line an insertion [in the hand of Sir J.L.(1)], the entry in the shillings column altered to illegibility.
84. Note in the r.h. col. opposite [hand of Sir J.L.(1)]: *accompted for in this accompt.*
85. Perhaps 9d.
86. For this purchase see p. 17.

		£.	s.	d.
100v *cont.*	Marton and Tolesbie allowed	131	00	00
	Lowther Milne	5		
	Egleston all but £2-3-1	100	15	
	Garnet Crofts with Jo	1		
	Skellans besides wheat	4	11	
	Dividend at York	41		
	in part of St Bees rents	73		
	Thwaytes rent qr. 14s 8 walk milne 11s-11*d*	11	06	7
	Cariages their	2	10	2
	part of Milne rent	4	18	
	Thirnbie rent	3	10	6
	Sleagill rent	0	17	6
	Turnebanke Jo L	8	10	
	Cringleings	4	5	
	Milnefield	5		
	Mr Tankard	7	8	4
	John Brians rent	3	15	

the £73 of St Bees is Hensingham £19 Preston £22 pecke £3
Habers £10-10s tythe (*erasure*) St Bees £21–£73

	ould Saltpans	13	15	
	St Bees coles w ff quo	6	15	10
	pecke milne K	3		
	Braisto[n][87] Eynsides K	8	2	6
	Knipe in part	3	8	7
	[*Change of ink: same hand*]			
	Newton Milne	4	5	
	Thwaytes Milne	7		
	Hens Thweytes		14	4
	Jo Musgrave	10	6[88]8	
	Weata rent paid	2	10	
	[*Change of hand—unknown hand*]			
	Hilton rent	7	15	[?][89]
	Hackthorpe rent	3	19	10
	of Thomas Sleddall[90]	30	0	

(*end of r.h.col., except note, see p. 45, n. 84*)

101r	(*l.h.col.*) [*Unknown hand*]			
	Leases			
	× Chappelhow tenement	2	0	0
	× Smith minority	0	3	4
	× Will Fletcher for 9 years Kand 1636	5	0	0

---

87. Blotted.
88. Altered.
89. Indecipherable.
90. For Sewborwens, see below, pp. 222–3, 223, n. 81.

	£.	s.	d.	101r *cont.*
× Thomas Wibergh and cleasby croft	0	16	0	
Mr Washingtons tythes	14	0	0	
× Meaburne demaine tyth	7	13	4	

Anunctiacon 1637[91]

	£.	s.	d.
× Meaburne per He Wilson	14	3	4
× Wharton crofts	3	0	0
× Eglestone then	100	15	10
Newton moulter	7	19	0
Preston tythe	22	10	0
Sainte Bees	20	0	0
Low Demaines	11	0	0
Hensingham tythe	17	0	0
Greenehow	2	15	0
Holmes	10	10	0
Hens	1-	6-	8
Rottington tyth	1	6	8
Willyam Ion and Mich. for Meaburne	40	0	0
× Hall garth	7	0	0

Leases (*r.h.col. ends opposite here, except see note below*)

	£.	s.	d.
× Cowpers tenement	6	10	0
× Fees and devident at Yorke	85	0	0

Whi*tsun* Rent added upon assignment.

	£.	s.	d.
Thomas Powley rent	0	0	5
× Newton finable	10	12	9
× Lowther rent	11	3	10
× Knipe rent	3	10	9[ob]
× Sleddale towne	4	5	0
× Crosby towne	12	1	9
× Sleagill towne	0	17	6
× Thirmby rent	3	13	6
St Bees	6	17	6[92]
× Threlkeld	[93]15	12	6
× Bampton finable	6	4	7

| | 75 [-0- 1½][94] |

	£.	s.	d.
free rent theire 12s 6th 15s 10d	1	8	4[95]
for all these and their fines I let them my sonne payeing now	82[96]		

---

91. Altered from 1633.
92. Figures have been altered to read thus.
93. Partially obscured by a blot.
94. Total of Whit. rents.
95. Note in r.h. col.: *paid to* (blank) *£01-6-0.*
96. Whole note an insertion [in the hand of Sir J.L.(1)].

101r *cont.*	Demaines	£.	s.	d.
	Bampton free rent	0	12	6
×	Lowther Mill	5	0	0
	Murris rent	0	5	0
×	Meaburne rent	16	19	5
	Meaburne killn decayed	0	0	0
×	Meaburne milne	8	0	0
×	Crosby services	3	0	0
×	Bampton demaine	34	10	0
×	Newton millne	4	5	0
	Cowpers tenant right	0	3	4
×	Braiston and Enside	8	2	6[97]
	Knipe Boons	0	4	3
×	Morton and Tolesby	131	0	0
	Salt pans and Coles	13	10	0
	Coles @ 6d per tune	30	0	0
×	Skellans and Sheepe	7	10	0

£263-2-6[98]

	Morgages			
	Clifton towne and town end	10	0	0
	Leases			
×	Mr Washington lives	10	0	0
	Atkinsons wardship and lease	12	0	0
×	Devident at Yorke	50	0	0

(end of l.h.col. r.h.col.) [*Sir J.L.(1)'s hand*[99]]

	W Chappellhow tenement	2		
	Mr Washington	14	10	
*	Hall garth	7	0	
*	Thomas Wibergh	0	16	
	Newton Moulter J L	7	[?]	0
	Meaburne demeine J.L.	14	3	4
	Eglestone[1]	85	3	5
	of Saint Bees rent at Wills accompt	20		
	Mich Mounsey in part	15		
	Hallgarth	7	0	0
	York all paid and allowed	66	1	5
	More their	50		
	Meburne tythe only	2		
	More[2]—	1	10	

---

97. A figure in front of 8 has been erased; 2 has been altered to read thus.
98. Figures [perhaps in hand of Sir J.L.(1)], *recte* £263-2-0.
99. Entries marked * may be in an unknown hand.
 1. A large blot obscures the end of this line.
 2. This line inserted and partly indecipherable.

	£.	s.	d.	101r *cont.*
Cowpers tenement in 2 oxen	6			
Wharton crofts J L	3			
Newton Multure A	7			
Lowther Milne E L	5			
Meburne Milne me	8			
* Newton moulture by Edmond	0	6	0	
Meburne rent paid	16	9	5	
Brayston and Ensides set by Jo	8	2	6	
Marton and Tolesbie paid therof for wheat	130-10-		0	
Skellans in part	5-10-		0	
Dividend at York	60			
Part of Newton Milne —	3	0	0	
part of Saint Bees	6			
Jo Lowther for ould rents	82			

(*r.h.col. ends, save note opposite Whit, Bampton free rent entry, see above,
p. 47, n. 95*)

h.col.) [*Unknown hand*]				101v
Lam*mas*				
× Hackthorpe	4	2	3	
× Hilton towne	7	17	7	
× Thwaites	12	6	10	
Demaines				
× John Brian rent	3	15	0	
×!Edward Willan Cringleings	4	15	0	
× Thwaite Mill	5	15	0	
× Chr Lowther for coles (*erasure*)	20	0	0	
John Musgrave for Thrimby	16	5	0[3]	
Salt pans and coles	13	10	0	
× Highfield	13	0	0	
× Meaburne peat rent	1	8		
Morgages				
× Thomas Wibergh Croft	0	16	0	
Leases[4]				
× Mr Washington tyth (*interlined*: expired)	⟨13	0	0⟩	
× Mr Edens annuity	⟨ 3	6	8⟩	
× Smiths minority (*interlined*: spent)	⟨ 6	3	4⟩	
Michaelmas Demaines				
× Wharton croft	3	0	0[5]	
× Mill field	5	0	0	
× Rayslace	10	0	0	

3. Noted in r.h. col. [by Sir J.L.(1)]: *allowed for accompt*. For Musgrave see *D.N.B.*
4. The three figures for this section have all been struck out. [The two interlineations are in the hand of Sir J.L.(1)].
5. Note in the r.h. col. [by Sir J.L.(1)]: *received by me.*

		£.	s.	d.
101v *cont.*	Holmes	10	10	0
	Low demaine	11	0	0
	Coles	10	0	0
	Sainte Bees	0	0	0
	Rottington tyth	1	6	8
	Orchard	1	1	0
	Grenehow	2	15	0
	Wm Ion for Meaburne and stock	65	10	10[6]
	Henery Wilson	14	3	4
	Giles Moore lands	20	0	0
	Low banke	3	0	0

Leases
Fe for the kings stewardship		8	0	8
fe and divident		90	0	0

(end of l.h.col.)

(r.h.col.) [Sir J.L.(1)'s hand]

Rayslack paid		⟨20	0	0⟩
By Edmond Burn Helton		7	15	0
Hackthorpe to Do:		3	19	10½
Meburne peat rent allowed in Jo Winters wage and				
5s5d to them with Rowl Cooke			*(blank)*	
Rich Winter Cringle Ing		4	15	0[7]
Mr Edens annuity paid		3	6	8
Thwaites Milne		5	15	0
Tho Wibergh paid me		0	16	

(end of r.h.col. except for notes indicated, see p. 49, n. 5)

102r *(blank)*

102v *[Hand of Sir J.L.(2)]*   2 Octobris 1637

After my ever memorable and moste deare and loveinge Father Sir John Lowther knight and one of his Ma*jesty*s right honourable Councell established in the north, had finished the painefull course of this life wherin he was exceedinge lawbowrious both in the generall care (and in a manner sole government of the cuntry, and in the manageinge of his owne estate ⟨and⟩ to the best advantage as appeareth by all his bookes and prudent consideracons, and which is a *(erasure)* principall motive and incuragement to those whoe God hath ordayned to succede him to an imitation of those singuller wayes wherin he soe wareley walked And shall more fully appeare in a more proper place) he departed this life after a fortnights sickness (conceived to be a hott fevor) on Friday mor
nieng beinge the 15th of September 1637 my Mother, Brother Kirkeby, my sister his wife, and my wife with Mr Teasdall the Parson,[8] and others then present in soe myld and gentle mannor, his strength considered, as could be; and to the greate

---

6. Figures altered.
7. Figure altered.
8. For Mr. Teasdale see p. 74 below.

comforth of all present his last words beeinge gratious God be mercifull
to mee; And as I am confidently perswaded he was merciful to him upon
his hartie repentance. Soe I besitch him that he will be mercifull to us that
are members of him and directe us in that course of life which may be
most to his Glory and our eternall comforth; Amen

Now that I may give an accompt as my worthie Father and Greategrand-
father Sir Richard Lowther[9] and summe other of oure Ancestor*s* have
formely done before me, of my beginninges and *pro*ceedings in estate, that
it may appeare to our posteritie, what every one in his tyme hath done
for the continuation and advancement of oure auncient familie (as I may
say without arrogancie) since I know none of greater antiquite not that
it is a thinge to glorie in, but as a tooken of Gods blesinge unto us. And
that this if it be well, may be a motive to those that shall succede me (*erasure*)
to doe the like or better, howsoever they may see (as I my selfe desired
to doe) what others did before them and what is amisse (*erasure*) or omitted
may throught observation, and the wisdome which in tyme to cumme will
teach, may be recitified. And will be a pleasure to see the diversitie and
alteration of tymes, and how thinges grow to maturitie in tymes of peace
and what (*erasure*) chainge warr and troubles and an unsettled governmente
doth produce.

Upon the mariage of my wife (*interlined*: I being 20 years of age) which
was the first of february in the first yeare of King Charles, with who I had
£2000 portion in the purchas of the Mannor of Threlkeld. I had in setled
in [*sic*] poss*ession* for my wives Joynture

	£	s	d
The demayne of Hackthropp lett formerly to Mr Clyburne at per annum	90	00	00
The demayne of Threlkeld let by me for but I had but, for 7 years, for it £50 of my father	58	00	0
Sledall demayne valued at £40 but lett only at	30	00	0
Shapp tyth rent	10	00	0
Somma totalis per annum	188	00	0
But I sowld Threlkeld demayne soe rested	130	00	0

This for about 3 years did but serve us I Beinge at the
Inns of Court and my wife ⟨at⟩ with mee at London
for neare one year.
For 3 years after I saved yearly somewhat for stockinge
my ground and was with my father for about i year paid
for my table soe that in 1629 vide foll. 6[to] I had in stock
£524.

---

9. For Sir J.L.(1)'s account of his doings see A1/1, ff335–361, Appendix I; no
similar record by Sir Richard Lowther is known.

	£.	s.	d.

102v *cont.*

Before Kand 1632 I had as appeareth their likewise in stock and banckt £600[10]

But in Mich teareme 1630 I was caled to the barr and then presently after beginn to practise law at Yorke before my father & then begunn my estate first to increase.

103r[11]

the Joynture lands before beinge — 130 00 0

the first thinge I bought was Cowpland park for Rich Salkelds life, my father haveinge formerly purchased the reversion[12] which cost me to Will Mowson £14. And was lett to Webster £14-00-0 — 004 13 4

I likewise disbursed to Sir Edward Musgrave for Newton and Allonby tythe £240-00-00 besides charge of fine and pardon[13] 20 00 00 which is in trust when he payeth me my monie to reconvey it and is lett at £40 per annum but the monie will purchase per annum — 015 00 0

Then in 1633 I sowld the tenants of Threlkeld to 4 penie fine for which wee hade near £1200 in 4 years time; and had 2 parts of it my father a 3d part.[14]

Jan 1634

I bought (*erasure*) the Mannor of Litle Strickland of Mr R Crackenthropp for £300-00-0 which is only (*interlined*: with) 20s per annum paid the King[15] — 066 05 0

1634

I bough Hugh Walker Houlmes near the Waterfals brigg which cost me litle but my father in a suit was against him wherin I advantaged him as much worth per annum — 002 00 0

1634

I there about bought Copperthwait tenement and added to Sledall demayne and sowld (*erasure*) 3 parts of the Bawfeild and 2 closes caled the Stritings in lew therof which is not good in law by the deeds yet lett them enjoy them soe they use themselves, as is fit, my new purchased better by per annum — 001 10 0

1632

(which I forgott) I (*erasure*) Built the mill at Lowther

10. Doubtful reading.
11. Top l.h. corner of MS missing.
12. See above, p. 28.
13. i.e. The conveyance of the property.
14. This agreement, which re-stated all the customs of the manor, was enrolled in Chancery as a decree (P.R.O., C78/1205/no. 7; copies also in C.R.O., D/MH/VII, p. 31, and Threlkeld B.1, 2). For Threlkeld see above, p. 18.
15. For the rental of purchase see above, p. 15.

Craggs wherein ther was since question made by the Lord   £.   s.   d.   103r *cont.*
Warton but by the opinion we held and by law, that
question was quietted, it cost me £040:00:0   005 : 0   0

1634
My Mother and I joyntly built the paper mill at
Ambleside, but by my Speciall helpe beinge the Kings
Steward for the Richmond fee which cost me
£010-00.0   002   00   0

June 1635
My father and I purchased the Manour of Marton in
Cleveland of Mr Wildon as appeareth by this book
fol 92. My part cost—£1100:00:0[16] And one halfe
after lett by me above   085 : 00   0

1635
That year after and the next year, I lent Mr Goodyear
£400,[17] And to Jo. Hanson £60 which will purchase
above per annum £460   30 :   00   0

1636
I bought George Bowes part of Messuage and tenement
at Marton which cost £20 : 00. 0   001   10   0

1636
I sowld Threlkeld demayne (*interlined*: except the Wood)
which was then in Chr Hawkines possession for about
£1100 which was troublesome to (*interlined*: me) beinge
ill land and troubled with water and not farmable.[18]

August 1636
My father and I purchased the Mannor of Wensladale
of the 2 Allens at London wherin I had much trouble
in passinge the assurance which gave mee first occasion
precisely to look into the manour of conveance.[19]
And the one halfe for my part cost £1275, per annum   085 : 00   0

May 1637
I bought a tenement in Setbusk[20] of one Whiteheade
for convenience which cost me £057 lett at   004 : 10 . 0

Then bought [*sic*] of Abraham Medcalfe his part
of a tenement at Newhouse which cost £040   003 . 6 .   0

---

16. See p. 39; for Marton, see p. 37.
17. For the significance of this mortgage, see below, p. 64.
18. Sold to Wilfrid Irton of Threlkeld; deed: Threlkeld B.7. Purchased in 1624, above
    p. 18; see D/Lons/Letters 1630, for an attempt to sell, when the ownership
    of the timber was disputed. There is a 1636 timber valuation in Threlkeld B.13.
    See p. 52 for the 1638 enfranchisement of the tenants.
19. See p. 42; for Wensleydale, see p. 40.
20. These four tenements are all in Wensleydale.

		£.	s.	d.
103r *cont.*	Allsoe then bought Wilfrid Moors ⟨3ᵈ part of⟩ his tenement and lett again to him which cost £090	007[21]06		8
	Allsoe a 3ʳᵈ part of Rich Medcalfs tenement in Cotterdale which he had by lease cost £022.0.0.	002	06	8
	Given by my father in Crosby Demay*ne*, 200, per annum	012	00	0
	These particulars cost beside the joynture £3698 revenuew per annum	⟨496 - 16 - 0[22]⟩ 398	16	

103v June 1637

My father and I as appereth foll 95 did purchasse of Mr Moore Symondston wherof cost in present monie £800:00 and is worth per annum but was to clear[23]

	£.	s.	d.
	050	00	0

Soe the particulars of the other side beeinge 398 : 16. 8

The total revenew of or as good as inheritance is 448 : 16 : 8

Indetted then to Mr Wildon Mr Alle*n*s Mr [*sic*] Mr Moore, parcells in Wensledale Mr Hutton Mr Blencoe—about— £2050

	[£]	
I have in dettes owinge me above	0750	
In rents of my owne and per discent (*interlined*: and fines) dew at Mart 1637 per litle booke	0800	
In rents and fines generall at Chan*g*e per [*sic*] at per booke[24]	0300	
In annuities and detts omitted which maketh upp	0200	2050

all beeinge or might be paid by Cannd.

Besides my personall estate which I estimate this viz 60 catle remaininge haveinge lately sowld £30 worth		160
12 horses and mares worth		060
400 of the great kind of sheep and hoggs		120

---

21. Figures altered.
22. Figures altered and line struck out.
23. Above, p. 42.
24. Sir J.L.(2) intended to record fines in A1/8, ruled—up for the purpose; very few entries, none for many manors, were made. The *litle booke* of the previous paragraph is not extant. Most particular fines from 1648 are in the book of fines 1648–1698.

		£.	s.	d.	
Househowld stuffe and Husbandrie geare	150				103v *cont.*
Cropp of Corne and haye better than	120				

fines to receive of the tenants for the
generall fine of Crosby save purchases of
£11 rent beside that dew of Mart and Cand
before mentioned to be paid at long
dayes or in 3 years about in all   £2000

    Soe the total personall estate is   2600

Whereof only £1000 profitable the fines
only cuminge in but yearly the use wher
of is   080. 00. 0.

The yearly revenew which I had by descent upon my
fathers death ⟨*viz.*⟩ in possession—viz:

Miche*lmas* Millfield halfe years rent per Michael Kitson   05. 00. 0.
apris son mort
05.00.0
Martinmas fineable.

	£	s	d
Bampton halfe years rent per Alphabet	06.	04.	9
Crosby	12.	02.	9
Lewes and Winster (*erasure*)	00.	11.	0
Knipe then	3	10	9
Lowther then	11	04	2
Newton then	10	12	9
Thrimby towne then	02	02	6
Thrimbie Grainge tenants	01	10	6
Thwaits and Walkemill[25]	10	06	0
Sledall omited in the order	04	10	11
Slegill likewise omitted	00	17	6
Threlkeld fine certaine most of it	15	12	6

79 : 05 : 11
Demesnes the rents then dew

Lowther mill	05	00	0
Marton et Tolsby	131	00	0
Crosby services	(*blank*)		
Cowpers tenantright	00	01	8
Newton Mill	04	05	0
Hens and Cariagis at Thwaits	03	07	4
Towne tearme ther then	00	13	4
Burtrybank and farr hay closes	09	00	0
Highfield then with stock of 400 sheep[26]	23	00	0

25. *and Walkemill* probably inserted later.
26. *with stock of 400 sheep* inserted later.

		£.	s.	d.
103v *cont.*	Skellans then with stock of 400 sheep[27]	07	10	0

183 : 17 : 4				
Kandlemass	Hackthropp fineable	04	03	4
	Helton then finable	07	17	7
	Estreats per Jo. Musgrave	08	00	0
Demesnes	Sewborwens then	30	00	0
	Millfield	05	00	0
	Lancelott Walker for Weatey	02	10	0
	Burthrybank	09	00	0

66 . 10 . 11				
Annunciation	Halegath only Jo Jackson	07 : 00 .		0
07 : 00 : 0	Total of this side is £349.13.2[28] ⟨Hall⟩			
	Newton Moulter then forgotten	07	19	0
		349	13	2

104r[29]   Whitsunday rents fineable

	Bampton halfe years rent	06	04	7
	Crosby then	12	02	9
	Lowis and Winster	00	11	6
	Knipe then	03	10	9
	Lowther then	11	04	2
	Newton then	10	12	9
	Sledall then	04	10	11
	Slegill then	00	17	6
	Thrimby towne then	02	02	6
	Thrimby Grainge	01	10	6
	Thwaites and walkmill[30]	⟨10	06	0⟩
	Threlkeld then fine certen	15	12	6
	Tho Pawley of Sledall imp*rove*d rent	00	00	5

69 . 06 . 4[31]				
Demesnes rents then dew				
	Lowther mill	05	00	0
	Marton et Tolsby	131	00	0
	Murres rent	000	05	0
	Crosby serves	(*blank*)		
	Newton mill	004	05	0

27. *of 400 sheep* inserted later. Cf. Whitsun demesne entry for figure of 100, see
     below, p. 57.
28. Figures have been altered to read thus.
29. Top l.h. corner of MS missing.
30. *and Walkmill* probably inserted later.
31. Altered to read thus.

	£.	s.	d.
Cowper tenantright	000	01	8
Knipe boones	000	04	3
Skellans with 100 sheepe[32]	007	10	0

⟨Highfield with sheep⟩   (*blank*)

148. 05. 11

Lamasse rents dew:

	£.	s.	d.
Helton towne finable	007	17	7
Hackthropp with Strickland[33]	004	03	4
Thwaites then	012	06	10
Demesnes then Highfield with stock of 400 sheep	23	00	00

47 : 07 : 9   Hilton tyth then forgotten   17 10   0

17 . 10 . 0

Soe the totall some of this page [f104r] is   282 . 04   0

The some of my fathers land at the other page [f103v]   349 13   2

The totall of all is at the full as now it is   631. 17   2

Demesnes then in my fathers hands not letten, but
valued in this book at my fathers entry, fol 7°b dearer
than they will now give, and as others are lett, viz.

	£.	s.	d.
Greenerigges and Brackenbergh	038.	00.	0
Thrimby Inge and Mills Close since bought	005.	00.	0
Owld Parke with the 2 hay closes added	032.	00.	0
Rowland feild waled new by my father and faules	024 :	00 .	0
Whaleinge[34] well mended by Wale-inge[35] and gutters	010 :	00 .	0
New Parke much as it was but the woodds in Whalebancke decayed by ill Springinge	030 :	00.	0
Below the house: Dawlands remayne-inge the low part thereof beeinge given to the Parson in my tyme in lew of tyth out of the demaynes of Lowther and Hackthropp	007.	00.	0

yet he never had anie tyth in kinde in
my tyme but 6 grasses in Greeneriggs

---

32. *with 100 sheepe* a later insert. Cf. Michaelmas entry, above, p. 56.
33. *with Strickland* probably inserted later.
34. i.e. Whale Inge.
35. i.e. Walling.

104r *cont.*	⟨for⟩ in lew of tyth for which he was given the Low Crofts and High Crofts bought of the tenents	£.	s.	d.
		003.	00.	0.
	The Low Flatts lett for formerly to the parson	022.	00.	0.
	Buckhoulme and Esklaymoore lett formerly	026.	00.	0.
	The orchards and gardings better than before that besides the Chapell beinge formerly a poowle	003.	00.	0.
	Boones moultermalt carages, perquisite of Courts	012.	00.	0.

Soe the totall remayneinge in possession not letten
at Lowther as valued at the highest though the grounds
be impaired   212 : 00.   0.

The totall of the rents and grounds lett as above is   631 : 17.   0

Soe the totall in possession Sur Mort del Peire   843 : 17.   2
The totall of my owne Inheritence on the value of it
in mortgages per ut ante   448 : 16 : 0
Besides £2600 in detts and fines whereof use profitable   080 : 00 . 0
The yearely casualties of fines   080 : 00 . 0

Soe after Cand 1637 to have in revenew besides
my detts paid   1452 : 13 : 10

J Lowther fils Jo Low*ther* M*iles*

(*Here begins an annual "diary" recording the most important events, purchases and disbursements year by year. In the hand of Sir J.L.(2), but in differing styles and inks: an asterisk at the beginning of a paragraph indicates a change of style or ink.*[36])

104v	1637 Soe the Inheritence beeinge at my fathers death[37] of his and my owne ⟨purchases⟩ clear beside the use of my stocke aboute	1400.	0.	0
	Ther remayned lands lett to pay legacies viz Egleston part of Wensladale Bampton Thwaites Asby qr per annum about	0500.	0.	0

36. A1/1, ff271–285, *Memorable observations* etc (Appendix III), is another "diary" which abbreviates events recorded here, but which has additional agricultural contents.

37. Sir J.L.(1)'s will, with the special commission for proving it from the Prerogative Court of York, and a copy of the arbitration of the will by Sir Richard Dyot, are in Lowther B.IV.17; probate inventory: D/Lons/L, wills and settlements, no. 2.

Soe the total revenew in all was then	1900. 0. 0	104v *cont.*

The personall estate of my owne with detts for fines et my detts all cleared — £2600

My fathers personall estate with which I retened, in detts goods househowld stuf qr — £2700

    Soe the total personall estate was — £5300

Out of which revenewes and detts I paid in that yeare and the yeare followinge for my fathers detts as appeareth by his owne booke to Mr Willdew, Mr Allens, Mr Moore *Mr* Peniman, *Mr* Lancaster[38] — £2500

1638   I paid my Mother upon a hard agreement Contrary my fathers will — 0500

1639   M[*sic*] I bought Mr Coles (*interlined*: last) part of Standraw[39] which cost me — 1000

I paide my Brother Christh the last part of £1000 given to him — 1000

And the Baronetshipp putt upon mee[40] — 0850

1640   I Built 2 sids of the Court viz the stable side and the gatehouse part. Which cost me with leade Cutt woorke etc at the least — 0400
I wainscoted the new midle tower and armor — 0050

I Bought out Crosby demayne which cost with what I laid out before, beside the buyinge in of severall leases I had in it[41] — 0670

I Bought out Shapp tythe Rectory which cost with what I had owinge upon it[42] — 0750

I waled that part of the Owlde Parke towards Brackenburgh Lymed Rowlandsfield Suites at Law with Sir Ja Belingeham, James Webster, my Liveries[43] — 0200

---

38. No such book survives, but see Sir J.L.(1)'s inventory.
39. In Wensleydale, abstracts: A1/6, f119; for Wensleydale, see p. 40.
40. G.E.C., *Complete Baronetage*, II, p. 440.
41. Crosby, see p. 14.
42. Shap, see p. 18. This purchase is explained below, p. 153.
43. No record of these lawsuits, or the livery payments, could be traced in the P.R.O.

104v *cont.*	I have in detts besides mortgages about as I compute for fines arrear for catle, lent monie and other things and rent arrears[44]	4000		
	In catle horses sheepe viz 2000 sheepe £600 140 Catle £400 30 horses and mares £150	1150		
	Househowld stuff, plate (*interlined*: books Clothes) and other goods qr about	1000		
	Soe the total disbursed and remayning in monie goods and detts is	14070		
	I should receive in 3 years and one halfe viz unto the Anutiation 1641—£6600 in personall estate £5,300. Soe the totall of this beeinge[45]	11900		
	It appearithe ther is saved and gained by good orderinge and disposeinge things in this 3 years and one halfe to live out of it	02170		
	*1641 I built the oxhouse the barne above it, and kilne upon Whalebanke which I wrought out of Whale quarrie which cost about	200		
	I paid my Brother Will his first half legacie	500		
	I bought a burgage house in Appelby of John Winter (about 1639: which I forgott) to make me free from towll which cost but about	010		
	I bought Thursby tenement in Cotterdale And the Moore tenement there which cost [46]	060		
105r[47]	I new inclosed Beanslacke close which cost walleinge in one quarter of a year and leading	050.	4.	0
	I new built the house of Skellan Heade	010.	0.	0
	*About this year I bought in Powley tenement and the parcells in Thrimby field which cost mee about	100.	0.	0.
	1642 * I paid my Brother Will the last part of £1000	500.	0.	0
	I new brought the water in lead to Hackthrop house which cost	060.	0.	0
	I Bewtified the hall porch (*interlined*: and stayere case) at Lowther Peylasters[48] and other woorke cost	040.	0.	0

44. *and rent arrears* probably inserted later.
45. The figure *£14070* apparently inserted later on this line.
46. In Wensleydale, see p. 40.
47. MS damaged in top l.h. corner.
48. i.e. Pilastres.

I payed my Sister Frances	1000.	0.	0	105r *cont.*

And this year was the (*erasure*) parlement wheirin by the troubles litle profitt was made[49] in Westmerland besides the losse in Yorkshire of my rents whereof I got but litle

1643
1644 In these tow years the warr continuing and the Scots beeinge in the cuntrey ther was noe profitt made, (*erasure*) but plundered by Brigges[50] souldiers both Hushowld stuff Lynninge Clothing; Arms ammunition horses catle sheepe lost in these aboute 0500. 0. 0.

1645
1646 In thies tymes the troubles still continued and I paid in sesses 1642 untill then in Yorkshire above 1500. 0. 0

And in Westmerland and Cumberland about 0500. 0. 0

I paid for the the [*sic*] sesse, of the 5th and 20th part in Yorkshire and Westmerland[51] 0300. 0. 0

I lost by the break of one Delaney a Merchant above 0450. 0. 0

I paid for my Composition of Gouldsmith Hall 2000.[52] 0. 0

I was licked for the 20th part againe at Haberdasher Hall (*interlined*: for £2000)[53] which cost mee above 0100. 0. 0 and was forced to stay in London neare a yeare about that and my Composition

*1647 This yeare the tymes continued pro ut I paid my sister Kirkeby hir leagacie given to hir Children of 0500. 0. 0

I contracted to grant and convey Crosby demesne to my sister Dodsworth in Lew of the latter £1000 in full of hir portion intendinge if please God to add as much in lew.[54]

I new walled the Crossewall in the New Parke and Cutt

49. Rest of paragraph a later insertion [by Sir J.L.(2)].
50. Col. Briggs, Parliamentarian commander of Westmorland forces in the Civil War, J.P. and Sheriff, 1644; later, with Sir J.L.(2), an agent of Lady Anne Clifford, and her under-sheriff (*Hist. MSS. Commission, 13th Report*, App. I, p. 186; D/Lons/L, letters, 1649; P.R.O , C5/384/17).
51. This figure agrees with *Calendar of the proceedings of the Committee for the advance of money*, ed. M. A. E. Green (1888), p. 652.
52. Agrees with *Calendar of the proceedings of the Committee for compounding*, ed. M. A. E. Green (1888–92), pp. 1024–25. See also p. 84, n. 40, below.
53. Agrees with *Cal. com. advance of money*, p. 652. For Lowther's rental when his sequestration was lifted, see p. 76, below.
54. For Crosby see p. 76; finally sold to John Dodsworthy, below, p. 68.

105r *cont.*   the high part of the wood which I sowld for £80 for Coleinge for the forge at Whinfell

I Burned the Banke at Bearslacke which I had lately inclosed and sew 16 bushells of wheate and Rye upon it which cost   0040. 00. 0

I likewise Bought Stainton in the Bishopprick of Durham in Nicholas and Jo Pearsons name in trust worth per annum and soe lett for £62 which cost   0930. 0. 0

And exchainged it the next year for Mr Fulthropp lands at Marton of equall value lett at £62 per annum.[55]

105v * In this year (*erasure*) upon Wednesday the 9 of February about 7 at night depparted my most dearly and intyrely beloved wife Dame Mary Lowther daughter to Sir Rich Fletcher and Dame Barbara daughter of Crackentropp of Newbiggenge after wee had beene maried and lived a most happie peaceable and loveinge tyme together of 22 years and 10 dayes and had 11 children and shee then at hir accompt of the 12th whereof it pleased God shee dyed not delivered whereof she (*erasure*) had an apprehention all the tyme of hir beeinge with Child. Shee had a greate breach about 7 weekees before shee dyed which brought hir weak yet shee recovered that and at the 5 weekes end had another breach ⟨untill when⟩ and upon Sunday at night the sixt weeke had a third breach untill when she felt the child to stirr and the issue of Blood Continued with hir until Wednesday night shee dyed in which tyme shee was hourely[56] afflicted which extremitie of sickness, and yett no travell upon hir to deliver the birth yet in all her sickness was singularly patient penitent and full of ejaculation and prayers that God would be merciful to hir that he (*interlined*: would) pardon hir sinnes and receive hir soule. Gave hartie blessinge to all hir Childeren beeinge 8 then liveinge and all about hir, gave mayne signes and tokens of Deare love to mee by imbraceinges and prayeres for mee and myne and towld mee they were all my owne. Shee was a pious, prudent, painefull lowborious loveinge charitable hospitable woman free from anie (*erasure*) affectation, pride, conceiptedness a lover of building Contriveinge, of houses, gardians and makeing of alterations rather for convenience than magnificence, shee knew when to spend and to pare; A lover of hir husbands friends and Kindred above hir owne. A good Accounteant who keepe my books of accoumpte for about 20 yeares and in the receipt and disbursement of above £20000 I cannot say I ever lost £5 soe careful shee was to give content and keepe

---

55. This paragraph written subsequently to that recording the purchase of Stainton.
56. Doubtful reading.

all perfect and strayght in which tyme wee never (*erasure*) but
one purse which shee kept and was a faithfull steward. She
loved hir Children dearely and was very careful to have them
piously and prudently educated. And in short shee was a
woman both for hir person and partes not to be paralleled
and in whom I had as much Comfort as could be desired in
a woman to good for me or this worlde. And therefore the
Lord hath taken hir to himselfe wheir I am fully assured shee
injoyeth the full frewetian of perfect bliss and happinesse to
which place the Lord Almightie bring us for (*interlined:* his)
deare love of his Sonne and our Saviour Jesus Christ the
righteous amen amen.

Jo Lowther[57]

1648   *   In this yeare the Scotts with Duik [*sic*] Hamilton
entered Carlile and these Cuntreyis I beeinge and liveinge then
in Yorkshire the spoyle and losse was soe greate of all sides
that noething was made, for I lost 400 sheepe about 10
beevees[58]; spent 100 bushells of malt 50 of bigge 10 of otemeale
50 of otes 10 wheate; loste in meadow and good grasse above
£150 in corn upon the ground £20 and 16 horses and mares
worth £100 besides the whole profit of 30 kine; soe that the
losse was apparently about £800 at Lowther besides the whole
profit of the rest of my estate went in Quarter and Sessements.
Soe noethinge but losse was in that yeare.

Only in the latter end of that yeare I bought for Dick[59] the
tenement of Threlkelds in Lowther which cost, in regard of
the conveniencie, viz   £560

1649   In the beginninge of this yeare I was forced to take
the land and grassinge belongeinge to Barney Lowther tenement in Lowther in a debte in my Sonne Christ. name yet
the same was singerly useful beinge mixed with Threlkeld
tenement and is now intyre and by this meanes by makeinge
sume exchange for Hugh Newton Close adjoyninge ⟨at⟩ to
Esklamore I may have the kine to goe in Skelands and
Buckholme and milke them at the back of the Low Orchard,
or it is near for tylage. It cost beeinge about 9 acres and
3 grasses   £32

Corne was this yeare in the Springe; wheate 30s per bushell
Pease £1-4s-9d Bigg £1-2s-0 Otes 14s and soe I paid and malt
at 16s.

105v *cont.*
106r

---

57. The neat and uniform hand and some of the interlineations suggest that this
    tribute to his wife was copied into the book from a draft.
58. Doubtful reading.
59. i.e. Richard Lowther, P.V.4.

106r *cont.*   * In September in this yeare my Uncle Rob et me purchased
Maske in trust for our children which cost intyrely £13000;
and I have the ellection for £500 to have the whole, or if I
disliked to accept of £6,500 as the moitee cost, God grant it
paid beeinge a deepe ingagement the tymes considered; and
2 of my Daughters that are cuminge on for mariage to be
provided for; it stands but about 15 years purchas and a halfe
and the houses have cost above £3000[60]   £6,500

1650   *   About 8[ber] Sir Hen Bellingham dyed and my sonne
haveinge received noe portion ⟨he⟩ wee were to have a
Composition in (*erasure*) Goods and monies of £3000 but vide
the storie after beeinge forgotten in his place.[61]

1650   *   September this yeare I bought out Mr Goodyeares
lands which I had formerly in mortgage[62] which cost in reddie
payment with that brought before beeinge £42 per annum but
I gave him other land for 40s per annum part of it soe declaro
£40 per annum cost mee then.   0.600

And he hath only the house cotages and sume smale yards
worth £20 per annum yet remayninge which is the securitie
for severall rents dew and payable by him beeing £128-12s per
annum and this hath compleated the lordshipp and made it
intyre and is beter by £10 per annum then the present rent
but I lett him it againe for 21 years at that rent.

The next monethe after October I sowlde the Mills at Bannard
Castlebrigg end for £450 beeinge but lett formerly at £20 per
annum but but [*sic*] that yeare at £30 per annum. Which I
did in regard they were then in good request and stood only
upon countrie now beeinge tyed to them and Lord Sir H Vayne
a potent man who had formerly prohibted the tenants of the
towne to grinde by amercinge of them at the Courts, and
beeinge chargeable in repaires and a good rate did all minde
mee to sell them hopeinge to bestow the monie better if
Please God

106v * 1651   At Whitsuntyd I bought a parcell of land at Maske
that (*erasure*) cost at £4 per annum   £50

1651   September the 20th beeinge Teusday I maried my Daughter Ellinnor to Christo. Wandesford of Kirkelington Esqr shee
beeinge 18 years and a halfe and had been (*erasure*) then
Governesse of my house since her mothers death beeinge but
litle after 14 years at that tyme; in which tyme both in my

---

60. In Yorkshire, *V.C.H., Yorks N.R.,* II, p. 402. The trust is enrolled in P.R.O.,
    C54/3743 m 13. See below, pp. 68; 86 P.III.12.
61. Paragraph a later insertion by Sir J.L.(2). See below, p. 170; PP.V.1, V.2.
62. i.e. at Marton, see p. 53, for the mortgage; for Marton see p. 37.

106v *cont.*

presence and absence when, whe had manie souldiers quartered, she carried her selfe whith so much temper sobriety and
discretion as was much beyond her yeares and much to my
contentment and her owne honor and credit. I gave in portion
£2000[63] viz £1000 in hand and £1000 within a year after pun
certaine agreements to repay £1000 if shee dyed without issue
liveinge. (*erasure*) I was to to [*sic*] lend or ingage for £1500
monie towards payment of detts the estate was lyable unto;
they beeinge very greate viz about £4000 that was chargeable
upon it and £4000 more charged upon the English and Irish
estate. And yet ⟨yet⟩ ther is about £3000 of that sume not
legally chargeable but the younge man desiring his fathers detts
should be paid agreath to more than he needeth. They will
probablie have about £400 per annum at present after the
Grandmother and Brothers death £200 more. After Mothers
death £400 more and after 21 years for 2 annuities of £250 per
annum ended £250 per annum more; soe in all then £1250 per
annum and my Daughter to have a Joynture of £300 in
England and £100 out of Ireland to be made good.

The Irish estate likewise to cum in after detts and legacies
paid and discharged accordinge to his fathers will which as yet
is very uncertaine both for the unsetling of the tymes there and
the charges upon it and sum question by ther nativis unto part
of it; it is said it was worth above £2000 per annum besides
a portion and other lands worth £500 per annum worthie the
lookinge after; but as yet neglected; I kepe them for 6 months
not upon contract but for ther good and setle them in our way.
Shee may be a stay to all the rest if please God I should be
taken from them.

I paid upon the mariage that yeare £1000.

In November this year I went to London and in regard I
found my selfe inclyned to mallencoly and wantinge suitable
societie and foreseeinge my Childeren as they came to be men
and women were like to leave mee and setle elsewhere and not
findeinge that contentment in my eldests sons Mariage by a
suitable temper to mee as I (*erasure*) hoped I was upon these
and other considerations beeinge not then 46 years of age
and reasonable good strength resolved to marrie if I should
light of a person of a temper suitable to my desires wherine
my ayme was to have one that were religiously disposed of a
gentele and sweate condicion of good parentage and comely
Person and of about 35 or 40 years of age. God haveinge
blessed me with 4 sons and 4 daughters I was not covetous of
a new (*interlined*: numerous) bread of Children yet consider-

---

63. Altered from £1000.

106r *cont.*   inge my estate my owne purchases and what advantage I might
have by my marriage conceived I might with as much reason
and justice conferr a hansome estate upon (*interlined*: the
eldest) son by a second venture, as well as

107r   my father did upon a second son by the first venture; and the
rather since I was resolved to leave a better estate to my eldest
then was left mee or ever was belongeinge to the house,
which if it were but as well[64] husbanded (*erasure*) by (*erasure*)
those that succeed as it hath beene by us viz my father and my
selfe (*interlined*: these two last ages) (*erasure*) there would be
an increase of estate rather more to be envied then desired;
for a moderate fortune is mostle easilye kept, freest from
hazard, dainger and envie; the rewine of manie families as is
to apparent these tymes; and therefore when it is at a fitt
proportion to preserve; not inconvenient to spredd the familie
into branches that they may be a strengtht to the ancient
⟨familie⟩ (*interlined*: house),[65] an addition of a familie to the
Comonwelth ⟨the⟩ and may prove as fortunate as anie of the
name. Upon the former, and other considerations I was invited
to the thoughts of a second mariage And upon enquirie was
informed by letter from my Uncle Rich Low. at London of a
person that might happily suite with my desires for I had
formerly given her a tast of my intentions and haveinge
formerly showne my dislike of some proposed for severall
reasons was better informed to ⟨meete⟩ fix upon such as might
be sutable to my affections; Soe that cominge to London in
9ber 1651 it hapened that the partie who was commended to
her was occasioned to repaire thether about freeinge of her
Joynture and sume other estate of her sons from Sequestration
at Haberdashers Hall. And haveinge an oppertunitie shortly
after of an interview and beenge well informed of qualitie
Birth, condicion estate and other circumstances; And a good
likeinge and affection beinge setled, it proceedeed afterwards
to a treatie ⟨betwixt⟩ wherein wee had none to arbitrate
betwixt us and was shortly after happily concluded, but by
reason her estate was not then cleared shee was not willinge
to a perfect consumation untill that was done, which beeinge
done, the mariage tooke effect the 9th of April 1652 which
was at her lodgein in Russell Street in Covent Garding beeinge
private as the tymes then required[66];

She was daughter to Sir John Hare of Stow in Norfolk eldest
sister to Sir Ralph Hare Baronet, Widow to Wolley Leigh
esquire who was son of Sir Frances Leigh of Adington in

---

64. Partially obscured by a blot.
65. *Familie* has been struck out and *House* interlined over it.
66. A copy of the marriage settlement is in Lowther B.III, 5.

Surrey and Grandchild to the Lord Coventry late Lord Keeper
her Mother beeinge ⟨the only⟩ his Daughter by a former wife
by whom he had likewise the now Lord Coventry his eldest
son by that venture. Shee had one son and one daughter to
Mr Leigh her former husband; Shee had a joynture of £700 per
annum at Torpe in Surrey and elsewhere but covenanted to bee
and continew of the value of £800 per annum which was
made by the advice of the Lord Coventry her Grandfather[67];
I was content she should dispose of her personall estate for
her Daughters portion beeinge noe wayes provided for, and
leave the dispose

1652   of her son to her freinds though otherwayes at first
conceived but would not insist upon it though it might have
been benificiall to him if it had beene otherwayis but in
matters indifferent I was willinge to leave it that tyme might
give the trew testimonie what had been best; I thought it
touched upon mee to wayve the trust and to confir it upon
others, yet since the profit could not be much to stand with
honestie and the trouble and certaine in an intangled estate
and the expectation more and the blame most if things had
not succeeded well by management at such a distance as Kent
and Surrey, I was content to admitt of those consideracons to
balance the former haveinge what I had free from accompt or
suspicion of ends upon him; Wee went presently after mariage
to Thorpe her joynture where wee stayed about 6 weeks to
setle all there with the tenants which I found anserable to
what was said and soe came to London; and were at Marton
upon Midsomday after ⟨which⟩ part of which I setled for her
joynture and the rest (*erasure*) and part of Wensladale upon
the issue mayle betwixt us. And since our mariage unto this
17th of 9br [16]52 wee have not had a crosse woord and I
thanke my God have noe reason but rejoyse in my choyse
shee being a most affectionate loveinge and observant wife,
and a lover of my freinds, Children, the Cuntry and a Cuntry
course which I most feared by reason of sume arguments
before and in tyme of treatie; It cost mee at that tyme at
London before our return to Lowther   £1000

in expenses and extraordinares upon that occasion in juells to
her, Coach and horses and Cloathes and other occasions
besides about £300 more of her halfe years rent dew at our
Ladie day before mariage which was spent likewise for her
Cloathes and household charge. And this is a breviate of my
proceedings, and the perfecting of the woorke wherein both
shee and I were more tymerous, then in our former choyses,
by reason of the remotness of freinds to both distance of

---

67. A copy of Woolley Leigh's marriage settlement is in A1/8, ff334r–339r.

107v *cont.*   Cunteryes difference of the condicion of Cuntryes and manor
of liveinge betwixt north and south and the difficulty of trew
understandinge for anothers tempers, condicons, and estates,
to which wee were soe much both straingers unto but by
relation; yet where there is honestie and trew noblenesse of
both sides ther cannot bee anie considerable mistakes, as it
hath proved to the full contentment of both parties which I
pray God may continew to his glory and our Comforts.

In this yeare about Whitsuntyd I contracted with my Unckle
Rob to sell him my moitie of Maske which wee purchased
joyntly[68]; for £500 profit for which I was to have £7000 and
£7000   consideracon from the tyme of the contract until payment.

At my goeinge to Marton at this tyme viz June [16]52 I
purchased of Mr Foster part of his land at Towlesby joyninge
to Marton Manor about (*erasure*) £35 per annum which cost
mee[69]   £520 00 0

And in this month of 9[br] I paid my Daughter, Wandesford   £1000.00 0
the remaynder of her portion of £2000 beeinge
besides 15 moneth keeping her hier husband and servants
gratis which I did not promise; and the 17th of 9[ber] shee bore
her eldest son Christopher when I witnessed at Lowther.

108r * 1652.   I likewise about this tyme contracted with my Brother
Dodsworth for the saile of the Lordshipp of Crosby beeinge
the rent of the tenants about £23 halfe of it at 2 penie fine
certaine the rest arbitrary but poore and Scout Green mill
rented at £7 per annum for the some of £950 in regard the
rent was ill paid
£950   the fines worse and troublesome to compound and was
convenient for him haveinge sould him the demesne before as
part of his wives portion intendinge to bestow that and the
price of Maske formerly sowld upon some considerable
purchas.[70]
     * 1653   My Brother Will and I lent Cousen Midleton of
Stockell to receive his land beeinge to be sowld by the
Parlement £6000 to have £1200[71] per annum for 7 years at
Whitt and Mart, after my part beeinge[72]   £3500.00.0
And to receive halfe beeinge £600 per annum[73] to begine at
Whit 1653 first payment
     *In June in the same year was likewise contracted with Sir

_____

68. See above, p. 64. P.III.12.
69. Tolsby, see p. 37.
70. See above pp. 14, 61, for Crosby Ravensworth. P.IV.13.
71. Altered from: *£5000 to have £1000.*
72. Noted by Sir J.L.(2): *betwixt us.*
73. The rest of the sentence is a subsequent insertion.

Jo Mallery for £4500 then lent to have £500 per annum for
21 years out of Studely in Yorkshire at (*erasure*) St. Andrew
day and Midsomer payable at Leedes and London as most
convenient this contract I made at London in my returne from
the Bath in which my Brother upon letters joyned.

108r *cont.*

And at the same tyme I agreed with Mr Faulkner ⟨for⟩ neare
Burrey Brigg for £2800 to have a lease of lands for payment
of £400 per annum for 12 years ⟨from⟩ payable at (*erasure*)
Christen and Midsom after at Egleston and Leedes whereof
My Cosen Northleigh[74] had halfe and my my [*sic*] Brother
and I the other halfe soe I was set and was to have £100 for
my part for 12 years after

£0750

In August (*erasure*) after in that yeare I bought of the Earle
of Annandale in Scotland the Mannor of Plumpton in Cumberland[75] beeinge Copiholds by decree,[76] but setled by his
father at that tyme (*interlined*: he) had only a lease for years
from the Crowne (*interlined*: viz from Kinge James) soe can
be noe good estate to bynde the sucesser nor the purchasser
who claymeth by

£2350

the grante of the Inheritance from Kinge Charles (q^d nota)
and consider well of it is £140 per annum rent at 2 years rent
for a fine as decreed with large heriots and other profitts it
cost mee £2350 all to ⟨be⟩ paid within 3 monethes, but I could
have had £200 for the bargaine after <u>Articles</u> before assurance
passed besides I gave £10 for a gratuitie to assist in it

In June in this yeare I went with my wife and Daughter
Barbara in our Coach to the Bath for a great payne in my
Hippe Thy and legge and stayed but there 10 days and soe
into Surrey and soe to London wher I made the above said
bargaines and came downe through Norfolk by my wives
freinds at Stow and Sir Will Armines and came hombe in
August it cost mee about that Journey about but I hope the
bargaine well quit, cost besides my cure

£300

653   *   In September this year I bought of Richard Cowper
part of his tenement beeinge free land at Sledall ajoyneing to
my owne lett at £4 per annum and hath manie convenences
by the Common, it cost

108v

£050.00.0.

* Vide foll 16^b a Computation of my estate reall and personall
untill this tyme.[77]

---

74. A London merchant who married a daughter of Robert Lowther, PP.III.12,
III.16, III.17. See J. R. Woodhead, *The Rulers of London 1660–1689* (1965),
pp. 122–123.

75. Title deeds in the Plumpton box, see pp. 8, 190.

76. For 3 copy exemplifications of this Exchequer decree of 1612, in 1631, see
Plumpton B. 2, and A1/8, ff234r–236v.

77. *Recte*, f15, see above p. 10. But the 1653 hand is much like the 1654 hand.

108v *cont.* * March the 27th 1654   I purchased of Mr Sandford and Mrs
Ramsey[78] his mother there Moitie of the Manner of Helton
Flecon, and ther moietie of the tythes of Corne and Hay with
the tyth Barne for[79]   £555:00.0
Paid all in hand which maketh that Lordshippe Compleate
and intyre giveth mee the sole comand for Common and
Turbary which was unsetled before in regard they claymed all
the sheepe heafe as belongeinge perculiarly to Sattery Parke
which now they cannot; I bought it in my Son Richards
and Will Atkinsons name in regard of the tymes and my eldest
sons unsetlednesse yet intend it shall allwayes goe and discend
with the house of Lowther. I had it reasonable in regard ⟨of⟩
that tythes and tenants were houlden the most uncertaine and
doubtfull to purchas.
In the end of the last yeare (*erasure*) and beginninge of this
viz betwixt Martinmas and May Day I new waled Rowland
field about 11 quarters high for to add to the Parke when I
(*erasure*) plowed the low playne next Cragges to bringe it into
good land beeinge much before shrubes and most overgrowne
with Brackes and much mossed; I had generally all that winter
30 or 40 men at woorke gettinge of stones and walleinge there
beeinge a smale low wale before but was forced to cleare all
and inlarg the groundwoorke of the inside to make it above
1 yarde at the bottome and had 2 draughts and 2 stone cartes
dayly leadinge. I take it cost mee by my estimate of booke
waiges and my owne servants and Catle imployed in (*interlined*:
and) about £80   £080:00.0
I intend a Padacke course in it to the fowlds for a Refuge;
a woorke pleasant in doeinge and may be soe for the future
to a good Husband for many uses in it beeinge with an easie
charge, it may be made stainch against all vermine and keepe
anie speciall goods safe and in vew. Besides it is a fine dry
feedinge ground, and worthie to be kept safe and may be
improved by fotheringe whaleinge hay upon it and placeling
manie builds and shelters as I doe haveinge soe many quaries
of stone in every part of it.
* In April 1654 I bought of Henry Dent the rest of his tenement
in Symondston[80] (*erasure*) to pay per annum £4-12s-0d; it cost
mee in hand   £0600.00.0
June   In this moneth I bought the moitie of the Manor of
Nunthropp adjoyneinge upon Marton of one Mr Keelinge but
it was in the name of Nutt and others intrust for him. It cost
mee besides Charges   £2200

78. Sandford's mother, see P.R.O., Wards 9/163, f30; also p. 186, below. Helton
     was part of her dower (*CW2.* XXI, p. 199).
79. Deeds: Helton B.I.22. For Sandford's mortgages see below pp. 73, 74, 186, 194,
     196.
80. In Wensleydale, see p. 40.

and was lett for £146 odd monie besides £5 paid out to the
Curate; but is better the rent. I bought it for the nearnesse
and conveniencie to Marton, more then anie pleasure in the
ground but Marton Moore may be watered by it.[81]

ptember   In this Moneth I bought of Mr Birkebecke of
Horneby the old rent of £1.8.0 and his interest in the Short
Wood which he valued to be full 2 parts of it. I had a part
in it before I bought of Cowper soe that now I accompt I
have the most part in it. This cost mee in readdie monie   0120
For the tytle as delivered mee by Mr Birkebecke, and Mawsons
pretenc vide the booke of the Evidences in the White velum
cover.[82]

tober 1654   I bought of Cleasby of Thrimby the two closes

called Dudgollinges in Thrimby feild whether the water is that
serveth all the High field and the high part of Greenrigg for
£12 and exchanged a close called Rawlerbanke for the other
2 closes of Dudgowlinges with him Soe that I have   £24:00.0.
all the 4 closes a thinge most necessarie and convenient for
watering all my high grounds. It cost in monie and exchange
above £24
This moneth I disbursed to Mr Whelpdale upon a demise and
redemise for 7 years and a halfe of his lands at Penreth and
Kirsgill £500 to have one hundereth pounds per annum for
7 years and a halfe at St Andrew Day the odd £50 to be
paid at St. Andrew day 1654   £500. 0.0.
This moneth or in 7ber before I disbursed the like sums of
£500 to Mr Swinburne upon the like Securitie of Maricke in
Yorkshire for to have £100 per annum at Whit and Martinmas
yearly for 7 years and a halfe[83]   £500. 0.0.
This moneth I likewise bought of my Cousen Dudley the
Manor of Yeanwith with the Poke Mills tenants and wood;
in reversion after his and his wives decease; but was to have
libertie to fell and springe all the wood and to have £5 rent
per annum and they to take backe an estate from mee for
her 2 lives. It was valued at £260 per annum with the old rents
and Mills. It cost mee £2100 all in monies to be paid in 6
moneths; it may prove a deare or cheape purchas. But in regard
of hansumenesse of the seate the nearnesse to this house and
the prospect   £2100

---

81. In Yorkshire, *V.C.H., Yorks N.R.*, II, pp. 228–29. P.R.O., C.54/3799, m.22 gives
    the names of the trustees; Lowther bought it in the name of his mother and
    his Yorkshire agent John Pearson. Abstracts: A1/6, ff120v–121v.
82. Inserted subsequently [by Sir J.L.(2)]: abstracts: A1/6, ff122r–123 (see p. xxvi).
    Short Wood is in Melkinthorpe; see p. 15 for a rental of this purchase, and
    pp. 72–3, for further purchases.
83. Thomas Swinburne of Barmpton, Co. Durham, esqr.; deed: Miscellaneous
    Yorkshire Deed B.

109r *cont.*   of the woods and grounds from the window made mee adventure to give more than anie other would, and take the contingencie of there 2 lives; which may be longe; yet in regard I have a present command and may cume to my heire or posteritie I did not value the monie since an opportunitie lost could not be recaled for double the price, besides I had then monie to spare all which invited mee; it was agreed that if (*erasure*) shee overlive him that the general fine be divided betwixt us to avoid dispute for without our joyninge (*erasure*) per adventure nether might get it[84]; but it hath beene since find it was better by £400 in regard of the wood that I valued at £350 only. I paid 8 years for the reversion.[85]

This month I lent likewise Sir Will Carleton £200 upon (*interlined*: his) lands at Carleton and Penreth to have £40 per annum at Whis and Mart for 7 years and a halfe this made upp £500 to have £160 per annum for that tyme.   £500

I agreed to receive back the monie lent to Sir John Mallory by £2250 which I was better inabled to pay the latter payment of the former somes by mee paid and undertaken.

* I agreed this moneth to lend unto Mr Wivell for younge Mr Beckwith £500 in which my Brother Will sent halfe upon expect of a Match for 7 years to have £100 per annum of one halfe viz 050   £250

109v   * 1654   In December this year I purchased of Mr George Mawson his lands tenants and tenements together with his part of the Short Wood which he estimated unto the halfe part, so that now I have the whole wood but smale part that one Pearson my tenant claymeth want but about £7; soe that his land beeinge £14-5s in possession and 13s 4d rent (*erasure*) besides 18s 4d allowed him for soe much he held of mee; and his part of the Short wood cost mee in present monie   £307:10

By this meanes I have (*interlined*: one of) the finest parcells of wood in the Countie which I intend to make severall[86] And by this means all questions and disputts are ended[87];

* 1655   In Apill [*sic*] this yeare I purchased the Maner of Rosgill[88] beeinge the tenants and Royaltie which is £14-12-10 ob old rent at least 10dob. which cost mee after 30 years purchas and a litle (*interlined*: more). This I was invited unto by reason of the Commons adjoyneinge and former disputes, to barr Webster; and to keepe others in order, and for the

---

84. From here to end of paragraph a subsequent insertion [by Sir J.L.(2)].
85. Deeds: Yanwath B. 2, 3. Lowther got possession in 1671, below, p. 193.
86. This sentence an after-thought [by Sir J.L.(2)].
87. This also a second after-thought. For the Short Wood see p. 71 and below this folio.
88. From the Wormsley family; deeds: Rosgill and Wet Sleddale B. 11. Rosgil tyth was conveyed separately for an additional £106. Both purchases were in trust for Lowther through his mother and steward.

109v *cont.*

nearness to Sele*ro*n, all Bampton and my other lands by which
I have ⟨most⟩ all the townes and Lordshipps upon the River
of Lowther from the rise to the fall into Eden except only
Shapp: and Thornthwaite and Askham this secured by the
moietie of the tyth of Rosgill.

£440:00

*In August this yeare I disbursed upon ⟨a rent charge⟩
Whitbysteades and Askham[89] rent for £34 per annum upon
bond for Whitbysed for 7 years at £12 per annum for 8 years
out of Askham towne rent the first payment of (*interlined*: of
that) rent to begine at Whit 1656: and the £34 to begine at
Kandlemas 1656: for 7 years, which cost mee

£236

*In (*erasure*) October this yeare I bought of Pearsons father
and son the last part of the Short Wood haveinge now the
whole and sole interest to dispose thereof which is fitt to be
kept inclosed and preserved and this cost mee £8-10s beeinge
but accompted the 18th part of the whole.[90]

In 10ber [16]56 or ther about I purchased the rent charge of
£50 per annum out of Preston on Tease

£600[91]

1656　　In the beginninge of this yeare I bought Willington
Hall of Mr Fulthropps of £100 per annum and after in
August exchainged the same againe with Mr Fulthropps for
rent charge of £100 per annum to be issueinge out of Certaine
lands in Stranton Seaton Hatlepoole and elsewher to be paid
sesse free for ever which cost[92]

£1475

110r

In August 1656 my Brother Will and I purchased the Lordshipp of Great Preston and Astley neare Swillington of Mr
Darcie son to the Lord Darcie of the yearly value in all of
£343: but improvable after 5 years £45: for cole mynes and
£80 more after 2 lives which cost in all £6100 my part half
cost[93]

£3050

About or before this tyme I exchanged Willington Hall I baugh
[*sic*] before of Mr Fulthropp for a rent charge of £100 per
annum out *of* Stranton Seaton and other places I had £50
allowed mee in exchange.

1656　*　In 9br this yeare I perfected the purchase of the
moitie of the lease of Askegarth Rectory, ⟨with⟩ Mr Clape-.

89. Whitbysteades is also in Askham (E.P.N.S., XLIII, p. 203). From Lowther's
annual rentals the £34 seems to have been paid on behalf of Mr Sandford
of Askham by one William Langhorne, see below, e.g. p. 94.
90. See above, this folio, and p. 71.
91. The whole entry a later insertion [by Sir J.L.(2)]; the figure £600 either erased
or obscured by a blot.
92. Probably Willington Hall near Bishop Auckland.
93. See p. 85 for rentals which include further details of the purchase, for sale
see p. 157.

110r *cont.*   ham the other moitie it cost us about £775 for my part[94]
⟨beside charges about the⟩ provinge the Lease from Trinity
College   £775

About Lamas before this yeare I bought the tenement at
Marton that belonged to G Anderton which is worth about
£13[95]-6-8 per annum and it cost present monie   £200

In 9[br] this year I procured Mr Teasdell Parson of Lowther
to resigne to Will Smith Clarke; and confirmed the same by
presentation, and agreed to take in the High Holme the
Millfield and the Winterage of the Low Holme and all the
tythes (*interlined*[96]: of the ⟨purchased⟩ tenants) ⟨for⟩ which
I lately purchased, and for which noe Composition nor
prescription was; to avoyde the danger of haveinge one putt
upon as in the tymes of libertie; and uncertaintey.

And for this I agreed to pay viz for the Millfield and tyth
of the tenants £5 per annum at Martinmas yearly and the 6
catlegates as formerly[97]

* In January this yeare my seacond Son Richard returned from
travell out of France and cost mee that year above £150 and
in the same Moneth I agreed to bynde my Christopher my
third son to a Turkie Merchant one Mr Buckworth[98] for 7
years and I to finde him cloathes for about 5 years or soe
beinge as he continewed in England and was to give in monie
with him £300 soe they 2 cost mee that yeare   £450

* The 2d of March 1656 I disbursed upon the Mortgage of the
Powdun Closes of Mr Sandfords adjoyneinge upon Yeanewith
Wood beeinge 4 in number worth per annum about £16[99]   £200[1]

110v–111v [*Unknown hand*] *Rental of all Sir J.L.(2)'s estates for the year beginning
Martinmas 1637 (written and arranged as f70r (pp. 33–4) above)*

112r–113r   *Rental of all Sir J.L.(2)'s estates for the year beginning Martinmas 1638
(written and arranged as f70r (pp. 33–4) above).*

---

94. Rest of paragraph an insertion [by Sir J.L.(2)]. Modern spelling: Aysgarth,
in Wensleydale, Yorkshire, *V.C.H. Yorks N.R.*, I, p. 213; abstracts A1/6,
f.125v–133r. D/Lons/L, letters, 1663, Clapham to Lowther: Clapham acted as
Lowther's agent collecting his rents. For Wensleydale, see p. 40.
95. See p. 37.
96. Interlineation in a different ink.
97. Valuation of the parsonage 1656–1658: above, p. 15. Nightingale gives bio-
graphical details and comments on the presentation, Nightingale, *Ejected*,
pp. 1235–1237; and see p. 245 below.
98. A copy of Sir J.L.(2)'s bond under the apprenticeship indenture shows that
Christopher was first apprenticed to Mr Wm. Denis of London, and then to
Mr Buckworth (A1/6, f133v). For Buckworth and Dennis see Woodhead, *Rulers
of London*, p. 41.
99. Deeds: Askham B.I.4; see p. 70.
1. The annual diary is continued, in A1/4a, on p. 152 below.

ange of hand, unknown hand] *Rental of Sir J.L.(2)'s lands in Wensleydale,*   113v–114r
Martinmas 1638. Gives name and descriptions of each property, annual rent,
commencing date and term of lease, and details of rents previously charged
for that property. Total annual rent due £338-16-0d.[2]

nd of Sir J.L.(2)] *Rental of all Sir J.L.(2)'s estates for the year beginning*   114v–115v
Martinmas 1639.

(The following description of the rental is intended to serve as a general formula
for all Sir J.L.(2)'s subsequent rentals; It will not be repeated. Deviations
from this format will be noted.

The page is divided into two columns, the rental in the l.h.col., and notes of
receipts and payments in the r.h.col. Each rental comprises:

1. *under the heading FINEABLE, rents of the customary tenants of the*
   Cumberland and Westmorland manors;
2. *under the heading DEMESNES, rent of demesnes in the two counties,*
   Yorkshire and elsewhere;
3. *under the heading MORTGAGES, payments due from lands mortgaged*
   to Lowther as security for money lent by him; and
4. *under the heading LEASES, rents of a few properties leased to Lowther*
   and sub-let by him, and receipts of fees paid to Lowther as, for example,
   Steward of the Honour of Penrith.

Entries for customary rents name the manor concerned; Cumberland and
Westmorland demesne properties are entered individually, and not under
manors. Rents from estates outside the two counties appear to have been
collected locally, and paid to Lowther once or twice a year; it is these
collected sums which are entered here.

Payments due under each of the four categories given above are listed alpha-
betically under the feast days when due, beginning in each year with Martin-
mas, and ending with Michaelmas in the following year.

Sometimes sub-totals are given for each category of rent on each feast-day,
and for each feast day; a total for the year is sometimes given)

[The rental, and most receipts, are in Sir J.L.(2)'s hand; a variety of inks
were used.]

Rental of Wensleydale due Martinmas 1640. Gives names of properties and   116r–116v
tenants, details of leases including rents. Includes a note of lands in hand,
value £50. Total of all properties is £431-8-10d. Followed by notes of changes
in the rental as leases fall in; concludes with a note that the total rent due
20 February 1641 is £462-15-5d, but that more increases are due. Many
alterations.

---

2. The addition on both pages is in error, but contemporary alterations make it
   impossible to offer a correct total.

117r–118v   *Rental of all Sir J.L.(2)'s estates for the year beginning Martinmas 1640, (arranged as f114v (p. 75) above).*

118v–119v   *Rental of all Sir J.L.(2)'s estates for the year beginning Martinmas 1641, (arranged as f114v (p. 75) above). Concludes with a calculation of the totals due under various headings, [hand of Sir J.L.(2)]*

Mar rent was then	£992-10-0	*Which is worth in land per annum	100-0-0
St Andrew day rent	029-05-2	In leases per annum £73	
Candlemasse rent	102-06-10	which is worth in land	030-0-0
Ladie day rent	160-04-0	Soe the total beeinge	2350-0-0
Whit rent	483-00-0	And deduct for mortgages	
Midsumer rent	024-00-0	and leases not worth soe	
Lamas and St James day	035-04-0	much as the rent by	0066
Michelmasse rent	203-11-6		
Flatts and Hay closes	016-10-0	Then there remayneth	
In my owne hand at Low-		clear rent of inheritance	2284-0-0
ther and Hackthrop	304-00-0	Casualties of fines cum	
		omnibus anis maybe	120-0-0
totall is	2350	profitts and use of stock	
Wherof ther is in		profitable	200-0-0
mortgages per annum*	123-0-0	Meaburne in reversion	
		apris mort de mere	230-0-0
		J.L.	

120r–121r   *Rental of all Sir J.L.(2)'s estates for the year beginning Martinmas 1642, (arranged as f114v (p. 75) above).*

121v–122v   *Rental of all Sir J.L.(2)'s estates for the year beginning Martinmas 1643, (arranged as f114v (p. 75) above).*

122v   *Rental of Sir J.L.(2)'s estates as let after the discharge of his estate from sequestration,[3] (the basic arrangement of the rental is as f114v (p. 75) above): rents due Martinmas 1646.*

123r–124r   *Rental of all Sir J.L.(2)'s estates for the year beginning Martinmas 1646, (arranged as f114v (p. 75) above).*

124r   *Statement of [half-yearly] rent due for Thrimby Grange £3-10-10d. with note of deductions to be allowed totalling 11s-8d.*

124v–125v   *Rental of all Sir J.L.(2)'s estates for the year beginning Martinmas 1647, [hand of Sir J.L.(2)][4]*

---

3. See p. 61, above.
4. In this rental the l.h.col. marginalia are often in the same ink as the notes of receipt in the r.h.col. This ink is often different from that used in the l.h.col. entry. Differing inks are often used to record separate receipts.

A perticular de rents Mart*inmas* 1647 Alphabetically   124v

paid + Bampton owld rent then	06	06	6	paid per Jo Knot	06	05	6[5]
Crosby pro ut per line	12	02	9	paid in 2 parcells 8:11:6			
paid + Winsters above the rent	00	04	8[6]	paid 2s.6d. and the rest allowed in sesses			
paid + Knipe rent then	03	10	3	paid £3 in part paid 10s3d in full			
Lowther as by booke	11	04	2	qr what paid to my sonne paid all but about 8s.			
paid + Newton rent then	10	12	9	paid per W Atk[7] £10.10.5d.ob paid in full			
paid + Sledall then qr.	04	07	6	paid in full then part for Jo Lowis			
Slegill then	00	17	6	3 yrs arrears and allowed for grasses out of it			
Strickland parva	03	02	6	paid in part £4.12.4d. and 11s6d			
Thrimby towne	02	00	4				
Thrimby Grainge	01	10	6				
paid + Threlkeld then	15	12	6	paid in full £15.12.6.			
paid + Thwaites owld rent	09	14	10	paid this	09	14	10
paid + Walkemill Silver then	00	09	10	paid this	00	9	10
Demesnes then							
paid + Mr Adamson for (*interlined*: part of) Hackthrop half years rent	41	00	0	paid in part 9ber [16]47 £10 more after £10 more £9 paid Jan [16]47: £10 paid £2 in full			
paid + Appleby Burgage	00	02	0	paid 2s			
paid + Bampton demesne	34	10	0	paid Januar [16]47: £23.12.0. and £10.18 in full			
paid + tyth hay then there	03	00[8]	0	accompted I thinke qr			

---

5. *Sic.* The figures in the rental column are altered to read as they do.
6. Altered from 6.
7. i.e. William Atkinson.
8. Perhaps £03 10 0d.

124v *cont.*

	£	s	d		£	s
+tyth corn given Jo Knot	00	14	0			
paid + free rent ther hafe	00	14	0	paid this per J Kt[9]	00	14
paid + Burtrybank rent	09	00	0	paid	09	00
+Highfield part to Rea for 3 years	06	00	0			
Crosbie rent this yeare	55	00	0	paid in part £25.04.00 paid and per Ron Lam 04-16-0 and paid more	10	00
Highfield another part to Muncas	11	00	0	This to begine next year[10]		
paid + Crosbie Millne the like[11]	06	10	0	paid this	06	10
paid + Lowther Millne	05	10	0	paid this	05	10
+Marton with Mr. Goody*ears*[12]	233	00	0	vide the particuler notes of accompt		
paid + Millfield £4.10s.	05	15	0	paid in part £4.10s.[13]		
paid + Newton Millne now[14]	04	10	0	paid £3.5s. paid Elliner £1.5s. in full	4	10
paid + Scoute*gree*ne Millne	03	10	0	paid this to W W	03	10
paid + Shapp tyth halfe with the tyth rent	30	00	0	paid £11 in part paid 1 Jan: [16]47 £8, allowed the rest		
paid + Skellan with stock	07	10	0	paid £4 2s2d paid in full to J.L.	3	7
paid + Sledall Millne	02	10	0	paid this	02	10
⟨ +Hayton tenement to Warriner halfe (*erasure*) with Ralf closes[15] ⟩				} This is dew at Mich [16]47		
paid + Thrimby Grange	16	12	1	paid all but Mr. Adamsons 10s	16	00
paid + Thwaites Carages	02	11	0	paid this	02	11
paid + Hens there	00	16	6	paid this but 15s		

---

9. i.e. Jo: Knot.
10. The two Highfield entries squeezed in in a different ink.
11. i.e. this year, as in the previous Crosby entry before the Highfield interlineation.
12. i.e. Mr Goodyear's mortgage, see p. 53.
13. This figure altered and difficult to read.
14. *Then* struck out, and *now* interlined.
15. All this entry in l.h.col. struck out.

	£.	s.	d.		£.	s.	d.	124v *cont.*
paid + Towne tearme 5 years and misse 2 years and this should be the 3rd yeare since the running gressum paid	00	13	4	paid this	00	13	4	
paid + greenehewes ther	00	05	3	paid this	00	05	3	
swine take	00	01	4					
paid + Thrimby Gill	02	00	0	paid this £2				
paid + Thrimby free rent	00	03	4	paid	00	03	4	
paid + Waytey + Will Smith	02	10	0	paid and paid £2.10s for [16]48	02	10	0	
+ Wensladale pro ut (*erasure*) particular	467	09	10	vide the particular notes. dbes. arrs.				
£1019:0:8 Mortgages Clifton	28	00	0	paid my wife in part £7 paid Jo. Low per Rich Wilkinson £7 more by him £2-10s and paid £2 per Jo Knot in full of the towne end rent				
Row Stephensons 1 day per weeke arr £8-10s								
eases Stephen Parker wife this yeare only	00	16	0	paid by her 3s secured per Musgrave this year				
paid + Earle de Annandale fee	01	00	0	paid this not paid[16]	01	00	0	
+ Paper Milne	01	00	0	paid				
Edward Garnet which endeth this next[17] yeare and £4. arrear last yeare from accompt	03	03	0					
+ for Whalefeild	01	15	0	yet to be paid				
St Andrew Day Horsdale rent	01	15	10					
paid + Emanuel Bird (*interlined*: for use of £90) £43.7.1.[19]	07	04	0[18]	paid mee	07	04	0	

16. *Not paid* in a different ink.
17. *next* interlined.
18. Altered from £5-10-0.
19. Before the alteration to the Bird entry, correct total £42-19-10d, after £44-13-10d.

		£.	s.	d.		£.	s.
124v *cont.*	Candlemas Hackthropp owld rent	03	19	10	qr what paid to ⟨my sonne⟩ Ellinor	3	7
	paid + Helton	07	17	7	paid Jo Low	07	17
	St. Andrew day demesne then Jo Knot for High-field[20]	12	00	0	This to be paid the next year	12	00
	[21]Crosby services not setled		*(blank)*		*(blank)*		
	Arkengarthdaly[22]	32	00	0	+		
125r	Candlemas 1647						
	paid + Beareslack Bradley wife	10	00	0	paid Jo Low 10.0.0 and given back by mee 5s		
	paid + Burtrybank then	09	00	0	paid W Watson	09	00
	paid + Sledall Carages at 1s6d[23]	⟨01	02	6⟩	paid to Jo Low and allowed in sesments accompted		
	paid + Smithy at Lowther	00	10	0			
	paid + Rich Mathew for Simpsons (*interlined*: ground) and Willans	02	10	0	paid and allowed this	02	10
	paid + Subworens part of the rent	20	00	0	paid Feb: [16]47 £19.0.0. paid £1 in full J.L.		
	+ Jo Knot for High-field	12	00	0	this to be paid the next yeare		
	the other halfe Leases then				paid £5 in full[24]		
	paid + Rich Tompson for Threlkelds mynoritie to pay only	2	10	0	paid Jo Low: £2 10s £2 10s at Cand 1648 in full of this dett		
	paid + Midleton Robt. Jackson	04	06	0	paid and secured		
	Frances Pearson	06	03	0			

---

20. This entry interlined in a different ink.
21. l.h. margin of MS damaged.
22. i.e. Arkengarthdale, Yorkshire.
23. *at 1s-6d* interlined. *£1-2-6d* struck out.
24. This whole entry an insertion.

125r *cont.*

	£.	s.	d.	
+ Rich. Wilkinson for the Mynoritie of Perey	⟨03	00	0⟩	paid the 14th May [16]49 £1.0.0 paid all[25]

02:19:7[26]

Annuntiation 1648

	£.	s.	d.	
+ Mr Adamson for part of Hackthropp dew at Mart before but spared from Cand.	⟨42 41[28]	00 0	0⟩ 0	paid Ell[27]: Jan [16]48 £20 secured to be paid in Cand £8 paid per Will At and paid £3 in full + vide the notes
paid + Egleston Abbey	105	15	0	
paid + Esklamore with £10	10	00	0	paid W.W. £6 paid Elinor: £3.12s0 paid all
+ Highfield Rea for 3 years	08	00	0	this to (*erasure*) be paid next year 1649[29]
paid + Kelthwaite	12	00	0	paid W.W. £6 paid me more £6
paid + Newton Moulture	07	19	0	paid me in part £1 the rest secured
paid + Pessiebrow and Houlmes	12	00	0	paid W.W. £4-14s paid in full with 10 busles of otes
paid + Chapelhow Croft*				paid W.W. £2.00 and £1-10s and £1-10s per Jo H paid in full.
paid + Subworens the rest	12	00	0	paid Will W: (*erasure*) £11 and £1 in full
paid + Thrimby Graynge	16	12	1	paid W.Wat £14.5.3 the rest allowed
+ Thwaites Milne	05	15	0	paid £5.10s but arr for Mich 1645 £2. 12s.

30:11:1[30]

Penticost 1648

	£.	s.	d.	
paid + Bampton finable	06	04	6	paid in part £6. paid in full
Crosby pro ut per lin	12	02	9	paid W W £3 paid mee £1.5 paid July [16]49 £1.13s.0.

---

25. *paid all* in different ink.
26. Total of £102.19.7 correct but see entries annotated 21 and 24 on p. 80.
27. i.e. Ellinor Lowther, P.V.8.
28. Altered from £24.
29. This entry in l.h.col. an interlineation.
30. Total of £230.11.1d. correct, but see entry under note 29 above.

125r *cont.*

	£.	s.	d.		£.	s.
Winster above the rent	00	04	8			
paid + Knipe rent	03	10	3	paid this per Jo K	03	10
paid + Lowther pro ut per lin	11	04	2	paid in part to W W £9 for Low and Hak[31]		
paid + Newton then	10	12	9	paid Elinor this	10	12
paid + Sledall then qr	04	07	6	paid per W W £2 paid £2-2s1d in full in all	04	2
	00	17	6			
Sleglill [*sic*] then						
Strickland parva	03	02	6	paid in part Jan [16]48 £5		
Thrimby towne	02	00	4			
Thrimby grainge	01	10	6			
paid + Threlkeld then	15	12	6	paid Elinor £15.12.6.		
Demesnes then						
paid + Appelby Burgage	00	02	0	paid this	00	02
paid + Bampton then	38[32]00		0	paid W W £13.6.8. Jo Pearson £18 5s the rest allowed for corn per note		
paid + Tyth hay there	03	00	0			
paid + Free rent there	00	13	4	Secured per Ed Cley		
Crosby services	02	10	0			
paid + Knipe services	00	04	3	allowed to Jo Knot		
paid + Lowther milne	05	10	0	paid W W £5	05	10
paid + Marton then	233	00	0	vide the note de annus		
paid + Millne field but to allowe 5s for walinge	05	15	0	paid W W and paid more £5 10s for Mart [16]49	05	10
Morterpitts then	02	10	0			
paid + Newton Milne	04	10	0	(*erasure*) dew by the Bayliff (*interlined*: now secured)		
paid + Scoutegrene Milln	03	10	0	paid this to W W	03	10
paid + Shapp tyth and tyth r[en]t	30	00	0	paid May [16]49 £4 and secured paid to Mr Washington £22.10s. qr vide the note of accompt.		
paid + Skellen with stock	07	10	0	paid W Wa: in part 7.10s[33] in full	7	10
paid + Sledall Millne	02	10	0	paid W Watson	02	10

£407.04.6[34]

31. i.e. Lowther and Hackthorpe.
32. Altered from £34-10-0.
33. Altered from £6-10s.[0d].
34. Total correct but neglects £3-10-0 from entry under note 32 above.

	Mortgages	£.	s.	d.		£.	s.	d.	125r *cont.*
	Clifton towne and townend	28	00	0	nothinge paid this years but paid for Mart after qr[35]				
	Leases then								
paid +	The Earle of Annondale	01	00	0	paid this				
+	the paper milne	01	00	0					
	Frances Pearson last pe[36]	06	03	0					
	Bishoppes fee was[37]	01	06	8					
£37.9.8.									
	Midsomer 1648								125v
paid +	Helton tyth Ex[ecuto]res John Langhorne	20	00	0	paid per Ed Langh: in part £15 mee per Ell £04.10s.6. and 9s6d. in full				
	Thrimby Carages qr				(*blank*)				
	Wensladale qr what dew if not putt in Mart. r[en]t				(*blank*)				
	Lamas 1648								
paid +	Hackthropp owld r[en]t	03	19	0	paid per W.W. at book	03	19	0	
	Helton r[en]t then	07	17	7	paid W.W. £7.13.8 more[38] 1s 6d.				
paid +	Thwaites St.Ja. day	12	04	3	paid Ellinor	12	4	2	
	Demesnes then Flatts then with sheepe	10	10	0	paid per Chr. Tompson £2.10.0. paid per Fr. Harison 9br [16]49 for this year £2.10.[0].				
+	Meason tyth silver but I sufer Jo Knot to have it	00	15	10ob.	given to Jo Knot				

35. This entry replaces the following, which was struck out: *paid W W part of towne rent 6.13.7.*
36. i.e. payment.
37. Sir J.L.(2) was appointed steward of the court of the Bishop of Carlisle in 1636, (C.R.O., D.C.C. Register, vol. VI, p. 441), fee 4 marks a year at Martinmas and Pentecost.
38. Smudged.

		£.	s.	d.		£.	s.
125r *cont.*	Morterpitts then Leases then John Hudson	02	10	0			
		3	00	0			
	George Simpson then Michelmass 1648	01	08	8			
	paid + Bampton demense	38	00	0	This is paid set downe on whis befor		
	+ Egleston Abbey	106	15	10	vide the note of arrears		
	paid + Hackthropp grasses	01	08	0	paid this to mee	01	08
	paid + Sledall demesne	36³⁹00		0	paid mee £22 and a note of charges of £8.13.4, and £7.13.0 in full		
	Reaslack with stock	20	00	0	(*blank*)		
	paid + Thwaites Millne	05	15	0	paid £5-10s per J.W. but arrear for Mich 1645— £2.12.1⁴⁰		
	paid + Hayton tenement to allow Hayton 16s per annum out	02	10	0	allowed all this in sessments (*erasure*)		
	Leases All the fees pro stewardshippes vide received nil Buckholme and Wiber ground for 1648	15	10	0	paid 9br [16]49 in part £15 and arrears part use of that for a year and 10s principall		

Concludes with [*hand of Sir J.L.*(*2*)*, transcript of heading:*] Ground lett for 1649 not in this rentall. *List of properties rents and receipts* (*arranged as above*).

126r–126v [*Unknown hand*] *Rental of Wensleydale, Martinmas 1647. List of 56 tenants' names, with rents due, arranged under Townships.* [*Total: £434-3-10*].

Rental concludes [*in hand of Sir J.L.*(*2*)] *with a note of the tenants' names and rents due from a property called the Lunns, before* [*£25-8-2d*] *and after improvement, £32-19-10d. This includes some improved rents, some additional rents, and some unchanged rents.*

---

39. Altered from £32.
40. Thwaites was settled in trust by Sir J.L.(1) in his will for payment of debts. This trust was accepted by the Committee for Compounding and the estate was not sequestrated (D/Lons/L, Composition papers), see above, pp. 58, 61.

Rental of Clifton Town as paid Martinmas 1648.   127r
Customary rental, names of 42 tenants with [half-yearly customary] rents
due. Total [half-year] £10-5-0d.[41]
Hand of Sir J.L.(2)] Note of the services performed by Clifton tenants, with
value as commuted.

Unknown hand] Half-year's [customary] rent of Newton Reigny as received   127v
at Martinmas 1647.
List of names of 41 tenants, with [customary] rents due. Total £10-12-5½d,[42]
plus 2d for smithie, noted as added by agreement.

Half-year's [customary] rental of Sleddale as received Martinmas 1647.   128r
List of names of 21 tenants, with rent due. Total £8-9-6d, with a note of
out payments, total 7s-4d. [Apparently for a whole year.]

Hand of Sir J.L.(2)] Rental of all Sir J.L.(2)'s estates for the year beginning   128v–129v
Martinmas 1648, (arranged as f114v (p. 75) above).

Rental in unknown hand, title in hand of Sir J.L.(2); transcript of title:]   130r
A note of the rent of Helton and Heltondale purchased of Mr. Sandford,
1654. *List of names of 17 tenants, with [customary] rent due. Total £10-15-6d.*

Change of hand, hand of Sir J.L.(2)] Note of tithes payable by, and services
performed by, these tenants.[43]

Unknown hand] Half-year's rent of Marton as received Martinmas 1648.   130v
List of names of 32 tenants, details and acreages of properties, with note of
rents due, total £265-1-8d.[44] *With a note [in hand of Sir J.L.(2)] of an*
additional purchase, half-year's rent £21, and notes of rents to be improved,
to yeild a further £17 half-year's rent.

List of goods bought [at Marton] from Mr. Wildon, now in Jo. Pearson's   131r
house there.
Rentals of all Sir J.L.(2)'s estates for the years beginning Martinmas 1649–   132v–138v
Martinmas 1655, (arranged as f114v (p. 75) above).

(Blank)   139r–140r

Unknown hand] Rental of Great Preston,[45] *Yorkshire [n.d.] giving, in tabular*   140v
form for each property: name of tenant and yearly rent due, acreage, length
of lease; with note of a free rent of 5s., and coal mines and lime quarries
leased for £45 per annum. Total [in hand of Sir J.L.(2)] £230-12-0d.

Followed by a similar rental of Astley in the lordship of Swillington,
Yorkshire, total [in hand of Sir J.L.(2)] £113. With total [in hand of Sir J.L.(2)]
of both: £343-12-0d.

---

41. The rents of two tenants and [a tenement called] Lowther Bridge are noted
    as *unpayd*; the total in the MS appears to be £10.5.6d. Lowther had just
    foreclosed his mortgage of this property.
42. This total appears to be wrong.
43. For this purchase see p. 70.
44. This figure is much altered in the text.
45. For this purchase see p. 73.

140v *cont.* [*Hand of Sir J.L.(2)*] *Note that 6s-8d rent is to be deducted, for which Mr. Tyne-dale is to make allowance; total £343-5-4d; half-year's rent is £171-12-8d.*

141r–141v [*Unknown hand*] *Copy of the previous rentals of Great Preston and Astley, with notes of the value of improved rents and reversions. Concludes with the calculation*

£185-7s[46]	at 17 yeares purchase	£3150-19-00
	the reversion of £60[47] after 2 lives at 8 years	480-00-00
	Colemines and lime quarrys for 5 years	
	£45 per annum	150-00-00
	Colemines and lime quarrys after not much valuable	
113	at 17 yeares for Astley	1921-00-00

185:7
113:0
———
298:7

142r and v   (*Blank*)

143r–144v   [*Title and first item of rental, hand of Sir J.L.(2); thereafter unknown hand*] *Rental of Maske, Yorkshire, [n.d., 1650] giving names of 121 tenants in alphabetical order, rents due, and, variously, details of their properties and their title thereto. Total £877-10-7[48]*

145r–146r [*Unknown hand*] *Rental of Thorpe, Surrey [n.d.], giving names of 28 tenants[49] and their properties, date of lease and term, and rent due. Total £736-15-0d,[50] with notes of outgoings totalling £168. Concludes, [in hand of Sir J.L.(2)] that total is £718-15-8d after improvements and outgoings, plus £19 for property at Blackhouse, details of which are specified.*

       (*f146 is the last folio to be numbered in a contemporary hand. For the purposes of this edition the following folios are numbered consecutively.*)

146v–[149r] [*Hand of Sir J.L.(2)*] *begins on f[149r] and runs backwards to f146r: List of freeholders in Westmorland, n.d. incomplete.*

[149v]–[150r][*Unknown hand*] *Rating of the Barony of Kendal for bridge repairs, 16 January, 10 Chas.I [1635]; with notes of meetings about repairs, 21 August 1635.*

[150v]–[151r]   *Rating of Demesnes in the Bottom of Westmorland,[51] 14 August 1635, with subsequent alterations.*

[151v]–[155v]   *Rating of customary and demesne lands to pay a subsidy, Westmorland*

---

46. i.e. the rent of Great Preston without the mines and quarries.
47. The reversion of the manor house and demesnes of Great Preston.
48. Figure accurate to within £1, but damage to MS forbids greater precision. For Marske see above, p. 64.
49. No names are given for properties where counterpart leases were missing when the rental was written. For Thorpe see above, p. 67.
50. *Recte* £753-15-8.
51. For the Barony of Kendel and the Bottom of Westmorland see *N&B*, I, p. 13.

18 April 18 Jas I [1620] with later ammendments [in hand of Sir J.L.(1)]
temp. Charles I.

Copy of a precept for appearance for subsidy assessment [annotated by Sir   [156r]
J.L.(1)].

(Blank)   [156v]–[159r]

nd of Sir J.L.(1)] (Heading:) A note of my stock of goods 1619.   [159v]
Number and value of sheep, with note of some purchases.

Note of the purchase of 2 kine and a calf for £5 from my uncle Cliburne.   [160r]

List of Sir J.L.(1)'s cattle, horses and mares, and sheep 7 November 1618;   [160v]
with note of cattle stock to 12 December 1619.

Blank)   [161r]–[164r]

known hand] Notes of odd accounts c.1604.   [164v]

SIR JOHN LOWTHER (d. 1675)'s LONG VELLUM BOOK

D/Lons/L, A1/4a

tal unknown hand; receipts, hand of Sir J.L.(2)]   [3v][52]–3r
ental of all Sir J.L.(2)'s estates for the year beginning Martinmas 1656.
he format of this rental is the same as those in A1/4 (see p. 75 above),
ith two exceptions. Firstly the rental is written on the verso of each folio,
nd the receipts entered on the recto of the following folio, i.e. on the facing
age. Secondly, for four estates lump sums are entered in the annual rentals,
ut the four also have separate rentals of their own, following the format
f the main series:

Maulds Meaburne, rentals 1663–1675[53]; Cartmel; Kirkby Lonsdale;
Preston Richard, rentals 1667–1675.[54]

he main sequence of rentals will continue to be described as for "all Sir
L.(2)'s estates", but this phrase is to be understood as here qualified.

ental of all Sir J.L.(2)'s estates for the year beginning Martinmas 1657.   3v–6r

---

2. The book begins with three unfoliated leaves, the first two blank, but with the
rental for 1656 beginning on the verso of the third. Placed inside the book are
four lists of sheriff's writs, arranged under term due for return, due 1661–1662.
Between [3v] and f1r a sheet of calculations is bound into the book.
3. Came to Sir J L.(2) in 1659 after the death of his mother, whose jointure it
was; see p. 161 below, and pp. 108, 111, 146 for the rentals.
4. Acquired by mortgage, 1667; see p. 146 below for the rental, and pp. 179–80,
186–7 for the mortgage; abstracts: A1/6, ff147v–149r. There is a customary
rental of Kirby Lonsdale in A1/8, f154; and a demesne rental for 1667 in A1/9,
noted by Sir J.L.(2) as: This beeinge altered there is noe further accompt of it.
The Preston Richard customary rent appears only as a lump sum. See p. 147.

	£.	s.	d.
3v Martinmas 1657			
+ Bampton old rent[55] part of it Moulter rent to be knowne	06	04	6
Clifton towne rent 9:14:2	09	14	2[56]
+ Helton rent take Mr. Sandfords[57] of Askham and 9d			
paid mee per Langhorne	05	07	9
+ Knipe rent then 3:10:3	03	10[58]	4[59]
+ Lowther rent as I take it qr. 9:16:1	09	16	1
+ Newton rent	10	12	9
+ Plumpton rent with the parcell of meadow out of which			
I allow the Bayliff if the Streets will not pay it	69	14	5
+ 1:13:4			
+ Rosgill rent	07	06	2
+ More a free rent at Christmas per Heydall	00	00	6
+ Sledall then	04	02	2
+ Slegill	00	17	6
+ Strickland parva	03	02	6
+ Thrimby towne rent	02	00	4
+ Thrimby Grainge rent	01	10	6
+ Threlkeld rent	15	04	6
+ Thwaits old rent	09	14	10
+ Walkemill Silver then	00	09	10

Demesnes tythes and free rents

	£.	s.	d.
+ Appleby Burgage rent in Antho Riggs possession	00	02	0
+ Bampton lett Jo Knot with 3d.4d. for Bushlips	38	03	4
⟨ + ⟩More for Langhornes tythe the moitee besids	00	12[60]	6
The other parcell seconded from the schoole			

---

55. Rest of line a subsequent insertion.
56. Clifton entry a subsequent insertion.
57. Rest of entry an annotation.
58. Altered.
59. Altered from 3d.
60. Altered.

	£.	s.	d.	
Paid Will Ak for Bampton rent	06	04	6	4r
Paid for Clifton rent 9:9:2 only 6s. arrears for Hartley wife		(*blank*)		
Paid Helton besides 9s. paid to me	05	07	9	
Paid per Jo Baxter to T.P.	03	10	4ob	
Paid Will Atk in manu 9:10:10 and to Hug.New 3s.4d. and Fallowfield 1s.10d. in all	09	16	1	
Paid Will Atkinson Newton rent	10	12	9	
Paid in part 56:00:0 and 12:01:1 and 1:13:4 allowed, in all	69	14	5	
Paid Rich Cawper to Tho Pear*son*	07	06	3	
Paid mee 006d.	00	00	6	
Paid Tho Pearson	04	2	1	
Paid to Will Simpson per Antho Clayburne	07	00	2	
Paid Tho P	15	14	2	
Paid Will Atkinson in full of this and carages	12	15	8	

Paid Tho Pearson Mart [16]57, 0 2s 0
Paid per Jo Kt to Will Atk qr of him for the accompt
in full qr   35 00 0
The rest allowed upon note[61]
⟨Paid more⟩

---

61. This line a subsequent insertion.

3v *cont.*	+ Bampton free rent then	00	14	0
	+ Beareslacke lett to Guy	11	10	0
	+ Bearslacke lett to Jo Knot halfe rent	10[62]00		0
	+ Burtrybanke halfe	06	15	0
	+ Fulthropps rent charge (*erasure*) out of Seaton and Stranton	50	00	0
	+ Helton (*interlined*: towne) tyth hay that was Mr. Sands[63]	01	15	0
	+ Helton (*interlined*: dale) tyth farme by prescription[64]	01	00	0
	+ Highfield and Hirpellhow £11.10.0.	11	10	0[65]
	+ Highfield (*erasure*) the rest with Powley tenement	07	10	0
	+ Hallgarth to Geo ⟨Whinfell⟩ Hayton	08	10	0
	+ Marton per rentall about[66]	316	13	4
	+ Nunthropp per rentall	072	11	3
	+ Newton tenement beeinge Millers lett the miller	02	00	0
	+ Newton Mill to him	06	00	0
	+ Preston upon Tease rent charge	28	00	0
	+ Preston Greate and Astley beside the improvement	85	16	4
	+ More for use of £500 for the coliery £15	(*blank*)		
	+ Sledall Mill	02	15	0
	+ Sledall tenement to Tho Jackson	02	10	0
	+ Shapp tyth to Noble Smith the halfe misplaced[67]	53	10	0
	+ Thrimby Grainge with Stocke 15	15	00	0
	+ Thrimby Dudgoldinges to Cleasby	01	14	0
	+ Thrimby free rent by Mathew	00	03	4
	+ Thwaits Cariages	02	11	0
	+ Hens then	00	16	6
	+ Towne tearme 5 years and misse 2 years this The 6th yeare and at the 7th yeare to the runninge gressom ⟨which is part⟩	00	13	4

---

62. Altered.
63. i.e. Mr. Sandford's.
64. *by prescription* added later in same hand; for prescription see below, pp. 162–3.
65. Altered from £23.0.0.
66. *About* a later insertion.
67. *misplaced* a later insertion.

Paid mee	00	14	0	4r *cont.*
Paid p Guy to mee in part £6: paid me in full £5:10	11	10	0	
⟨Paid⟩ to allow for horse grasse [68]2:8:0 ⟨qr horse⟩ paid my wife	05	16	in full	
Paid Tho Pear	06	15	0	
Paid per Jo Pear: accompt marked ff	50	00	0	
Paid Tho Pearson	01	15	0	
Paid to Will Atk per Langhorne in the 6.7.6.	01	00	0	
Paid Will Atkinson	11	10	0	
Paid mee this dew	07	10	0	
Paid Tho Pearson 1s allowed for (*interlined*: sesse)[69]	08	10	0	

} vide the particular of the arrears for 1657:

This is dew at Lam (*interlined*: Cand) after and allowed in repairs

Paid me per Tho P 9br [16]58 part of the £14–£6 for that now dew	06	00	0
Paid per Jo Pear: account marked ff	28	00	0

This accompted for at May [16]59

Paid ⟨mee⟩ Tho Pear: £2 and £3 before in full of this years rent	2	10	0
Paid mee per Jackson	02	10	0
Paid in monie 41:6:6 in a note of dis*bursements* £12.3.6.	53	10	0
Paid per Will Atk booke with 4s sesse	15	0	0
This 1:14:0 was paid to mee in 9br 1658 dew for this yeare			
Paid to Will Simpson	00	03	4
Paid Will Ak in the towne rent	02	11	0
Paid for hens with allowance[70]	00	15	0

noathinge paid this yeare

---

68. Altered from £1.8.0.
69. This phrase added later.
70. *with allowance* a later insertion.

3r *cont.*	+Greenehew then 5s and swinetake 1. 7d. in all	00	6	7
	+Watey to Will Smith	02	10	0
	+Wensladale per particuler about	467	09	10
	+Wilkinson for Hackthropp feild that was Mawsons	00	10	0
	+Clifton towne end forfited	19	00	0
	+Rob Wilkinson mortgage	02	10	0

£1376 17 7[71]

Leases then Jo Atkinson of the dales 2nd payment of 7 years and a halfe	20	00	0
+[72]Sir Will Carleton the 4th payment of 7 and a (*interlined*: halfe)	50	00	0
[73]Mr. Challinor next martinmas			
+Mr. Midleton of Belsa for 7 years at Mart and Whit this the first	50	00	0
+Cosen Midleton the 5th payment of 5 years and a halfe	300	00	0
+Edward Meason the 4th payment of 7 years and halfe	02	00	0
+George Nelson wife the 5th payment of 6 years	10	00	0
+Paper Mill a long lease	01	00	0
+Mr. Sandford the 4th payment of 8 years	06	00	0
+Mr. Swinburne the 6th payment of 7 years and a halfe	50	00	0
+Mr. Wivell the 6th payment of 7 years and a halfe	25	00	0

£464: ⟨467⟩ £1840: 17. 7

4v	Saint Andrew day [16]57:			
	+Forsdale rent charge per Ja: Metcalfe	03	15	10
	+Lowther Brigg tenement per Emanll Bird	07	04	04

71. *Recte* £1390.11.0.
72. This entry a contemporary insertion.
73. This entry an insertion.

Paid per Will Smith allowed him 5s for walling	02	10	0	4r *cont.*
vide the particuler of the arrears				
This is said to be secured in his other bond				
Paid to Tho Pearson	19	00	0	
Paid mee upon accompt				
Paid by Jo : Metcalfe to Tho Pearson Jan [16]57	20	00	0	

Paid per Jo Pearsons account after Mart [16]57 beeinge			
the first payment	50	00	0
Paid me the £4 for this and Whis before	02	00	0
Paid Mr. Drumand and £1.5s.0 viz 9s use of the £10			
(*interlined*: dew at Whis last) and 16s dew at Lam. Whis			
[16]57			
paid mee at June [16]58 10. 0. 0. for Whis [16]57 and £5			
in part of this Mart. [16]57			
Paid Tho Pearson per Wil Atkinson of Whitehaven			
Paid Tho Pearson	06	00	0
Paid per Jo Pear: accompt marked ff	50	00	0

Demesnes at Penticot 58[74]   5r

paid
new secured

---

74. At this point the first eleven entries now found on f5v (p. 98) below were
written in error, and then deleted. As a result the notes of receipts are squashed
in the l.h. margin.

4v *cont.*

Leases then

+ Mr. Whelpdale the 4th payment of 7 years and a halfe	100	00	0
+ Mr. Tankard the 9th payment of 12 years	050	00	0
+ Candlemas Hackthropp old rent	04	00	0
+ Helton my owld part qr beside the mill rent	07	09	3[75]
+ Melkinthropp with Tompson	01	00	9

⟨Milne tenement at Newton⟩[76]
Demesnes then

+ Asby with stocke besids £1 abatement	22	10	0
+ Bampton John Knot besides the tyth accompt.	38	00	0
+ Hackthropp feild to Ch.Hudson and Robley and one grasse	00	15	0
+ Melkinthropp tenement to Chr. Wilkinson	06	17	6
+ Rosgill Carages with one lately to be aded	02	00	0
+ Sledall Cariages at 1s 6d a peece	01	02	6
+ Stewardson for Cowper tenement lett	04	00	0
+ Sewborwens to Aray halfe	16	00	0
+ Quale tenement lett to Fallowfield besides allowed for my sheepe keepinge £1	00	13	0
+ Howcarle to W Allkinson to begine next Candlemas £7.10s.[77]			
+ Jo Baxter for Punderhackes at Cand [16]58[78]	04	10	0

Leases then

+ John Aray the 6th payment of 7 years for Mr Sandford at Lam and Cand[79]	10	00	0
Lancelot Iveson for 7 years to begine at Lam next £30[80]			
⟨ Will Aray for Mr Sand*ford* at Lam [16]58 for 7 years⟩			
+ Will Langhorne for Mr Sandford the 2nd of 7 years	34	00	0

---

75. Altered.
76. This line, a contemporary insertion, has been deleted.
77. This line interlined.
78. *At Cand [16]58* inserted in same hand.
79. *At Lam and Cand* inserted in same hand.
80. This line inserted, see p. 154 below.

paid £63   5r *cont.*
accompted

paid £3:16:8.
paid £7 9s 2d
paid W Atk

accompted
paid my wife £38[81]

paid by Hudson and Robley	00	15	0
paid once in part 6.13.0 pd mee 4s 6d in full	06	17	6
paid Wil Atkinson in part	01	13	0
paid mee p Tho Noble 1.1.0. and 1s 6d allowed for his owne	01	01	0
paid mee with 3s 10d in sesse	04	00	0

June [16]58 £6 and £11 in part of the next rent

paid mee 13s 4d and now determined beeinge sowld away

paid Tho Pearson per Ramsey	10	00	0
paid to Tho Pearson	34[81]00		0

---

81. This figure partially blotted out.

4v *cont.* + Tho Lancaster the 4th payment of 7 years and halfe	01	12[82]	6
Mr Richardson to be added the next Candlemas £50[83]			
+ Miller tenement at Newton	⟨01	00	0⟩

Anuntiation 1658*

⟨ + Bearslack to Jo Knot this year			
+ Bartribanke the other half 6.15.0.	06	15	0
+ Egleston Abbey	95	15	10
+ Highfield to Rawley and Wilkinson	07	10	0
+ Highfield and Tarneber another part of it to J Kt	11	10	0
Lowther Moultermalt 1 pecke for every 20	02	10	0
+ Newton Moulter rent	07	19	0
+ Sewborwens the other halfe	16	00	0
+ Thrimby Grainge to Webster et al	15	00	0
+ Thwaits Mill	05	17	6

Leases Then

+ Emanuell Bird	15	00	0
+ Thorpe rents with the Nativitie before about dureinge our joynt lives	300	00	0
£800. 17. 6.			

Penticost [16]58

+ Bampton old rent	06	04	6
+ Clifton rent the mortgage forfited manie years	09	14	2
+ Helton late Mr Sandfords	05	07	9
+ Knipe rent	03	10	3
+ Lowther rent as I take it	09	16	2

---

82. Altered from 0s.
83. This line inserted.

	£	s	d	
this 1. 12. 6. is cleared by Sutton	01	12	6	5r *cont.*
this is allowed for repairs viz and £1 before dew (*interlined*: at Lam)	01	00	0	
paid this to Tho Pear per booke	06	15	0	
paid mee	07	10	0	
paid Will Atkin per Jo Knot	11	10	0	
paid Will Atkinson in 2 somes	07	19	0	
paid my wife £11 part of the £17 shee received soe arrear £5 paid T.P.	05	00	0	
paid Will Atkin : with 6ᵈ allowed for sesse	15	00	0	
paid mee per Jo Wren Bayiff 9br [16]58	05	17[84]	6	

this accompted and new secured per Ja Bird and he to pay £20 per annum at Mich and Lad: day for 7 years in part

vide the accompt

	£	s	d	
paid mee part 6. 2. 5. the rest allowed for collecting				
paid mee in full of this halfe years rent[85] in monie allowed out of it 2s 6d	09	08	10	
paid mee	05	7	9	
paid mee per Baxter	03	10	[3][86]	
paid to Will Simpson per Geo: in part 9.12.4 and 3s 4d Bayliff and 4s abated				

---

84. Altered.
85. Rest of entry inserted in contemporary hand.
86. Blotted out, with the final word of the line below.

4r *cont.*	Mures rent then finable	00	05	0
	+ Newton rent with Smith rent 1d[87]	10	12	10[88]
	+ Plumpton rent	69	06	5
	+ Rosgill rent	07	06	3
	+ Sledall then	04	02	1
	+ Slegill then	00	17	6
	+ Strickland	03	02	6
	+ Thrimby towne	02	00	4
	+ Thrimby Grainge	01	10	6
	+ Threlkeld rent	15	04	6

£949 18:11

5v	Pentecost 1658			
	+ Appleby Burgage misplaced before	00	02	0
	+ Bampton free rent	00	13	4
	+ Mr Fulthropps, rent charge out of Seaton etc	50	00	0
	+ Lowther Mill lett for 36 bushels of bigg and malt and 6 of shirlline valued at £6[89]	06	00	0
	+ Melkinthropp let to Wilkinson	06	17	6
	+ More his son for a parcell thereof in Hacktrop	⟨00	10	0⟩
	+ Marton with Nunthropp rentall	387	13	4
	+ More at Newham Mr Westropp rent charge and as much at Mart	20	00	0[90]
	+ Newton Mills	06	00	0
	+ Preston upon Tease rent charge	28	00	0
	+ Preston and Astley my Bro: Will the (*interlined*: writing) beside the improvement to be added when dew	85	15	0
	+ Shapp tyth one halfe to Noble, Smith etc.	53	10	0
	+ Sledall mill not certainly lett	02	15	0
	+ Threlkeld Kilne to accompt for was sumtyme	02	10	0

---

87. This entry inserted.
88. Altered from 9d.
89. i.e. Skilling.
90. This entry inserted.

paid my wife 10. 12. 10[91] and 5s to mee for tyme
paid and accompted for by booke
paid mee 7.4.9. per Rich Cowper and 1s 6d arrears per
Atkinson paid mee in full

5r *cont.*

paid mee per Noble and given 1s 6d[92]	04	2	1
⎧ paid mee July [16]58	07	00	2[93]
⎨			
⎩ paid mee this	15	04	6

6r

paid Will At June [16]59 for this and Mart followinge	00	04	0
paid in part to mee per Jo Kt 11s and 1s for Aray			
paid per Jo Pear: account ⟨Mar⟩ Whis [16]58	50	00	0
vide Geo note of what is arrers of Corne if anie			
paid mee with 10s allowed in sesse	06	17	6
This is to be made payable at Mart [16]58 and soe after			
vide the accompt of arrears of Marton			
paid per Jo P account (*erasure*) the first payment	20	00	0
paid mee in the £14 paid per Tho Pearson this rent	06	00	0
paid per Jo Pear: accompt with 4s sess[94]	28	00	0
This accompted for in May [16]59 with my Brother			
This paid my wife 9 July [16]58 with 14s abated for sess	£53	-10 -	0
paid mee for this tyme in full viz beforehand	02	10	0
paid this yeare as it came to	01	17	0

---

91. Altered from 9d.
92. *and given 1s 6d* a later insertion.
93. *Sic.*
94. *with 4s sess* a subsequent addition.

5v *cont.* + Rob Wilkinson mortgage as good as inheritance	02	10	0
+ Helton tyth rent per Will Langhorne next Whis	15	00	0
+ Helton Mill next Whis and Mart [16]59	04	00	0

Leases then

Sir Will Carleton the 5th payment of 7 years and ½	50	00	0
+ Cos Midleton the 6th payment of ⟨7⟩5 years beside			
120 paid for 10ᵐᵒ	300	00	0
+ Mr Midleton of Bellsay the 2ᵈ payment of 7 years	050	00	0
+ ⟨George Nelson widow⟩ Edward Meason the 5th pay-			
ment of 7 years and a ½	02	00	0
George Nelson widow the 6 payment of 6 years	10	16	0⁹⁵
+ Paper Mill a long lease	01	00	0
+ Mr Sandford the 5th payment of 8 years	06	00	0
+ Mr Swinburne the 7th payment of 7 year and a ½	50	00	0
+ Mr Tanckerd but paid at Midsomer the 10th payment			
of 12 years	50	00	0
+ Mr Wivell the 7th payment of 7 years and and [*sic*]			
a halfe	25	00	0
+ Asby Grainge with stocke	22	10	0

Midsomer

+ Helton tyth lett to the tenants wherof give £5	20	00	0
+ Helton tyth that was Mr Sandfords let to Judson	15	00	0
+ Helton Mill not yet lett in manus domini⁹⁶		(*blank*)	
⁹⁷Lanc Browne et al for Sir Will Carleton next Mids to			
pay for 6 years and a halfe 18.10.0.			

Lam*mas* [16]58

+ Hackthropp old rent	04	02	2
+ Helton old rent that was my owne anciently	07	09	3
+ Melkinthropp rent	01	00	9
+ Thwaites St James tyde	12	04	3

---

95. Altered so to read from £10.0.0.
96. *in manus domini* a subsequent insertion.
97. This entry a later insertion.

6r *cont.*

paid this and that dew at Martinmas (*erasure*) as by the
debt booke

} This dew Whis [16]59

allowed and secured per Hen Robinson 20⁰ June [16]58
in part of this and former arrears for which Sir Will hath
a note   123 00   0

accompted per Brother Will   300 00   0
paid per Jo Pear: accompt   50 00   0

paid mee
paid about Feb [16]58 of Wid Nelson in part of £5 arrears
at Mart [16]57 and this 10.16.0 to Will Simpson 9.14.0.
paid per Will Atkinson[98] of Whithaven to Tho Pearson
paid mee
paid per Jo P accompt for Whis [16]58   50 00   0

accompted for by Bro Will   50 00   0

paid mee per Henry Robinson the full payment   10 00   0
vide the arrears upon accompt

paid W At in part £10 paid mee £5 in full   15 00   0
paid my wife per Judgson [99]now lett to Will Langherne   15 00   0

paid per Will Atkinson 3.16.4 beinge all dew qr
paid per Geo: to my wife [1]qr for 6d wantinge   07 08   9
paid mee per Chr Wilkinson   01 00   9
paid my wife then   12 04   2

---

98. An estate officer of the Lowthers of Whitehaven
99. Rest of line added later.
 1. Rest of line a later insertion.

5v *cont.* + Demesnes then. Heltondale tenement bought of Holme beside lokeinge to my Shepe	05	10	0
+ Mill tenement at Newton	01	00	0
Leases + Tho Lancaster the 5th payment of 7 years and halfe	01	12	6
+ John Aray the 7th payment of 7 years	10	00	0
+ Lancelott Iveson of Leedes the first payment of 7 yeares	30	00	0[2]
⟨Will Langhorne the 3rd payment for 7 years	34	00	0⟩
+ Will Aray the first payment of 7 years at one payment yearly	20	00	0
Mr Richardson ⟨halfe⟩ the first halfe year of 7 years as much at Candlemas	50	00	0[3]

Michelmas [16]58

+ Egleston Abbey	95	15	0
+			
+ Highfield to John Knott this year	41	10	0
+ Hackthropp grasses to Hudson qr	01	05	0
Lowther grasses about 12[4] about qr[5]	01	00	0
+ Reaslack for Wenington	19	00	0
+ Sledall to Tho Noble	36	00	0
+ Thwaits Mill to Caward	05	17	6[6]
+ Mr Dudleys £5 remitted for the use of £100	05	00	0
+ Leases then Emanuell (*interlined*: James) Bird at Mich at as much at Ladie Day	10	7[7]00	0
+ Thorpe my wives Joynture about	300	00	0

£1769   19   7

Will Jamson for Sherflatt halfe rent and shepe	04	00	0
Arkendall what can be made of it which was only	02	00	0

---

2. This line inserted, see p. 154.
3. This entry inserted.
4. Altered from 11.
5. *about qr* a later insertion.
6. Altered from £6.0.0d.
7. Altered.

6r *cont.*

paid mee 4.17.6 the rest allowed for salveinge but to pay it
all next year

paid mee 9br [16]58 part of the £14—£1.0.0.   01 00 0

This ended by payment a grosse some per Sutton the
Quaker

paid my wife per booke   10 00 0

paid upon accompt per Bro Will May [16]59:

paid Will Atkinson   20 00 0

paid to Will Atkinson   50 00 0

paid the rent now dew pro ut per booke qr[8]   95 15 0

paid Will Atkinson 8br [16]58 £30 in part allowed £10
for Old Park
given to my son Jo. L. 01.15.0.

paid mee per Jo Wen bayliff with 4s 3d sesse allowed   18 15 9
paid mee with 9s 1d rent   36[9] 00 0
paid per Jo Wentington to my wife 5.17.6.

paid by Ja Bird to Geo and he to my wife   10 00 0
vide the accompt of arrears

paid me per wife

---

8. *qr.* added later.
9. Altered.

6v   *(Arranged on verso and recto as the 1657 rental)*

Additions for 1658 in lew of
Substractions quod nota

Mr Westropps rent charge out of Newham			
Jo Pearson hath the writeinge Whis & Mar[10]	040 : 00 .		0
+ Mr Anderson upon £100 *(erasure)* to have £6-13-4	⟨006 : 13		4⟩
qr how setled			
Mr Midletons lease for £100 per annum for 7 years			
begininge at Mart [16]57 qr et vide of Jo P	100 : 00		0
Mr Johnson by my Brother Will qr how setled upon			
£500 lent at 2 tymes	*(blank)*		
× More my Brother Will for £500 upon the Collery to			
pay at Christ [16]57 and misomer [16]58	030 : 0.		0
× Howcarale to lett not yet setled lett since[11]	007 : 10[12]		0

In *(erasure)* manus domini 1657: as valued

Above the house viz Greenerigs	40	00	0
Thrimby feild new walled and Thrimby Inge	10	00	0
The 4 hay closes better then	12	00	0
The old Parke and Springe	26	00	0
The Heades £3 Rowland feild £24 fouldes £3	30	00	0
Whale Inge	12	00	0
New Parke as improved besides the deare	30	00	0
Cotdikes with the rest of that tenement and grasses[13]	06	00	0
The 4 crofts about the house	05	00	0
Dawlands Bankcrofts and the High Holme Clarke Croft and Calfe Garth and Ravencash[14]	15	00	0
The House gardens 3 orchards and Jackcroft and Ridgencote	08	00	0
Thwaite landes with that added	07	00	0
Sherflatt with that of Barnes tenement and the litle new inclosed part at the heade of it	08	00	0
Millfielde with that of the Parsons I have	18	00	0

---

10. *Whis and Mar* a subsequent addition.
11. *lett since* a subsequent insertion.
12. Altered from 00.
13. *and grasses* a subsequent insertion.
14. *and Ravencash* a subsequent addition.

This proceeded not

This £30 per annum ended the £500 beeinge accompted for

paid to Tho Pearson 15to 9ber [16]58 for Greenerigs dew
Mich [16]58   21 : 00   0
Greenrigg and Thrimby let to the 2 young Simpsons
at £42 per annum at Mich [16]58 and Ladie [16]59   42 00   0
The rest of Thrimby feild called Punderhackes lett to
Jo Baxter at   04 10   0
The 4 hay closes the heades and Old Parke and £10 for
the winterage of Burtribanke to Jo Knot with the 2
Bearslackes Thorneburge and Hirpletthow and 400 sheep
and the Heafe at Helten at £83 per annum at Mich and
Ladie pro ut ante.   83 00   0
only I had the summerage of the Old Parke this yeare
for which I rebated £20.0.0.
paid Will Atkinson part of the rent dew Mich [16]58 £30
This lett part of it to plow for halfe part for otes and the
hay ground at the 4th locke; and 40s per annum to Lanc
Chapelhow dew at Cand [16]58[15]

This lett to Will Jamson et al for 4 years at £8 per annum
at Mich and Ladie day   08. 00.   0

---

15. *at Cand [16]58* written on line above.

6v *cont.*	The two flatts were formerly £24[16]	22 00	0
	Buckholme as growne over with wood £8 the High		
	Close of Clifton £8 and that part of Esklamoore		
	adjoyneinge £8 in all	24 00	0
	Skellan with that part of Esklamore added	16 00	0
	Boones services and Mill better then	20 00	0
	Helton Mill and Killne valued about since lett at[17]	08 10	0[18]
	Wood Sailes perquisits of Courts and the casualtie of		
	fines in this Lordshipp about	20 00	0
	A grant of 20 bushel of Salt, a barell of Hearinge, a		
	lode of Killinge and Pickeled oysters yearely out of		
	St. Bees and Whitehaven or else £5 in lew thereof,		
	which I receive, worth	05 00	0
	Smithie at Lowther (*erasure*) with the stiddie	00 10	0

[*change of style hand of Sir J.L.(2)*]

Lett Chr Simpson from the first of Aprill [16]59[19]		
Skellans £16 Eshalmoor Buckholme and Higclose £24		
and Flats £24. From the 15th of Aprill, and Thwait-		
lands from the 10th of May [16]58 at £8	72 06	8
(*erasure*) 3rd of the bone peates £1.6.8 and 20 days		
shearing and 20[20] days mowinge in all the Cropp to		
be made as good againe[21]		
to pay at Mich and Ladie day yearly	(*blank*)	
Memorandum that Will Simpson had his goods in the		
Millfield from Mid Aprill to the 3d of May [16]59		

7v   [*Heading in hand of Sir J.L.(2), rental in unknown hand*] A perticuler of the rentall of Mauldesmeaburn as lett and jeast valued by my mother July 1658.
Rental giving names of properties in hand and land use, value £112 a year; and giving names of properties let with, in most cases, name of tenant and amount of rent, £122-3-0d.[22] No value given for coals and peats. [Total value £234-4-0d.]

8r   [*Hand of Sir J.L.(2)*] *Note of the number of Sir J.L.(2)'s sheep let with named properties of his, with name of tenant and value of, but not number of, sheep, [n.d.].*

---

16. *were formerly £24* a subsequent addition.
17. *since lett at* a subsequent addition.
18. Altered from £08-00-0, presumably when let.
19. See p. 159.
20. Altered from 29?
21. *as good againe* a subsequent addition.
22. *Recte* £122-4-4.

(*blank*)

8v–11r   *Rental of all Sir J.L.(2)'s estates for the year beginning Martinmas, 1658,*
          (arranged as f3 (p. 87) above.)

  11v   *[Hand of Sir J.L.(2)] 1659. Notes of purchases of land in Wensleydale.*[23] *Gives*
          name of township and vendor, purchase price and rent per annum: With notes
          of the subsequent sale of some purchases; and of fee farm rents.
          [Unknown hand] Note of mortgage payments due to Sir J.L.(2) from the lands
          of Sir William Carleton in 1664/1665.[24]

  12   *Copy document headed: a particular of Milby*[25] *given in upon the purchase*
          [by Sir J.L.(2)] 21 September 1659, copy signature of Thomas Tanckred.
          Note of 11 tenants' holdings in the manor of Millby giving type of land,
          acreage, and rent. [The purpose of numbers in the l.h. margin is not clear.]
          With a note of quit rents to be paid out, and that the common is now stinted
          by the tenants. Total acreage 215a. 8rds. 3p., annual rent £236-16-6d.
          Out payments total £5-12-7d.

12v–13r   *[Change of hand, unknown hand] Copy of a survey of the manor of Millby made*
          May 30 1654; gives, under the name of each tenant, the acreage of each piece
          of ground that he holds. Concludes with a like survey of Mr Tancred's grounds
          at Ellinthorp and Thorton Ings.

13v–16r   *Rental of all Sir J.L.(2)'s estates for the year beginning Martinmas 1659,*
          (arranged as f3 (p. 87) above).

16v–17r   *Rental of Maulds Meaburne, Martinmas 1659.*[26] *Lists names of 85 tenants,*
          sometimes with place of residence, and [half-year's] rent. Total £17.[27] *Similar*
          rental of free rents payable at Martinmas only, total 12s-2d. from 9 tenants.

17r–17v   *[Change of hand; unknown hand] Rental of Meaburne demesne February*
          1659 [–60], total £264-8-0d. Concludes with notes [in hand of Sir J.L.(2)] of
          deductions to be made from this total.

18r   *(blank)*

18v–22r   *Rental of all Sir J.L.(2)'s estates for the year beginning Martinmas 1660,*
          (arranged as f3 (p. 87) above).

22v–23r   *[Top half of page: unknown hand] List of ratings of constabularies in Yorkshire,*
          n.d. (continued on top half of f23r).

22v–23r   *[Bottom half of page: hand of Sir J.L.(2)] Rental of Meaburne as due Candlemas*
          1662, total £244-5-2d. Concludes with a cross reference to the next rental,
          fol. 35b. Receipts are entered on bottom half of f23r.

---

23. Wensleydale, see p. 40 above, see also p. 157 below.
24. See pp. 72, 178.
25. See pp. 157–8, below.
26. Noted in the same hand: *to be made more perfect.*
27. £16-5-5d.

*Rental of all Sir J.L.(2)'s estates for the year beginning Martinmas 1661,
(arranged as f3 (p. 87) above).*

	£ – s – d		
'and of Sir J.L.(2)] Memorandum that it appeareth in the yeare begining at Mart 1661 ut patet (*interlined:* ante) I have in revenew in lands of inheritance and leases and other profitts pro ut ante patet per particulars and in right of my wife and other wayes	5555	18	0
Whereof appeareth to be in leases neare expiringe manie of them [28]as appeareth after viz			
In leases at Mart [16]61	565	19	10
At Candlemas ut patet	267	10	0
At Ladie day after	312	13	4
At Penticost after	390	00	0
At Lamas after	182	00	0
At Michelmas after	310	00	0
Soe the total in leases then	2028	03	2
Which deducted out of the former whole revenue resteth	3527	14	10
to which add (*erasure*) not mentioned in aforsaid revenew being in another rentall, At Meaburne	240	00	0
Item in Demesnes in my owne hands at Lowther	200	00	0
Item my son in right of his wife £100 (*interlined:* in possession) and at Hackthropp not formerly mentioned	100	00	0
above	100	00	0
Item Yeanewith in reversion after a life ⟨upon⟩	250	00	0
Soe then the total is	4417	14	10
Out of which deduct for Son Ralph about	1000	00	0
Item for my son Richard setled and given about	300	00	0
In all	1300	00	0
Soe then resteth of inheritance to my eldest	3117	14	10
Item may add to this in casuall fines per annum about	150	00	0
Item the beinefitt of my ⟨fines⟩ generall fines of my tenants at my death will goe neare to purchas £200 per annum if well and discretcly manuged and rightly tymed and ordered[29] with those most tractable first	200	00	0
Item I have bought (*erasure*) an addition to the rent charge of Preston upon Tease of Mr Sayer since per annum	064	00	0

Marginal folio references: 23v–26r; 26v; 26v cont.

Beside the beinefitt of woods, charge in Buildinge (*interlined:* wallinge) at

---

28. Rest of the line a later insertion.
29. Rest of line a later insertion [by Sir J.L.(2)]; last two words uncertain reading.

severall places which hath cost me above £3000 and this is cleare without anie charge upon it save to make good my debts and legacies which may be uncertaine.

But as the case studd at Whitsontyde 1659 I did estimate my personall estate then in leases debts rent arrer howsehould stiff etc by a particuler estimate to be worth about £20,000 and I thinke it not much lessened which if it soe continew (as I will make a perticular estimate,) then I haveinge but given out in legacies about £11,000 there will about £9000 remayne to add to my (*erasure*) heire, which will purchas at 15 years purchas (as most I bought at that rate) £600 per annum which if bestowed in land or is as good would make my eldest sons revenew above £4000 per annum which is sufficient for a Northeraine gentleman and more than double I had left mee; this will increase if you live in the North which I advise; though you live plentifully and use all your tenants and those you deale with to full content-ment; And by prudent management (*erasure*) may purchas £200 per annum and spend £1000 per annum besids which is to much; and that £200 per annum (*erasure*) in tenn years will be besids the yearly beinefitt £2000 per annum; which if I live and all succede well I may doe and if I dye those that succede mee will have the like advantage to doe it consideringe what I doe other wayes yearely to my other children not yett provided for as I (*erasure*) intend but have (*interlined*: intend to) declared my mynde therein both by will and a lease;

27r[1]

$£ - s - d$

A perticuler estimate of my personnall estate at Whisuntyde 1659 viz

1659
In leases for years as worth in present monie

	£	s	d
Jo Atkinson of the Dales	070	00	0
Sir Will Carleton	500	00	0
Mr Midleton of Belsay in Northumberland	400	00	0
Cos. Midleton of Stockell	800	00	0
Edw Meason	015	00	0
Paper Mill then	020	00	0
Mr Sandford	024	00	0
Mr Swinburne of Bishopricke	250	00	0
Mr Robt Wivell	075	00	0
Mr Whelpdale of Penreth	250	00	0
Mr Tanckerd of Braneton in Yorkshire	500	00	0
Hen Robinson of Penreth	085	00	0
Mr Menell of Thornabie	500	00	0
Mr Mathew Richardson	400	00	0
My Brother Will for my part of Great Preston	3000	00	0
Totall leases	6900[30]00	0	
Wensladale rents and debts there arrears	0800	00	0
Mr Challernor of Gisbraw lease forgott	0400	00	0

---

30. Altered from £9,600.

Marton rents and debts arrer	1100	00	0	27r *cont.*
Debtts per (*erasure*) Alphabett pro ut	6000	00	0
Rents arrears at Whis heare	330	00	0
Rents now due at Whis [16]59	1500	00	0
Fines arrears untill then	200	00	0
Horses about 26 valued at	150	00	0
8 Oxen and 50 Sheepe	080	00	0
Househoulde stuff plate and lingen etc	1000	00	0
Monies upon accompt with my Son Christopher	877	00	0
More upon my Brother Will accompt book mereley	270	00	0
More upon my wives and Will Atkinsons bookes	0200	00	0
More upon my Son Kitts private accompt	0200	00	0

The totall then is	20007	00	0

Thorpe rents arrears forgotten	100	00	0
Lancelott Ivesons lease of lands forgott	250	00	0
Will Langhorne of Helton for Mr Sandford	150	00	0

	[20507	00	0]

By this may bee seene what increase of both
reall and personall estate is made after or
what disbursed for mariage of Daughters
and preferment of younger childeren or
other expences

Vide foll 156 : a : and 165 : b :[31]

nknown hand] *Rental of Wensleydale, 1661. Gives, in alphabetical order,*   27v–28r
names of 79 tenants, occasionally with residence, and amount of rent.[32]

and of Sir J.L.(2)] *Rentals of all Sir J.L.(2)'s estates for the years beginning*   28v–34r
Martinmas 1662 and 1663, (arranged as f3 (p. 87) above).

Part of a rental dated Candlemas 1664.[33]   34v

(Blank)   35r

Rentals of the manor of Maulds Meaburne from Martinmas 1663 to Candlemas   35v–38r
1671/72, with notes of receipts, (arranged as f3 (p. 87) above).

Rentals of all Sir J.L.(2)'s estates for the years beginning Martinmas 1664–   38v–48r
Martinmass 1666[34], *(arranged as f3 (p. 87) above).*

Rental of all Sir J.L.(2)'s estates for the year beginning Martinmas 1667,   48v–51r
(arranged as f3 (p. 87) above). [Hand of Sir J.L.(2)]

---

31. Added by Sir J.L.(2) later.
32. See p. 40 above.
33. Noted as: *This is misplaced vide foll: 39b*, [by Sir J.L.(2)].
34. ff46v–47r are blank, but the rentals are complete.

48v Mart*inmas* [16]67

+ Bampton old rent	06	04	5
+ Clifton out of which allowed 2s 6d for collectinge	09	08	10
[35]Cleburne about £3			
+ Helton then	05	08	9
+ Knipe then	03	09	6
+ Lowther out of which allowed 3s 4d to the Bayliff	09	11	3
+ Newton with the increase and smithie	10	13	0
+ Plumpton with the medow out of which allowed: 1:13:4.	69	14	5
+ Rosgill allowed his cariages for Collectinge and 6d free rent	07	06	9
+ Sledall allowed his 2 Carages	04	02	2
+ Slegill Strickland and Thrimby	07	10	2
+ Threlkeld then	15	05	6
+ Thwaites this yeare again old rent with walkemil silver and hens carages and 5s greenhew in all	13	13	8[36]

Demesnes then

+ Appleby Burgage	00	02	0
+ Bampton to Jo Knot with the Barnesteade	38	03	4
+ More for Schoole rent 10 : Beachefott 12s 6d Sadmanhow 2.15.0.	03	07	6
+ More free rent then	00	15	7 +
+ More for Thornebergh and Herplethow	11	10	0
+ For the use of the 400 sheepe	05	00	0
+ More for Heltondale tyth	02	15	0
+ Punderhackes the last rent for [16]66[37]	02	00	0
+ Beareslacke of Jo Powley and Powley tenement and sheepe	14	08	2
+ Beareslacke another part and Thrimby feild to Guy Coperthwaite pro ut at Mart before vide the particulers	10	01	0
+ Haycloses and Heades to Geo Laybourne the Keeper	08	10	0

---

35. The whole line a contemporary insertion.
36. Altered to read so.
37. Altered from [16]67: the line inserted.

paid Geo Mo: 6.4.5
paid my wife 9. 8. 10
paid W.At. in part of Cleyburne rent: 2.16.2[38]
paid my wife 5. 8. 9.
paid Geo. Mo. 3: 9. 6.
paid Geo. Mo. 9. 8. 0.
paid W. At. 10.12.⟨9⟩10

paid W At. 65: 4: 7 in part Accompted for the rest

paid Geo Mo: 7.6.3. paid mee 6d ob in full
paid in part 3.18.6. and 3s 6d for Dale head in full
paid Will At 7.00 in part and 10s in full
paid W At 13.5.–[39] in part paid £2 in full

of which paid Geo Mo: £11 in 2 parts free rent arrears 2.8.0; and
collectinge 5s 8d

paid 2s

{ paid my wife per Jo Knott wife £40 9br [16]67. viz and £2 for Sadamanhow
  and Jo Knot paid mee 8s 4d for the odd 3s 4d for the barne and 5s odd
  for Sadamanhow (*erasure*) and for the school rent pro tyth of Beckefott,
  now dew and at Cand next, beeinge for [16]66 and [16]67. pro ut per
  his acquittance

{ paid my wife per Jo Knot 21: 05: 0 beeinge 5s (*erasure*) abated
  for Punderhackes

paid my wife with 2s given backe againe

paid Geo. Mo: June [16]68 in part £10; vide the accompt at Mart [16]69 postea
paid Geo Mo: 9br in full 8:10 0

---

38. The whole line an insertion.
39. Illegible.

48v *cont.*	+Burtrybancke to Ri. Wilkinson et al	07	00	0
	+Hall Garth to Geo Hayton	08	10	0
	+Heltondale tyth per prescription of Sandford tenants	01	00	0
	+Heltondale Mill to	05	00	0
	+Helton mowinge and shearinge wants corne leadinge	02	00	0
	+Lowther mill in my owne land[40]		*(blank)*	

+Marton with Darlington, Preston rent charge West-
ropps, Fulthropps, Skelton, Nuntropp Ayton Thorn-
aby in Jo P collection above 760 02 10
+Millby besides free rent deducted 115 11 8
+Meaburne halfe at severall days per the rentall pro
ut about 120 00 0
+Murreys grasses to Rich Wilkinson 001 00 0
+Newton Mill as now lett too deare 007 00 0

+Punderhackes This year to Robert Wilkinson 004 00 0
+Shapp tyth to Richard Smith and Thomas Noble 053 10 0

+Sledall Millne to Rich Wilkinson 002 15 0
+Sledall tenement at Dalehead I to beare all rents and
sesse 005 12 6
+Suborwens now and at Lamas halfe accomptd at
Mart [16]68 .... 023 05 0

+Thrimby Grainge halfe (*erasure*) to Jo Webster et al 015 00 0
+Thrimby free rent per Mathew 000 03 4
+Watey to Will Smith[41] but better 002 10 0
+Wensladale by the perticuler rentall about 565 13 11
+Worshall in Yorkshire by Sir Will Midleton cleare rent 100 00 0
+Yeanewith a parcell neare the walke mill to Chr Meeson 00 10 0
+Whale tenement to Jo Wilkinson forgotten and to pay
5s rent and services 04 00 0

---

40. Note [by Sir J.L.(2)] *for 26 bushels of bigge and now to lett* then struck out
and *now* [£]*5.15.0* inserted. Difficult to read.
41. Rest of line a subsequent insertion.

paid my wife; £7:

paid W A 8.10. 0.

paid my wife £1: 0: 0

paid mee £5 and given backe 10:ˢ

paid mee per W Lang: 2: 0: 0

lett for 36 bushell of Corne whereof 2 to be skillin used to be above 40 busel.

vide the particuler arrere

vide the particuler arrear

vide Meaburne rent arrears in the booke before

paid mee £1: 0: 0

paid Geo Mo: February [16]67 in part of former arrers 13:07:6, Nota £14

paid W At July [16]68 and arrears then 13s 6d of ⟨This⟩ the last rent. and this ⟨yeare⟩ rent Soe now arrer 7.13.6 paid

paid mee in part 2:0:0 per Rob Wilkinson

paid Jan [16]67 by Emanul Noble £40:0:0. Paid after to Will At £56.15.0 in full of this and Whis rent after.

paid W At July [16]68 for this and the rent 5.10.0

paid Will At 5:01.4 the rest allowed in sesse

paid Geo: Mo July [16]68 in full of the last and in part of this £19: and arrere yet of this rent £19.0.0 vide his accquitance

paid Geo Mo 9br [16]67: £15 but I gave them backe 10s

paid W Atk 3s 4d

paid mee 2.10.0.

vide the accompt

vide the Marton arrer

paid mee per Meason wife 7br [16]68 0:10.0

vide the note of arrears at Cand [16]69 in the bonds

48v *cont.* + Wiber closes and Buckholme to Frans Lowther
    forgotten   2085 : 11 : 1[42]   28 00 0

Mortgages then and St Andrew Day

+ Reaslack now againe from Sir Will Hudleston   19[43]00 0
+ Clifton Towne End to Birkebecke et al   19 00 0
              ⟨Walke Millne⟩[44]   00 00[45] 0
+ My last Mortgage or estate with Sir Jo my son in law
    upon Clifton for which I disbursed for my part £250
    Whis [16]67
+ Slegill tens mortgaged to pay £6 per annum at Whis
    and Mart [16]68 for 3 years first at Whis [16]68[46]

Leases then

+ Rumley widowe now Chr: Brawhams the 12 of 7 years
    and ½   05 00 0
+ Mr Fulthropp the 13th of 7 years   90 00 0
+ Mr Humphreys the 13 of 7 years and ½   50 00 0

+ Paper Millne a longe lease cleare   02 00 0
+ Mr Sandford the use of Pawdens out of his old rent
    a mortgage   06 00 0
+ Mr Blackburne the 11th of 7 and ½   50 00 0
+ Mr Skelton the 10th[47] (*interlined*: last) of 7 and ½ 50 00 0
+ Mr Lee the the [*sic*] 9th of 7 years   50 00 0
    Lanc Chapelhow tenement Mortgaged untill £20 with
    use be paid   02 00 0
+ Will Langhorne the 3[d] of 7 years   20 00 0
+ Mr Denton of Cardew the 4th of 7 and ½   50 00 0
+ Mr Birkebecke the 6th of 7 and ½   50 00 0
+ Frances Lowther for Todd the 4th of 7½   05 00 0
+ Jo Lowther the 2[d] of 7 years lent £700   50 00 0
+ Kirkeby Lonsdale and Churchtowne at Carmell should
    be about halfe yearely and this the 1st of 14 years 200 00 0
+ Mr Simpson the next Mart [16]68 to pay £35 for 7 and
    halfe for Fairebanke then and at Whis after   (*blank*)

---

42. Subsequent insertion.
43. Figure altered.
44. This subsequent insertion in a different ink later struck out.
45. 10s here erased.
46. The whole of this entry a contemporary insertion.
47. *9th* struck out, *10th* substituted.

paid and secured this £28

49r *cont.*

paid Geo Mo: in manu 17 : 10 : 5d. in sesses if allowed 1.9.6ob given back 1s.
paid my wife £19.0.0.
Thwaits mill lett to͵pay at Mart [16]68 9. 10. 0.

This begins not to pay before Cand and Ladie Day next quod vide[48]

new secured at Whis [16]69
vide Marton accompt cleired
paid Geo Mo: 9br [16]67 £50 : paid W At: 9br [16]67 for Whis [16]68: pro
ut—£8-10-0 paid before hand.
paid per Cos*en* Teasdell all ferme part of £4–£2

paid Geo Mo: £6
accompted after
accompted and new secured
accompted in the purchas

(*blank*)
paid my wife £20
new secured
accompted vide the accompt Mich [16]68
paid and secured
paid W At: 10br [16]67: £48: 0: 0 and given back 2.00.0. paid in full £50

vide the rentall in booke towards the end[49]

(*blank*)

---

48. Unclear whether this refers to the Clifton and Slegill entries, or just to Clifton.
49. See p. 146.

49v   Cand*lemas* [16]67

+Hackthropp old rent	qr	03	19	9
+Helton then		07	09	3
+Melkinthropp old rent		01	00	9

Demesnes then

Asby with stock	22	10	0
+Bampton demesne and tythes	38	00	0
+Sadamanhow then 2.05.0 Schole tyth 10s Beckefott 12ˢ 6d in all	03	07	6
+Atkinson tenement and Caldickes to Jo Cos. Pinfowld	07	00	0
+Barnefield to Dick Stephenson	08	00	0
+Chr. Ritson for part of Atkinson tenement	02	00	0
+Coniwaren to Watterson	01	10	0
+Howcarle to Tho Robinson out of which the widow £1	07	10	0
+Melkintropp tenement vide how devided before	14	00	0
+feild land to Richard Hudson that belonged to it	00	10	0
+Rosgill carages besides 3 allowed the Bayliff	01	13	0
+Rosgill tyth morgaged per Rich Smith for Warmsley	12	00	0
+Sledall Carages besides 2 allowed Noble	01	02	0
+[50]Stewardson tenement ther	04	00	0
+Skellans to the Parson and Noble	18	00	0
+⟨Mr Sandfords morgage of Powdunns	12	00	0⟩[51]
+Guy Copperthwaite for that of Westgarths and other pro ut at Mart [16]67 patet	10	01	0
+Clifton cariages dew per Warkeman	03	00	0
More for Clifton mortgage for my £250 per Cos*en* Teasdell and Lady Day qr	00	00	0

---

50. This sign perhaps erased.
51. All this line struck out, see note in receipt column.

paid W At qr 3.17.9
paid Will At 7.9.3.
paid Will At Feb [16]68

paid Geo Mo the 8th of June [16]68 in part £10
secured and accompted

secured and accompted for part of the (*blank*)
paid mee in February [16]67 in part £4 paid mee more Lam [16]68 in
full   £3: 0. 0
paid Geo Mo (*erasure*) May [16]68 in part of this and former arrears
£2 and arrears upon accompt Mart [16]68 £11.16.0
paid my wife £2
paid to Will At 8r [16]68 1:10:0
paid Geo Mo: the 3d of July [16]68 in part £5:0:0 paid mee 1o9br [16]68
1:3:4 in full
paid per W At his part 3.13.0 paid per Pearson in part £2 to W At: per
Geo Mo June [16]68 £3 paid July [16]68 per Tompson £4 to W At.
paid Will At February [16]68 10s
paid Geo Mo 1.13.0
paid Geo Mo £12: dett to Smith £6 and 10s and 10s paid Mr Wormsley in all
£19 and fee farme rent paid 4s
paid Will At 19s6d abatinge for Hayton tenement that Wariner had
paid Geo 3:11:6 and 7s 6d in sesse
paid W At per Antho Noble 2.5.0. paid more by him 2.5.0. and paid per
Mr Smith 5.10.0 and £8 allowed for the prescription monie in full
This 12 per annum is sett downe as paid at Whis and Mart: and soe not
to be sett againe as dew

paid Geo Mo: 7b: [16]68 £10: in part of this and former arrers,[52] vide the
accompt Mart [16]69
paid Will Atk £3. 0. 0.

next ⟨Mart⟩ Cand begines

---

52. Rest of entry a contemporary addition.

Leases

49v *cont.*	+Lan Smith 7 of 7 and ½	05	00	0
	+Francis Harison untill all detts be runn of	04[53]10	0
	+Jo Nickelson the 5 of 7 years	10	00	0
	+Tho Nickelson the 5 of 7 years	10	00	0

+Robley and Mill the 7th of 8 years   03   06   8

+Nickelson and Bushe the 12th of 7 years   02   00   0
+Jo Wilkinson above the hall the 10th of 7 years and ½   03   00   0
  John Wilkinson of the Dale the like   03   00   0
+Jo Lancaster the 5th of 7 years   20   00   0

+Guy Coperthwaite the 4 of 15 years[54] for Westgarth
  or Jo Knot   04   06   8

+Richard Hudson for Robert Wilkinson the 2d of 7 years   02   06   8

+Rich ⟨Hudson⟩ (*interlined*: Sutton) the 8[55] payment
  of (*erasure*) 15 years   01   10   0

Lady Day [16]68   ⟨Spitle⟩

+Burtrybanke the 3d yeare of 7 to D Wilkinson   07   00   0
+Egleston as lett Cleare r[en]t   98   04   7

+Highfield and intacke to Powley with Sheepe   14   08   2
+Punderhackes (*erasure*) (*interlined*: to Robart Wilkin-
  son) halfe yerely £2   00   00   0
+Lowther dry mouwlter worth above   02   00   0
+Newton dry Moulter   07   19   0

+Thrimby Grange the 3d of 7 years   15   00   0

+Newton tyth now and at Lam after, the first ⟨year⟩
  (*interlined*: payment) for the last years rent but I restore
  5s for repaire of the barne   20   05   0

---

53. Altered from £4.
54. Rest of entry a later insertion.
55. Figure altered.

50r *cont.*

paid per Pearson per accompt
paid in manu 3.1.6. in sesse 15s2d in the Law busines 13s4d in all 04 10 0
paid mee the 18th of February [16]67 £10 the last payment
paid my wife per Will And 6thFebruary [16]68 per Tinckler in part of this
debt £5.0.0. paid per Tho Nic: February [16]68 more to him for use and
charges—£6. 0. 0. and £1 yet arrear of This secured at Cand [16]69
paid my wife 9 [16]68 in part of arrers—£6:00.0; new secured per lease of his
land.
paid mee part of the £4 Aug [16]68. £2
new secured in the £54 mortgage

paid W At February [16]67 in part 12:16:0 paid him 3o April [16]68 in part
5:1:5 of Tho Jonson 2: 1: 6d paid 2s6d in full

paid mee per Jo Knot (*erasure*) 7 [16]68—1. 6. 6. beeinge all that made of
my part as is said
paid Will At per Hudson 1:3 4 and allowed per Wiber in work at Cleburne
1. 3. 4.

arrears in all now 5:10:0 more use 10s in all £6 of which paid in 20 Sheepe
£4 (*erasure*) dew per Bainbrig 17s and yet arrear by Sutton 1.3.0. for which I
had a litle Heffer; and since paid me 1.12. in full.

paid Geo Mo: 7.0: 0
paid Will At per 41: 16: 10 paid my wife per Will Simpson £17:0:0 56vide
the accompt
paid mee July [16]68 14 08.0 in full

paid mee by Rob Wilk July [16]68 £2 in full for Punderhackes
(*blank*)
paid Will Atk July [16]68 3.13.0 qr for the rest paid more Aprill before
4.6.0. in full
paid Geo Mo £15 with sesse 2 p[ar]ts

paid W At Aprill [16]68 in part Rob Pear: £4; paid him April [16]68 per
James Nichelson; £4.0.0. paid Tho Waterson then in part—£5.0.0. of
Symond Watson in part £2.10.0.

---

56. Rest of line a later contemporary insertion.

49v *cont.* +Catterlen yet to lett for 1668 qr when to pay Mar
and at qr   22   00   0
+[57]Son Leighs Mortgage of Thorpe Shireland Norfolk
as good as land next Lady day £100

Leases then

+My wives estate at Thorpe about	300	00	0
+Mr Denton the 5th of 7 years	030	00	0
+Sir Edward Musgrave the 4th of 7 years	050	00	0
[58]Rob Cuthbert for Ringefeild then about for the rent [16]67	030	00	0
Clifton mortgage the other halfe qr about	015	00	0

Whi*tsun* [16]68

+Bampton old rent	06	04	5
+Clifton then	09	08	10
+Cleyburne qr paid Geo July [16]68 in part 2:16:3ob		*(blank)*	
+Helton then	05	08	9
+Knipe then	03	09	6ob
+Lowther with 3s4d allowed the Bayliff	09	11	3
+Mureys rent finable	00	05	0
+Newton with the Smithie	10	13	0
+Plumpton abateinge 1 13 4	69	06	5
+Rosgill allowed the Bayliff 2 Carages beside	07	06	3
+Sledall allowed the Bayliff 2 Carages[59] besides Warrinds allowed 3s6d	03	18	6
+Strickland Slegill and Thrimby	07	10	2
+Threlkeld then	15	05	0

Demesnes then

+Appleby Burgage	00	02	0
+Bampton free rent then	00	14	4
+Helton boone plowinge at 2s6d a plough (*interlined*: out of which) ⟨and⟩ given the Bayliff his	03	02	6

---

57. All this a later, contemporary insertion.
58. These two entries later insertions.
59. Rest of entry a later note.

paid Will At 15.0.0. and to Geo Mo 5-15.5 in sesse 1:4:7 in full   50r *cont.*

vide the accompt and arrears
paid W At Aprill [16]68 in part £20; Soe arrears then £10 and £5 of the
former arrear paid after 9br [16]68 to my wife part of £45
paid Will Atk: £50

(*blank*)
paid per Chr Teas*dale* to Will At May [16]68 23:10:5 (*interlined*: beeinge)
for my part for [16]67 as I take it

paid Geo Mo 6. 4:5
paid 9.6.4. and 2s6d allowed

paid Geo 5. 8: 9 ⟨ob⟩
paid Geo 3. 9. 6 ob
paid Geo Mo 9:4:9 ob and 3s2d ob abated for Chapelhowes, and 3s4d
the Bayliff.
paid W At Whis [16]63 quod vide
paid W At 10: 13: 0
paid W At Cand [16]68—part 57:07:6, accompted for July [16]69
paid Geo Mo: 7.6.3

paid ⟨Geo⟩ Will Atk 3.18.6
paid Geo Mo: 7.10.2
paid Geo 15.5.0

paid (*erasure*) W At: Cand [16]68
paid my wife 10br [16]68 part of £3

paid mee with 7 bones allowed

49v *cont.*	+Heltondale Millne	05	00	0
	+Horpletthow and Tarnebergh to Jo Knott	11	10	0
	+More for Sheepe £5 Heltondale tyth 2:15:0 Punder- hackes in my owne hand	07	15	0
	+Hay Closes and heades to the Keper beside his allowance	08	10	0
	+Lowther Millne lett for 36 bushels of Corne of which 4 Skillin			
	+Marton with all Jo Pearsons Collection save what is abated of late and in my owne hand was vide ante[60]	760	02	10

50v

Whi*tsun* [16]68

+Meaburn (*erasure*) was about then £90 some what I have in my owne hands	90	00	0
+Millby then	115	11	8
+Newton Millne then but deare	007	00	0
+Shapp tyth the 6 payment of 7 years	53	10	0
+Threlkeld kilne used to be	02	10	0
+Sledall millne forgott before	02	15	0
+Warshall then from Sir Will Midleton	100	00	0
+Smithie at Lowther to Salkeld and Sledie	00	10	0
+Slegill mortgage as good as land to Will Farrer for £100	03	00	0
+Mr Sandford mortgage likewise of Powdon (*interlined:* for £200) paid out of Askham	06	00	0
+Cleyburne in my owne hand [61]what I can make of it			
+Spitle ⟨for⟩ my Grandchild the first rent after ⟨his dea⟩ my sons death	31	00	0
+Hacktropp lett to Sands and Hudson my owne though I paid my Son before he died 800 upon it	60	00	0
+⟨Casterton it seems is at Ladie day and qr about with free rents qr	20	00	0⟩
+(*erasure*) Kirkeby Lonsdale and Cartmell and tyth etc new mortgag next Midsom	100	00	0

---

60. *vide ante* a later insertion.
61. Rest of line a later insertion.

paid Will Atk £5   50r *cont.*

Secured and accmpted for

paid me 8.10.0 July [16]68 and given back 5s

vide ye perticuler rentall

51r

vide Ions accompt of arrears
vide Milby accompt what arrer
arrear of Newton Mill upon accompt with this rent £14.13.6 vide ante this 7
and the former rent paid Will At £14 15s 6
paid Will Atk part of the £56 paid July [16]68 for which I gave an
acquitance allowed 40s for 2 last years as an addition for Mr Howards tyth,
and to pay 20s after.
paid Geo Mo for it 1 05. 0 and 8s for a hare cloath
paid W A for this and Mart before 5. 10. 0.
vide Marton accompt
paid and allowed per Geo Mo['s] boke 10s
paid Geo Mo. June [16]68: £3: 0: 0

paid Geo Mo June [16]68 in part £5 and allowed her £1 in full and that
together with £10 paid by mee and £9 allowed in the use of £200 maketh
upp the £25 wee should have paid to Starr soe that we owe noethinge for that
£25   .

paid W A in part Aug [16]68 £13 paid more in part 8r [16]68 per Colison £17.
The rest allowed in sesse per note

paid Geo Mo July [16]68 £60 (*erasure*) but given backe again £2

⟨paid W Alk 17br April [16]68 in part £15⟩ dew at Laide Day before and
then paid

(*blank*)

Leases then

+Mr Fulthropp the 13 payment of 7 years ended[62]	⟨90	00	0⟩
+Paper Mill a longe lease cleare rent	02	00	0
⟨+Mr Humprey the 14th of 7 years ½⟩ the last payment[63]		00	0
+Mr Blackeburne the 12 of 7 and ½	50	00	0
+Rumley now Brawham The 13th of 7 and ½	05	00	0
+Mr Denton the 5th of 7 and ½	50	00	0
+Mr Skelton the ⟨9th⟩ (*interlined*: 10th) of 7 and ½	50	00	0
+Mr Birckbeck the 7 of 7 and ½	50	00	0
+Todd per Fr Lowther the 5th of 7 and ½	05	00	0
⟨+Mr Preston for Cartmell and Kirby [Lonsdale] for which vide the particuler rentall⟩ now made upon a new release[64]	200	00	0

Casterlen demesne tyth qr if not dew now   (*blank*)

[16]68

Midsomer Asby then with stocke	22	10	0
+Helton tyth to Judson	35	00	0
+Thornthwaite tyth of the demayne upon a rent charge	07	00	0

                              Leases then

+Mr Browham the 6th of 7 years at at[65] one tyme	20	00	0
+Carterlen tyth of the demesne per Mr Richmond at will	04	00	0
Lamas +Hackthropp old rent	03	16	6
+Helton Then	07	09	3
+Melkinthropp	01	00	10
+Thwaites at St James tyde[66] as formerly viz towne rent 9.15 3 more services monie 1.18:5 forest meale 0:11:1 in all 12. 4. 9	12	04	3

                              Demesnes

+Suborwens then	23	05	0
+Newton tyth (*interlined*: half now) for the last years profitt to Waterson et al	20	05	0

---

62. *ended* a later addition.
63. *The last payment* a later note.
64. An annotation.
65. *Sic.*
66. Rest of entry a later date.

51r *cont.*

ended vide the accompt
paid per Cos*en* Tea*s*dell for part of the £4 £2
This £50 was paid befo*r*ehand and more paid viz at July [16]68 £48:12 0
beforehand for Mart next [16]68 in full of all payment
paid pro ut per account quod vide and £52 arrear at Mart [16]68
new secured at Whiss [16]69 per Mr Browhams
new secured
This 50 is included in the new securities for 7 years and $\frac{1}{2}$ beginge at
St. Andrew day [16]68
vide Eg: accompt June [16]69 paid all but about 12s use arrer
paid and secured This £5

vide the particuler arrer towards the end of the booke; and altered into
£100 per annum

paid 8r [16]68 to W At £30 vide the arrear then paid Geo Mo all former
Jan [16]68 19.18.0.
secured per tenement dew Cand [16]69
paid Geo Mo June [16]68 £7

paid W A 20: 4 0
This £4 assigned to Mr Pearson[67] for part of his stipend
paid Geo Mo then 3. 16. 3   qr
paid W At 7. 9. 3.
paid Will Atk February [16]68 1. 0. 9.

paid Geo Mo Aug [16]68 12: 04. 0

vide the accompt what arrer at Mart [16]68 viz £50:10.0

paid per Waterson to W At £4 per Pearson £6 per Nicholson £6 per Watson
2.10.0 paid more per Row Nick. more £5. 0. 0. and only 10s arrer per
Waterson[68]

---

67. Curate of Newton Reigny, Nightingale, *Ejected*, pp. 451–453.
68. Discrepancy here between rent due and monies paid.

50v *cont.*   + Tho Duffield for £60 part of Jo Sandersons tenement
to pay at Lam [16]68 and Candlemas after for 7 years

this first payment	05	10	0
+ Lenard Smith the 7 of 7 and ½	05	00	0
+ Nickelson and Bewsher the 12th of 7 years	02	00	0
+ Jo Wilkinson of the Dale the 11th[69] of 7 years and ½	03	00	0
+ Jo Wilk above the Hall the like	03	00	0

+ Catterlen tyth begineth this year should be beside £4

for the demesne [70]£23 per annum not yet lett	20	00	0

+ ⟨Chr Ritson of Holme qr if now dew for Hugh Chapel-
row £1⟩ at Mich after

⟨ + Tho Duffeild to pay £60 for Sanderson £11 per
annum at now and Cand after for 7 years, this first

payment	05	10	0⟩

Mich*aelmas*

+ Egleston Abey cleare rent	98	11	3
+ Arkendale tyth with oare cleare rent cleare	32	00	0
+ Sledall demesne Then	36	00	0
+ Mrs Dudley remitted for the use of the £100	05	00	0
⟨Reaslack to Wennington as formerly	19	00	0⟩

Leases

+ Thorpe my wives about	300	00	0
+ Mr Denton the 6th of 7 years	30	00	0
+ Sir Edw Musgrave the 5th[71] of 7 years	50	00	0

+ Ritson and Holme ⟨for Jo of the Dale⟩ (*interlined*: for
Hugh Chapelhow) in part his dett to pay 40s per
annum at Mich [16]68 and Lady Day [16]69 for

7 years this the first	01	00	0

+ More Chr Ritson of the Towne Heade for John of
Dale in part of his dett to pay at Mich [16]68 and Lady

[16]69 for 7 years at £3 per annum	01	10[72]	0

⟨ + Christ Ritson for that of Jo⟩ (*ends*)

---

69. Altered from 10.
70. Rest of entry a subsequent note. Further annotated in same ink as the figure
column: *first at Lamas next.*
71. Much altered.
72. Altered from 0s.

paid Will At: 8r [16]68 5:10.0 The first payment
paid and accompted per Deane March [16]72
paid mee lam [16]68 part of £4 for this and the rent before £2
Lett this yeare to Chr Ritson for 7 years at Mich [16]68 and Lady Day [16]69
to pay £3 per annum
new secured in the £54 mortgage at Cand [16]69 quod vide

let to Parker to pay £20 per annum for 9 years the first payment at
Lam [16]69 but to abate £1 the first yeare if he say he loose by it

putt before

paid Geo Mo: in part of arrears of Birkebecke £7. 0. 0. vide the note of
arrears at Mich [16]69[73]
this £30 paid Rob Simpson about Mich [16]69 soe use of it arrears for one
yeare
paid to Will Midleton (*interlined*: to my wife) 1º Jan [16]68 £35 in sesse
18s. given backe 2s in full
(*blank*)
Set downe as at Mart

vide Thorpe arrears
paid my wife 9br [16]68 45 for this and £15 arrer before in full untill now
paid Will Ak 8r [16]68 £50

paid mee Mich [16]68 £1:0:0

paid mee Mich [16]68 1.10.0

---

73. Interlined: see above, Whit leases.

51v–74r   *Rentals of all Sir J.L.(2)'s estates for the years beginning Martinmas 1668–1673[74], (arranged as f3 (p. 87) above.*

     [ff58v–67v rental pages in an unknown hand.]

74v–78r   *Rental of all Sir J.L.(2)'s estates for the year beginning Martinmas 1674, (arranged as f3 (p. 87) above). [Hand of Sir J.L.(2).]*

74v Mart*inmas* [16]74

+ Bampton old rent	06	04	5
+ Clifton out of which allowed 2s 6d for collectinge	09	08	10
+ Cleyburne qr what paid for services	02	16	4
+ Helton then noe allowance	05	08	9
+ Knipe then	03	09	6
+ Lowther allowed 3s 4d	09	11	3
+ Newton with the Smithie	10	13	0
+ Plumpton out of which allowed 1:13:4	69	14	5
+ Rosgill besides 2 carages allowed	07	06	9
+ Sledall (*interlined*: beside) 2 Carages allowed	03	18	6
+ Slegill Strickland and Thrimby	07	06	11
+ Threlkeld then [75]sans allowance	15	05	0
+ Thwaites with other smale rents	14	11	9
[76]More hall Thwaits towne tearme		13	4
+ Yeanewith old rent	06	16	3

[Change of hand, unknown hand]

+ Appleby Burgage	02	02	0[77]
Bampton demesne with Bamestead and Sedamanhaw	⟨40	08	4⟩[78]
	50	00	0
More schoole rent of Tyth 15s and Beckefoote £1-5s 0d in all	02	00	0
Free rent there halfe yeare	00	15	7
John Knott for Greenriggs	24		
more he for the shepe rent then	05	00	0
+ Beareslacke and Powleyes Tennement to Powley	14	08	2
Beareslack and Thrimby closes to Guy Copperthwaite	10	01	0

---

74. The 1672 rental concludes, in the same format, with a rental: *A perticuler of Mr Standfords halfe years rent the first halfe year of 4 years viz at Lam and Cand 1673.*

75. Rest of line a contemporary addition.

76. This whole line inserted after the Yeanewith entry was written.

77. *Sic*: an error for 2s 0d.

78. These three figures struck out and replaced by £50-00-0.

paid Geo Mo 6.4.5.
paid Geo Mo 9r [16]74 qr in part 08:18:4 the rest abated for which vide
Mart [16]73
paid Geo Mo 2:16:4
paid Geo Mo 5:8:9
paid Geo M 3:9:6 ob
paid Geo Mo: –9–4–2 the rest allowed quod vide Mart [16]73
paid Ge Mo 10:13:0
paid in part to Geo Mo. £40: paid more to him 26.4.11 and arrear for
Jo Sanderson 1:16:2
paid Geo Mo 7.6.3. and 6d free rent arrears due at Xmas
paid W At 3.18.6
paid Geo Mo 7.06.11
new secured per Irton[79]
paid Geo Mo £13 and the rest allowed pro ut as at Mart [16]73 and the 13s 4d
(*blank*)

paid Geo Mo in part 5:8:4 paid him more in part at Mart [16]74 1.5.0. arrers
6s 6d

[*same hand*]
paid Will Atk Lam [16]75

} All lett now to pay £50

(*blank*)
(*blank*)
paid Geo Mo 14.8.2
paid Geo Mo in part of former arrears quod vide £10 paid him more June
[16]75 in part £10 (*erasure*) now with Cand rent the arrca₁ 31:14:0

---

79. Perhaps Mr. Christopher Irton of Threlkeld, see p. 53.

74v *cont.* +Burtreebanck to John Wilkinson of Pinfould	14	00	0
+Hallgarth to George Hayton	08	10	0
+Haycloses to the Keeper	08	10	0
+Heltondale prescripcion money	01	00	0
+Heltondale Mill to Roberton	05	00	0
+Helton boone sheareing at pleasure	02	00	0
+Cleyburne demesne to Lowther with 120 Sheepe and £20 lent money	23	00	0
+Wiberge for another parte of the demesne with +60 hoges and Cows and £10 lent +money and an outshot of hay to be lett	} 06	10	0
Mill Inges lett next yeare to Wibergh 2	2	00	0[80]
+More they 2 for Birckeraiyne and Milne Inge in our owne hand	05	00	0
+More Cleyburne Milne to Dalton	02	10	0
+Lowther Milne per Mayson	05	10	0[81]
Marton in all with former rentall collected per NP	872	05	0
Meaburne in all now and Cand about	120	00	0
Millby besides free rents deducted	115	11	8
+Newton Milne	007	00	0
Moores Grasses to Richard Wilkinson 13 @ 1s 6d	001	00	0
+Skelton and Cotdickes halfe rent and halfe rent [*sic*] lett to Mayson	012	10	0
+Shapps tythe now besides deductions	050	08	2
+Sledale demesne with 4s the new close	040	00	0
+Warners Tenementt [*sic*] at Sledale to Noble	005	12	6
+Sledale Milne to Wilkinson	002	15	0
Spittle to Willson qr if not now at	028	00	0
Suborwens to Aray	023	05	0

---

80. This line a subsequent insertion.
81. Altered from £4-00-0.

75r *cont.*

paid Geo Mo 14. 0. 0.
paid Geo Mo 8.10. 0.
paid Geo Mo 8.10. 0.
paid Geo Mo 1. 0. 0.
paid Geo Mo 5. 0. 0.
paid for Whis and this Mart [16]74 to Geo: April [16]74 pro ut £5 in full

paid Geo Mo 23. 00. 0.

paid per Wib: to Geo. Mo: 9r [16]74—6.10.0.

paid Geo Mo March [16]74 £5.0.0.
paid Geo Mo October [16]74 qr how this is paid
paid Geo Mo 1st qr rent 2.10.0 paid March [16]74 more 2 qr £2.10.0

paid W At Aug: [16]75 £7. 0. 0. and the rest new secured part of £14
arrear pro ut paid at Mart [16]73 quo vide 0:10:0, soe arrear now 1:10:0
whereof paid Geo.Mo: April [16]75 in part (*interlined*: £1) paid him more
June [16]75 per Rob Lowther[82] qr more soe qr £1

paid Geo Mo 9br [16]74 12.10.0
paid Geo Mo in part £40: paid more to him March [16]74 in full £10.8.2.
paid Geo in part Feb [16]74 £20 paid more to him
    24.14.6 the rest paid out in sesse
paid Geo Mo at Whis after
paid Geo Mo the 4th of May [16]75 in part of this and Whis rent before £30
paid Geo Mo June [16]75 in monie 12:5 :0 and in 2 oxen £11 for this rent
⟨but qr for 8.5.0 arrers at Mart [16]73 soe qr⟩

---

82. Not a member of Sir J.L.(2)'s family, see *The Registers of Lowther* ed. J. F.
    Haswell (CW.PRS 1933) pp. 41–6, 189.

74v *cont.*	+Sands for Hackthorpe demesne	060	00	0
	Casterton to my Grandson	020	10	0
	free rent there	002	05	0
	+Reslacke with stock	019	00	0
	+Thrimby Grange	015	00	0
	+Thrimby free rent	000	03	4[83]
	+Thwates Milne qr what it is about	008	10[84]	0
	Wensladale was about now lessened	580	00	0
	+⟨Whale tennementt to John Wilkinson allowed in wages	004	00	0⟩[85]
	+Townend Tennementt Mortgaged	019	00	0
	+Thorneberge and Herpletthowe to Robt Wilkinson	011	10	0
	+Watey to ⟨Will: Smyth⟩ Gibson	002	10	0
	Yeanewth demesne to Cous. Teasdell	062	00	0
	+More for the Bancks to Mr Bird	002	00	0
	+More the Tenter acre to Meason	000	10	0
	More Wood demesne halfe rent	050	00	0
75v	Mart*inmas* [16]74			
	More Poke Mills halfe rent	011	00	0
	Mr Rookesby the first 4 yeares upon Mortgage	027	00	0

Leases then

Paper Milne a long lease	002	00	0
Mr Skelton the 13th payment of 7 and ½	050	00	0
+Mr Fothergill the first payment	020	00	0
+Sir Richard Sandford at Martinmas (*erasure*) The first payment at £200 per annum	100	00	0[86]
Mr Simpson the 12 payment of 11 and ½	042	10	0
+Sonne Wandesford [secured by][87] lease the 12 of 7 and ½	⟨065	00	0⟩
+More he upon bond the 7th of 7 yeares	⟨050	00	0⟩

---

83. Figures much altered.
84. Figures altered.
85. Whole entry struck out.
86. Altered from £200.
87. Expanded contraction.

paid to us (*interlined*: Geo) £20 and to Geo Mo: £40 in full   75r *cont.*
paid Will At 1 May [16]75 iń part £15.0.0.

paid Geo Mo in part, Jan [16]74 £10.8.0. paid W A Lam [16]75 £8 and
sesse 12s in all 19
paid Geo Mo 9br [16]74 ⟨£14.0.6⟩ 14.16.6. the rest in sesses
paid Geo Mo 3s 4d.
paid Geo Mo Jan 8.10.0—lett to Andrew Trawton for this year £10

sowld unto Bird.
paid Geo Mo 19.00.0
paid Geo Mo 9br [16]74 11.10.0
paid Geo Mo 2.10.0.

allowed per Mr Bird £2. 0. 0.
paid mee May [16]75—0.10.0 per the woman
(*blank*)

76r

(*blank*)
(*blank*)

(*blank*)
(*blank*)
paid Geo Mo: 9br [16]74—20: 00. 0

paid Robt Simpson in parcells 100: 00 [0]
(*blank*)

Son Wand[88]: new secured to pay Whis and Mart [16]75—£200 Whis and
Mart [16]76—£200
more Whis [1677] £100 and Mart [16]77 £70 in full in all £570

---

88. Wandesford.

	£–	s–	d
75v *cont.* Catterlen tyth to Mawson qr this yeare when due	000	00	0
+ Sonn Trotter the 8 halfe payment of 7 yeares	054	00	0
+ Allam[89] lease at Xmas about 12 yeares in being	108	06	0
+ Margaret Briham.to pay at Mart and Whis £4 16-0d	002	08	0

Cand*lemas* [16]74

	£–	s–	d
+ Hackthorpe old rent qr	003	19	9
+ Helton then	007	09	3
+ Mellkinthorpe now with abatement only	000	18	0

Demesnes then

	£–	s–	d
Asby with stock then	022	00	0
Bampton demesnes and tyth et al	050	00	0
+ Ritson for Lowbottome part of Atkinson tenementt	002	10	0
+ Coniewarren to Stephenson this yeare	001	10	0
Howcale and Wibergh tennementt besides 20s	010	00	0
Melkinthorpe tennementt to Pearson et al	014	00	0
+ Feild land in Hackthorpe feild to Tho Hudson	000	10	0
+ Rosgill carages besides 2 of Cowpers	001	13	0
+ Sledall Cariages besides 2 of Nobles	000	19	6
Guy Coperthwaite for Beareslacke	010	01	0
+ Buckholme and Highcloses a Mortgage	018	00	0
+ Slacke to Hugh Newton	000	16	0
+ Rosgill tyth mortgaged as good as Inheritance	012	04	0
+ Mr Sandfords Mortgage now and at Lam	030	00	0
Capt. Hanby for Gilmanby and Colerye	022	10	0
+ Turnerers tennementt at Yeanwith	007	00	0

---

89. i.e. Alum mines in Yorkshire.

(*blank*)
accompted for 7br [16]75   76r *cont.*
accompted for 7br [16]75
paid Geo Mo ⟨in part⟩ February [16]74 £2 and sesse and rent ⟨£8⟩ and
paid mee Whis [16]75 for that rent 2.6.0 and the rest allowed

paid Geo Mo qr 3.17:11
paid Geo 7:09 6
paid W A (*erasure*) July⁹⁰ 0:18:0

(*blank*)
(*blank*)
paid Geo Mo 2.10.0.
paid Geo Mo. 1.10.0
(*blank*)
(*blank*)
paid Geo Mo May [16]75 0:10.0
paid Geo Mo 1.13.0.
paid Geo M 19s 6
arrer. Now per account pro ut agreed on by him 31: 14 [0]
paid Geo Mo February [16]74 £15 the rest abated for Buckholme
paid Geo Mo then 16ˢ
paid Geo Mo May [16]75 12.4.0.
paid Geo Mo pro ut by particuler February [16]74—£30

Jo Low to receive it

---

90. *July* written below the erasure.

75v *cont.*	+Woodhouse at Yeanewith to Willson at this time	050 00 0	
	Kerkby Lonsdale rent vide the particular rent ⟨all £212:4s:6d.⟩		
	+Thrimby Carriages at 2s a peece by agreement yearely	001 02 0	

Leases and Mortgages

Clifton Mortgage determinable qr how long to Warkeman and Robinson	023 10 0	
Tho Duffeild the 14 and last paymentt of 7 yeares	005 10 0	
The three Browhams in part of Rumley debt the 7 of 7 yeares vide	005 00 0	
+Brihams widd*ow* and Mr Burton for Walkers tennementt and to allow rent and sess out of it	(*blank*)	
Teasdell for Mabell his wife to pay yearely qr and see the account	(*blank*)	
Francis Lowther the 4th halfe yeare of 7 yeares	025 00 0	
+Cous: Rich: Lampeley the (*erasure*) ist halfe years of 7 £84-6s[od]	020 00 0	

Ladie Day [16]75

Egglestone Abbey then	098	04	7
+Highfeild and sheepe to Powley	014	08	2
+Lowther drie moulter about 8 bushells	002	00	0
+Newton drie moulter	007	19	0
+Thrimby Grange then to Webster et al	015	00	0
+Casterton to Henry Johnson	020	10	0
Francis Lowther by his tennants Mounsey of Staynton[91] et al [secured by][92] Mortgage for £250 this yeare	015	00	0
Clifton Mortgage determinable	023	10	0

---

91. *N* interlined.
92. Expanded contraction.

Jo Low received

paid Will At: [16]74 £1 in part and paid mee 2s more per Guy Coper.
for Cleasby.

paid Geo Mo per Wark: about February [16]74 first £8 more after by him £5
and paid Will At more £10 and allowed my corne pro ut per account 11.0.0.
and arrear at Ladie Day after per account £28.0.0. vide the arrear at
Ladie Day [16]75 postea per Warkman then £28
(blank)

(blank)

(blank)

aid W At March [16]74 £20:00.0

(blank)
(blank)
ide Geo Mo account for the corne
aid my Grandson
aid Geo Mo May [16]75 14.19.8 in full
his turned arrear to J L

aid Geo Mo Aprill [16]75 in part £14
aid per Geo Set downe upon Ladie Day [16]74 quod (*erasure*) vide in full
f this rent per Robinson; and Warkeman arrer now at this tyme upon
ccount quod vide £28.0.0.

75v *cont.*	+ Newton tyth now and at Lam as good as Inheritance	020	10	0
	+ Mr Denton the 11 halfe yeare of 7	045	00	0
	Ritson and Holme for Hugh Chapelhowes	001	00	0
	+ Ritson of Townehead for John of Dales	001	10	0
	+ Mr Browham the 10 halfe yeares of 7	012	10	0
	My wives Joynture about	300	00	0
	+ Catterlen tyth the 1st payment of 3 years due at Lady			
	Day and Lam to one Carleton et al per lease	009	10	0
76v	Whi*ts*un [16]75	03	18	6

[*Change of hand; hand of Sir J.L.(2)*]

+ Bampton old rent	06	04	5
+ Clifton then	09	08	10
+ Cleyburne then	02	16	4
+ Helton then	05	08	9
+ Knipe then	03	09	6
+ Lowther to allow out of it 3s4d vide Mart [16]73			
and [16]74	09	04	2
Mures rent finable	00	05	0
Newton then	10	13	0
+ Rosgill and 2 carages allowed	07	06	3
Sledall 2 allowed	03	18	6
+ Strickland Slegill and Thrimby then	07	06	11⁹³ob
+ Threlkeld then	15	15	0
Yeanewith then	06	14	9

Demesnes then

+ Appleby burgage	00	02	0
Helton plowinge	03	02	6
+ Helton Millne	05	00	0
+ Hackthropp demesne then	60	00	0

93. 11d altered from 3d.

dew to J L   76r *cont.*
paid W At at twice Aprill [16]75 £45:0:0
(*blank*)
paid Geo Mo March [16]74 ⟨in part⟩ 1.10.0.
paid Geo Mo July [16]75 12-10-0
(*blank*)

This dew to J.L.

                                                               77r

[*same hand, no change*]
paid Geo M £6 - 4. 6
paid Geo Mo 8.18.4 and 2s6d for collectinge
paid Geo Mo June [16]75 2.16.4
paid Geo Mo June [16]75 5.8.9
paid Geo M then 3.9.6 ob

paid Geo Mo 9.4.2
(*blank*)
(*blank*)
paid Geo Mo 7.6.3
(*blank*)
paid Geo Mo 7.6.11 ob
paid per Lamaman to Geo Mo 15.05.0
paid Geo Mo in part 5.11.9

paid Will At Lam [16]75 for these 2 last years 8s
⟨*blank*⟩
paid Will At 5.0.0 June [16]75
paid Geo Mo June [16]75 20.00.0 more paid Hayton to returne as paid
to George £40 in full

76r *cont.*	Greenerriggs to Jo Knot	24 00	0
	More he for the sheepe rent then	05 00	0
	+Lowther Mill then to pay a qr beforehand	05[94]00	0
	+Hay closes the Keper	08 10	0
	Marton all in that collection about quod vide	875 19	7[95]
	Meaburne then about vide the rentall	90 00	0
	+Milby beside out rents quod vide about	116 00	0
	+Cleyburne to Lowther omitted in its dew place	023[96]00	0
	+More to Wiberghe Lowther Birkerayne[97] at Mart next		
	a halfe years rent	⟨05 00	0⟩
	+More to Wibergh 6:10:0 and Millrig in all	07 10	0
	+More the Mill to Dalton	02 10	0
	⟨Newton⟩Shapp tyth to Rich Smith	50 08	2
	+Skelanes and Lowther Croft	12 10	0
	+Sledall Millne then	02 15	0
	Threlkeld Kilne used to be about	02 00	0
	Mr Rookesley mortgage	27 00	0
	Mr Duckett Mortgage then	36 00	0

Leases

Paper Mill a longe lease	02 00	0
Mr Skelton the 14 of 7 years and ½	50 00	0
Mr Simpson the 14th of 7½	42 10	0[98]
Son Wandesford upon a new lease to pay £200 per annum at Whis and Mart [16]75 ⟨to begin⟩ [16]76 and £100 at Whis [16]77 and £70 at Mart [16]77	100 00	0
Sir Richard Sandford the 2nd payment of 7 years	100 00	0
+Son Trotter the 9 of 7 years	054 00	0

---

94. This figure has been altered.
95. 7d altered from 6d.
96. This figure has been written over a misplaced entry of £116.
97. Rest of entry an annotation.
98. Figures altered.

(*blank*)
(*blank*)
paid Geo Mo Aug: [16]75 in full of Whis rent and Lam rent beforehand
beeinge the 4 qr by rent beforhad
paid Geo Mo June [16]75 8:10:0

paid all but sume ⟨arr⟩ smale arrear quod vide and Sir Will Tanckerd £15
use monie arrears
paid Geo Mo June [16]75 £23

putt at Mart after
paid mee June [16]75 6:10:0 and 4s given backe for an arrer, and to abate
for the Cand next rent quod vide
paid to Mawnan
paid W At July [16]75 in part £40:00.0
paid Geo Mo May [16]75 12.10.0
paid Geo Mo June [16]75 for this and Whis rent before 5.7.6 and 2s6d given
[back].
(*blank*)
(*blank*)
paid Will At June [16]75 in part £22

(*blank*)
(*blank*)
(*blank*)

(*blank*)
(*blank*)
accompted for 7br [16]75 when paid above

76v *cont.*

Allam rent a lease in beeinge about 10 years[99] at			
Midsomer	108	06	8
+Margaret Bryham for Walker tenement	02	08	0
+Jo Knot qr for Westgarths qr	03	17	4

Midsum*mer* [16]75

Asby with stocke	22	00	0
+Helton tyth with Heltondale	40	00	0
Thornetwaite rent charge	07	00	0
+Allam rent at Skelton should be as good as inheritance			
about 12 years in this lease	108	06	8

Lam*mas* [16]75 +Hackthropp old rent	03	16	6

+Helton old rent	07	09	3
Melkinthropp beside what sowld	00	18	0
+Thwaites at St James tyde	12	04	3

Demesnes then

Bowes with the toll and Collery	22	10	0
Mr Sandfords mortgage as good as land	30	00	0
+More upon Powduns then for the whole years rent for			
Mrs Winches life	07	04	0

77v

Lam*mas* [16]75 Rutford tyth at Lamas uncertaine but			
should be about	07	10	0

Leases then

Francis Lowther the 5½ years payment of 7 years	25	00	0
+Cous Rich Lamplugh the 4 halfe years of 7 years	20	00	0

Mich*ael*mas [16]75 Egleston Abey	98	11	3
Arkendale tyth clear rent the whole years rent	32	00	0
My wives joynture about	300	00	0
Hayclose during the lease in beeinge	045	00	0
[1]And after as it can be lett their beeinge £14 per annum			
paid out of it			
Will Ritson for Hugh Chapelhowes tennement qr			
how longe	01	00	0
Christ Ritsons for Jo of Dale upon account which			
payes not the use of the monie arrear		*(blank)*	

---

99. *At Midsomer* an annotation.
1. This sentence an annotation.

putt after at Midsum
paid mee 2.6.0. the rest allowed
paid mee Aug [16]75 3.17.6

paid Geo Mo July [16]75 in part of former arrears 15:10:0
paid Geo Mo 7br [16]75 40:00:0
(*blank*)

accompted for when paid

paid Geo Mo 3:16:5
paid W At 7.9.3
(*blank*)
paid with deductions to W A as at Lam [16]74 12:4 8

paid per Mr Will Sand in part 25: and £5 arrear per Mr W. mich.

paid my wife Lam [16]75 (*erasure*) for this £7: 0: 0

(*blank*)   78r

(*blank*)

paid W At Lam [16]75 £20: 0: 0

                         (*all blank*)

78v–127r   (*Blank.*)

127v–129r   *Rental of Maulds Meaburne, from Whitsuntide 1672 to Lamas 1675, (arranged as rentals for the whole estate, see p. 87 above).*

129v–134r   (*Blank.*)

134v–137r   *Rental of Lands at Kirkby Lonsdale and Cartmel which Lowther entered at Mid-summer 1667, until Lady Day 1675, (arranged as rentals for the whole estate, see p. 87 above).*

137v–144r   (*Blank.*)

144v–146v [*Unknown hand*] A Perfect Rentall of the Tythes of Wool Lambes hay and other rents due out of the Rectory of Shappe for the yeare 1664.
List of names of 194 tenants, grouped under townships,[2] with the value of their tithe rent under the headings of wool, lambs, hay and other rents. Concludes with a breakdown of the rents under the feast days when due. Total rents £91-17-0½d.

147r [*Hand of Sir J.L.(2)*] The extract of the years profitt of Shappe Rectory for 1664 when I had it in my owne hand is as valued upon the former particulers. *Total £122-13-2d.*

147v–148r   (*Blank.*)

148v [*Unknown hand*] *Lists of rents paid out of Sir J.L.(2)'s estates, 1661.*

149r [*Hand of Sir J.L.(2)*] *List of out payments from lands purchased, and leases taken, 1665–1667.*

149v [*Unknown hand*] *List of rents due Whit. 1661 from Marton, Thornaby, Nunthorpe, Preston* (Co. Durham) *and Ayton; names of tenants with amount due, including rent charges, at Whit. 1661 (some due Mart.1661). Residence of tenants not always given.*
Totals: Marton, Thornaby and Preston: £459-11-8[3]; Nunthorpe £70-8-4; Ayton: £67-9-6; with additional purchases, totalling £83-10-0, [noted in hand of Sir J.L.(2)].

150r [*Hand of Sir J.L.(2)*] Observations upon the rentall on the other side (f149v).
Notes about the estates of the individual tenants, calculation that in 1661 £460-1-6d would be left to Ralph Lowther.[4]

150v   (*Blank.*)

151r [*Unknown hand*] *Rental of Thorpe as paid at Michaelmas 1665.*
List of names of 29 tenants, some notes of their estates, and rents due. Total [half year] £392-1-2d.[5] With a note of a rent charge of £90 per annum; and £10 per annum payable to the vicar.

---

2. See p. 20 for the names.
3. This figure has been updated; *recte* £460-1-0d.
4. P.V.16.
5. Thorpe in Surrey. *Recte* £392-1-10d.

Hand of Sir J.L.(2)] A Rentall of Skelton [Yorkshire] as sent by my son   151v
Trotter against Whit [16]66.[6]
List of names of 29 tenants with rent due; total, free of sesses, £120-3-0d.

Unknown hand] A Perticular of Cleburne as valewed September 1667.[7]
*List of each piece of land comprising the demesne of Clibburn, under the
headings of meadow and arable; gives name of each property, acreage and
rent due, with some names of tenants. Concludes with a summary, [in the hand
of Sir J.L.(2)]: acreage of demesne 123; valued at £55-11-4d [per annum],
let for £60; plus customary rents £5-10-0d. and mill rent £5, total £12 [sic].
Overall total £72.*

Hand of Sir J.L.(2)] Rental of Kirkby Lonsdale as given to Sir J.L.(2) in   152r
September 1667[8]. *List of demesne properties, with names of 6 tenants and
rents due, total £127; and total of customary rents at Preston Richard, £20,
and Kirkby Lonsdale, £34. Total £181.*
*Rental of leasehold lands and houses at Church Town, Cartmel [Furness],
made 20 September 1667 by Jo. Marshall, Mr. Preston's steward.*
*List of names of 9 tenants, with some details of their estates, and rents
due, total £206-5-0d.*

Unknown hand] Rental of Wensleydale, 1660, including the Lunds.[9]   152v–153r
*Rental arranged in alphabetical order of 94 tenants' names, with rent due,
total £556.13.11. Concludes [in the hand of Sir J.L.(2)] with notes of some
additional rents due, Lunds £33-0-7, others £8-18-4.*

Notes on the preceeding rental of Wensleydale, dated 1661.   153v

(Blank.)   154r

[Half year's] rental of Egleston Abbey, for Lady Day 1657; gives names of   154v
12 tenants with rent due, total £97-7-1d.
Change of hand; new hand perhaps Sir J.L.(2)] Rental of Egleston for 21 years
from Lady Day 1662, 7 tenants total, half year, £97-12-1d. *With notes of
outpayments; and changes in the rental up to 1671.*

Hand of Sir J.L.(2)] A rentall of lands and inheritances intended to be left   155r–155v
to the heires of my house at Lowther 7th 8br 1664.
*List of Cumbrian manors with annual revenues grouped under headings:
customary rents, services, demesne rents (some individual properties named);
with annual values for the Yorkshire and Co. Durham properties.*

In personall estate the 10th of 8br 1664 as estimated vide foll 27th before[10]   156r

---

6. See p. 177 for purchase.
7. See p. 181 for purchase.
8. See p. 179 for mortgage. This rental is an altered copy of one in A1/9. The
   A1/9 entry includes some receipts, for which also see p. 146.
9. See p. 40.
10. See p. 110, above.

		£	s	d
156r *cont.*	Rumley lease worth as valued in present monie	050	00	0
	Alexander and Edmond Metcalfe	040	00	0
	Mr Challenar	100	00	0
	Mr Fullthrapp	350	00	0
	Sir Will Carleton about	500	00	0
	Mr Humphrey per Dobson of Barwis	350	00	0
	John Metcalfe	100	00	0
	Cuthbert Win	050	00	0
	Mr Blackburne upon Maricke Abbey	400	00	0
	Mr Lee upon Cleyburne	400	00	0
	Henry Westgarth lease of 15 years	030	00	0
	Mr Skelton upon lands in Bishoppricke	400	00	0
	Mr Richardson yet arr*ears*	100	00	0
	Son Trotter about	200	00	0
	Jo. Webster	020	00	0
	Nickelson, Tinckler, Lancaster for Mr Sandford	250	00	0
	Ralph Jackson	050	00	0
	Mr. Nevison	035	00	0
	Will Meason of Carleton	090	00	0
	total of leases	3515	00	0
	Item in debtes and rents arrer at Marton	1400	00	0
	Wensledale dets et rents arrer	1000	00	0
	Thorpe in like maner pro ut per the rentalls and abstracts	1000	00	0
	Other rents arrer at Milby and in Westmerland	0500	00	0
	Debtts pro ut by debtt booke per the Alphabett letter	6000	00	0
	Item horses as in the last accompt quod vide better then	150	00	0
	Catle 8 oxen 20 cowes 12 two yeare olds 12 yearings besids fatt catle to kill	150	00	0
	Item 40 sheepe about in my possession besides those lett out with the land	50	00	0
	Item in howshold stuff (*interlined*: as before but) soe much better	1000	00	0
	In payne per ferm Will Atkinson & Geo accompts	1000	00	0
	Mr. Peryer disposed per line pro ut	4400	00	0
	Item more per line prepared for the purchas of Yarm etc	3000	00	0[11]
	Item fines arrer about	0100	00	0
	Item rent arrer at Michelmas last & Martinmas now at hand	3000	00	0
	Totall then	⟨265	00	0⟩
	Item in trade for Italie & Affrick in Kitts orderinge besids £1500 I lett him have in part of portion	2300	00	0
	Soe ye Totall	28565	00	0

11. See p. 174, below.

By these 2 leaves may be estimated the increase and decrease of Reall and   156r *cont.*
personall estate and what alteration since the former estimate vide foll
26 & 27

Change of style] Soe that in 1661 my land intend for my heires (*erasure*) though
not my son Jo. (soe much) who followeth not my advice at all in his course
of life (nor sheweth anie affection ansnerable to my love and care) having
beene then ut patet foll 26, quod vide about.   £3531 14 10
The same is not much altered though much at one since I bought Bemont
Hill·lease & other things not mentioned in the last particular

And for my personall estate it was in 1659 valued at about £20,000 and
is now computed as above unto about £28,565 besides all portions of my
Daughters paid since then & monies paid my 4 sons for their several advancements and other great disbursments as may in part (*erasure*) bee seene in
the severall years untill the 7th 8br [16]64 amountinge upon an estimate
to about £10,000 will make the total increase to be £18565 from (*erasure*)
1659 unto 8br 1664 beeinge 5 years

Note I sowld of Thwaites in this tyme which did lessen the land revenue
soe much & increased the personall estate though in this tyme I added
severall thinges of like value.

Hand of Sir J.L.(2)] *A summary statement of the total revenues due at the various*   156v–157r
feast-days in the year beginning Martinmas 1664:

	£	s	d
Leases	1750	00	0
Lands of inheritance	3632	19	3
Profit per annum from money lent or invested capital			
£20,000	1200		
Demesnes and revenues in hand	200		
Yanwath in reversion	250		
Revenues of John Lowther, son of Sir J.L.(2)[12]	250		
Casual fines per annum	150		
	£5682	19	3
Like summary, Martinmas 1668:			
Leases	1499	14	8
Lands of inheritance	4487	11	0
Profit per annum from money lent or invested	1200		
Demesnes in hand	200		
Yanwath in reversion	250		
Casual fines per annum	150		
	£6287	11	0

From which deduct revenues to be left to Ralph Lowther[13]

12. P.V.1.
13. P.V.16.

156v–157r *cont.* *£1000 per annum; and Richard Lowther*[14] *(the manor of*
        Meaburne and Asby demesne) £250 per annum; total £1250   *1250*

        So clear income to descend to the next head of the family,
        having provided for his younger sons and daughters out of his
        personal estate and leases: *£5037 11   0*

        Followed by an alternative calculation of revenue, (continued on f157r).

		£	s	d	
157r	*Like summary of revenues at Martinmas 1672:*				
	Leases	*1411*	*6*	*0*	
	Lands of inheritance	4731	0	0	
	Demesnes in hand and casual fines	270	0	0	
	Lands omitted from the total above	200	0	0	
	Profit per annum from money lent or invested	2400			
	Total lands of inheritance and use of stock, per annum				£7601
	Deduct for Ralph Lowther and his two brothers[15]	1200			
	for Richard Lowther	300			
	Interest	2400			
					3900
	Total of inheritance to descend to Sir J.L.(2)'s heir				£3701

157v [*Hand of Sir J.L.(2)*] Etatis mea 68
        A particuler estimate of what is to discend to the heire of
        the familie Jan [16]73 as intended viz
        Inprimis Lowther Hackthropp, Clifton, Melkintropp Hel-
        ton, Bampton Knipe, Rosgill, Sledall, Thrimby Stricklande
        Slegill, Shapp, Yeanewith, Newton Plumpton Threlkeld,
        Spitle, Casterton, with a valuation of £200 per annum for
        the generall fine as appears by the particulers in foll
        155b[16] doth amount unto   2026-8-10d
        Some £20 of the cassulaties of Clifton sowld in lew of
        w[hic]h Hartley tenement is added and some at Lowther
        at Lynelandes
        To which is added since not there mentioned viz
        In Westmerland Cleyburne better then   070
        Item Kirkeby Lonsdale and Preston Richard about   200
        Item Thwaites mortgage as good as land in Cumberland   060
        The lease for 3 lives of Newton and Caterlen ⟨about⟩   040
        Mr Sandford Mortgage as good as lands about[17] being
        above 1300 dew upon the 2 estates   080

---

        14. P.V.4.
        15. PP. V.17, V.18.
        16. Note by Sir J.L.(2): *In which there is litle alteration.*
        17. *about* a later insertion.

Thornthwaite tyth quitted 7 years	007			157v *cont.*
In Yorkeshire and Bishoprick to discend pro ut foll 155				
Egleston pro ut	197			
Arkendalle pro ut	032			
Toll of Bowes with land and Collery from Hanby[18]	45			
Darlington and Ringfield, last at lease for 21 years	75	6	8	
Rutford tyth in Mortage for 4 tymes the worth about	07	10	0	

Thornaby £70 bought with the £20 rent charge and above
£500 more arrer upon Mortgage fitt to go together (*erasure*)

above £100 per annum	100	
Preston rent charge besides the arrers upon it ⟨of inheritance⟩	120	
Mr Fulthropp rent charge out of vide [*sic*]	100	
Warshall bought of Sir Will Midleton	200	
Skelton lett cleare for	124	

More the Allam mynes lett for about 15 years yet in
beeinge and then may be renewed or answer soe much rent

about as now answered	216	13	4
Mylby besides the out rents about	235		
Wensladle besides about 4 or £5 sowld off about	500		

£4435-18-2d.[19]

Besides his hopes of part of Bemont Hill £90 per annum
But nota I have lymited £60 00:0 per annum out of Milby
to Will Lowther[20] my Son Johns Son by the second venture
for his preferment and mayntenance beeing other wayes
unprovided; but what his brother John will thinke fitt to add
to him as he shall deserve.
And I intend to reserve Kirkeby Lons and Preston to sell
or setle upon my Son Rich to helpe his advancement.

(*Blank. Between ff171–172 two loose letters*)	158r–193v

1. Barbara Beilby to her father Sir J.L.(2), from Grange, n.d.[21] With some
   calculations on the reverse.
2. (damaged) to Sir J.L.(2), n.d.

land of Sir J.L.(2)] The Accounts settled Betwixt my Brother Willum and	194r–196r

my selfe the 26th May 1657.
Accounts, comprising receipts and disbursements, of monies loaned, borrowed
and invested, and payments of rents, 1657–1659. Concludes with a memorandum
signed by Sir J.L.(2) that all accounts between him and his brother up to 26
August 1665 are cleared.

(*Blank*)	196v–201r

---

18. *from Hanby* added later.
19. £4435-18-10d.
20. P.VI.4.
21. See p. 167.

201v–202v [*Unknown hand*] *Accounts of money handled by Christopher Lowther,*[22] *Sir J.L.(2)'s son apprenticed to Mr. John Buckworth a London merchant trading with the Levant, October 1657–August 1659.*

203r   (*Blank.*)

203v–205r   *Accounts of monies received upon bills of exchange, giving name of person upon whom bill is drawn; also receipts of interest due to Sir J.L.(2), 1661– 1665.*

205v–213v   (*Blank*)

214r–215r [*Unknown hand*] Disbursements by Mr Peryer 1660.
        Accounts of monies invested in mortgages and bonds, with related charges for legal searches and letter postage. 1660–1664.[23]
215v–226v   (*Blank.*)

227r   *Here follows Sir J.L.(2)'s annual diary of events, continued from p. 74 above. (*in margin at beginning of paragraphs indicates a change in ink or style. Many of the financial transactions are also dealt with, from 1661 onwards, in A1/9. Where Lowther writes £600-00-0 the 00-0 is omitted.)*
        For the most considerable somes disbursed by mee J.L.Bt. since the entry unto my estate after the death of my father Sir John Low. Kt. which was in 7br 1637 untill the 25th March 1657 beeinge neare 20 years vide a former Longe vellum covered booke marked on the backe side (A) and for what is remarkable since heare followeth onely this (*erasure*) first perticuler was a (*erasure*) litle before March [16]57.
        1657 In the begininge of this Moneth 1656 I purchased the moitie of the Rectory of Shapp with the Advowson of the Vickerage of Mr Wharton and Mr Crackentropp who had the same in mortgage I haveinge formerly purchased the other moitie and had per a grant and Release from Mr. Dalton the present Vicker to avoyd his pretence of clayme that he had made under some estate from Mr Wharton, as for a pretence of £2 per annum alledged to have beene formerly paid out of the said Rectory but this was only done to avoyd a claymorous man for he had not the least shew of right that ever I could perceive. (*erasure*) It cost mee (*erasure*) (*interlined:* to) Wharton and Craik £550 and to Dalton £22 besides above £10 formerly soe cost me in all (*erasure*) upon   £600
        By this meanes I have the whole Rectory to dispose which

---

22. Noted by Sir J.L.(2): *my son Christophers accompte.*
23. The four sets of accounts just calendared should be compared with A1/9. *Mr. Peryer,* who also figures frequently in the diary below, is probably Mr. George Perryer (d. 1678, P.R.O., Prob. 11/358, f102) a prominent London Scrivener (*Scrivener's Company Common Paper, 1557–1628. With a continuation to 1678,* ed. F. W. Steer (London Record Society, IV, 1968), pp. 119, 122, 123, 126). He witnessed Sir J.L.(2)'s will (P.R.O., Prob. 11/350, f. 20).

227r *cont.*

formerly was inconvenient, both to devide and observe ther
tymes and seasons for Collectinge. Is is [*sic*] worth about
£54 per annum but I lett my part formerly for £60 (*erasure*)
but I accompt both part together worth besides the free rent
and sesses £105 per annum.[24]

In this moneth of March 1657 I perfected the Inclosure in
Thrimby feild adjoyneinge unto Greenerigges; which I had
formerly by mortgage from Simpson with other parcells of
ground that I exchainged and had from Henry Westgarth
and others; which was very convenient to Add to Greenriggs
for the better wateringe and some medow for winter to use
at pleasure. I accompt it cost me first and last above   £050
and I suppose it may be worth about £4 per annum

In or about June 1657 I purchased a tenement in Heltondale
for my Sheepe beeinge convenient for keepinge a flocke of
wethers in Winter and Ewes and Lambs in Somer. I was
to have £5 10s per annum for it and he to pay the rent and
he to keepe mee 200 wethers in Winter and Somer and
looke to all my other Sheepe in Somer tyme. It cost mee
beeinge well built   £090

I likewise in August this yeare bought in Jo Smith tenement
and the Walkemill in Strickland adjoyninge unto Studsall
and Millbrowes at Hackethropp which cost mee   £030
which I bestowed upon my Grandson Jo: Lowther

In 8br [16]57 I purchased the tenement at Howcarle as
comandinge the Cornage round about and a fitt grassige
for the tenement at Melkinthopp.[25] It cost mee in monie
£40 and fines arrere £40 in all   £080

657 In 9br in this yeare I inclosed the Corner from Eshlamor   227v
Gate to the Church Gate with a good wall as I had formerly
determined wherein I found noe opposition nor dislike of the
tenants they all helpeinge to gett stones and wallinge and I
believe it cost wallinge gettinge and leadinge which was done
with the coach horses about   £015
beeinge a conveyance from the low orchard to goe around
about to Buckholme and soe to cume round againe to
Bradgarde.

In this moneth I built the Kilne at Heltondale haveinge
(*erasure*) (*interlined*: finished) the Mill but the somer before
both which cost mee at least with stones 2 pro ut   £050
I hope it will be better than £10 per annum.

In January this yeare I disbursed unto Mr. Mathew Richard-
son upon Sandscales in Furness to have £100 per annum
at Lam and Cand [16]58 for 7 years   £500

This yeare about 10br I disbursed unto Mr. Westropp upon

24. Shap, see p. 18. For Mr. Dalton see Nightingale, *Ejected*, pp. 1190–1194.
25. How Carl, Clifton (E.P.N.S., XLIII, p. 188); see pp. 155, 195; 193.

227v *cont.* lands at Newham to have a rent charge of £40 per annum
at Whis and Mart [16]58 for ever, but J. Pear. promised a
redemption as is said qr   £500

In this yeare I setled an old debt of £500 dew by Mr. Midleton
of Bessay to have £100 per annum for 7 years at Mart [16]57
and Whis [16]58 for 7 years   £500

* In or about January this yeare I lent my Son Christopher
for to begin trade but to be at my dispose though I intend
it for him if he doe well.
It was £500 but his Master recaled his trade and admitted
lent   £100[26]

In the begininge of this yeare I did disburse to my brother
Will upon the collerie at Preston to be made good to mee
out of it and the lease of Preston which my Brother hath
and not yet secured to me (*interlined*: since it is paid).   £500

I likewise lent my Brother upon Mr Johnsons land near
Swillington (*erasure*) halfe of which was lent before, not yet
secured to mee though in part accompted for.   £500

* In March this yeare my Brother Will did disburse for mee
£300 upon a lease (*erasure*) to have £60 per annum at Lam
and Cand 1658 for 7 years unto one Lancelott Iveson upon
Houses and Landes in Leedes.[27]   £300

In the yeare 1657 I disbursed in these summs above besides
all ordinary expences £3815[28]

* 1658   Aprill this yeare 58 I walled the New Orchard under
Brodegards about neare 3 yards high which is like to be a
place for frewte if anie will doe it. Cost mee I beleive
neare £50.   £050

In May (*erasure*) I bought in the interest and tenantright
which Lycocke claymed in the tenement at the Towne Heade
as heire to Atkinson his Grandfather it cost mee in monie
£13 and in arrers of 3 fines and £20 upon a mortgage and
20 years rent arrears in all it studd mee in above £150 though
worth but about £8 per annum; but it was neare and convenient and I bought peace by it.* I new repaired the house
and Barne then.   £100

228r * 1658   In June this yeare I highered the Lowside of Rowlandfeild wall above 3 quarters the Deare leapinge out that way,
it cost mee above £20   £020

* In this moneth I disbursed £500 upon a lease or rent charge
of £100 per annum for 7 years and a halfe to begine at
Martinmas 1658 upon the Lordshipp of Gisbrough to Mr
Challenor which was contracted for by John Pearson.   £500

---

26. *£100* altered from £500. This entry an insertion, which explains the alteration
27. Deed: Yorkshire Estates Box.
28. Figures altered. Includes the £600 for Shap.

228r *cont.*

About this tyme I bought Seamers lott and land at Marton
lett to Will Arrsum for 2.6.8 which cost mee[29]   £035
In September ⟨I agreed to⟩ (*interlined*: the 11th I) maried
my 2nd Daughter Mary to Mr. Trotter of Skelton Castle
and to give hir £2000 portion viz £1000 upon mariage and
£1000 at Lam [16]59 to have £300 per annum Joynture and
he in present neare £500 per annum and after 6 years in
which he is to pay his brothers £1200, to have £200 per annum
more and after his Mothers life £120 more beeinge hir
Joynture in all £800 per annum and above, all now (*erasure*)
lett.   £1000
I then allowed Jo Pearson towards the repaire and new
walinge the house at Marton.   £0060
The 11th of 9br [16]58 beeinge Martinmas day and hir birth
day was my daughter Mary Maried in pursewance of the
former agreement and are to stay with mee about six or nine
Monethes.
The 29th of this moneth about 4 a clock in the Morneinge
died my Eldest Daughter by my now wife beeinge Elisabeth
after hir Mothers name and beeinge upon two years want
tow monethethes old who had beene a weake sickly Child
since she was wained of the Nurse, though about one moneth
before shee died shee was growne much stronger and like to
have lived; and died very gently and quietly as in a sleepe
so that one Daughter entered upon the cares of the wordle
and the other left the wordle with all the cross accidents
thereunto God grant us all to be rightly prepared for that
appoynted tyme.
In february [16]58 I bought of Mr Fletcher of Little Strick-
lands all his tenants there beeinge 40s rent and granted him
Capelrigg in fee which paid mee 19s 9d rent. Soe I had 20s 3d
more rent then I granted to him (*erasure*) for which paid
him in hand £40 and he to pay the 1s 3d free rent formerly
dew out of all his lands at Little Strickland, by this I have
the towne intyre except sume few freehoulders which pay mee
in all 10s 4d rent.   £40
I lent him then £60 more for which I have securitie
Att the same tyme upon the civell intreatie of the Lewctenant
that quartered at Penreth I paid Wibergh for his pretended
interest in the tenement at Howcarle £10; and gave to his
Mother 20s   £10
per annum dureinge hir life to be paid at Cand [16]59 and
soe yearely. Soe had both there releases and bonds and the
tenement clear which stand in above £100 out of purse
with fines.[30]

---

29. Marton, p. 37, above.
30. See p. 153, above.

228v 1658 About this tyme I purchased a parcell of Land in
Wensladale at Setbuske caled the Calfe Garth of one (*blank*)
which cost   £20 00 0
and is lett for about 30s per annum.[31]
In the latter end of February I tooke upp a good part of the
water Pipes at the well heade for about 70:yards which was
all decayed beeinge above 50 or 60 holes in a yeard most
part and rotten away and yet the water came prittie well
beeinge well laide in clay soe that it run out at one hole
and in at another as observed when it was opened, and cast
new pipes (*erasure*) of a larger boore, which after-ages may
compute the Continewance of, if this booke be pireserved soe
longe, for who laid them first is not knowne though it
(*interlined*: were) worth the rememberance who did soe
necessarie a woorke. I uncovered all the pipes untill the
⟨low⟩ High Orchard wale and placed stones for markes to
lyne it from one greate stone to another to know where the
piple lyeth to finde anie deffects in future tymes; and I left
noe defect soe farr, haveing made the water to be stoped to
stand back soe farr and soe were anie hole was the water
leyed it, and soe mended it wherein there was not past 3 or 4
places defective soe that it may now continew manie years if
the well heade doe be kept locked and a grate kept upon
the pipes to keepe leaves froges and rubish to enter in, which
causeth often openinge and tryeinge the pipes which is a
greate decay and prejudice to them as hath beene founde
by experience. I have left about 140 pairs of pipes redie cast
and burnt supposinge there had been more needs then
I found to use them; this cost mee about   £20
In the begininge of March this yeare I burned a greate
Lymekilne in the New Parke and laide it upon the same
(*erasure*) on both sides the new house all but sume 4 semcastes
next the Cross Earth hedge which is not yet lymed nor the
high ends above the hause all through unto the house.
This cost about   £15
There was 14 fother of coles in it and about 20 fother of Great
logges beeinge three lyers of wood besides the Brandereth.
The other p[ar]t above the house and about the kilne was
lymed the yeare before.
*   1659   Aprill the 20th I was (*erasure*) at Marton in Cleaveland
and I bought of the 3 Menells of Tornaby near Stockton
and a lease of lands there and elsewhere for 7 years and a
halfe to pay £100 per annum for that tyme that first payment
to begine at Mart 1659, which cost mee as good as reddie
money[32]   £500

31. Wensleydale, see p. 40.
32. See p. 166.

The Same Moneth I came through Wensladal and there I
bought of 9 tenants, as by a particulir in ⟨the⟩ this booke
appeareth, severall Lands ⟨and⟩ Messuages and tenements
of the rent of £53:13:4d. per annum, which cost at 15 years
purchas³³

659 In Aprill I contracted with Mr Swaile and Sir Tanckerd
for the purchase of Millby³⁴ adjoining upon Burow Briggs
beeinge about £237 per annum at 16 years purchas and to
allow the debt of £2140 dew to my Cos Northey³⁵ my
Brother Will and my selfe in the first payment and to pay
the remaynder at Christmas and Midsom after; and my Son
Trotter beeinge to Convey Easton in Cleaveland with £20
per annum out of Skelton in lewe and exchange for the third
part of Skelton which my Son Trotter had from Mr Stapleton, and beeinge to take a lease for 94³⁶ years backe againe
from Mr Stapleton with hard Covenants to pay £200 per
annum rent. And Millby faleinge out to be neare adjoyninge
to Mr Stapleton, and Easton convenient for mee beinge neare
Marton, and my Son Trotter beeinge desirous to be freed
from the Lease and ingagement for the rent of Easton wee
all agreed that I should have Easton³⁷ ⟨at £180 per annum
as it is lett and £20 per annum at Skelton to make it upp
£200 at 15 years purchas, which will be £3000; and Mr
Stapleton to have Millby as I was to have it at 16 years
purchase and to pay the over pluss of the purchas to Mr
Swaile and Mr Tankerd as I was to doe; and I to discharge
them of the said £3000. But in regard my Son Trotter had
but a Condicionall estate in the 3ᵈ part of Skelton from
Mr Stapleton, it was agreed that Milby should be conveyed
to my Son Trotter and then he to grant it to Mr Stapleton
with provisoe for quiett enjoyeinge of Skelton which may be
made perfect when Mr Stapletons Son attayne his fullage
of 21 years³⁸⟩ or (erasure) if his (erasure) Sons happen to
dye; before that his life by me. Soe as that Easton cost mee
with the £20 in Skelton³⁹
Whereof I paid and allowed my Cos North my Brother and
my Selfe £2140, and the rest to be paid at the Nativitie and
Midsom after
* About Martinmas last [16]58 I agreed to sell my part of
Preston and Ashley to my Brother Will which cost mee

228v cont.

229r

£805

£3000

---

33. See p. 108 for rental; for Wensleydale, see p. 40.
34. See p. 158.
35. P.III.17.
36. Altered from 99.
37. From here to n. 38 the text struck through with two diagonal strokes.
38. End of deletion.
39. See over.

229r *cont.* £3050 for a rent charge of £610: per annum to begine at
Whis 1659: but he after desired to buy it out and pay in my
monie which I shall not much stand upon and which was
after done accordingly.⁴⁰

    * In August this yeare I lent Mr Nevison £180 to have £50
per annum for five years at Cand [16]59 and Lam [16]60
yearely by equall portions; upon a lease of certane lands
in Newby for 30 years pro ut remised yealdeinge the said
£50 per annum for five years which cost   £180

    About or before this I paid my Son Trotter £1000 beeinge
the last part of his portion besides £60 I gave him (*erasure*)
which he bought a Coach and horses with of Mr Leigh of
Cleybourne   £1060

    * In October [16]59 the bargaine betwixt my Son Trotter and
Mr Stapleton not (*erasure*) proceedinge as was agreed⁴¹; I
purchased Milby myself in Son Trotters name beeinge
£231:03:11 rent cleare besides £5.12.0 free rent paid out;
which cost mee after the rate of 16 years purchas   £3699 2 8

    of which paid in hand and allowed to Brother Will Cos
Northeigh and my selfe he ought us £1940.2.7d. the rest
beeinge £1759:00.1 to be paid at 2 six moneths⁴²

229v 1659 In 8ber 1659 I perfected the bargaine formerly agreed
upon and desired by my son Trotter to supply him with
£500 which was paid to Coll. Overton for soe much borowed
of him   £500 00 0

    upon the purchas of the third part of Skelton from Sir Will
Darcie for which I am to have £100 per annum paid to Jo
Pearson for 7 years (*erasure*) at Cand and Lam, the first
payment to begine at Cand next [16]59

485 I received or had allowed mee upon the purchas of Milby from
═══ Mr Tanckerd £480 which was owinge mee by him upon
the rent charge dew by him⁴³

    *⟨I likewise paid for my Son Trotter to Coll.Overton more
the some of £500 for the last part of my Daughter Marys
portion Makeinge paid in all to him by my sons desire
£1000   £⟨500 00 0⟩

    This is made paid before ⁴⁴⟩
This yeare I lett all my Demesne at Lowther save the
(*erasure*) New Parke Rowlandfeild Whaleinge Dawlands and

---

40. See p. 73.
41. Above, p. 157.
42. Deeds: Yorkshire Estates Box; abstracts: A1/6, f137v–139r. Details of estate
above, p. 108; see also p. 157. Cf. *V.C.H., Yorks N.R.*, I, p. 369.
43. For the mortgage see above, p. 110 and Yorkshire Estates Box, letters:
Northleigh to Sir J.L.(2), 6 Oct. 1657, and enclosures. Marginal figure altered.
44. This whole paragraph struck out and annotated. See p. 177 for Skelton.

the smale parcells about the house to Jo Knot Christo
Simpson junior.[45] Soe I did but litle woorke abrode this
yeare besides in 7br and 8br wee had 10 of oure best horses
dyed of a generall sicknesse; of which above 400 dyed in
Penreth and proportionably all about, soe were disfurnished
by that meanes to doe our necessarie woorke but were forced
to use oxen in steade of horses.

In this moneth I purchased of Mr Thoby Humprey the water
Corne Millne and certaine Messuages and lands at Greate
Ayton, the mill at £38 per annum at 13 years purchas, and
£8:02:0 in land at 14 years purchas and a halfe in regard
I pay most sessements and repair the millne which cost mee
in hand   £583.02. 4
haveinge had rebated besides (*erasure*) the said som £9 in
regard of present payment and £19:06:8 likewise deducted
out of the purchas for a free rent of £1.6.8 paid for the Mill
which was dew to the Crowne formerly soe the cleare rent
except taxes beeinge £44:15:4 Cost in reddie monie as above-
said £583:02:4[46]

I likewise agreed for a farme there if I like of 88.17.0 at
14 years purchas and a halfe in regard I beare all grand
sessements which will (*erasure*) amounte unto £1288:06:6
to be paid at Christmas (*erasure*) next and Midsom 1660   £1288.06. 0

* The 1st of 9br 1659 beeinge Tewsday and All Sls day about
two of the clock afternoone there came six men habited like
Souldiers[47] with swords and short pistolls beeinge a (*erasure*)
raynie day and pretended to search for Armes, and sent for all
the servants both Men and Women pretendinge to take a note
or list of all there names and then caried them all into the
old Low Towre with my wife and hir daughter, and after
caried mee into the Low Pantery and ther with sword knife
and pistoll bent threatened to discover all wee had and tooke
my watch out of my Pockett then one wisheinge the rest to
forbeare a while from present mischeefe they then caried
mee into Backhouse loft and then used the like terror and
threats to discover, and after sett one as sentry at the doore,
and soe went to search in our chamber and then findinge the
Low Newtowre a more secure and convenient place they
brought all the servants together with my wife and Daughter
into the New Low Towre and Locked them all upp and
then went and made my wife and daughter open all the lockes
Trunckes and Chests, and tooke our plate Money and sume
Jewells which they found as not fearinge anie thinge at that
tyme After this they brought my wife and Daughter and

---

45. For a rental of this, see above, p. 106.
46. Great Ayton, see p. 166.
47. For the significance of this disguise, see p. 248, below.

229v *cont.*   putt them into the rest of the Servants, but at her desire.

230r   they after brought her owte to mee, and when they had taken all they pleased and putt them upp about them and sought all places with Candles they came to us and then caried mee out and threatened to carie mee away with them except they had more monie upon which my wife beeinge much affrighted and beeinge within 6 weeks of hir tyme of Childbed shee was forced to give them all the owld gowld shee then had about hir in (*erasure*) 2 purses one of mine and another Shee had before oure mariage beeinge about £20 with my wedinge ringe, And then conniveinge not to prosecute about it they putt us both to the rest of the People and locked us all in and then ⟨went⟩ leaveinge a Candle burninge at the Stayres heade beeinge then growne very dark they went away, and before wee cauld out a Staincher out of the backe window they were gone about 4 myles for they mett Will Atkinson cumeinge late from Penreth at the Schoolehouse and caried him backe as farr as Howcarle and he was just cumed hombe as they gott out of the window. One of them stodd with the horses at the out Gates and braught all pasengers in that came that way from Penreth and delivered them to one that stood at the High Court gates, who brought them upp and putt them into the Low Towre even as they came; Soe that wee were in all soe inprisoned of owne house with those that were then at woorke with us, these persons viz. first my selfe wife her Daughter and our litle Boy Ralph Geo Mounsey (*erasure*) John Askeugh Hugh Walker Richard Stephenson Thomas Millne 3 Slaters viz. Jo Steeley and his 2 men, Francis Harison and Rowland Stephenson John Bradley Christo Simpson man. Those that were brought in were Will Robinson Hugh Chapelhow Smith John Warkeman Hutchinson son Hen Clarke John Wilkinson of the Dale Jo Wilkinson above the Hall Christo Ritson and Leonard Martine that braugh breade hombe. Women there my wives Chambermayd Bridget and Issabell Nunn Parsons Mayde Great Besse Ritson wife Will Miller wife. Wee lost more then wee did well know but since it pleased God to preserve us all without bodily harme wee have greate cause to Prayses him the preserver of all that trust in him; and hope through his Mercie to recover those losses amongest divers others; when those malefactors will (*erasure*) have another accoumpt to make if not heare yet elsewhere for I see litle hopes of ever recoveringe anie thinge againe though manie judge of some very suspicions, but without pregnant proofe of the Persons or Sume thinge taken to discover them there is noe likely-hood of discoverie sume beeinge disguised especially one with a redd Periwigge.

* The names (*erasure*) of the Persons that Robed us as was
after confessed by one Hillery that was executed at Yorke
for other Roberys were
1 Tristeran Barwick not yet taken,[48] said since to be hanged
at London
2 The 2 Hillerey our Nursess husbands brothers one of them
after hanged at Yorke and the other in Jeole ther[49]
and hanged at Durham
3 One Hall that was shott with a Pistoll of his owne going off
4 One Willson of Kirkeby Hill that was after executed at
Yorke for other fellonies
5 One Rockley a gentlemans son not heard of soe that by
providence they ⟨all⟩ neare all cumed to ther deserved
deaths though not by my procurement
* In lent assises at Yorke Barwick was condemned for
breackinge the Church at Chester and before execution died
as though—poisened the day before; and one Fowcet who
Robed my Son Wandesford and was my Son Richards Man
was condemned for horse stealinge in Engla[nd].

* The 16th of 9br 1659 about 4 of the clock in the morninge
it pleased God of his mercie to take to himselfe (*erasure*)
out of this miserable wordle my Deeare and loveinge Mother,
the Ladie Ellinor Lowther beeinge about 76[50] years of age,
Shee had beene sickly in hir Midleage but for this 22 years
since my fathers death had beene very healthfull save only
for a moneths sickness one year since.
She used constantly to cume once a moneth over to us and
was withall upon Friday after our Robery to see us and after
went hombe and was at Crosby [Ravensworth] Church on
fott both forenone and after and fell sicke upon Munday
next day thought to be a cowld and sent for mee upon
Fryday after where I found hir sicke and then after a litle
discourse shee called for hir will and wished mee to see it and
tell hir what I thought and my tow sisters beeinge made
joint executors I towld hir I thought if shee pleased to give
out in legacie what shee pleased and then to make us all 4
executors but shee then said that might add more to those
that have had there proportion but I towld hir shee might
helpe that; but shee said then the will might be writ over
againe which I towld hir neede not since ether the executors
might be putt in and a codicell annexed to it wherupon
shee said shee would consider of (*erasure*) particulars when
my sisters came and would send for mee if shee were worse
and then setle it but my sisters cumeinge next day I heard not

---

48. Rest of entry a later note, with a second annotation [by Sir J.L. (2)]: *but not soe.*
49. Rest of entry a later note.
50. Altered and blotted in text, 76 in margin, in contemporary hand.

230v *cont.* from hir untill tewsday after and when I came shee was past
speech or knowledge of anie. (*erasure*) And soe shee
continewed with sume strange panges of death and then
continewed that night as in a deade slumber and short
breathinge and Rutlinge and sume coughinge[51] as stoped
with pleagme but could gett noethinge upp and soe departed
without further motion the next morneinge (*erasure*) expressinge ⟨a desire⟩ a litle before ⟨of⟩ (*interlined*: a) desire
to be disolved and to be with hir saviour. Shee was a very
sober frewgall temperall and myld woman a litle toe
persimonius and negligent of repair of houses and fences
which were very rewenous but otherwayes very good and
pious. She left my sisters and gave them in monie and
specialties as good as I collected neare £1800 or 2000 and
to my Brother Will which she said he had received of hirs,
about £900; and she had given me about a yeare before £100
and £20 per annum as shee alledged out of Asby (*interlined*:
worth) about £150 more and to my Son John at severall
tymes about £110; and in smale legacies to me my wife and
Children about £50 which was all I had from hir in all hir
tyme. I paid hir in monie att my fathers death £500 and shee
had about £240[52] per annum (*erasure*) of which shee spent
but litle, only what shee lost in badd debts, and lived 22
years a widow; this is the short accoumpt of hir condicon
at hir death who was brought to Lowther and buried in my
fathers grave where his scull was found with hare fresh on his
heade and Beard. I hope shee is now in a blessed and happie
estate; where God grant us all (*interlined*: to rest), in the end
of (*erasure. Interlined*: our dayes and) these troublesome
tymes. (*The rest of this page is left blank.*)

231r 1659 February about this moneth I purchased from Jo: Knot
a smale tenement adjoyninge to Bampton demesne caled
Sadamanhow of the rent of 1s8d for £60 he ought mee. Said
to be very fitt for that demayne as joyinge[53] the demayne
to it and the Comon upon the other side a fitt outgate for
the sheepe to the Coman for which he is to pay per annum
£4 10s 0d. I valueinge my Lords right at about £20 beeinge
soe cheape rented as it was. Soe as it cost asbefore   £60
Item in that moneth I took a mortgage of that tenement of
(*erasure*) John Holmes at Heltondale Heade beeinge now lett
to Will Langhorne Bayliff for 9s per annum and of the rent
of about 12s for which I lent him £20 and if not redemed
within 3 years I to pay £40 more for the full purchas of it.
It is more convenient for a (*letter erased*) keepinge a flock of

---

51. Blotted: uncertain reading.
52. Altered from £250.
53. The initial letters, *ad*, of this word struck out. Bampton, see p. 18.

sheepe then anie in the Dale and is accoumpted the best
dale for wethers in those forest fells and if it happen into my
hands I meane to sell that other tenement I bought of Richard
Holme which I bought for the same purpose, this lyinge much
more intyre and more convenient for keepinge the sheepe   £20
then the other and besides the house stands in Bampton Parish
where I have a tyth lambe (and may in tyme cume to have
the wooll) but the sheepe goinge both in Bampton and Helton
parish one may the better deale for the tyth since the
proprieters (*erasure*) cannot soe punctually make good a
certaine demand. Albeit at present I pay noe tythes for my
Stocke within Askeham Parish; for which I know noe cause
except Mr Sandford pay sume composition or prescription
for that and the rest (*erasure. Interlined*: as for) Askeham
and Helton of whome I bought the moitie of Helton and soe
may be free for my part upon that cause, viz, because he
hath the donation of the Vickerage of which qr. or else it
were good to pay sume smale composition that in tyme it may
becume a prescription the rather because most of the sheepe
goe upon Helton side and racke only to Bampton side but
if I have this tenement then the Ewes may renew there within
Bampton soe that I may have the tyth lambes by that right
and then may goe upon Helton heafe most part and soe may
have the wool by the Prescription or other Composition of
which qr. Nota that Mr Sandford payes 20s or a horse grasse
in lieu of all tythes.[54] In the same moneth I purchased the
tenement of Christopher Wilkinson and his sons in Quale[55]
to have a third part in possession and the other two parts
after the old mans death beeinge above 80 years of age which
I intend for my keeper of the Parke as nearest and most
convenient ⟨to⟩ both to the Parke and Rowland feild, which
he is to enjoye only at pleasure by lease at will leaste he
cume to Clayme a tenantright as Cragge hath done for that
at this end of the Parke which was without all question part
of the Parke as may appeare by the wall and Groundwoorke
pulled upp. This cost mee in monie paid and owinge to mee
£80 and accoumptinge the losse of my fine and Lords right   £80.
which
I account at least £50 more it stands mee in as if it were
freehowld unto £130 and is worth in all if (*erasure*) all in
possession at least £10 per annum sume say £12 but I thinke
it to deare of that and would not have bought it but for this
end only to preserve the Deare the better.
At this tyme I bought 2 closes or parcells of land at (*space*) in

---

54. This sentence a subsequent insertion by the same hand in a different ink,
    extending into the margin.
55. See pp. 177, 196.

231r *cont.* Wensladale adjoyninge upon the Haylands which ley conveniently for to hinder anie pasage that way without my
licence which Norton who basely troubles mee about that
ground would make use of to my prejudice. It is (*erasure*) to
be lett againe to one Whaley of whom I bought it at £5
per annum at Mart [16]60 yearely for which I paid 15 years
purchas   £75.

231v 1660 In Aprill I Bauugh of one Chr Rowthland at Hardrow
Beck lett to Trenie Metcalfe att ⟨£5 per annum as others⟩
6-13-4d per annum som for 8s free rent paid out
which is adjoyinge on the farr side the water upon my owne
land. Cost: £94
Item bought of Roger Taylor ⟨another⟩ halfe a tenement
at Burtersid adjoyinge upon my owne there lett at £5 per
annum free from rent. Cost £75 which I paid him in
hand.[56]   £75
The 12th of this moneth I was elected knight of the Shire for
this Countie (*erasure*) haveinge noe intention or thoughts of
it but was only desired to goe alonge with Sir Tho. Wharton[57]
to countenance him; He, Mr. Brathwaite of Ambleside,[58]
Mr. Burton[59] and Mr. Thomas Wharton of London[60] all
standinge for it and haveinge lawboured it above 6 weekes
yet when I appeared but at Appelby All the whole Gentry
of both sides the fell and all the whole Country in generall
did all overrewle mee to stand which at there intreatie I did;
And whole Country did Unanimusly macke choyce of mee
for the first knight nullo contradicentie.
But before it came to pollinge Mr Brath*waite* and Mr Tho
Wharton relinguished standing and Mr Burton pressed the
poll (*interlined*: against Sir Thomas) wherein I caried it above
300 votes from him and 150 from Sir Thomas Wharton who
had lost it if I had not joyned to assist him with my seacond
votes, which he most civelly acknowledged that he came
under my winges. This was done without ever maneinge anie
Person for it and all that were lawboured by all the other
4 and Mr Baynes[61] that intended the like did all turne and
appeare for me there beeinge not one negative vote against
mee in the whole Baronry; and the most in these parts

56. These three purchases in Wensleydale, see p. 40.
57. Sir Thomas Wharton, younger son of the third Lord Wharton, G.E.C., *Complete Peerage*, XII, pt. 2, p. 602. See p. 173.
58. A prominent committee man and lawyer.
59. See *D.N.B.*; *N&B*, I, pp. 363, 586.
60. See E. R. Wharton, *The Whartons of Wharton Hall* (Oxford, 1898), pp. 30, 59 *et seq.*
61. See W. W. Bean, *The Parliamentary Representation of the six Northern Counties* (Hull, 1890), p. 597.

except sume ingaged People about Orton Branton and   231v *cont.*
Cleyburne which were inconsiderable. But observe that the
bills of charges of that night expences in the intertaynement
of the Cuntry cost Sir Thomas and mee joyntly £180 which
was £90 a peece, which at former taymes cost not £5.   £90
Soe much is tymes altered; but the number of people was
greate beeinge thought to be above 3000 men and wee paid
for all that was spent by Mr Brath*waite* and Mr Wharton in
regard they resigned and would not stand (*erasure*) in
opposition.
And upon tewsday the 17th wee are for London the
Parlements beeinge to sitt downe the 25th instant to which
I pray God grant a good successe and a happie closeinge
of all differances; and restore the Church and State to its
pristine splendor and puritie.
* My Wife and daughters went to London and brooke upp
house; and the Parlement ended in Christmas after to the
full Content, restoringe the Kinge Queene Nobilitie and
Gentry to a greate part of ther right and closed with an act of
oblivion to all but what were excepted about the Kinges
death and was stiled by the Kinge the healeinge and blessed
Parlement it cost mee in expences there at that tyme before
wee came downe which was not untill March after.   £500
But I settled my business at Thorpe and elsewhere in those
parts[62]

560[63] About (*space*)   this yeare I bound my Son Hugh   232r
an Apprentice to one Mr. Masters[64] a Turkie Merchant for
7 years with whome I then gave in monie besides other
accomodations; ⟨(who doth well though was mild)⟩   £300
I then gave my Son Richard who went over with the Lord
Primate of Ireland in hopes of Preferment beeinge his owne
desire, but fear it will not answer the expectation   £250
I likewise about August [16]60 furnished my Son Christopher
⟨to⟩ besides £150 formerly, to helpe him in Stocke for his
Adventures for Constantinope whither he went in 9br after as
factor beeinge not 4 years since he was bound, but beeinge
hopefull and towardly in his profession I lett him have to
incurage his indevors   £400
In or about 9br [16]60 I was gladd to ⟨lett⟩ lend my Son
Wandesforde to helpe him out of debt ⟨in⟩ which he had
contracted at London, he and his wife and Children haveinge
been sicke, which he secured me by Bests land, and a lease

---

62. This sentence an after-thought, inserted at the bottom of the page.
63. Altered from 1661.
64. Possible identification: Woodhead, *Rulers of London*, p. 113, see below, p. 167.

232r *cont.* of (*erasure*) Thimblely and Kirkeington to be paid with
consideracion in 3 years tyme; principall[65]   £500

About 9br that yeare lent Mr. Fulthropp £900 upon securitie
of land in Bisopricke; of which Jo: Pearson hath the
securitie to pay £180 per annum for 7 years to begine at
Wis [16]61   £900

About 10br [16]60 I lett my Brother Will have £1500 to
redeme his Son in Lawes land Sir Francis Blands estate from
one Mrs. Moore at London which he is to pay at Mids and
Christ[16]61[66]   £1500

And that Somer I paid Mr Harpers the £1288.8s formerly
agreed for the farme at Ayton (*erasure*) sett downe before but
not p(er)fected untill then.[67]

1661 The 31the of May [16]61 I purchased of Mr Menell
certaine lands at Thornabie neare Marton of the yearly value
of £53-13-4d. which cost mee with £500 I had formerly lent
in all £800 the £300 to make upp the £800 beeinge to be paid
at Midsom and Martinmas next in full; (*erasure*) and to finde
sufficient tenants for 21 years at that rent and pay a 3d of
taxes; this standinge to 15 years purchas[68]   £800

* But agreed afterwards to pay only £750 and to have £50 per
annum rent[69]

In June this yeare I contracted for a lease of Barwis demayne
from Mr Humprey for 99 years to have £100 per annum
for 7 years and a halfe, the first payment to begine at Mart
1661: for which I have paid £100 in hand and assigned my
Brother Will or Mr Peryer to pay £400 more in full befor the
1st of August next or else to use from that tyme unto it
to be paid.   £500

I had agreed with him (*erasure*) for the purchas of it and
was to have given him 15 years purchase for it ⟨as⟩ if he
found mee good tenants to likeinge which he pretended he
would doe at £60 per annum but could not and I thought to
deare (*erasure*) at that rent soe it braugh on this bargaine
and he sowld it to Dobson of Dufton with an exception of
my lease.

* In June and July I unriped the Hall at Meaburne and new
slated it all with slate gott (*interlined*: in) the Edgeclose which
cost mee 15s a roode gettinge and 5s leadinge and 11s
slatinge. I likewise took downe the tow longe houses one

---

65. Noted [by Sir J.L.(2)]: *besides £500 before lent.*
66. *CW₂*, XLII, p. 75. His d. Jane married Bland in 1660.
67. Great Ayton, abstracts: A1/6, f140r–142r (*note*: f141 is missing; the last deed
    on f140 is dated 1654 and the first on f142 1660). See p. 159.
68. Yorkshire, *V.C.H., Yorks N.R.*, II, p. 298. Deeds: Yorkshire Estates B., see
    p. 156.
69. This whole sentence squeezed in between the paragraphs.

adjoyninge to the Hall and the other to Fletcher house and
new walled them which cost 4s per roode ten quarters high
and soe proportionablie as it was higher. The wood worke
cost (*erasure*) mee £10 I bough 42 oke trees at Greate
Strickland wood of my cosen Dalston which cost mee £20
besides leadinge which I did with my owne tow draughts
save about tenne fothers I had neightbours that did helpe
mee. The whole charge of them (*interlined*: with) the
Brewhouse Backhouse Playsteringe and laths, lyme etc. cost
above £100.

261 In July this yeare I agreed upon a mariage for my
Daughter Barbara with Mr. John Beilby of Mickelthwaite
Grainge neare Wetherby of an auncient familie; I was to give
£2000 whereof to pay upon Mariage £500 and £1000 at
Nativitie after and £500 last part at Midsom after viz:
[16]62, whereof I paid before hand upon bond, the mariage
beeinge agreed to bee the 12th of 7br, shee was to have
Killerby neare (*interlined*: Scarbrough)[70] beeinge £300 per
annum in Joynture and they to have there diett with there
father and Mother (who are aged) or £50 more in Monie if
they live from them. Soe ther is 3 of my 4 Daughters by
my first wife that are maried or to be maried into Yorkshire.
His estate is accoumpted well worth £800 per annum besides
he hath purchased about £70 per annum that ley conveniently, with part of the portion though hee be indebted
for it to his Unckle Sunderland from whome as likewise
from an other Unckle by the Mother side is expected sume
considerable estate, they haveinge above £1200 per annum
betwixt them (*erasure*) to which he is in hopes of a good part
they haveinge noe Children; and have a good respect for
him, which maketh the Match besides the estate beeinge well
wooded worth 4 or £5000 maketh it more considerable,
with a sober Man;
In ⟨the⟩ July in this Moneth my ungracious Son Hugh who
had cost (*erasure*) mee but the last yeare byndinge an
Apprintice £300 besides £100 more in fittinge him in
Cloathes and teachinge Did runn away from his Master and
gott of his monie £200 and of myne from Mr Buckworth
£100 from Mr Peryer £60 and at Thorpe £30 and about £50
more upon his accoumpt; besides that he tooke up in Cloath,
Lyninge and other thinges of Kid the taylor (*interlined*: and
others) about £150. Soe that he goatt of (*erasure*) his
Masters and myne and others to the value of neare £600
besides the £400 he cost byndinge and puttinge out beeinge
in all above £1000; And this of a Sudaine and never expected

232r *cont.*

£100

232v

---

70. *Killerby neare Scarbrough* written in a different ink.

232v *cont.* from his Master or anie other; And to agrevate this
abominable act he had the impudence to cume downe post in
August to Penreth, where wee heard of him and seised upon
him (*interlined*: at Emont Brigg) and caried him to Socke-
bridge as beeinge unwillinge to looke upon him; And then
(*interlined*: he) framed a Story to my Wife and Daughter
that he came purposely to acquainte us with a greate fortune
he had got one Mrs Cutler worth £10000 and that he had
bought £300 per annum at Tyton neare Barnet and had
manie servants and had putt out abouve £4000 to certaine
Aldermen at London: And write a letter to his wife and
Master and severall others for the confirmation, and wished
them and others to give us full assurance thereof by the
next post, which beeinge delivered with soe manie circumstances gott sume creditt and beleife; (*interlined*: with sume)
And at the weekes end when an accoumpt was expected;
he writ a letter and left upon the table in the High Towre
where he was camed (*interlined*: privatly) expressinge all was
false and untrew and that he was maried but not to such a
fortune (*erasure*) nor such a person; And soe in the night gott
the keyes of the dore and soe gott

233r [16]61 gott [*sic*] away. Wee never knew where he went unto
nor what became of him, but I never expect more good of him
beeinge given over to all villanie and as wee suppose thought
to (*erasure*) have gott sumething upon this pretence of
Mariage to such a fortune but he had gott to much before
for soe lewd ends. And I fear his end will be miserable[71];
* In September I was invited by Sir Ja. Peniman upon the
motion of my son Trotter to a meetinge at Egleston Abbey,
about a treatie of a Match with his son and my Daughter
Frances, And after sume conferance about the sume; how
fitt and convenient a Match it might bee for hir to be seated
next to hir Brother Ralph on the one hand and hir sister
Trotter on the otherside; And how suitable they were for
years hee about 19 and shee about 17; and he beeinge his
only son and haveinge upon a former vew about 2 moneths
before beene much taken with hir and hee agreeinge to make
him £1000 per annum besides all his (*erasure*) personall
estate; I was content upon those consideracons and Sir Ja.
much desireinge it to give her £2300 portion a third upon
mariage a third upon six monethes after and a third at six
monethes after that and he to setle £350 Joynture and £400
present mayntenance though he thought £300 might serve in
regard he intended to give 3 or £400 for them to begine
the wordle with; which wee left unsetled for as he left
the portion partly to mee Soe I must (*interlined*: not) stand

71. See below, p. 179.

to strictly with him, since hee professeth and I partly beleive
he might have had £4000 with Mr Elwis Daughter and yet
had rather take £2000 with mee; Soe wee agreed in few
woords that night, upon likeinge of the younge foolkes of
which there is litle doubt, but thinke not to hasten the
mariage for about a yeare that he may have the advantage
of sume more breedinge at Ines of Court haveinge beeinge
[*sic*] 2 years at the Universitie; which if please God to take
effect all my 4 Daughters will be maried into Yorkeshire
not farr distant; And though the estates be not greate yet
they may by providence increase it, And it is difficult to finde
greate estates and Men capable (*interlined*: and) unmaried
and fitly qualified in all respects soe thought fitt not to
sleight oppertunities when offered; there beeinge so manie
that have Daughters Sticke upon there hands and cannot
bestow them but are forced to lett them bestow themselves;
And finde yet more towardlynesse and contentement from
my Daughters (then my sons) who have beene all dewtiefull
and directable, as I thought fitt.

The 12 of September my Daughter Barbara was maried
upon the former agreements and setlements. It cost them
in Gloves and fancies above £120: wee had most of the
Gentry in the Country 3 or 4 dayes and about 20 horse
with him out of Yorkeshire a weeke, and then wee all sett
them hombe; at Burowbrigge there mett us neare 80 horse
and that night cost them above £25 and the next day wee
went to the Grainge and stayed there 4 dayes were wee
were intertayned with greate freedom of Musicke and
feastinge 4 dayes. Then my Brother Will Lowther invited all
the Companie to Swillington where wee had the like
intertaynement.

»61 And from thence wee went to Skelton Castle to my son
Trotters and stayed there 4 dayes, And from thence were
invited unto Sir James Penimans to Ormesby; and from
thence to Marton, Soe to Egleston and soe hombe haveinge
not had one shower on all the journey but one in our way
from Marton, the way at that tyme of yeare beeinge all dustie
betwixt Burowbrigge and Wetherby Grainge at that season;
and this is the accoumpt of that affaire;

In December this tyme I paid my Daughter and Son Beilby
£1000 makeinge £1500

In 9br before I was elected High Shiriff of Cumberland
unexpected, though I had both the Secritorys, the Earl of
Carlile and my Lord Cowper of the Privie Councell all my
freinds, but it was said the Kinge Consulted his owne and
the Kingedomes saftie and therefor the tymes beeinge
daingerous he would have one he knew faithfull. And soe

233v *cont.*   had a dispensation to live at hombe and entered upon that office the profitt and expence shall be found after wards in a speciall accoumpt for that purpose for future information.[72]

About this tyme I purchased of Mr Sayer a rent charge ⟨of⟩ out of Preston upon Tease of £64 which with £56 rent I had before maketh it upp £120 per annum; which £64 cost mee: £800

This Moneth I lent unto Mr Blackeburne upon an anuitie of £100 per annum for 7 years and ½ the some of £500 to pay at Whis and Mart [16]62 and soe yearely.   £500

The same tyme I bought certaine houses and lands at Darlington for convenience of that Markett and in my way to Marton part (*interlined*: of the land) beeinge Coppihowld land howlden of the Bishopp which cost[73] mee at 15 years purchas beeinge lett to one Rob Cuthbert the Bayliff of the Towne for £35.06.0.[74]   £530

* In 7br befor I gave my Son Christopher an addition of £200 to helpe him forward in trade which maketh   £200
which with [*sic*] £300 cost byndeinge (*interlined*: an Apprintice)[75] maketh £1100

* The (*space*) of January my Son Jo haveinge caried his wife upp to London without and against my likeinge, he serveinge as Burgess for Appelby; Shee fell sick sume say of sume ulcer or gangeringe which shee would not discover untill to late and dyed, how as yet I know not certainely, Shee was one of the Coheirs of Sir Henry Bellingham but had only £100 land at Spitle and Casterton with hir and about £2500 in monie and goods which cost much in suite about it; and the tytle to the moitie of Beamond Hill a Coppihold in Bishopricke after the Ladie Belinghams death though Allen Bellingham claymeth the same by way of covenents of Mariage but not beeinge passed by Surender and beeinge noe equitie, I suppose he will doe noe good though he now seu in Chancery about it.[76] Shee was a good hansome yellow hayerd woman and knowinge enough and very handie and neate in her house; though somethinge humarous and conceipted when shee sett upon anie thinge shee desired; and pashonate and very oft apt to spleene fitts; and growne very grosse and corpulent in bodie. Shee

72. See pp. 87n., 52, 172
73. The word *cost* abuts against *£530* in the marginal column.
74. Abstract: A1/6, f143r. P.R.O., C.6/212/35 is a suit by Sir J.L.(2) against Cuthbert in 1673 over rent arrears and debts owed by Cuthbert.
75. Interlined in the style of the subsequent January entry.
76. There are two chancery bills which relate to this dispute, but not to the £2,500: P.R.O., C.5/378/25 and C.10/53/125. See also pp. 64, 244.

hath left tow hopefull Childeren a Son and a Daughter who   233v *cont.*
if they prove well and continew towardly must be my care to
educate and in sume measure to provide for if they neede it
in my life tyme; What my son will bind himselfe unto I know
not, but his good and prudent setlement will much conduce
to the prosperitie of our familie

662 The 24th of Aprill was my Daughter Frances maried to   234r
Sir Ja: Penimans Son Accordinge to our former treatie
and agreement,[77] the estate setled and shee a rent charge of
£325 per ann[um] for joynture and I to give £2300, at
Midsom [16]62 and Nativitie and Midsom after (*interlined*:
neare) equally if shee or anie child by hir be liveinge at the
respective tymes of payment. Sir Ja and his Brother the
Dockter was ther and maried them And was present Sir Geo
Fletcher, his Brother Harie, Son Wandesford, Son Trotter
and severall other Gentlemen and neyghtbours; and Sir Ja:
sheweth a greate affection for hir and the like to his Son
beeinge his only child.

In June I did give my Son Richard £200 to helpe him in
his Irish undertaking and purchas of sume lands he was in
hopes to get a collery in, makeinge £400 since he went for
Ireland besides £100 in setinge him forward when he went
over[78] in all £500   £200

This Whisantyd ⟨I⟩ and Midsom I paid my Son Beilby
£500 in full of £2000 for his wives portion ⟨in full⟩ the
sume of   £500

And about the same tyme I paid my Son Penimans father
the sume of £750 the first payment of ⟨his⟩ my Daughters
portion out of my rents at Marton; ther beeinge £750 more
dew at the Nativitie next, and £800 in full at Midsom [16]63   £750

This Whisantyd I lett Jo Pearson have £200 to pay £40 per
annum for 7 years   £200[79]

In September I ordered my Son Christopher more £200
makeinge £400 since he went over sea, makinge in all⟨since
his⟩ with his byndinge Apprintice at least £1300[80] (this
not yet paid) 8r [16]62   £⟨200⟩

*In 10br viz 1⁰ 10br I paid Mr Skelton upon a rent charge
of £100 per annum for 7 years and ½ begininge at Midsom
[16]63 and St Andrew day upon[81]   £500

---

77. See p. 168, above.
78. Rest of line a later note. For letters of Richard mentioning the colliery see
    D/Lons/L, letters, 1661.
79. This whole entry a later insertion in the same style.
80. Rest of entry an annotation in the same ink as that used to strike out £200 and
    for the next paragraph.
81. *Upon* added as an afterthought.

234r *cont.*   In 9br before I bought more of Mr Menell one rent charge
of £20 per annum for ever out of all his lands at Thornabie
to begine at Whis [16]62 which cost redie monie   £300
Jo Pearson hath the writinges yet not delivered to mee.[82]
Which I have now.[83]
I paid my Son Peniman the 2d payment of his wives Portion
beeinge   £750
 * This moneth I (*erasure*) in part finished the wainescott and
woode worke in the Chapell with together with [*sic*] Playster
woorke and the Roofe and guildinge costs about £80   £080
 * This yeare the charge of my Shiriffaltie besides the profitt
of the office which might amount unto about £250 cost mee
about £400 besides as may appeare by Perticuler bookes of
the Profitt and Charge.[84] For a short estimate Coach and
4 horses £130 Cloaths for myselfe with sadle pistolls and
other furniture about £170. Liveries beinge 40 at my owne
cost wherein I gave all my Bayliffs and Servants cost about
£120; Item in Lyninge Pewter Brasse and other necessaries
about £60; Item in Provision for the housekeepinge at the
Assises in Wine Beare Beefe Mutton Breade Wheate guifts
for presents above £120; Item the charges of the 4 sessions
about £40; Soe that I suppose[85] I lost bye it £400. But I
had noe Crosses by the Goale; but all was done with creditt
and good opinion.   £400

234v 1662 In February this yeare I lent Meason of Carleton upon
a lease and bond £100 to pay £20 per annum at Lam and
Cand [16]63 for 7 years and ½ in Geo Mounsey name[86]   £100
The 6th of this Moneth lett Mr Lee of Cleyburne have £500
to pay £100 per annum for 7 years upon the Manor of
Cleyburne to be paid at Whis 1663 and the 30th of 9br   £500
1663 In Aprill when I was at my Daughter Penimans I bought
of Bartholomew Milburne a Cotage and land at Marton
beeinge soe neare and mixed with the rest lett at £3 per
annum which cost redie monie at 15 years purchas which
I intend shall goe with that estate at Marton[87]   £045
A litle before that tyme when I was at London I bought the
lease of Ringe or Dringe feild at Bemont Hill of Mr Purefoy
and gave it my Son John for his Boy to incurage him
to providence[88] as hoped to have it joyned to the Moietie of

82. The whole of this line written in after the note of the rent charge.
83. This line added after the line in note 82. For Thornaby, see above, p. 166.
84. None of the books noted on p. 87, nor Sir J.L.(2)'s Sheriff's Book seem to
be these referred to here.
85. Uncertain reading.
86. *In Geo Mounsey name* a later insertion in the same hand.
87. Marton, see p. 37.
88. Word smudged, reading uncertain.

Beamont Hill[89] (*erasure*) which beeinge Copihold should   234v *cont.*
discend to his son after the Ladie Bellingehams death
which cost mee in redie monie besides charges about;
beeinge a ⟨lease⟩ Colledge lease newly renewed for 22 years;   £385
About the same tyme I gave my Son Jo: towards his extra-
odinare expences (*interlined*: £100) besides £100 a litle before
when he went upp to the Parlement, beeinge at my motion
chosen Burges for Appleby 1663 ⟨before⟩   £200
About Whis [16]63 I bought of John Pearson the tyth
corne of Marton[90] which I had lent him monie partly
to bye it; and was able to repay it; It cost mee at 10 years
purchas beeinge a lease for three lives of Jo Pearsons sons,
now renewable by mee, £600 beeinge lett againe for £60
per annum free from all charges or deductions soe better
upon that accoumpt then in another place besides the
Conveniencie as arrisinge out of my owne tenants   £600
And I wish my Son Ralpe should have it, he payinge to my
Eldest son what it cost mee
In June and after I builded the Coachhouse and Stable
in the end of it new from the ground which Cost in all
materialls buildinge above; when[91] not putt that use may
serve for other good uses as for a woorke house more
proper then that I use now   £080
In January the 25th I lett my Son Christopher have £740[92]
makeinge in all received by him £1500 besides £400 he cost
mee upon his byndinge Aprintice and Clothes. Which £1500
I intend to make upp £2000 in full of his Childs part which
beeinge paid soe earlie in my life by mee I accoumpt it
better then £3000 besides I putt into stocke then with him in
trade £1000 all which I have bond for Which is with my will;
but only now paid to him which I intend to bee for himselfe   £740
Item as I say lent him to trade for my use   £1000
In this Moneth I paid Sir Philipp[93] Musgrave for Sir Tho
Wharton[94] for the purchas of his Captaines place and
Companie of the Standinge Armie in Ireland for my Son
Richard which he desired £250 and am to pay him at
Whis next £250 more in full beeinge in all £500; besides

---

89. See p. 170.
90. For another entry of this purchase, which has been crossed out, see below on
    this folio; a further entry below relates to an additional purchase of Marton tithe.
    Marton see p. 37.
91. *when* appears to be inserted, and may suggest that the clause it introduces was
    an afterthought.
92. The figure 4 scratched out before *£750*.
93. The second *i* interlined; for Musgrave see *D.N.B.*
94. For Wharton see p. 164, also *Calendar of State Papers (Ireland), 1669–1670,
    Addenda 1625–1670*, pp. 384, 388.

234v *cont.*   £500 and above he [Richard] hath had since he went into
Ireland Soe that this may be a Stay to him for my life
intendinge him Meaburne and Reavegill at my death which
is worth neare £250 per annum and well housed which
hath lately cost mee above £150   £500

⟨About Whisontyde Before I bought in of John Pearson
the tyth Corne of Marton for 3 lives beinge a Bishopps lease
for which I am to have £60 per annum cleare rent which
cost mee in debts and other monie John and his Son Mich
aught mee with (*erasure*) (*interlined*: selinge[95]) of the the [*sic*]
£40 per annum (*interlined*: and more) I had lent him before
towards the purchas of it; Soe that it cost mee in all.
This twice set downe[96]   £600⟩

About January this yeare I contracted for the purchas of
Mr Sayers lands at Yarm Eyscliff Ayslahy and Preston for
£6746 but not yet finished, and to lend him besides £1300
which I suppose will cum in the next yeare[97]

I bought of Mr Westropp and Jo Pearson the rest of
Marton tyth cost   £200

235r 1664 In the begininge of this yeare I bought of Rumley of
Emont brigg the Poake Mill houlme[98] to add to the tenement
at Lowther brigg end for better conveniencie and to save
hedging and water etc worth £1-10-0 per annum for   £17

In Aprill I bought of Mr Whelpdale—Newton Rigg closes
to add to Subarwens[99] for better advantage and way to
Penreth fell, and libertie in Penreth feild for sheepe and
goods, and lett the same to Jo Aray the farmer of Suborwens
for £8-10s per annum but hath beene lett for £10 per annum,
it cost   £135

This moneth I new layd most the leade pipes from the high
orchard wall unto the kitchinge though, and layde it a new
upon a levenell to have a discent all alonge without
raysinge or falinge as it layd formerly to low and rose againe
in severall places soe that now if anie default be in the pipes
above it doth noe harme and it lyeth not to deepe but
easie to find the defects if anie bee; beeinge noe mention in
former tymes when and by whom they were first layd beeinge
through tyme which weareth out all thinges much decayed by
often searchinge ripinge and boringe to try where the stopps
were which will not now need soe much as formerly; there
is a stone sett in the Midle of the high Orchard to direct

---

95. *Selinge* interlined over the erasure.
96. This whole entry struck out, as the last sentence, a later addition [by Sir J.L.(2)],
    indicates.
97. See pp. 176, 180, 191, for the outcome.
98. See E.P.N.S., XLIII, p. 206.
99. Sewborwens, p. 283, n. 81.

where the pipe goeth in a direct line from place to place.   235r *cont.*

*In July this yeare I set A Batlement upon Shapp Quire
new layd the leades upon it, I bought A tunn of leade that
new laide the Gutters and other places most defective;
which cost with woorkmanshipp above £30; though Rosgill
tyth and Shapp ⟨tyth⟩ demayne should have contributed
pro rata   £030

£200   ⟨About⟩ In this yeare I sowld Lowtherbrigg tenement and
Poake Mill Holme that I bought of Smith and Rumley unto
James Bird lyeinge inconvenient for mee; ⟨for⟩ by which
saile I gained of what they cost mee £50.[1]

In this Springe I walled the Crosse walle in the Birkes for
(*erasure*) the horse close and finished the rest beeinge A
convenient place for keepeinge 3 or 4 horses severall which
cost about   £010

In June [16]64 I gave John Lowther upon his travell   £100[2]

I new repaired the wall from Eshlamoore geate to the heade
of Skellans, and intend to (*erasure*) make a walle from
thence to the far end of Skellans beeinge now the worst fence
about the demesne.   (*blank*)

In July the last yeare I forgott to sett downe I new scoured
about Halfe of the Old Parke tarne which had never beene
made soe deepe and made the brest walle at the low end
of it.

I new made the Pond and traughes at the end of Whinine
Rigge which was very usefull that ground before most part
wantinge water; I new dressed the Newparke Pond in the
Playne, and the Pond in Rowlandfeild which I made new
beeinge none formerly there. This beeinge a very draughtie
Sumer there was want of water in Greenerigges and generally
all over the Country which moved us unto that woorke
that yeare. (*erasure*) By which may guesse how longe it will
neede before another dressinge.   (*blank*)

The last yeare I forgott to sett downe how I sowld the Lordshipp of Thwaites to Sir Willyam Hudleston for £1700 it cost
my father under £1000[3] Soe I gott by it £700 when paid

£1700   of which I have received one halfe and the land itselfe is
my securitie for the remaynder. It was remote and troublesome and I dislike tenant-right estates beeinge, more in
shew than substance and often cheated in fines especially at
such distance.

I bought part of Henry Westgarth tenement of Thrimby
adjoyneinge to our demayne which I lett to Guy Coper-

1. See p. 174.
2. This whole entry appears to have been squeezed in later.
3. See above, p. 26; for re-mortgage see p. 182.

235r *cont.* thwaite for £7 per annum but better worth which cost mee
about £100 and continew the old rent upon the rest; and I
have a lease for 15 years of the halfe of the rest of the
tenement for which I paid £20 in hand and lett the same
to Guy Coperthwaite for £3-10-0d. per annum cleare rent.[4]   £120[5]

235v 1664 About August [16]64 I disbursed for the trade of Guinie
in Africa by my son Christopher £1300; which was paid
Mr Ashburnham to have an accoumpt at 7 years end of
which 2 years was cum before my purchase of his interest
in it of which my Son Christ*opher* is to goe a third part,[6]
he (*erasure*) payinge mee a third of the £1300 with use; which
I was willinge he should doe, for his better inspection into
the preceedethings of which I am to have an accoumpt
and declaration of this from my Son Kitt quod nota[7]   £1300
* In Jan: this yeare I lent to Mr Sayer and Crouch upon the
assignment of a lease from one Wanakers with £1100 he
aught mee £3000 to pay £186[8] per annum at Whis and
Mart [16]65 for 2 years and the principall at the end of 2 years.
Mr. Paryer hath all the writings. This was turned from an
agreement of an absolut (*erasure*) purchas to a mortgage in
regard they could not compass and adjust the debtts betwixt
the creditors and them;[9]   £3100
First payment at Whis [16]65.[10]
In this moneth I lent my Nephew Brathwaite £500 upon
Winderwath demesne but only to be redeemable at 8
monthes, but was intended to have had a lease of it to pay
£100 per annum for 7 years for that £500; *but vaine hopes
of freeinge his Cumberland tenants made him chuse this way
and to mee all thinges of this nature are indifferent   £500
This moneth likewise I (*erasure*) disbursed to Mr Denton of
Warnell my freind £300 upon the assignment of Nag Close
lease for 11 years and of Hoale for 21 years payinge £60
per annum at Mich [16]65 and Ladie day after for 7 years[11]   £300
* Aboute January [16]64 this yeare I lett Mr Tho Birkebecke
have £500 upon a lease of his Bishopprike land to have

---

4. See p. 153.
5. Figure smudged.
6. An investment in the Royal African Company, see K. G. Davies, *The Royal African Company* (1957), p. 66. Christopher's Master, John Buckworth, was a Deputy Governor and Warden, *ibid.*, p. 69 and index. See below, p. 194.
7. *quod nota* a later insertion.
8. This figure has been altered.
9. See p. 174.
10. This line a later insertion.
11. See p. 190. Warnell B.3, and D/Lons/L, Miscellaneous deeds, M1 for the mortgage.

235v *cont.*

£100 per annum for 7 years and ½ (*erasure*) at Mids and
St Tho day [16]65 the first payment   £500
665 In March this yeare I exchainged part of the tenement of
Wilkinsons tenement at Qualle[12] for that of Grysbournes
above Qualinge Heade,[13] which I allow the keper at my will
for his service, and fothiringe my goods and Deare in Winter
in the Old Parke and the New Parke and Rowlandfeild
and gettinge the hay in the fowlds and 4 dayes mowinge
in the parke.
Besides I give him a horse grasse in Sumer tyme. The close I
value per annum at £5-10-0 but will be better after it be laide
beeinge ⟨all⟩ most plowed and out of hart when I exchainged
it valued besides the old rent of (*erasure: space*) drowned
in the purchas   £060
This summer I walled the owte wall at Skellans and added
a smale parcell to it of the moore it cost mee 2s a rood
wallinge (*interlined*: and gettinge) besides leadinge, cost in
all above   £15
* About August I (*erasure*) gave my Son Rich £100 which I
paid by my Son Wandesfords order in part of his rent which
makes £1100 paid to and for him since he went   £100
* In 10br this yeare I bought certaine closes and houses upon
them of Augustine Metcalfe at Setbuske[14] which cost mee   £180
for which to lett him a lease for 21 years at £12 per annum
Item in 9br before I disbursed to Mr Denton of Cardew the
some of £500 for which am to have £100 per annum for
7 years and a halfe at Whis and Mart [16]66 first payment
but for the last halfe yeare if well paid am content to reffer
it to Mr Thomas Denton of Warnell to dispose of[15]   £500
* I bought then of one Oswald Routh of Wensladale A parcell
of land called the Strands which cost   £33 15s.
lett for £2-6-8 per annum[16]
and lyeth convenient for the other.[17]
* In 9br this yeare I purchased that part of the Manner of
Skelton though it should have beene perfected longe before.[18]
It cost 15 years purchas and ½ beeinge £1860 all as good as
paid in hand and to have £120 per annum clear from anie
sesse or deduction, ⟨it⟩ I bought it in order to my Son
Trotters convenience for improveinge and inclosinge the rest

---

12. See above, p. 163 for this tenement.
13. i.e. Whale Ing Heade.
14. Wensleydale, see p. 40.
15. Deeds and letters: Cardew B., 3, 4, 5, 7. For circumstances see Phillips, Thesis,
    pp. 322–323.
16. This line is a later insertion.
17. This line inserted after the previous line. Wensleydale, see p. 40.
18. See above, p. 158; *V.C.H., Yorks N.R.*, II, pp. 408. Abstract of deeds: A1/6, f146.

235v *cont.* of the Manner to pay me for it when he is better able
though only at my pleasure, no wayes bound to it   £1860
But in regard I wanted Martinmas rent which I was to have
had, I paid only £1800.[19]

236r* 1665 About 10br [16]65 I lent Todd of Penreth £50 upon
Franc*is* Low*ther*, lease to have £10 per annum for 7 years
and ½ at Whis and Mart[20]   £050
In March [16]65 I lent Sir Edward Musgrave   £500
to pay £100 per annum for 7 years and ½ at Mich [16]66
and Ladie Day after (*erasure*) first at Mich [16]66: upon a
lease of Sealith Grainge in Abbey Holme[21]

* 1666 The 12th of June this yeare I purchased of Mr Will
Midleton of Belshaw then High Shirifff of Northumberland
the Mannor or Lordshipp of Nether Worshall upon Tease
for which I paid all in hand £3000[22]; viz by a bill of
exchange charged upon Mr Peryer and my Son Chriso.
£2000. Item by a bill Charged upon Jo Pearson at Marton
£600 and paid in monie heare £200 and in a bill Charged
upon Rob Simpson at Egleston £200 in all £3000 paid as
good as in hand   £3000
Nota he said he expected to be able to repurchas it at 4 years
end but I would not promise anie such thinge; though I shall
not be unwillinge Soe I be sure of a years notice and that
the monie be paid at London or where I neede it, though
I did not at the least undertake anie such matter.
Nota that I ame to have £200 per anum by a lease backe to
him for 21 years at Mart and (*erasure*) Midsom cleare free
from all charges and deductions whatsoever Which is considerable as the wordle goeth.
The 3rd of July [16]66 I purchased of Sir Will Carleton the
tyth of Newton and Catterlan in part of his dett which cost
mee upon accoumpt after £46-13-4 cleare rent besides £17-6-8
paid out to the Bishipp and Minster which after 10 years
purchas present monie cost mee   £466 13 4
The rest of his dett of £250 is secured per Frenchfeild but
nota I am but to have halfe of Newton tyth for 1666; and
I must not enter unto Catterlen tyth for [16]66 and [16]67
beeinge lett soe longe and allowe mee in the purchas for
⟨those⟩ those wants £64-16-0[23]
The 24th of July [16]66 beeinge St James his day was

---

19. This sentence written in the margin.
20. Nature of relationship (below, p. 194) with Sir J.L.(2) not established.
21. For circumstances see Phillips, Thesis, pp. 326–327.
22. *V.C.H., Yorks N.R.*, II, p. 262 (citing a fine) states that Lowther bought it
    in 1654. In 1659 he listed it as a lease (above, p. 110). Abstracts: p. xxiii.
23. See pp. 72, 108. For circumstances see Phillips, Thesis, p. 321.

sonsecrated the Chappell at Lowther by the Bishopp of
Carlisle, Bishopp Raynebow at which most of the Gentry in
the Cuntry was present, by which have powre to Chrissen
Sacraments Prayers and Preachinge for the Lordshipp of
Lowther else might be caled a conventickle. The (*erasure*)
Instrament is amongst the Pardons and Patents in the
Evidence Chist quod vide.[24]

* The 15th of 8r [16]66 my son Hugh haveinge beene longe
A Prisoner in Holland taken in A shipp as A Privater came
over for London beeinge redemed for £30 and dyed there
about a moneth after his returne of a Consumptuon
gotten by longe and hard imprisonment, who is said was
much reformed in his temper and sobrietie and dyed very
penitently for his miscariages. (*erasure*) Soe hope he is well
and freed from the dainger of further temptations and from
the miseries the future tymes are like to produce. Which
God divert from this sinfull Iland, haveinge manie
sumetombes of a Consumption;

In 7br before I agreed to lend my Son Jo £700 to pay his
extravigant detts he had contracted and to take the same by
£100 per annum in 7 years the first payment to beginn at
Whis [16]67, and all this will not yet free him, and all spent
without creditt or reputation; God mend him for I receive
noe greate content, but in the hopes of his Son whom I take
care to Educate and bringe upp in my owne way; And am
like to doe the like for his Daughter if shee doe well.

667 About ⟨June⟩ (*interlined*: May) 1667 I agreed for a
Mariage with my Grandchild Mary Lowther with Mr George
Preston son of Thomas Preston of Holker Esq and the 11th
of July [16]67 the Mariage was Solemnised but noe publiq
mariage but only freinds present. I gave in portion with
her as my [*sic*] with most of my owne Daughters which
was £2000 and undertooke to pay £3050 more (*erasure*) for
dischargeinge the dettes and mortgages upon the estate;
And for this £3050 soe undertaken, I am to have (for
£2000 part of it) £400 per annum for 7 years to be paid at
Martinmas ⟨and⟩[25] [16]67 and Whis after; and for the other
£1050 that beeinge forborne and not paid for 7 years more
will in that tyme amount to about £1800 which to cume of in
other 7 years to begin at the end of the 1st 7 years will be
£360 per annum for the latter 7 years; Soe that I am to have
£400 per annum for the 1st 7 years and £360 per annum
for the latter 7 years; besides the portion of £2000 paid of.   £5050

---

24. The instrument has not survived, but Lowther's application for a licence is
    Lowther B.II.7. St. James' Day is 25 July.
25. Ampersand struck out.

236v *cont.*   And I was to pay this £5050 in this Manor viz £1050 upon
mariage or one moneth after (which is paid accordingely)
an other £1000 within 6 moneths after that, and the other
£3000 within 3 moneths after that beeinge all to be paid in
9 or 10 moneths.

And I am to have my £400 per annum out (*interlined*: of)
Bigines (*erasure*) Kirkeby[26] Lordshipp and Preston Richard,
and the lands and inheritances of the Kirketowne in
Cartmell; ⟨but⟩ though if shee happen to dye that (*interlined*:
last) beeinge part of her Joynture then I am to have Holker
Demesne and Parke, mills, and fishings, in lew of it for 21
years; and the Inheritance of Westmerland to be (*interlined*:
all) defezanced upon payment of the afforsaid rents for
14 years. Nota that shee is to have in Joynture the Frith
valued at £200 per annum, and Church towne at other £200
but I to exchange Holcar demesne with the Church towne
for her life as before; this I did in the very juncture
of tyme of The Dutch invasion and Burneinge our shipps
at Chatham[27], when London and all England was in such a
consternation haveinge noe fleet to oppose them that noe
monie was to be gotten in all London the Bankers and all
men refuseinge to pay anie monies, and all men callinge in
there detts though to noe pourpose and it was litle better
in the Cuntry when we could (*interlined*: not) gett a 5th
part of our rents and scarce anie detts; the Dutch and
French with 2 powerfull fleets lyinge upon our costs, And
I relyed upon payment in of above £3000 by one Mr Sayer
and Crouch[28] at London intended to be imployed this
way, but gott (*erasure*) not one penie though under taken
by my Lord Bellases; but the Bankers failed him and hee me;
Soe was glad to use other meane to make good my under-
takinge, which I hope to performe if God blesse mee, and
that wee have noe invasion for then noethinge will be
expected but confusion from which Libera nos Domine.

£90   I paid after £90 and odd which made upp £1800: full £2000
and soe to have £400 per annum for 14 years.[29]

This Somer was a greate Draught for there was but one
shower upon the matter betwixt the Sowinge and reapinge of
the Bigg; wee new dressed a part of the Old Parke Tarne
the pond in Rowlandfeild mended the troughts in Whinie
Rigg; and in the highend of Greeneriggs and brought the
water out of the wells of that I bought of Hen Westgarth
and Cleasby (*interlined*: in Thrimby), that which came into

---

26. Kirkby Lonsdale.
27. See June 1667.
28. See p. 174.
29. This whole sentence a later insertion written into the r.h. margin and the text.

Thrimby Inge beeinge dried upp for 6 weekes together and
most of the Mills in the Contry stood for want of water
though ours by Lawboure and (*erasure*) new Halves and
diginge the dame both above and below the Mill it went and
manie came from Cleyburne Clifton Melkinthropp and all
part abouts, and catle were most starved for want of grasse
and ⟨very⟩ litle hay upon anie dry grounds and yet Bigg
generally good and otes as badd; a greate frute yeare of all
sorts and wee had the grapes come to reasonable perfection;[30]

1667 About the 26th of 7br I bought of Mr Lee of Cleyburne
the Manor and Demesne of Cleyburne for £1100 as good as
all paid in hand, which I was forced unto, haveinge lent
him upon it £500 upon a lease to pay £100 per annum
for 7 years but he faileinge in payment the dett was runn
with charges haveinge had a Judgement for possession at
Law after a suite in Chancery[31]; and besides he had made a
former estate to one Streete and Holt 2 Londeners for 500
yers for £500 of which £424[32] was arrer which I must
(*erasure*) likewise pay to redeeme that estate. Soe it will cost
mee above £1124 besides trouble and charges not valued for
which I have an absolute estate by way of lease and
release (*interlined*: and a fine); And after liverie and seison
given by word (*interlined*: by delivery of the key of the
door) as by a note or memorandum appears; But after the
estate passed I was content that if he paid mee the monies
dew upon it with the costs and charges (*interlined*: I should
be) in repairs and otherways I should be putt unto and gave
mee notice 6 moneth before hand within two years I would
reconvey (*erasure*) it and take my monie, and that was only
verball
In this Moneth my son John acquainted (*erasure*) mee by
letter of his Mariage at London, against his former promises
and professions to mee; this beeinge the 2d tyme he hath
offended in that kinde; I believe there is nether fortune nor
familie, nor freindshipp, (*erasure*) nor anie strength or
advantage (*erasure*) like to be by it but a probable charge,
to the lessinge of (*interlined*: our) familie by devidinge it,
and noe addition to support them, which putts mee to a new
resoulion[33] to setle my estate in an other Mannor then I had
intended it and only to allow him a Compitent subscistance

236v *cont.*

237r

£1124

---

30. In the MS the last two lines have been extended into the r.h. margin.
31. For the loan see p. 172. Deeds: Cliburn B., 10, 11. The suit is P.R.O., C.8/173/67.
32. It is not clear in the text whether 424 or 24 is intended; from the marginal
    entry of £1124, 24 is probably intended. The two London men are named in
    the deeds.
33. *Sic*, i.e. resolution.

237r *cont.* and the rest upon his son who is hethertoe towardly and (*erasure*) to other of my Sons more hopefull and deserveing.

* The 22nd of 8br [16]67 I bought out the Haylands Strands and the Tonnges in Wensladale for which I had 8 years suite with Major and Will Norton and it cost mee in suite about £100; and upon Will Nortons beeinge kild at London I agreed to give Major Norton £40 which I then paid him, and tooke in his purchas from the Citie of London which cost him but about £20; but beeinge in suite above 8 years and I haveinge still the possession I thought better to give £40 then renew the suite; the whole value beeinge not above £6 per annum[34]   £40

* The 9th of 9br this yeare I entered againe upon Thwaites[35] for non payment of my monie dew and arrer, both by vertue of A verdict at the Assises before and by vertue of a letter of Attorney from Sir Willyam Hudleston to deliver mee possession; and soe was to receive that Martinmas and Mich rent; the debt dew by him beeinge 1st 10br [16]67 about £1026 besides charges of suite at Sises about £14.0.0.

* In this moneth of 9br I entered againe upon Thwaites for non paym[en]t of the monie arrer beeinge above £1000 with the Consent ⟨of⟩ of Sir Willyam Hudleston after A recoverie at the last assises upon an Ejectment   £1000

This moneth I cutt the underwood in Ravenrash and fenced and sprunge the same and pruned the okes; it beeing a fitt ground to preserve only for wood and noethinge to be suffered to cum in it as I intend for my tyme and soe advise for the future; for okes will be precious;

* In January I gave my three Sons John Richard and Christopher beeinge all at London for ther better incuragement and contentment £300 viz to every one of them £100 Jo: beeinge said to be sicke and Dicke newly to cum out of Ireland   £300

[36]And my son Johns funerall and nurseinges cost mee beside another   £200
his funerall in all £200

237v * 1667 In 10br his [*sic*] yeare I disbursed upon (*erasure*) the Moitie of Clifton demesne that my son in law Sir Jo L had from Thomas Wharton; and am to have the assignement of (*interlined*: the) the Statute from Barwick Likewise to be

---

34. See p. 40 for Wensleydale.
35. See above p. 175; this paragraph is in the same hand, but a different style from the similar paragraph following. D/Lons/W, Thwaites Box contains many papers relating to this mortgage and re-entry. For Thwaites see p. 26.
36. Rest of the paragraph, including figures, added later. A full notice of his death is on the next page of the MS.

lyable upon both Clifton and St. Bees; but I to covenant not
to make use of it against St. Bees exceipt I be evicted out of
Clifton and this Cost mee which I paid at London about
July [16]67.

237v *cont.*

£250

Though I had the Manor of Clifton the Towne End tenement
and the High Closes adjoyninge upon Buckholme befor
for more than they are worth quod nota[37]

anuary The 8th of January 1667 at 4 in the morninge after
3 weekes indisposition it pleased God to take to his Mercie
my Eldest Son John Lowther beeinge then in his fortith yeare
of his age; Haveinge as was given out Maried one Mrs
Withines of Kent but about August before, though others
think he was maried 2 or 3 years before; and (*erasure*) in
regard upon the first notice about 3 years before[38] declareinge my dislike as an unfitt match for him haveinge nether
freindes nor fortune, he desired to free his thoughts of it,
(*interlined*: and) to goe to travell which he did [16]63 and soe
spent 2 years in France Italy Germanie and Antwarpe, and
then returinge hombe about the springe, and stayinge with
mee untill I had (*erasure*) provided and maried his only
daughter to Mr. Prestons Son of Holker,[39] and taken care of
his Son (*interlined*: and paid £700 for his debtts)[40] he went
upp (*interlined*: to London) in order to the Sitinge of the
Parlement in July, and then after declared his Mariage (*interlined*: in august) which it may bee, he not findinge answerable
to his hopes and not well pleasinge to mee, it may be gave
him some thoughts (*erasure*) not so contentefull to himselfe;
But However it pleased God to give him a short life after
which I beleive was shortened by aboundance of Phelemne
and (*erasure*) bad humors he had contracted in his Stomocke
(*interlined*: for some years before) haveinge often for divers
years complayned in a stopinge and payne in his brest and
Stomocke. I cannot commend him for anie extraordinarie
qualities, as not haveinge his bookes nor businesse, but
rather ease and idlenesse and (*erasure*) somethinge of late
inclyned to Companie I (*erasure*) suppose to devert humors.
And had (*erasure*) as little of, ill, beeinge well natured in
generall and well disposed and jealous in his religion carry-
inge homb the same principalls of religion he went to travill
with which is rare; he did not exceed in companie, nor was
given to anie publique or notorious vice, he was talle in
Person (*erasure*) and growinge a litle corpulent; he died with

---

37. See p. 85.
38. *London Marriage Licences*, ed. Joseph Foster (1887), c.865 gives 25 February
    1666/67.
39. See p. 179.
40. See p. 179.

237v *cont.* much tranquilitie and resignation and full assurance of pardon for his sines and future happinesse (*interlined*: leave the wordle); Soe this is my first borne Son and Hugh that (*erasure*) dyed befor my youngest son; I have overlived; and I besitch God it may prepare mee for my dissolution, by the sad consideracon of mortalitie; which is now augmented by the Newes of my Brother Sir Will Lowthers sickesse whose life is muche feared, which beginin with a paine in his arme which is feared may turne to a Gangeringe and hath putt him in a high fever of which the Docters say my son dyed and wee know not who shall be next but once more I besetche God to fitt us for his owne tyme amen. ⟨for⟩ He was a man of my owne temper and humor and one indeed loved mee soe well as I did noe lesse him then anie of my owne and if he dye not only his wife and children his freinds and cuntry but indeed the whole kingedome will perticipate of his losse, as A Member of Parlement in which he was eminent and jealous both for Kinge and kingedom beeinge not to be buyassed or taken of from the rewles of honor and Justice and ⟨for⟩ a fitt Member both in publique and private affaires and had advanced his estate to about £1500 per annum by providence and Gods Blessinge and maried 3 daughters well and His eldest son[41];

238r 1667 About 10br in this yeare I had a mortgage from Will Fairer of his tenants at Slegill for the loane of   £100
for which I am to have £6 per annum at Whis and Mar [16]68 for 3 years[42]
1668 In June of this yeare I bought ⟨of⟩ out of Roger Taylor of Wensladale[43] the rest of his lands and tenements valued to aboute £15 rent, cost as good as 16 years purchas besides as much bought of him and his father before; qr for the writinges from Ja Metcalfe   £240
In this moneth I disbursed upon a mortgage of Mr Fosters land at Towlsby ⟨4⟩ £500 besides £200 formerly upon a rent charge of £16 per annum, for which am to have alltogether £46 per Annum at Mart ⟨and⟩ [16]68 and Whis for about 9 years and then to redeeme beeinge the tyme of about his Sons should cume to full age[44]   £700
In the beginge of May my wife and I and my daughter Margt[45] went to London to setle our accompts at Thorpe where wee found our Recevier Mr Carill neare £500 in our dett for monie received and not accompted for; and after

41. But William lived until 1689.
42. Deed: Reagill and Sleagill B.
43. Wensleydale, see p. 40.
44. Tolsby, see p. 37.
45. P.V.20.

283r *cont.*

(*erasure*) 14 dayes stay there, and setlinge most of our leases
in our return to London I lent my Son in Law Sir Thomas
Leigh to redeeme him out of (*erasure*) severall ingagements
the sume of £3000 whereof I borowed £1000 of Mr Barker
untill the 19th of 8br and the rest Mr Peryer procured, for
which my son Leigh gave him £30 and I am to have £180
for the use of that and £20 per annum duringe my wives life
in lew of the Blackhouse[46] makinge in all £200 payable at
Ladie day and Mich [16]69. For which I have an assignement
of a lease of 999 years of his lands in Norfolk Sunbery and
(*erasure*) his part of Shewland which (*interlined*: was) mortgaged to one Pecke; aslikewise the assignement of 2 Judgements of Trusells and another for about £750 which will be
lyable upon Thorpe and Adington if neede bee (*interlined*:
after my wives life) (that I cannot get it from Thorpe; beeinge
there was a fine levied to lett in those Judgements by Sir
Francis Leigh). (*erasure*) And besides I have the grant of the
Revertion of Thorpe (*interlined*: and a rent charge of £1100
per annum out of Adington) to strengthen my Securitie all
which putt together may make good my securitie and if anie
part be sowld the dett to be lessened upon payment of the
monie to me and 6 monethes notice beforehand. If it should
please God my wife should dye before payment then the 2
Judgements (*erasure*) beeinge the first in order as is supposed
might be first layde upon Thorpe and halfe of Shewland; And
if my Wife should live soe longe as the dett should out growe
the securitie (*erasure*) they may be layde upon Adington
because of A fine that was passed by Sir Francis Leigh,
which letteth in those 2 Judgements at least quod nota. Nota
likewise I have a surender of Sunbury for my better
securitie.[47]

⟨About Mich 1667 forgotten in that yeare Thwaites before⟩
I ⟨lent⟩ disbursed upon a mortgage of Fairebancke both
freehowld and copihowld ⟨to have⟩ for £350   £350
for which to pay £70 per annum for 7 years and a halfe
⟨the fir⟩ at Martinmas [16]68 and Whis yearely, from Mr
Simpson.[48]

* In July my Ladie Pembroke sent mee a grant or warant for
My Lodgeinge for my Selfe and Servants in the Greene
Chamber and that adjoyneinge, for my life,[49] as a testimonie
of her Love and affection; In returne whereof I doe usually
send her a Buck at the Assises as beeinge better than hers
that lye abroad and not quiet;

---

46. See p. 86.
47. This sentence a later insertion.
48. See p. 189, below.
49. D/Lons/L Letters, 1668.

238r *cont.* * Son Wandesfords detts (*erasure*) of £650 turned to a rent of
£130 per annum upon Thimbelby for 7 years 1st at Mart
[16]68   £650 00 0
February [16]68 Mr Sandfords dett of £200 for which Mr
Orfer stands bound with £140 more lent and use of the
aforsaid sumes and of £100 dew by the tenants makeinge in
all[50]   £380 00 0
secured by deede and fine from Mr Sand*ford* and his wife
and Mr Winch and his wife to pay £22.16.0. at Cand yeare
for 4 years and the principall likewise at Cand 1672 pro ut.

238v* 1668 More lent after upon the same securitie[51] for Son Rich   £025
vide a[52] note of observations upon Mr Sandfords Setlement
that it is imperfect for want of licence and atturnement the
land beeinge in lease, soe that my estate if needefull may be
helped and made good thereby:
Nota likewise that there is £200 still dew upon the mortgage
of the Powdunes; which hath prioritie of his setlement by
neare 2 years[53] and £100 now dew upon the tenants securitie
of ther tenements
In this moneth of February upon accompt of receipts and
disbursements out of ⟨his⟩ (*interlined*: my Son Prestons)
estate ⟨and⟩ at Kirkeby [Lonsdale] and Cartmell[54] wee
(*erasure*) Changed the lease I had of £400 per annum for
14 years (*erasure*) And in lew thereof and of the principall
monie then dew upon accompt beeinge £3334.00.0 which
£334 (then paid him in monie)   £334
I tooke a grant and release of all condicons provisoes and
Covenants of redemption conteayned in the defezance he
had; with a new provision in the said Release that if he paid
£200 per annum beeinge the just use at Midsom and Xmas
[16]69 and £100 at Mids [16]70 and £3434 the remaynder of
the use and principall at Xmas ⟨70⟩ 1670 then he to enter all.
Nota that I had then likewise an assignement of all his interest
in the Rectorie of Cartmell for my further securitie haveinge
the deede from Suell to my Son Pres. and his father to warant
his estate;

---

50. Thomas Sandford's wife was Elizabeth, sister of William Orfeur of Plumbland
    esqr. d. 1681. See William Jackson, *Papers and Pedigrees mainly relating to
    Cumberland and Westmorland*, vol. 1, ed., Mrs. Jackson (CWAAS, Extra Series,
    V, 1892), p. 197; C.R.O., will of Bridget Orfeur, 1666. Sandford's mother's
    third marriage was to Mr. Winch (C.R.O., will of Mary Winch, 1680). See p. 70.
51. Rest of line a later addition, see p. 70 for Richard's involvement.
52. Altered from one.
53. Rest of paragraph a later addition, annotated [by Sir J.L.(2)]: *vide the accompt.*
54. For this mortgage see p. 179.

Nota that I am to have £150 per annum made good out of
Kirkeby and Preston Richard and £50 more cleare out of
Cartmell to be paid at Midsom and Xmas yearely for the said
2 years; in which tyme it is to be hoped ⟨it may⟩ somethinge
may be sowld to pay of the whole debt.

Nota I have the first defeazance ⟨in⟩ delivered in which is to
be safely kept untill all be paid; And nota that the covenant
therein (*erasure*) for Kirkeby etc to goe to the younger sons
can take noe effect untill those payments therin mentioned
be performed which is never like to be; and besides ther
beeinge a release of all covenants and provisoes by the
parties themselves doth vacate that covenant, if ever it should
be insisted upon; and besides I have the defeazance it selfe both
parts and they noethinge to shew for it, but however it will
be fitt to have a fine of all passed for better securitie and my
estate is fromm the Rawlinsons as well as the Prestons who
had the estate in Mortgage which see all the evidences and
the Charter of Kirkeby delivered in; but nota that ther is
wantinge the Deede of the Mannor of Kirkeby from Witherington to Geo Preston my sons Grandfather though their be
a Recoverie of it and the demesne (*erasure*) pro ut patet;

6]69 (*erasure*) March (*interlined*: the 27) [16]69 I burnte the
Limekilne on the Hall Bank which had about 16 fother of
Coles and 10 of wood; and sett most of it in the high end of
Barney feild unto the Knaw about 5 acres (*erasure*) to reduce
that course land to more use and value beeinge one close
nearest for tylage it is most clay; though lyme be more
proper for mixt ground, and that which is dry and broken
eareth or moorish. I (*erasure*) gave £1-15-0 for gettinge
stones and breakinge and couchinge the kilne with one to
helpe it cost about in coles and leadinge £5 in stone gettinge
breakinge and leadinge £3.0.0. in wood £2.0.0., besides
leadinge out by me a whole weeke with 2 draughts and 2
Cates; in all about £18.

* In this yeare and the yeare before I repaired the barne
(*interlined*: at Cleaburne) and new slated one side of stables
and oxhouse and mended the leade gutters and caried leade
from Lowther cost mee near about £50

In July this yeare I new built the Barne at Casterton[55] and
Repaired and new tymbered and slated the dweling house
and other charges cost mee about £⟨40⟩
£50

669 I then repaired the Water Mills at Kirkeby Lonsdale;
and built a new water well and Repaired the mill dam which
is very chargable that it takes away most of the profitts of the
Mill and not like to be helped it cost mee about (*blank*)

238v *cont.*

239r

---

55. Property of Sir J.L.(2)'s grandson, see p. 170.

239r *cont.* * I was at charges in gettinge and leadinge stones to the New oxhouse and Barne at the low end of it at Yeanewith, which formerly studd neare the Gardinge and Cousin Dudley upon a suit was at cost of walinge, and removeinge the tymber, and I found wood that wanted, and to inlarge it about 8 or 10 yards longer then formerly it will cost mee in wood and lawboure above £15 and her asmuch

    Nota that in these last years I found noe incuragement to purchas anie land, since the tymes have beene soe badd and unsetled (contrary to hopes) both by greate land taxes which went away with at least a tenth in one place with another; And low rates of all comodities as catle sheepe corne wooll that the tenants wee had, manie failed, and turned upp ther farmes, soe that I was forced to send servants into Cleave-land[56] Milby Wensladale and other places, and to keepe much in my owne hand to my greate trouble and losse; which was not my case alone but generally all England over Soe that what I spared I returned it for London to make what I could otherwayes (*interlined*: of it) and serve it as well as I could, untill tymes were more certaine; And that a fitt oppertunitie offered for a purchass of some considerable estate together, that may probablie howld the rent, for of late years one could not buy anie things but that it did fall of the rent, beside constant and troublesome taxes of all sorts, and horse charge and the like. And its very diffcult to finde a good purchas of (*interlined*: a) good tytle, in or near the way of ones other estate; well tenanted, and well neigh-boured, all which are considerable in a purchas;

    * In August I lent my Cous. Claveringe that maried my Cos Midletons Daughter of Stockell and his brother Mr Ridell of Gatesheade upon the Toll and land at Bowes and upon a Judgement entered by them of £500 defezanced (both) that upon payment of £15 at Cand [16]69 and £515 at Lamas [16]70; then to be voyd; they had the estate by Mr Tunstalls will and Mr Tunstall had it by purchas from Mr Hawneby but the estate is not worth the monie, soe much depend upon the Judgement if the other fall short

    About this tyme I disbursed upon the wood at Lambehagg in Skelton in order to the errectinge the Allam workes to Redshaw £440; whereof paid in part £120 the rest not paid but am to receive for the barke backe againe £149

    * This yeare I bought a parcell of land of Phillip Emerson adjoyneinge upon Selby Hagg at Skelton for Allom rock in it, and to compleate the other without which I could not have wrought the Allam workes as I intend, with my son

(blank)

£500

£440

---

56. i.e. Marton, Tolsby and Nunthorpe.

Trotters assistance, for way leeves and liberties to build
houses near Saltburne
The land I lett againe to Emerson for £4 per annum it cost
16 years purchas viz
I may have £150 per annum for the libertie to woorke
* In October in pursewance of my former intention my son
Trotter and I did joyne with one Mr Shipton a kinde of
Quaker, who had beene skilled in the Allome workes

239r *cont.*

£064

and had beene braught upp under his father[57] who managed
the Greate Allom workes under my Lord of Molgrave[58];
that wee should sett upp an Allom worke ether in my ground
or my son Trotters where most convenient and every one goe
a third of charge and profitt; for 31 years; only I was to
have over and above a full third part £100 for the benifitt
of my Rocke of Allom as most convenient, And my son
Trotter to have £50 per annum for the accommodations of
the house wayes etc and £50 to Shippton for his sallery when
imployed in the worke; and if anie ley downe anie part of the
Charge more than another to be made good by the Allom
workes as (*interlined*: an additionall) securitie; or rather to
enjoy the same untill reimbursed what shall be soe laide
downe; in which Lambe Hagge is included to be paid for
(*erasure*) by us all etc pro ut per the artickles, quod vide,
and what I disburse more than they[59];
* In 10br [16]69 I lent Mr Lanc. Simpson upon the release of
covenants of Fairebancke £250; for which he is to pay £15
per annum beeinge the use for 6 years first at Whis and
Mart 1670; and the principall beeinge £250 at Mart 1675
which said £15 use is to be paid with the former rent of
£70 per annum and for the said 6 years; makeinge the
yearley pay £85 per annum for 6 years; and the said ⟨240⟩
£250 principall at the end of the said 6 years viz at Mart
1675
* To which securitie is added a bond and Judgement (*interlined*: upon it) of £200 for performance of covenants of the

239v
[16]69
and
[16]70

£250

---

57. Thomas Shipton, Steward of the Earl of Mulgrave, managed the earl's alum
     interests from 1653 to *c.* 1665; his son Matthew worked for the earl in 1673.
     R. B. Turton, *The Alum Farm* (Whitby, 1938), pp. 174, 177, 182, 193.
58. Difficult to read, either Molgrave or Margrave. From the context I think
     Lowther meant to write Mulgrave (see previous note, and *ibid.*, pp. 66, 159;
     V.C.H., Yorks N.R., II, p. 407). But Margrave Park in Skelton was the site
     of an alum works and Lord Conyers and Darcy, who had an interest in the
     manor, worked alum, but I know of no Shipton connection (*ibid.*, p. 408; Turton,
     Alum Farm, p. 184).
59. Lowther's dealings with the Crown over alum mines are summarised in *Calendar
     of Treasury Books 1669–1672*, pp. 383, 389, 784, 1230; see also Turton, *Alum
     Farm*, pp. 191, 192.

239v *cont.*   deeds quod vide and cale for the fine of Mr Bird at Mr
Simpsons charges[60]

* Jan [16]69 I lent unto Mr Denton with the arrers of the
former rent charge of £60 per annum with £224.10.0. more
paid in monie to make upp his debt upon accompt the sums
of £450[61]; ⟨for which⟩ as dew at Michelmas before ⟨for⟩
upon a release of covenants of the former estate of Hayclose.
Bothell, with addition of the Toll of Penreth for 21 years and
land at Sebram and other personall securitie for performance
of covenants by Mr Lamplugh and 4 others; for (*erasure*)
which he is to pay £90 per annum at Ladie Day and Mich
[16]70 and soe for 7 years; save that the Mich rent is to be
forborne till Martinmas yearely by my consent in regard he
pretended his rent was but then dew   £450

In Aprill I agreed with Mr Henry Browham to lett him have
£125 to have £25 per annum for 7 years the[62] ⟨first payment⟩
at Mich and Ladie day the first payment at Mich [16]70 for
which I have the assignement of the Lease of Plumpton
tyths,[63] and in regard ther wants (*erasure*) a licence for that
assignement, I have further a lease for 99 years of the Brigg
tenement; for makeinge good the rent for 7 years   £125

* 1670   In June in pursewance of a former agreement I ⟨lent
upon⟩ paid further unto Mr Hanby £200 upon the absolute
(*interlined*: purchas) of the tenements and lands at Gilmanby
the Toll and castle and lands at Bowes, with all the Colleries
and Leademynes in the Manor of Bowes Bawbran Spitle
Stowekeld etc which maketh the whole sume paid £700 for
which I am to have £45 per annum at ⟨Mich and Ladie⟩
Lamas [16]70 and Candemas after; (*erasure*) free from all
sessements, upon a lease for 999 years made backe againe to
him and his son; with a provisoe for non payment to reenter   £200
Nota I keepe £100 part of the £700 untill he gett his quietus
est for beeinge Receivor to the Kinge; and the rent dew at
Lamas next to be deducted out of it. * He to pay all out
rents to the kinge and otherwayes; I am further to have 140
load of Coles (*erasure*) and 100 catle and 20 horse and 200
shepe towle free upon my note or tickett they are myne

* In July I bought of Wm Walker of Yeanewith the land at
Pokemillbankes with 4d rent in my Grandsons Jo. his name,
it was lett to Mr Bird for 40s per annum dew at Michel
next, but I have only 20s for that tyme, it cost mee[64]   £015

---

60. See the mortgage on p. 185.
61. See the mortgage on p. 176.
62. *The* should also have been struck out.
63. Plumpton, see p. 69.
64. For significance of lease, see p. 174.

670 This yeare about July [16]70 I should have bought of   240r
Crouch and Sayer Upper Worshall Eyscliffe and Ayslaby
and Preston but Mr Bellingham bought Worshall over my
heade and soe I would not buy the rest but returned my
monie to London to be (*erasure*) reddie for the first opportunitie[65]

* In August this yeare after I had beene with my Lord of
Carlisle at a foot race at Langanbye I fell sicke occasioned
partly by a cowld I gott then; And soe continewed in a kinde
of Rumatisme and distemper over my whole bodie but
especially my stomocke (*erasure*) all winter untill May that I
went to London, haveinge had all the Dockters from Yorke
as Dr. Taylor Dr Witie[66] ⟨and⟩ Dr Kempe and others. I
was 20 dayes in my Journey to London with my wife and
Daughter Margarett; And at London had Dr Fisher the
Kinges principall Phisition, Dr Whisler and Dr Wharton[67];
and in August followinge viz 1671 I was advised to Tunbridge
to the Waters, and after drinkinge of them for 3 weekes and
of Hepsom Barnet, North Hall, Winson and Suningehill
waters I recovered in my part my stomocke and sleepe, And
returninge to London I had a flux of humors ⟨that did⟩ or a
tumor that discended upon ⟨my⟩ (*interlined*: the) right side
of my codd which swelled to the bignesse of a Gouse Egg
or more, upon which by advise of the Phisitions and
Surgions I was Cutt by Mr Mullines[68] the Prime Surigion of
London, after the part was molified by stupes prepared by
the Appothicarie to extenuate the matter and make it more
fluent, upon cutinge whereof with his instrument ther
sprunge out as out of a springet, neare a Pinte of matter as
Cleare as Sacke, which wee kepte above 4 monethes in a
glasse without much alteration; and about 4 monethes after
was Cut againe and was then but about halfe a pinte of like
matter, after which cuting the part was as litle and as much
falen as ever it was; And the payne not soe much as lettinge
of blood, beeinge but only as a pricke with a pennknife: But
afterwards the matter increased, but not soe much as the
Surgion though safe to cutt it Soe I was advised to goe to
the Bath in Sumercettshire where after I had beene 3 weekes
and druncke the waters ther, and at my Nepew Sidnamans

---

65. See p. 174 for the mortgage; Lowther had already bought the nearby Nether
    Worstall, above p. 178.
66. See Wm. Munk, *The Roll of the Royal College of Physicians* (2nd ed; 1878),
    I, pp. 401, 413.
67. For these men see *ibid.*, pp. 347, 249, 255; for Wharton see *D.N.B.* also;
    Whisler was a distant relative, *CW2*, XLIV, p. 103.
68. See *The Diary of Samuel Pepys*, ed. R. C. Latham and W. Mathews, (1974),
    VIII, p. 41.

240r *cont.* at Brimpton neare Bristol which is a very good water for
stone and purgeing I returned hombe in June with my wife,
and left my Daughter at Schoole at London and sent my
Grandson Jo Low*ther* into France with my Grandson Kitt
Wandesford into an Academie in Paris for a yeare or 2; And
since my returne to Lowther have beene better in health,
though not freed from that tumor or swellinge in the same
part though not to that bignesse nor trouble as before, but
what it may grow to in tyme I know not but its a gentile
admonition and remembrance of mortalitie, and not to be in
love with the world.

This Journey and my Phisicke and expence cost mee above   £1000
But in the tyme I was at London which was a full yeare
from May 1671 untill May [16]72 I did disburse and lend
there sumes of monie (viz)

1671 About the (*interlined*: 21 of 8br) 1671 to the Earle of
Strafford upon a Mortgage of his Manor and Lands at
Wentworth Woodhouse in Yorkeshire and other lands
therin mentioned; and A Judgement and other securitie
which Mr Massam and Mr Peryer[69] hath; and

240v 1671 is for payment of £420 per annum at the 28th of Aprill
[16]72 (*interlined*: and 8br after) and for payment of the
principall beeinge quod vide at and upon pro ut; about 8be
[16]72   £7000

* 1672 June the 8th [16]72 I lent then per Mr Massam to Mr
Burcher upon securitie of land neare Yorke and dew the 8th
of 8br [16]72 with use for which Mr Massam hath the
securitie with a Judgement putt in the chest with Mr Peryer   £1000
Item ther abouts Lent for mee by Mr Peryer unto the Mr
Pebles Clarke of the Peace for the ⟨North⟩ (*interlined*: West)
Ridinge with my Brother Sir Willyam £1500 whereof my part
was £1000 dew and payable upon land and tyth securitie
about 8br 1672 with use pro ut per the securitie (*erasure*)
which Mr Peryer hath beeinge in trust for us both in my son
in law Sir Jo Low name[70]   £1000
July the 7th or ther about, lent more for mee by Mr Peryer
to my Lord St. Johns upon Breareton in the Bishopricke
besides his former dett of £2500 to pay about the 7th of
January [16]72 with use pro ut per the securitie Mr Peryer
hath quod vide   £1500

* In May this yeare I bought Burells house and lands at
Thórpe cost mee   £106

---

69. Mr. Peryer, see p. 152. Mr. Thomas Massam was a scrivener contemporary
of Mr. Peryer, but not in partnership with him so far as is known (Steer,
Scriveners Common⌐Paper, pp. 119, 122, 123, 126; Woodhead, *Rulers of London*,
p. 113). Massam witnessed Sir J.L.(2)'s will (P.R.O., Prob.11/350, f20).
70. Sir John Lowther of Whitehaven, Bt., P.IV.8.

240v *cont.*

Rosgill fines In August this yeare I compounded with the tenants of Rosgill for a generall fine upon the death of Mrs Wormeley,[71] wherein the tenants did submitt to mee for ther fine of 20 years old rent but in regard of ther submission, I was contented to take 16 years old rent of the old tenants, that were not chainged in my tyme, and 12 years old rent of those that had fined to mee neare before, which they kindly accepted; the rent beeinge neare £15 per annum did come

£200   unto about about [*sic*] £200; in 4 years tyme which was in regard a fine was questionable for the most part of the rent of those I had admitted tenants before

Clifton fines In the same moneth I agreed with the tenants of Clifton ⟨to⟩ in lew of the generall (*erasure*) fine ⟨dew and⟩ claymed by mee at Mr Wibers death, and to setle ther estates as customarie tenants payinge the old yearely rent, they (*erasure*) agreed most of them to pay mee 51 years the old rent as present payment from Michelmas [16]72, which

£800   would amount neare unto £800; and I to have a third of the Comons and my proportion for my old rent I have beeinge about 22s for Hartley and Howcarle tenements and Remeyes and Newnehow and somethinge else not bought[72]

Yeanewith fines In 8br before (*interlined*: [16]71) my (*interlined*: she) Cous*in* Dudley dyed at Yeanewith beeinge 18 years after I purchased[73] the reversion (*interlined*: after two lives) which then cost mee neare upon £2200 and is but about £220 per annum though valued to mee at £250 And in February last my Servant Will Akinson compounded with all the tenants there beeinge about £14 rent at 20 years old rent for a generall fine upon her death to be paid at 2 six monethes after

£250   which would come to about £250 and now I lett the high demesne for £100 per annum and the low demesne and tenement at £72 besides the Mill and rent per annum about £30

* About 10br [16]72 my son Christopher dyed of a consumption and I paid for his debts and funerall above   £200[74]

[£]700   * Nota about M [16]72 I received of my Grandchild Prestons[75] daughters portion £500 which I must be answerable for; and

---

71. She was the heiress of the previous lords of the Manor, the Salkelds of Corby. For the purchase see p. 72. In this case, in the cases of Clifton and Yanwith below, and generally under tenantright, general fines were payable on change of lord by death, but not by purchase.
72. For Lowther's foreclosure of Clifton, see p. 85. Deeds and enfranchisement: Clifton B.I.1. For Howcarle see p. 153. The last line of the paragraph is an insertion.
73. For purchase see p. 71.
74. The whole entry a later insertion.
75. P.VI.2, see p. 179, for marriage.

240v *cont.* I had of my sister Suson Hare[76] £200 putt into my hand at her desire to pay £10 per annum for the use of it about May [16]73

* About this moneth I subscribed for my self and Son Christo*pher* for the Royal Companie[77] £380 besides £120 was dew to me to make upp the sume in all   £500
transferred to my Son in law Sir John[78] in trust for mee quod nota

241r * 1672   The 3d of 9br [16]72 I tooke A mortgage of Mr Sandford his wife and son of part of the demesne mill tenants rents ⟨and all⟩ tythes, Sattery Parke etc and had a fine and recoverie thereupon; ⟨with a⟩ for £1200; with A defesance that upon payment of £60 per annum at Lam and Cand [16]73 and soe for 4 years and the £1200 at last Candlemas then to reenter. The use of the £200 part of the £1200 beeinge accompted and allowed before hand soe noe use to be paid for that untill Cand [16]76 beeinge the last payment of 4 yeares and then if not paid the use will be £72 per annum; and I am to have tenants boones to make good the yearely rent for the £60 per annum for 4 years

Notatt his former debts was included in this sume and the mortgage of Powduns allsoe.[79]

Nota that the 8th of 9br [16]72 I made the new Bridge in the end of the Millfeild for the better managment of Yeanewith demesnes, and for intercourse betwixt them, and our better accomodation; for which I cutt 7 or 8 of the best okes in Clifton Fitts worth £20 and in lawbourers and wages about £10 in all cost   £30
but I would not have it for horses, for spoylinge the ground on both sides; and wearinge the bridge

* The 15th instant I lent Sir Edward Chalenor upon (*interlined:* a mortgage of) an estate of land in Buckingehamshire £3000 haveinge had £500 in part before to pay £180 per annum halfe yeare and the principall at two years end, which will be fitt then to be called for since I like not soe well of the securitie; for which see the tytle to that estate in the Greate Booke of evidences[80] ther entered; Nota that Mr Massam hath the securitie with other writeinges; to be putt in the Chist for that use   £3000

* Nota that about ⟨February [16]71⟩ 10br [16]72 I lent unto Cous. Francis Lowther of Penreth upon a mortgage of his

---

76. Sir J.L.(2)'s second wife's sister, see p. 66.
77. The Royal African Company, see above, p. 176.
78. P.IV.8. This line a later insertion.
79. See p. 70.
80. See p. xxiii.

land at Penreth with what he ought mee before in all £250   241r *cont.*
to pay £50 per annum for 7 years (*erasure*) first payment to
be at Lamas and Cand 1673[81]   £250

* New yeare eve was the greatest flood of waters had had [*sic*]
beene knowne in memorie, which caried away my New
Bridge, And Langanby[82] bridge which had been thrice build
and cost each tyme the Country above £1000; butt all my
bridge save one planke was cast upp in the Ilands in
Buckholme, and Clifton and the furthest in the Mr Birds
ground below Lowther Bridge Soe intend to have it upp
againe next Sumer and make it higher which was the defect,
for the water went a yard over the topp of it which I see
my selfe; and bidd 2 or 3 floodes before the last which was
the greatest;

* About June this yeare I bought Hartley tenement that
adjoyneth on Howcarle[83] for the better inclosure of the
Comon formerly designed and to make a litle demesne there
together which cost mee £37 besides the generall composision
drowned in it beeinge 12s rent at 60 years purchas is more
£36 more Soe it stands me Consideringe the sinckinge of the
old rent at least in   £73
And I builded a new Barne upon it cost mee   £15

* About Aprill this yeare forgotten I bought of the severall
(*erasure*) fee farmes rents due to the Kinge out of Asby
Ayton; Egleston Abey, Marton, Shapp tyth, Hallgarth
Sledall, amountinge to about £14.17.2. (*interlined*: per
annum) in all at 16 years purchas cost about with passinge
the securitie about[84]   £240

* March the 22 [16]72 Lent at London by Mr Massam to Sir
Tho*mas* Garett for 12 months Securitie mortgage with him   £1500

* In this yeare and part of the next yeare my Grandson cost
mee in France in travel and in returne hombe above   £0400
And my sicknesse and Bath Journey and Phisitions above   £0200

1673 etatis mea 68   241v
In May lent Mr Peryer to Mr Moore of Lerpoole[85] upon
securitie of his land there and Sir Fr Radclifes securitie to
be paid pro ut quod vide with Mr Peryer £3200[86]   £3200
£3000   But I received then about of Mr Bramley £2000 and Pebles
£1000 towards disbursement; which was formerly lent
Witsunday this yeare I lent Mr Rookesly with the £300 he

---

81. See p. 178.
82. This word altered.
83. See pp. 153, 193.
84. See pp. 36, 146.
85. Liverpool?
86. The marginal figure altered, and this figure written for clarity.

241v *cont.*   ought mee before £600 more, makinge in all £900 upon the securitie of lands at Rookely[87] of the value of £70 per annum; secured likewise by the tenants for the rent for 3 years, redemable then pro ut   **£0900**

May the 17th lent Cous Anthonie Lowther[88] per Mr Massam and in Ger Bartons name   **£0600**

July the 10th lent then per Mr Massam to Mr Witherington and Sir Francis Radcliff *Securitie* ob etc   **£0500**

* Lent Cous*in* Sandford the younger upon Powduns for Mrs Winch her life to pay at Lam [16]74 and soe yearely £7.4.0. and £127.4.0. after her death pro ut[89]   **£0127 04s.**

The 30th of 8br [16]73 Lent per Mr Massam to one Mr Walron of Sumersetshire upon a lease for 1000 years of land and statute pro ut for 2 years to pay £210 at May day and the 1st of 9br yearly and the principall at the end of 2 years   **£3500**

Franc. Lowther lent omitted before to pay £50 per annum at Lam and Cand [16]73 for 7 years[90]   **£⟨250⟩**

Geo Fothergill lent to pay at Lady day [16]74 £200   **£⟨200⟩**

In 10br 1673 lent Mr Wicliff junior and other 3, *Securitie* bond dew pro ut; paid per Robt Simpson for mee he hath the bond in keepinge   **£200**

* In 9br of this yeare I cutt the springs of wood adjoyninge on Clifton ground from the topp of the hill to the waterside and sowld it for £26 and excepted all Oke Elme and Ashes, which was above 40 years growth, and might have had £30 for it above 16 years since but it decayed and grew thin and out of the way for use soe best for sale; and for to improve the wood the better   **£26**

In February I agreed to sell a smale tenement in Quale which was Chr. Wilkinsons[91] of 8s rent to one Bird to howld anothere tenement there for £60   **£90**

And to Jo Warkeman a tenement late Lanc. Chapelhowes of the rent of 6s8d for £30 at Longe dayes both which I purchased as uselesse to mee; both together £90

* But they are to continew to pay rent fines and services as others doe.

Item I took then of Jo Cragg a tenement that was Hugh Michells of 6s 8d rent in £26 debts besides 2 fines dew one upon forfiture to mee, and another if it had been sowld againe as it would, Soe I aacount it stands me neare £35 and but worth per annum above the rent about £2.10.0. per annum,

---

87. In Yorkshire.
88. P.III.14.
89. See p. 70.
90. Noted as: *set befor.*
91. See p. 163.

and I meane to plant the high end of the croft towards the
Scarr with Ashes for a shelter and ornament to the house and
lett the litle close next the well heade and the 2 acres and
$\frac{1}{2}$ in the feild.

* In 9ber [16]73 I sowld Hansom coppes at Thorne beeinge a
deare yeare for fire at London Coles beeinge then above 50s
a Chalder in regard of the warr betwixt England and Holland
£74   for £74 this beeinge the third tyme it hath been cutt since my
last mariage in the tyme of 22 years

* 1674 In July this yeare I lent Sir Rich Sandford[92] £700 which
with £348 formerly dew made upp £1000; for which I am to
have £200 per annum at Mart [16]74 and Whis after or within
20 dayes after (interlined: for 7 years) this is secured by a
lease of 999 years of lands at Howgill and Milburne not
intayled and by the like lease of Somerhouse and Morton
Tinmouth[93] beeinge my (interlined: old) Ladies Joynture and
assigned to Sir Rich to inable him to make securitie thereof
to mee; And, for further securitie of the £200 per annum the
tenants bound in 7 bondes, to pay the said rent mentioned in
the provisoe of the defezance; And though Sir Rich hath
made

A lease to his Mother for payment to her £100 for her life
and £900 to her sones and Daughters pro ut by the lease and
redemise which I have; (erasure) of the lands not intayled,
(erasure) yet my estate ⟨for⟩ of the same lands for my £300
formerly lent, and a release of Condicons made the yeare
after makes my estate good and to have precedence of her
estate of the same lands; Though I desire not to make anie
advantage but only for secureinge my just debt, of £1000 to
be paid £200 per annum pro ut ante

About June ⟨or July⟩ my Lord St Jo. and his trustees and Sir
Philipp Howard did grant and assigne ther interest of a lease
of 1000 years of West Harelsey and Rawneton to my selfe
and Jo Lowther my Grandson And ⟨wee⟩ covenant by Sir
Ph How. to pay £126 the 23 of June [16]74; and £135 the
14th of 10br after; And £4635 the 14th of June [16]75;
makeinge in all £4896 Mr Peryer hath the assurances and a
fine upon the estate formerly passed to secure it to my Lords
trustees,

* In May [16]74 my wife and I and Daughter went to London
in ordei to Match my Grandson Jo Lowther with (erasure)[95]

241v cont.

£35

242r

£1000[94]

£4500

---

92. Sir Richard Sandford of Howgill, 2nd Bt.
93. The last two properties are in Co. Durham.
94. Figure altered.
95. The word *Sir*, omitted in transcript, should have been erased. Letters relating
to his marriage negotiations are D/Lons/L, Letters, John Lowther, 1st Viscount
Lonsdale, to Sir J.L.(2), 3 October 1671 and 18 August 1674; marriage settlement: Lowther B.IV.14.

242r *cont.*   Katherine Thynne Daughter of Sir Henry Frederige Thynne
of Glostershire, and Neece to Secritorie Coventry and Sir
Will Coventry which was treated on by letters before and
he likinge the younge Ladie, it was shortly concluded, and
£5000 portion given in hand but above £1000 was spent ther
upon that occasion, And the 2nd of December they were
Maried at Henry the 7ths Chapell by the Bishop of
Rochester, and thereupon I setled in joynture Yeanewith
and other lands of above £750 per annum Joynture and
£100 more aded for mayntenance which was more then
ordinairie in regard of the relations

And I then lent the said £5000 and £6000 more in all £11000
to Thomas Thynne (*interlined*: Esq) her Brother who had
lately Maried the Earle of Winchelseys Daughter by whom
he had given by the Dutchesse of Somerset one of the coheires
of the Earle of Essex; the Manor of Drayton Bassett etc in
Staffordshire payinge out of it certaine debts and legacies
wherewith the same and Essex house were chargeable to the
Docter Wearener then Bishopp of Rochester; Soe for discharge thereof the Bishopps (*interlined*: executors) Sir
Philipp Warick and his Trustees all joyned in the securitie
by (*interlined*: the assignement of) a lease of 1000 years
worth above £800 per annum to pay the Consideracon yearly
for 3 years (*erasure*) viz (*erasure*) £330 halfe yearely the 11th
of May and the 11th of 9br the first in May [16]75; And
all ther writinges with the fines and other securities mentioned in the booke[96] of the severall securities were left in
Mr Peryers custodie in the chest for that pourpuse amongst
others[97]   £11000

* 9br   the 10th and 11th a lease and release of Grayrigge and
Lambrigge and the Parke ther; (*interlined*: from Mr Duckett)
with a provisoe upon payment of £72 per annum at Whis
and Mart [16]75 and [16]76 ⟨[16]77⟩ and £1276 at Mart
[16]77 to be voyd   £1200

A lease for 99 years of Grayrigg demesne mill tyth,
Bethom demesne for 99 years for collaterall securitie,
together with assignements of 2 Anuites (*erasure*) from
Tho Dalston and Mr Layburnes and also assignment of a
statue of £1600 for better securitie and the Mortgage of
Lambrigge Parke taken in upon payment of the monie to
Mrs. Ducketts trustees,[98]

242v–257r   *Account of the family by Sir J.L.(2)'s grandson, the first Viscount Lonsdale,*
with an autobiography. (ff247–250 missing).[99]

---

96. See p. xxiv.
97. *Amongst others* in another ink.
98. These properties passed to Sir J.L.(2)'s grandson, see Grayrigg manor box.
99. Sir J.H.(2) died 30 November 1675.

APPENDIX I

SIR JOHN LOWTHER (1)'S AUTOBIOGRAPHY

(D/Lons/L, A1/1, ff.335r–361r.)

[Hand of Sir J.L.(1). Changes in ink and style are indicated by an asterisk at the beginning of a paragraph. The MS is numbered pp. 1–33 in a contemporary hand in ink; and, in pencil, pp. 34–47 in a modern hand; both these numberings are here omitted. Throughout the for thee has been expanded silently. Words written as continuations from page to page are here printed on the first page only.]

335r   My sonnes I prayse God for you who hathe at this time made me a father unto (*interlined:* you) thre and one daughter. (*erasure*) I shall daylye pray unto him for you and that he may Increas your number, and posteritie so long as it shall please him, ⟨the Inlargeing whereof and long continuance being a great blessing⟩ not for that I am (*interlined*: not) (nor[1] wowld have you to be) Ambituos of the vaine[2] glorious tytle of antiquitie in your familie (although it be of great estimation and not to be contemned but (*interlined*: fōr) that it is a testimonie of God his blessing to your familie when he dothe inlarge it and maketh it florish like the brode spredding and fruitefull vine and doth continue and upholde it with wealth and woorshippe (*erasure*) without ⟨wealth⟩ whitch (*erasure; interlined*: wealth) the supporte and upholder of Gentrie and wordlie reputation nobilitie or gentilitie is a vaine and contemptible tytle hear in England and allwayes hathe bene; and of the contrarie the degree of wealth (*interlined*: is) the degree of gentrie[3] for of anntient times before the Conquest he that had so manie Hides of land was admitted as a lord to come [to] the Parliament untill afterwards it was upon the Barons wars limited to those onely to whome the King did send his writ, and yet at this day we have now waye knowen to make a Gentleman but his Competent wealth for the meintenance of sutch an estate dothe give him that tytle, though the way of making of knights (at this day verie comen) by the Kings laying his sword upon his showlder saying Rise up Sir Henrie hathe a particuler ceremonie as aforesayd: to whome at this day being manie poore ones one might say to manie as the Bishopp that met the priests and sayd God Morrowe Clearks to whome they replied we are no Clearks but priests then he sayd God Morrowe priests that are no Clerks[4] so may you

---

1. A different ink used for the interlineation, and to alter *or* to *nor*.
2. Smudged or struck out.
3. L.h. margin, note begins adjacent to *for: Vide Camden Britania f120. Cooke in his seventhe reporte 33. 34 and in his 9 reporte 124.*
4. L.h. margin, note beginning adjacent to *so* has been struck out; reads: *Nota Sir Richard Fletcher the chapman with whome I may allie.* Erasure by the same ink as n. 1. See P.IV.2.

say unto manie knights Good morrowe knights that are no gentlemen, wherfore my sonnes wherein I

speak to all your posteritie in you preserve youre estate if you will preserve   335v
your gentrie and nobilitie of Blood whitch is nothing els but a discent of
(*erasure*) Ritches, wherein I teatch not Querenda pecunia primus virtus post
numeros, but that by wisdome and good discretion you carefully governe
the estate and honor left unto you by your Auncestors, whereof I wowld
have you make conscience not to dissipate and in an hight of follie to
misspend that whitch you never toyled for, whitch daunger youth in their
pride and high conceyt of themselves apt to be flattered in their oune follyes
often fall into, consorting themselves with Companie above their calling,
els out of their weakenes triumphing and takeing glorie in the chaire and
to be the best man of the Companie and soe to consorte and have in their
companie base persons and Parasites and they to pay for all. Of whitch
extremes I wish you to take hede and ⟨an⟩ to have an especiall ceare in
the choyse of your Companie for it is a trew saying tell me with whome
thou wilt goe or be, and I will tell thee what thou wilt doe (for Quibuscum
vixeris talis eris). This counsell and direction more aptlye might have
followed in another place yet am I not sorie that it is placed here in the
Begining for that it is one principall thing next after the service of God
whitch I wowld have thee to regard and is a difficultie; for as we say a litle
wealth maketh the wits to wonder and I know ((*erasure; interlined*: maior)
est virtus querere quam parta tueri) for he that is bred and brought up with
wealth of meanes and enter to his estate and liveing meinteinining the (*interlined*: credit) porte state and hospitalitie of his Anncestors hathe or aught to
have as mutch care and trouble in the orderly spending disposing and
ordering of his estate as he that first purchased and acquired the same, who
in his beginings was not

tied by expectation of anie to keepe anie (*interlined*: sutch) state as he is,   336r
unto whome a great estate and manie frinds (I mean kinred) are left who
as they are a comfort so they are a charge especially unto the Head of
their house whitch charge and care he that can say (Ego meis maioribus
virtute preluxi) and is the first beginner and founder of a howse or familie
is freed of, and not troubled withall. Wherefore my advise is to thee to take
hede and not to think thy credit or reputation to consist in great expence
for that without order and great care may consume thee, even in Hospitalitie,
whitch is the honestest waste if it be orderlye, yet take care to prevent that
for Quantum quisque sua nummorum habet in arca tantum habet et fidei)
theirfore looke warilye unto the howse since thow art like to be a howse
keper for it was the Rule of a wise statesman to have his hospitalitie rather
plentifull for his degree then sparing and yet but to spend the third part
of his revenewes in his howse his estate divided into fower parts other tow
parts for Apparell wages and other ordinarie occasions and the fowerth
part to put in thy purse for extraordinarie events and things whitch may
happen. These precepts thus unorderly placed as they be, yet have they this
reason that if they be neglected and that by disorder and misgovernement
the revenew of Our familie should be spent and our posteritie be scatered
abrode as persons withoute note and of no regard and being of noe place

336r *cont.*   certein (whitch needs must followe the ruine of oure estate) then showld
all the residew and sequele of what I shall write be voyd and of noe effect,
since it is onely purposed unto my sonnes sedem et locum meum tenentibus.

336v   Bodin in his booke de Republica is of Opinion that (*interlined*: it were good
if) the Inheritance whitch came from our Auncestors by discent (*interlined*:
were) ⟨ought⟩[5] not to be forfeited for treason or felonie or other cryminall
offence for the forfeiture whitch is a punishment for example to kepe other
Offenders from the like dothe rather by the forfeiture produce the contrarie
affect for the Chyldren and familie whitch were meinteined theirby are
utterly left without meintenance and brought unto extreme povertie and
soe being fallen from their hopes and from the course they rested upon
being not brought up to labour cannot frame them selves to humble them
selves with their fortune but become insolent disperate and apt to attempt
anie stratagem whereby to live or rayse their fortunes, and wee soe by
the law given by God himself unto the Jewes and Israellites their fathers,
what regard he had for the discent the Continuance of ther Inheritaunce
in their tribe and families that if it were sowld away it showld revert in
their Jubile and that the Brother should rayse up issew unto his deceased
brother without issew as we have it translated a Rule seming contrarie to
the degree of mariage limited unto Moses; but in trewath an exception in
case he die without issew, and to that people onely as Beza in his Booke
de Repudiis and Callvin are of Opinion wherein they Aunswer the objection
of Juday his sonnes married to Thamer and the saying of Naemi in the
booke of Ruth as aforesayd and that the brother is taken sometimes for
the Coozen Germein who they are of opinion may marrie together

337r   howsoever may perhaps faintly prove the proposition and that I know a
weake argument or bad proose doth weaken and bring distrust to the cause
and impare the treweth before those who are not Juditious, soe allsoe the
Juditious will supply it with their knowledge and meditation, and my sonnes
I wowld not have you require at my hands an exact and orderly composed
treatisie for that my time ⟨is⟩[6] otherwise imployed and I am at this
present exercised in the practise of the Law whitch requireth an whole man
and all his time, and whatsoever I write now is at houres of leysure whitch
will make it a disjointed woorke, havinge forgotten when I begin to write,
what I writ last, yet how soever imperfect for the publique view yet doe
I hope and soe require that my imperfections be borne withall by you my
sonnes that shall read it to whome my naturall Imperfections are hereditarie
though the goodnes or vertew if anie be given me from above doth not
goe by discent but by the guift of God and Instruction; for whitch end that
if anie thing be in me Inclining unto good or that by example or precept
might move you theirunto I ⟨that⟩ who am the means to derive ⟨originall⟩
corruption unto you thought it my deutie to instill into your hearts sutch
drops of grace as I have received sofurfoath as I can that I who gave life
under God might adde somewhat unto it for use and ornament whitch I
am moved unto by this perswasion that what soever we receive or hear

5. Interlined and struck out in the same ink as p. 200, n. 1.
6. Smudged?

of our Auncestors we doe more willingly imbrace it and practise it then   337r *cont.*
we wowld doe from anie other though[7] reason be the same thing
from whome soever it procede yea as we say be it sung or be it sayde, yet   337v
surely hathe it not the like effect, and having found this to be trew In mine
oune experience for that I have ever given great regard to the sayings of
my memorable Grandfather and that it might be proved by infinite examples
as of ⟨him⟩ (*interlined*: one)[8] who when he was perswaded in the treweth
of Christiane Religion by a Monke and of the daungerous estate he stoode
in in paganisme and infidelitie did become Christiane yet when he asked
what became of his Auncestors who were kings as he was and that it was
answered that they were all in daunger of damnation, whereupon he revolted
and sayd he wowld rather goe to the divell with his anncestors then to God
with him, whitch example though it be not to be followed yet sheweth it
the great desier we have to be like unto our anncestors (*interlined*: yea) even
in evill things mutch More in good, yet verie manie of our English papists
led by their forefathers Errors at this day refuse our Church and congregation
upon noe other reason then for that they will be like unto their fathers, who
are not to be Guides unto our conscience (*erasure*) for then the Reprobate
Gentiles showld not have converted nor we from the Jewes. And in this
my purpose I was incouraged by the example of M C Cicero and of Oure
King James that now is of England the first of that name who have written
unto their sonnes Bookes of their offices and deuties as directions and guides
through the manifolde cumbers and passages of this wordeld, whitch I will
not take upon me to doe for it mutch excedeth my abilitie besides the
diversitie of occurrents are sutch as no man can meat with theim all and everie
particuler subject requireth a particuler treatise or particulerly to be observed   338r
and is best learned by experience and observation how to deall in theim
and to manage our affaires with respect unto the times the place and
persons, and the learning of negotiation and managing of our affaires by
precept is noted by Sir Frauncis Bacon in his booke of the advancement
of learning as deficient and imperfect and undertaken by fewe yet proposed
by Solemon and handled by him in his booke of Wisdome whitch he their
noteth and giveth manie of his Rules a coment or exposition and illustration
and the reason he giveth why it is so litle practised, in former ages to write
in this kinde, and In this our age allsoe when everie mans pen is so rumitike
that it is ever Runing, is not for the unworthines of the subject or that it
is not necessarie or that it is Impossible but that it is indeed Infinite and
knowen to few and yet necessarie to be given in precept so far as we can,
for (est quoddam prodire tenus si non datur ultra) and that whitch is not
begun shall never be polished, and though Solomon the wisest of men
and Jesus the sonne of Syrack hathe given manie excellent lessons (whitch
I wish you my sonnes to observe) yet the practise and length of time doth
perfect and amend everie good begining (for nemo simull invenit et perfecit)
and Sir F. Bacon their allsoe cyteth that the gravest and wisest of the
Romanes and of best experience were woont to come unto a publique place

---

7. Final *h* in a different ink.
8. Erasure and interlineation in same ink as p. 200, n. 1.

338r *cont.* at certein times unto whome manie resorted for advise In matters of Importance as the estateing their lands matching their daughters and other negotiations, to whome I may best compare our English Lawyers men best experienced in wordly busines yet everie

338v time hathe in it his alterations whictch must be observed and foloed for he that chaungeth from the times wherein he liveth and seteth ⟨either⟩ eyther after noveltie or innovation or antiquated antiquities doth antique like appear unto other men, wherein it is good to avoyd all singularitie of opinion and to approve that whitch is generally approved least in condempning the generall current singularitie appeareth in the end to be grosse and foolish. But my principall Intention is to leave unto you my posteritie With the evidences of my lands allsoe these undigested notes as evidences of my heart and minde whitch is the best purtreiture, and my owne observations and practise in my perticuler and somewhat toutching other generall occurrents in my time as occasion serveth Wherein I will with Jospehus in his bookes of the wars and antiquities of the Jewes professe and protest unto you that this woorke I take in hand is not to paint myselfe unto you and to extoll my oune actions (unworthie of comendation) ⟨unto you⟩ but sincerely and trewly to deliver everie thing whitch I shall set doune, desiring thee my sonne whosoever shall read me silently to passe over my infirmities and to adde what thou thinkest amisse, for noe humane woorke is perfect, and yet their are degrees tending to perfections of whitch mine howsoever the meanest yet thought I not good to be silent but rather thus to spende my Idle time then otherwise and to leave some memorie of me not vaynely to eternish myself for I know that of the life of man and all his actions in time ther is no more memoriall or token of ⟨the⟩ it then of the flight of a bird in the eier or in the winde whitch vanisheth

339r with the flyght, and howsoever the observations I write may be found better perhaps in manie others (*erasure; interlined*: and that) nihil dictum quod non dictum prius yet have I towld the reason why I wowld have thee know what I have practised for that it preceding from me thy anncestor though in a rude style yet may it perhaps move thee more then a Rhetoricall oration or a more polished writing, for allthough I doe mutch commend Eloquence in speatch and writing for that it dothe highly extolle and advaunce a good Action and their by doth more inamoure and draw the affection of the hearer to it and move him to the pursuet thereof and that it is able better to discribe everie action then anie can doe it and is theirby of great consequence and of an extraordinarie power to allure and move us unto vertew and of the contrarie can decypher and set foorth vice to be soe loathsome and so scandalous and so hurtfull to deterre us theirfrom and to bread in us a detestation theirof yet is their an error whitch manie men fall into by the love theirof to hunt so mutch for woords as they do loose their matter, whitch is especially to be avoyded besides substance is more to be insisted upon then forme whitch is but the accident especiallye in a man of authoritie and in a Judiciall place, wherfor howsoever in the authoritie of a father I might speake unto thee unlimited to forme, yet will I not so doe for I will not comand aniething but perswade since comaundment is vayne where their is noe constreint to inforce it, besides the matter I intreat

of is rather Counsell then comanndement, whitch I pray thee kepe unto   339r *cont.*
thy selfe and in thy familie who are bound to make
a favorable construction of my doings and to Intende the best since everie   339v
man aboundeth in his oune sence and noe man can trewly enter into the
depth and meaninge of an others conceit in his writeings and the verie accent
or manner of speatch dothe manie times alter the sence of the same woords
and maketh therin good or evill, theirfore since all things are good or evill
according to opinion and that of crosses and losses we may some times
make as good use as of benifits and pleasures theirfore I advise thee
not to be peremptorie in opinion nor selfe conceited, but willing to hear
and to be advised er thou deliverest thy opinion, whitch if it be subitane
is often upon better consideration recalled yet not without some toutch,
especially if it be in writing or publique whitch was a reason that moved
Dimosthones an Eloquent orator that he wowld not write, being theirunto
moved by cause as he sayd he might be contrarie to himself and often speak
ageinst his writings as our famous Lawyer the Lord Cooke Lord Chief
Justice of the Comenplees delivering his opinion contrarie to his bookes
⟨and⟩ being towld of it observed and sayde (dominum cognoscite vestrum)
forgetting the first part of the verse which is Actaeon ego sum dominus
etc whitch some then present sayde he had good occasion to Remember;
(this by waye of meriment and private for thee to laugh at, I hope to be
no great offence in an other age when he is gone.) Of these[9] directions
though thou perhaps might tell me I might have doone well to to have made
use of my self and to have beene silent (to that I answer I doe but speak
it unto my self in speaking unto thee of whome
thou art a member and discovering my whole heart unto thee I desier thy   340r
secrecie and soe shallt thou know us of this age and somewhat from us,
that may doe thee some good, and inable thy Judgement; and by compareing
times let (*interlined*: thee) see the time to come in providence as farre
differing from the time present as the time past differeth from the time
thow shalt live (*interlined*: in), yet by the waye let me advise thee and
learne out of my experience least thow learne repentance by thine oune
experience, that is, not (*interlined*: good) too mutch to busie the minde with
providence and forecasting of what thow wilt doe at sutch a time and at
sutch an age and soe of all other melancholie conceits whitch trouble a
woorkeing braine (*interlined*: a thing wherein I have erred)[10] least thou think
so mutch and of so manie things that thow forget to doe the effect of the
thinkeing, for manie times more time is spent in thinking of it then wowld
doe it and wee spend mutch time in thinking of that whitch we shall never
doe, and in care what we shall doe in times to come, before whitch manie
crosses happen may happen [*sic*] and oure purpose often alter. We neglect the
time present and care not for that whitch ought to be moste precius and
of whitch I advise thee to have a speciall regard yet not soe that thow use
onely a dayes care or care for the daye for the saying in the Gospell (Care
not for tomorrowe) hathe a larger extent, for we see the verie birds (their

---

9. *Whitch* struck out and *these* interlined over it.
10. Interlined in the same ink as p. 200, n. 1.

340r *cont.*   used as instances that they take no great care for foode or rayment and
yet they want not) have care as the swallowe the wood cock (birds best
knowen in oure clymate) doe chaunge their habitation and foresee winter
and somer and provide for it as the emmet[11]

340v   or pismire provideth allsoe in Somer for winter and generally all birds being
aierie bodies doe comonly a weak before a storme flock togither for their
temperature doe first feall the Chaunges of the eier and they resorte to
hedges and townes for foode and covert and the (*erasure; interlined*:
hedgehog)[12] will stop hir hole on that side the wind will turne unto before
it chaunge but first, she maketh it before she stoppe hir nest as all birds
doe providently and conveniently for safetie from daunger and nearnes of
foode soe must thou first set thy estate and house in an order and let the
times for all provision and disbursements beforeseme and apply those times
when they come allwayes observing to be beforehand with thy provision
and to doe it at the best time and rate least it cost thee double and in sutch
an Order things goe forward eatch knoweing his deutie and time yeaven
when thou slepest yet hereat cleyme no privilidge to slepe for without
oversight and a watchfull eie good orders may be broken, and theirfore
I am of opinion and have heard it well expounded by good Devines that
the (*erasure; interlined*: morowe) that must not be cared for is times a farre
(*interlined*: offe) and remote possibilities too mutch care for Childrens
Children, and ever for oure oune Children yea and for oure selves too, for
it is not he that strives nor he that runs the best that allwayes wins for
their are stumbling blocks in the wayes but as God giveth the blessing and
Increas, to whome we must leave the successe soe that we walke orderly
in our Callinge, for I have observed and thou shallt for that in everie calling
one of as good merit

341r   and desert having like wealth like favour and like woorth cometh not
(*interlined*: to) the same end that others in the same profession doe, and
some that have none of these become greater then he that hathe theim
all and he that hathe but one dothe manie times as well he that haythe
more, yet the Ordinarie waye is to be pursewed, for though the fables say
that fortune be blinde yet seldome doth she run into corners, but kepeth
the brodewaye where if thou wowldest she showld stumble on the cast to
mete hir, for their is she as Like to be as els where and stumbleth upon
thee moste in that walke thoe sometimes she goe by paths, and to cyte
the Instances of the great and supernaturall woorking of the almightie that
maketh Kings Beggers and Beggers Kings shall be an Idle labour for the
wholie Bible the stories of the Romaine Emperors our English stories and
everie time is and willbe full of theim, whitch I prey thee learne to knowe
and acknowledge, and theirin shalt thou see as in a glasse thine oune
frayltie and the omnipotencie and manifolde manner of woorking of thy
maker, whitch in thy private meditation I prey thee think upon, and it will
give thee great contentment and will reconcile thy wondering thought and
set thee at peace with thy self and all men whitch though perhaps upon

---

11. *Emmet* and *Pismire*, terms for the ant (*O.E.D.*).
12. Ink as p. 200, n. 1.

a sudden it may (*interlined*: be) disturbed and thou distempered yet when 341r *cont.*
thou art come into a better temper and in thy cowld blood thow wilt recall
thy self and represse and lay aside these sudden distempers of humane
thoughts[13] whereunto the best (*interlined*: of) our forfathers have often
fallen, and yet never finally and totally fallen. And that I may not seme
to prescribe
that unto thee whitch I have not in some sort practised my selfe and doe 341v
desier to doe and least thou may say unto me that you preatch patience
unto me (for sed tu si his fas aliter censies) I will speak unto thee (*interlined*:
by) example (whitch teatcheth better and moveth more then precept for
we care not for nor do believe their doctrine whose life is Contrarie and
a good orator that wowld move others showld in his action showe that
he is moved himself as the Cock that wakeneth others first beateth him
self with his oune wings and awaketh himself, before he Crowe) and theirfore
I will trewly set thee doune mine oune lief and my whole course not as
an example for thee to imitate (and ne plus ultra) but to give thee all the
help I can to stirre thee uppe to amend those things in thee, whitch were
faults in me unto whitch by nature thou art of kinred (for I doe assure
thee thou hadest an honest mother) and that by my oversight and neglects
as allsoe by my miscariage thou mayest beware and become better (for felix
quem facerint aliena pericula tantum) whitch (*interlined*: happines) I wish
thee and that though in this declining age for the generalitie we say seldome
proveth the sonne the fathers better)[14] yet doe I not doubte but that the
auntient woorth of oure Auncestors may be Revived in you whitch is at
this time, through want obscured.

26 decembris Anno domini 1612.[15]
And now to begin to declare unto thee, my self and mine oune lief, though
perhaps thow lookest for and requirest at my hands an auntient pedigree
to give thee an high discent, whitch manie (*interlined*: doe affect and some
undertake) whitch if they were strictly examined must have perhaps some
slips of Bastardie, or a feined father to fetch it farre as the Welsh men doe
who with ease will ascend unto the Flood of Noah but sutch is not mine 342r
intention for the treweth is I am as yet a straunger at home and in oure
evidence who are in my fathers custodie and I would have no untreweth
found in me, and oure beginning or from whence we came I cannot perfectly
tell, but this I presume of, that as I myself cannot tell soe noe man els can
tell or call us upsterts, for by good evidence without date, it appears Our
begining is without date, for I have Evidence under seall of the Veponts,
who writ theim selves de Veteri-ponte who lived in King Johns time here
in England where we of Lowther were witnesses amongst others of the best
ranke in the Cuntrie and in King Edward the second his time oure Anncestor
Sir Heugh of Lowther was his Attorney generall and afterwards Justice
Itinerant called Justice in Eier as appears in Fitzherberts abridgement of

---

13. *thoughts* added in the same ink as p. 200, n. 1.
14. It is not clear where this parenthesis commenced.
15. Date in l.h. margin.

342r *cont.*   the Law title Corone Pl (*space*) in the third yere of Edward the third as
allsoe in my Lord Cooke his seventh booke fol 7 in the cases of the
(*erasure*) statute of Winchester, who allsoe cites our anncestor in his
Cataloge of those that were lawyers whose families florish at this daye in
his Epistle to his second booke, but that Sir Heugh was no Anncestor that
Raysed or advanced his house for he was the sonne of a woorthie knight
and our house of Lowther was in oure familie long before that time
(*insertion*:[16] as appears by the charter of King Edward the first of a free
warrein and Parke granted to us in Lowther now in our evidences) though
names did take their setling but about that time as Verstigan in his booke
of English antiquities unto the King doth write as allsoe as Cambden, for
before they were called John sonne and Tom sonne, and had comenly but
one name

342v   as Adam our forefather of us all had whitch one name was given upon
reasons as his was signifieing earth or read cley whereupon he was made
and as thow mayest observe in the wholye byble, reasons given wherefore
moste were so called upon their birth, and as I sayed in or about the
Conquerors time the sayd antiquaries as allsoe Mr. Cotton are of opinion
that tow names to one man came into England, unto the Courtiers and
better sorte and in King E*dward* 2 time begun to be generall[17]; for they
saye that then they tooke unto theim names some from their trades as
smith ferrers, others from their place of Habitation as Clyfford who was
the sonne of (*illegible*) tooke his name of the Cliffes and Rockes as
they reporte in their writings, as allsoe Mortimer and Warren tow great
English families, and of divers names yet were tow brothers, whereupon
some have sayde that Veipont, Lowther and Musgrave were of one howse
and chaunged names by their habitation, whitch they collect by their Cote
armes whitch they give that is all of them bear six annules thre tow and

one in this order and they varied onely in colors for

Veipont bore gules and or, Lowther Or and Sable, Musgrave Aisure and
or, whitch variation of cowlers they say was the difference of brothers
Haralldrie being then not so perfect nor in the same fashion that now it
is, but what the treweth is I leave it to the fruitelesse labour of those that
will seartch for it, but this I know that Sir Heugh Lowther did bear tow
names, in E*dward* 2 his time as aforesayd and he and Sir Robert who tooke
Andrew Hartley Earle of Carliell were cyted in the great cawse in the Court
of Wardes betwixt (*interlined*: Franncis) the Earle of Cumberland[18] and the
daughter of George his brother (who cleymed the Countie of Westmerland
as heir in the generall tayle unto the Lord Veipont, whose heirs Clifford
and Leyburne maried and all survived to Clifford) for that they had made

---

16. The insertion is written in the l.h. margin, with a sign in the text, in the same
    ink as p. 200, n. 1. The document, of 1283, is still at Lowther. I have not
    been able to trace a text in the P.R.O. calendars.
17. R.h. margin sewn in.
18. L.h. margin, note: *sequitur*, see p. 224 below for this controversy.

notes that Andrew Hartley had taken Brougham Castle and Burned   343r
Clyffords evidence, whitch Castle was their in the owlde booke then showed,
sayd to be in the custodie of Sir Heugh Lowther, whitch they urged to this
end, for hear the question rested that they pretended whereas King John
gave unto Robert Veipont and to the heirs of the bodie of him and his
wife All his lands whatsoever in Westmerland (except knights fees ⟨howlden
of his person⟩[19]) and allsoe the Sheriffewicke of the same by the name
of the Bayliwicke, whether the heirs of Veipont before the statute of Donis
conditionalibus (whitch created an estate tayle) 1301 had sowld and retaken
the same and soe gained an absolute fee; whitch cowld not be proved, 2
and admit they had not then if the Kings had not granted the reversion
after it became an estate tayle, whitch they pretended he had because moste
offices found the discent in fee, (interlined: and) then was the estayte tayle
barred by the fines of George Earle of Cumberland, and they alledged that
the King had granted the reversion but the same and manie other evidences
were Burned by the sayde Earle of Carliell and although their be noe grant
recorded as divers were not in those times and some perished that were
in the Civill Warres of Yorke and Lancaster yet shall not a man loose
his lands theirfore but upon a generall isseu it may be founde, but this Office
past ageinst the Ladie Anne Clyfforde heir of the bodie of Veipont and
with Francis Earle of Cumberland heir male upon his brother George his
estate tayle by him made allthough the proofe was very pregnant of the
other side in the Opinion of Sir Thomas Strickland[20] who was the foreman
of that inquest and gave no verdict and some other understanding Gentilmen
with him yet the same being but an inquest of Office and their being above
twelve agreed their verdict was taken and so certefied and Allowed (interlined: my Coosen[21]) Tho. Carleton being then Eschetor.
* 2 December 1613[22]
And now to retorne unto my self leavinge oure petigree untill hereafter.   343v
I John Lowther sonne of Sir Christopher and Elinor[23] his wife daughter
of Willyam Musgrave of Hayton Castle, was borne at Lowther[24] and
brought up a schollar at Appelbie under Reginalde Bainebridge[25] untill
eightene yeres of age in whitch time yeaven in my Infancie I was provident
by nature for greater matters, and careless of lesse, and spent mutch time
and vaynely pleased my self in meditation what I might attein unto aspiring
at great matters and contenuing mean though since I finde mediocria firma
by nature to mutch Inclined to revenge even in my youth and to plotte
the means upon the present heat but upon a cowld consideration repentant
that ever I purposed it and apt to forgive whitch continueth in me still for

19 Perhaps underlined as the rest of the parenthesis rather than struck out; ink
    of both as p. 200, n. 1.
20 Of Sizergh Castle, Westmorland, died 1612.
21 Interlined in ink as p. 200, n. 1; he was later Sir Thomas Carleton of Carleton
    near Penrith, Escheator 12 Feb. 1608 (List and Index Soc., LXXII (1971), p. 31).
22 Date in l.h. margin.
23 P.II.2.
24 Baptized at Lowther 24 February 1581/82.
25 For him see CW2, XLIX, p. 239.

343v *cont.* I praise God he liveth not to whome I will not be a frind if he will be a frind to me observing that revenge provoketh an other Injurie, and is ever unprofitable and ungodly, and even in humane pollitie except by Just corection it disable the partie to rise agein it provokes a new Injurie. In (*interlined*: all) my mothers life I was greatly beloved of hir who died when I was about foureteene yeres owld[26] and my father was austere unto us all and kept us allwayes abrode, after eightene years I was sent to London to the Innes of Court and their admitted to the Inner Temple and there left with small means, unaquainted, without anie direction or help for my Studie,[27] in whitch time haveing a trew taste of my fathers wants I was constreined to husband a litle and to live of a litle whitch I did and applied the studie of the lawes verie close for allmoste tow years and red mutch whereby I atteined some generall uncertain knowledge but no certain Judgement whitch is geined by setled reading multum and not multa

344r in whitch time my Uncle Lancelot[28] in his absence left me the keyes of his Chamber where findeing divers writings of my Grandfathers, as a dede of feofment to the use of himself for lief with remeinder to my father intayle with power of Revocation and divers leases and annuities made to his younge sonnes and the same dede revoked, amongst others I found something by whitch it was like that he had suspended his power of Revocation and disabled himself to revoke[29] of whitch takeing advantage I copied the dedes and refused to give them to my Uncle to whom they belonged not but gave theim to my Grandfather Sir Richard whose estate being then declining through manie troubles by the follies of his younger sonnes, and he and my father being of a differing nature my father jealous and he grieving to be suspected and offences taken manie times betwixt theim, and especially in this that my father would never be drawn to consent to anie reasonable anuities to his younger brethren, for that it was covenanted otherwise at my fathers mariage and his charge of children was great, whereupon he had of himself (the covenants of my fathers mariage not being bindeing)[30] doubled the annuities whitch he wowld have required my fathers consent unto and let out Hackthroppe demein to my Uncle Willyam for 200 years,[31] for prevention whereof I copied the writings unknown to theim and did deliver theim to my Grandfather, and still reteined his love, at whitch time my father being Indebted and not able to meintein me was constreined to marrie me and sent unto me verie loveingly to knowe my Inclination theirunto and nominated unto me my now wife

---

26. Buried 6 June 1597 at Lowther.
27. Sir J.L.(1) was admitted to the Inner Temple in 1599 and called to the bar in 1609 (W. H. Cooke, *Students Admitted to the Inner Temple* (1878), p. 155.)
28. For his legal career see *CW2*, II, p. 10 *et seq.* Sir Francis Bacon was also of this Inn; he had Lancelot appointed a Baron of the Irish Exchequer in 1617 (H.M.C., *Hastings MSS*, IV, p. 52). P.II.6.
29. Similar deeds to those mentioned are in Lowther B.IV.17.
30. Marriage settlements of Sir Richard and Sir Christopher: Lowther B.II.4, 5.
31. In William's marriage settlement, 22 June 1600, deed: Lowther B.II.5. For the resolution of these problems see p. 220. P.II.8.

the daughter of Mr Fleming deceased whome I had sene being there with   344r *cont.*
my Coosen Tho. Carleton who was a seuter unto hir.
Upon whitch motion I entered into consideration how that my present   344v
meintenance was like to be taken away and my hopes and course overthrowen if I maried not I theirupon prayed unto God that if it were convenient for me and that I might like the woman it might procede otherwise
not and resolved to marie at whitch time my father had like hope yeaven
full assurance to have maried my wifes mother and the mariage cloth[32]
were bought by consent and licence gotten but that not succeding my
mariage was like allsoe to have stayed, but I foreseeing my oune extreame
was willing to goe forward and within six weaks maried my now wife[33]
wherewith my Grandfather was not made acquainted but yet afterwards
was pleased and if my father would have given him £200 having received
£1000 in mariage with my wife he wowld have estated all his lands upon
my father after his death and Wethoppe in posession, but I cowld not
perswade my father to give aniething and soe that oportunite was lost, but
in my mariage I had this difficultie imposed upon me to satisfie my wifes
frinds that my father had the remeinder of all my Grandfathers lands and
power to estate theim upon us and our issews and to augment our Jointure
after his decease[34] whitch I Cowld noe wayes doe but by the copies of those
writings I had tooke as before and yet I gave satisfaction theirin resolving
with my self so soone as my means and meintenance was setled to retorne
to my Booke and make it a profession to preserve oure estate whitch was
then to like to fall to decaye we being to manie to have gentlemanly
meintenance out of that smale liveing, conceiving besides it was not honest
to live in no profession
and that it was unfitte for me to professe anie other studie but the lawe   345r
in the opinion of the times, and husbandrie I presumed I cowld resorte unto
when I cowld not procede in profession ⟨but⟩ (*interlined*: and) considering
how that upon small beginings mutch painefull husbandrie is but litle sence
and buildeth but up a small fortune without long time, I resolved to goe
forward in my course of the studie of lawe partly howldeing myself bound
theirunto bycause I had begun it ever howlding it for a principle in all my
course that it was a shame to begin aniething soe unadvisedly as to be forced
to fall from it, if it were possible without extreme prejudice to be effected
knoweing this allsoe that paynefullnes and providence continued doth
advance and bring to great perfection the meanest profession or trade,
whereas chaunge of purpose and of course hathe manie vaine hopes but
bringeth nothing to perfection, wherein I was ever in all my courses con-
siderate of the means to the end for though finis be primus intentione yet
is ultimus executione, and I ever kept my self within my compasse and
undertoke notheing but that I cowld performe and was ever the maister
of my woord in great and small matters wherein I found mutch pleasure
and ease and did visible see trouble and dannger in the contrarie In whitch

---

32. R.h. margin tightly sewn.
33. At Candlemas 1601/2; marriage settlement 2 October 1602, Lowther B.II.5.
34. But see p. 212, n. 35.

345r *cont.* my course I was not so Ingaged but that if crosse fortunes and great mens
disfavors oppressed me but that I cowld ever with safetie retire my self
into the cuntrie with some advantage during my life to be geined by my
profession if I lived but in my oune howse, besides the help in the government of my oune estate and the understanding theirof.

345v For I approved that opinion that it was not good for anie man soe farre
to ingage himself and his fortune in one course that if fayled he were
undone as the fable of the two frogs expresseth it well that in a drought
in somer having removed to manie pooles and all dried uppe the one advised
to goe doune to a deepe well Whitch was not like to be drie but the other
desired to be satisfied how they showld doe if that showld be drie allsoe,
for it was soe depe they cowld not get out agein, whitch when they cowld
not satisfie they wowld not enter into it but rather take other courses wherein
their is allwayes hope, and that if one doe fayle they may undertake another,
upon whitch considerations returning to my booke to spend my youth in
it whitch I then neglected I sawe ther was no other time for it, I left my
wife in loveing tearmes perswading and prevayleing with hir modestie and
honestie for bothe our goods, and once a year came doune to se hir. In
whitch our mutuall absence we bothe I dare professe it lived honestly and
avoyded the temptation of companie and oppertunitie the greatest allure-
ments that might be, in whitch time my wife lived with hir mother at no
charge to me for hir diet nor mine when I came, by means whereof my
estate at Meaborne being but then of the yearly revenew of £72 did meintein
us and with some casualties and our providence Increased yearly soe that
I praise god it is now bettered and I have a thowsand pounds in personall
estate saved out of that and my practise of the law this tow years[35] and
£20 a year of Increas of Jointure whitch I had by my Grandfathers decease,
not being otherwayes Inritched by anie fortune or frind no not by mother
in law who was (*interlined*: a) ritch widowe of[36] whome

346r * March 1617[37]
I never had aniething given me of valew yet[38] geined I an opinion of the
Cuntrie by hir ritches that what she had I might have, whitch I did know
was not soe for hir hart was addicted onely to hir sonnes and to advance
theim esteming one of the woorst of theim above all hir daughters, of whome
neverthelesse she did thinke well and loveingly as they well deserved; they
being all honest and discreete and competently matched as their state then
was the eldest to (*interlined*: John) Ambrose of Lowick the second to John
Senhouse of Seascales the third to Anthonie Barwys of Hilekirke and the
youngest to me whoe am now soe busied with other mens cumbers the subject
of my profession that I have noe time to attend this woorke, as by my notes
in the margent thou mayest perceive whitch shew when I writte these things

35. i.e. about 1612. For further comments on his finances at this time see p. 27.
    The increase of jointure was granted 19 December 8 Jas I 1610, Lowther B.IV.17.
36. On f346 *from* has been struck out and *of* inserted.
37. L.h. margin.
38. L.h. margin, note: *of whitch matter of opinion I allwayes made a principall use
    in all my course for the wordeld is ruled with opinion and, misled by it generally.*

and in this tow years allmoste not once haveing time to take it in my hand, 346r *cont.*
for I have for the conveniencie of my practise tied my selfe to a great
Inconvenience that is to kepe tow houses one at Meaborne bycause I cannot
lett it and am allwayes addeing to it where I live in somer another I take
in Kendale where I live in Winter, betwixt whitch (I ([*sic*] attendeing the
markett daye in my house for the resorte that come to me for my profession,)
doe travell manie times especially when my wife is at Meaborne once a
weke upon the night not loveing to stay longer then my business lasteth
otherwise I should ride in the morrow upon the Sabbeth or the Lords daye
whitch I have done as not directly satisfied whether it be one of the
comandments to kepe that[39] day since it was altered to the eight day by
the apostles, and since noe direct precept but the authoritie of the church,
upon whitch occasion I will a litle relate unto thee the travell and peins
of a a [*sic*] lawyer of whome I may say this that as he is generally a mover
in other mens cumbars and an auther of theim to if he be not
a verie honest man soe hathe he this recompense that he never hathe rest 347r[40]
but is allwayes in Cumba himself, for In riding to tearme, at tearme
forenuoone he goes to the hall in somer in heat winter in wette and cowlde,
stands there bare headed at the barre, bears the burthen of his oune follye
and of his clyent allsoe, the discurtesie of his adversarie, and discountenance
of the Judge if he observe him not though ageinst reason (*interlined*: manie)
times, and soe he stands swetting intollerablely in somer, and in winter
otherwise Distempered after dinner he is tied to his chare, and to read
evidences while he can sea, and to advise and be advised, without rest if
he be in great practise, and if in mean it is not woorth followeing abrode
and terme being done he retournes to circuet and cuntrie practise and soe
never hathe rest and is moste a straunger at home, whitch howsoever the
divines preatch ageinst in regard (*erasure*) some with sutch Infinite peyns
gette great geins, yet is their peins sutch as in my opinion cannot be
recompenced with money, and sutch as hardly anie honest man can continew
to the end; though upon the contrarie the divines whose studie is no more
have great advancement; and at mutch ease deliver upon a quishion what
they have forethought or studied without Interruption whitch is a verie
comendable profession and fitte for younger sonne if the first steppe to
preferment theirin be not though perjurie, whitch I mutch fear and partly
know is generall, for lesse esteme of simonie for I thinke if the man deserve
the place, for the temporall promotion to the benefice he is bound to a
thankfullnes to the patron and may contract for it (*interlined*: but for the
othe), and simonie is Intended in the Scripture onely of the purchaseing
the holye ghost, and soe now of the spirituall ordination, if anie holines
doe come by the ordination and Imposition of hands whitch the papists
make one of the Sacraments we none and soe haveing toutched these things
by the waye; I will shew thee my course and means in my profession,
wherein I am a hope without a parte, for I have noe great protector

---

39. L.h. margin, note: *quod dubitas ne feceris.*
40. ff346v and 347r have been written upside down, and thus transposed, as indicated
by the page numberings.

346v[41]   Noe Judges extraordinarie favor, nor Courtier nor great Lords protection
whitch is my losse in profitte yet freeth me of manie base and dishonest
services whitch I showlde be tied unto for theim if I had theim and did
use theim mutch in the great busines of the woordeld, for I know noe man
out of his oune means can rise to be great and good, but by percimonie,
and the honest Indevors in his profession he may be Indifferent, and above
the moste whitch I thinke to be sufficient, and safest, bothe for god and
the wordeld, but of the contrarie I have the great discurtesie yea malice
of the Lord Willyam Howard whoe is moste powerfull in the cuntrie by
his hard dealing and manie sewets, and in court by his Kinred, whoe sayed
unto me, Intreating him for my father not to medle in the purchase of Helton
whereof we had the moyatie by leas and the other moyatie by eschaunge
with Mallorie, the reversion whereof he purposed to purchase[42] to Incumbar
us with sewets he answered me that if his sonne[43] showld forget the
unkindenes of oure house he wowld disinherit him, to whitch I replied that
he cowld not charge my father nor me with aniething whitch he acknowledged, and if he had wrong by my Grandfather or my great uncle, it was
not in reason ([44]nor Christiaintie to be Imputed to us, and then he
concluded he wowld say notheing to me but temperately, but Judge thou
of this temper and this Inhumaine speatch, and I towlde him that in my
practise since I was not of counsell with him, he must pardon me to be
of counsell ageinst him wherein I wowld be honest to my clyent and
temperate towards him whitch he cowld not except[45] ageinst but ever since
privately where he cowlde he Indevored to hinder me and if he cowlde have
catched at the least occasion that cowlde be he wowlde have overthrowen
me if he cowlde, and I of the contrarie not findeing him to be Intreated
did openly shew my self

347v   ageinst him, and at severall offices where he was a comissioner bothe for
the lunacie of Sands where he wowlde have defeated my brother Fleming
of his Rectories Impropriate at St Johns and St Bridgets and St Leonards
besides Calder, I opposed him to his face and did shew his Indirect cariage
and Justefie our selves when with an overbearing he wowlde have cast an
aspersion upon me, for procureing an order out of Court to be had whitch
he had denied us at a former cession, yet his power with the Jurors was
sutch that he did make theim hoodewinke, and finde that whitch I toulde
him that I hoped he showlde never finde a Jurie that wowlde finde for they
might as well finde him seisor of my mannour of Meaborne, but he answeres
we showlde not be heard for he had private direction from the Lord Knowles
Master of the Wards contrarie to the open order in Court whitch howsoever

---

41. See p. 213, n. 40. The word *protector* has been interlined here in the same ink
as p. 200, n. 1.
42. The Lowthers acquired part of Helton from Sir John Mallorie in 1511 (deed:
Helton B.I.23). They leased part from the Crown. I have found nothing to suggest
that they purchased the reversion, indeed the lawsuit mentioned above p. 17
gave them an absolute title; Lord William was not apparently involved in the suit.
43. Hand sign in l.h. margin.
44. This parenthesis not completed.
45. Smudged.

I was assured was untrew yet was it in vein to question it further for the 347v *cont.*
Lord Knowles who maried his nece wowld have affirmed it and did, in
whitch manner of opposition I found easier to yeald then to intreatie
bycause he generally used his power to defend the unjust cause, whitch
I allwayes did make a publique scandall to him though I did seldome prevayle
that he had famam ultricem and upon all occasions in other mens busines
I left noe means untried or attempted wherby I might putte him to trie
his strength bycause I did knowe the King did not love him for his religion
and taxed him for his Infinite oppression wherein the King was continually
remembred by manie petitions of his oppresion and some times he was
drawen
into suspition as daungerous to the state, by reason of his religion and 348r
in that he having noe estate at the 42th or 43 yere of Quene Eliz. hir reign
showlde purchase of hir and pay for his part of the Dacres lands, and ever
since be at a great charge in building, stocking his grounde and other
purchases and yette still to be ritch and the means how not discovered,
wherefore it was sayde by the pope or papists money, but all this discovered, and how he plotted a Sheriffe of his faction and Justices of peace
in Cumberland allwayes, and howe he Joines himself in everie mans actions
and is still of one side where it notheing concerneth him, and manie
particulers cyted halfe of whitch wowld make a mean man a comon barretor
and the Infinitenes of his oune sewets whitch have bene 20 or 30 ageinst
Mr Salkeld, Dacres, Sir H. Curwen Sir Ja Bellingham and all others with
whome he had to doe, and yet by his power with the Jurors, whome he
terrifieth, and with the Subtile persons of the Cuntrie whitch all depend
upon (*interlined*: him) he effecteth what he list, in soe mutch that a Juror
being asked whie he gave his verdict for his purpose, whitch he had in part
made knowen to his frind was ageinst (*interlined*: his) conscience, he
answered their was mercie with God if (*interlined*: he) offended him but
none with the Lord Willyam, with whome I standeing in this sorte it was
a speciall care I had to doe noe unjust thing whereby he cowlde aniewayes
disgrace me or draw me into question, and yet upon all occasions where
a particuler was like to fall betwixt him and me I avoyded him and theirin
desired to purchase his favor ut ne noceat seming to stand ageinst him in
other mens busines for the Justice of their cause
and to give theim a Just satisfaction whitch he cowlde not but approve in 348v
me, but I being to purchase some of Sandfoorths lands in Knipe and
Bampton of one Mr Rookebie to whome Tho Sandfoorth had mortgaged
the same, and the Lord Willyam being likewise verie desirus of it, yet broke
with Mr Rookebye, I had the writings theirof delivered from Mr Rookebye
and the Indenture whereby Mr Rookeby sowlde the same to the Lord
Willyam, and had agreed with Mr Rookebie for the price whitch was but
£250 for £10 rent, and the tenants wowld have payed it all in a fine by
reason of the death of Sandfoorth uponn whose death a generall fine was
(*interlined*: due) in whitch bargein of £250 I hadde geined clearly £300
at the least for it is woorth £500, yet I knoweing Mrs Sandfoorth the wards
mother to be a Cumbersome women, and full of evill reporte (for whitch
I made hir pay a hundreth markes by year whitch she had concealed from

348v *cont.*   the King and hir husbands creditors at the office upon a melius Inquirendum)
I resolved to let it passe, and did offer to yeald my bargein to the Lord
Willyam and sent it to him by Mr Dudley[46] whitch he accepted and the
tenants payed the purchase and he hath the land for notheing; since whitch
I had noe requitall but as mutch unkindenes[47] as before, for he thought
I durst not buy it (*interlined*: for him) though I made another shew but
the trewth was their was Imperfection in the conveyance, for Rookebies
conveyance and fine from Sandfoorth was Bainton for Barton or Bampton
whitch will avayle him (*interlined*: or his) for soe mutch and wowlde surely
have bene objected ageinst me and it was but to kepe Rookebie harmless
for bonds entered for Sandfoorth and soe subject to Incumbrance all whitch

349r   I perceived and theirfore did forbear and not for hope of his love but fear
of his trouble whitch may in time fall upon his for I have caused Mrs
Sandfoorth and hir sonne enter to Banton to avoyde his fine within five
years theirof whitch he hathe levied as I think by the right name, but
notheing of this being perceived by him I pleinly perceived his love was
not to be purchased with price nor prayer, and theirupon I resolved to
stand upon my gard, and yet still when I had power to pleasure him in
that, whitch cowlde not hurt him greatly, In busines wherein I had to doe,
to doe it soe that it were without wrong to Comon honestie (*interlined*:
to gein) him ut ne noceat onely. And if not ⟨and⟩ in other things where
I cowlde and had Just occasion while he stoode contrarie to oppose him
and make him be opposed at other mens charge, In myne oune I durst not
vente, for the victorie with losse I allwayes abhorred, and never practised
nor will advise anie other to spend towpence to get one, whitch manie doe
unles a man out of his superfluitie may spare it, and perhaps shall spend
it as Idlely, In whitch course I found him to be greatly desirus of Mr
Salkelds[48] lands in Sleddale etc whitch my mother had for securitie of £800
whitch he payed as sewertie for Sandfoorth for Askham tythe barne, whitch
my brother Fleming and I had conveyed in our names, whitch Lands he
desired partly because they Joined upon Thornethwayte but especially to
be revenged upon Mr Salkeld, and to continew him in sewets, and soe to
undoe him, and he thought he cowlde not have theim but through my means,
and theirfore he sent me threatnings that he would purchase a part of Helton
if I wowld (*interlined*: not) and I conteinued the threatnings

349v   and returned answer how unrespectedly my last kindenes was requited, and
wowld not move in it unlesse I might perceive how I might have requitall,
since in that if he did not purchase it, if I did I must pay for it, and soe
I might purchase else where if I missed that, and soe that matter depending
in suspence, I was occasioned to confront him agein about the wardshippe
of my Nephew Barwys whitch in right belonged by the Kings Instructions
to my mother in law as to the nearest, his father and mother dieing near
togither and she being the Grandmother who cowlde have noe benefitte

---

46. See p. 222.
47. The *un* in *unkindenes* is interlined.
48. See above p. 9 for Mr. Salkeld and Lowther's mother-in-law (Agnes Fleming)
    not mother; mortgage 10 August 1613.

by his death,[49] wherein the Lord W*illiam* Interposed himself and opposed   349v *cont.*
us though we petitioned within the month and had a writte to finde an
office yette did he soe plotte with the Sheriffe[50] that we cowlde have no
Jurie whitch plotte we got the Eschetor to certefie and othe made of it,
yet stirred uppe the grandmother of the fatherside to be a competitor whose
sonnes the one being a Bankerupt and the other haveing spent all were
next in remeinder if the ward died without issew, all whitch though we
alledged and offard to give to the wards sister in mariage whatsoever we
received in mariage with the ward above the Kings composition yet we
cowlde not prevayle, but he got a comission, and did publiquely affirme
that the petitions we made to the Lord Viscount Wallingforde[51] who maried
his nece toutcheing that Wardshippe he gave us the answer, all whitch I
pressed and the Justnes of oure cause ageinst him before the Lord of
Wallingfoorde and the Counsell of the Court soe that all the Counsell were
satisfied but the vicount who wowld not yet the best offer being to be taken
for the King they purposed to have catched me and overtaken me by tricks
and theirfore called the Lord Treasorers secretarie whoe did solicit for
the Lord Willyam and the other grandmother to se what he offered whoe   350r
offered but a hundred markes for the ⟨land⟩ bodie and ten pounds for
the land with whitch offer I being not made acqueinted they demaunded
of me what I wowlde give according to a Rule I had obteined to be heard,
wherein if I had offered lesse, then I showlde have bene Justly rejected
therefore I at the first woord offered the full valew whitch was £300 for
the bodie and fortie markes by year for the third part of the land whitch
onely the King was to have whitch offer the other partie was admitted to
hear, and wowlde not give so mutch whereupon the counsell of the Court
resolved I showlde have it, but they preyd time afterwards to talke with
the Lord Willyam whoe sayde (*interlined*: privately) he wowld give £500 of
his oune purse er we had it, and I being soe deleyed pressed the Lord
Wallingforde that I wowlde petition the King if he wowld not admits
(*erasure*) us to compound for the wardshippe and shew how the Lord William
had published that we showlde never have it allthough by the Kings
Instructions we were to have it, and yet theirin offered to follow his direction
and to seeke oure peace at the Lord Williams hands if anie wayes we
might have it, wherein I cowlde have discovered that practise that might
have avayled the King £5000 by year in the Court of Wardes, whitch is this
that when anie servant of the maister of the Wards is to be gratified, whitch
everie man that taketh a wardshippe by the Instructions is to swear not
[to] doe and not to give aniething but to the King for anie favor, the practise

49. Richard Barwise of Islekirk, his father and mother (Grace d. of Agnes Fleming)
    both died in 1616. The *Kings Instructions* are his general instructions to the
    Court of 1610 (P.R.O., S.P.14/61/6).
50. Sheriff: Richard Fletcher of Hutton-in-the-Forest (P.R.O., *Lists and Indexes*
    no. IX (1898), p. 28. Escheator: Roger Otway of Midleton (W. Farrer,
    Records Relating to the Barony of Kendal, ed. J. F. Curwen (Cumb. & Westm.
    Arch. & Arch. Soc., Record Series, V, 1924), pp. 102, 105, etc.
51. Sir Francis Knollys, Master of the Wards; Lord Knollys 1603, cr. Viscount
    Wallingford 1616 (G.E.C., *Complete Peerage*, I, p. 400).

350r *cont.*   is that he that dothe give shall take the graunt in anothers name whoe
knoweth notheing and he shall swear he giveth notheing and after assigne
the wardshippe to him that gave money

350v   whitch hapened in our case for the Lord Willyam was the means that
Fraunces Dalavell his neces usha showld have a hundreth marke to crosse
us and to get the wardshippe for the grandmother of the other side, and
soe it was passed in one Robinsons name to hir use whome the Lord Willyam
used but as a shaddow for he causeth as I think Sir Jo Dalston or himselfe
to disburse the money and will not let the grandmother whose name he
used to have wardshippe but hathe since offared it to us if we will let him
have Mr Salkelds Lands,[52] whitch was his unjust purpose in the begining
though he covered his pretence with other shadowes, that whoe wowld doe
the best for the ward showlde have his furtherance, but being driven from
those howlds by our offers he was forced openly to shew him self by whitch
means it appeared in this particular what evasion they have to deceive
the King in generall in all matters of that nature, whitch petition I shewed
the vicount Wallingfoorde to daunt him and the Lord Willyam but they
were so strong that they cared not and I cowlde finde noe means to second
me to the King though I offered that occasion to the Lord of Cumberland,
the Lord Wootton and other their opposites, whitch durst not meddle and
Sir James Fullerton a woorthie Scottish knight near the King and prince
willed me to desist for that the king loved theim best that did deceive him
moste, and did not love his profitte nor the moovers theirof, and wowld
thinke it was my oune particuler that moved it, and the Treasorer being
his brother the Earle of Arundell, his nephew Pembroke the Chamberlain
and Arundels brother in law, and the Lord Knowles his nephew all of the
counsell were soe powerfull that I haveing tried the utter moste in anothers
cause and at their cost, did desist whitch let it be a caution to thee not
to be to confident

351r   in a Just cause whitch I was not but onely desired to trie his strength and
to second Mr Salkeld whoe had expressed all his oppressions to him and
all the cuntrie in a petition to the King whitch I (*blank*) whereby the King
was greatly incensed against him and sayde Mr Salkeld showlde be helped,
whitch was countenanced by the Lord of Cantaburie the archbishoppe
and Mr Secretarie Winward but was soe crossed that Mr Salkeld cowld
get noe answer but the maister of request towld him it was in some of
the Kings pockets or under some quishion in his chamber, but it had noe
effect, though the ground of it was that the Lord Willyam showlde have
answered an Information exhibited ageinst him for recusancie, whitch I
directed to disable him by conviction theirin to sew others whitch sewet
Mr Attorney stayed by direction from the King as he alledged, but the

---

52. Fine of Wardship: £300; rent of lands: £26-13-4d. p.a. (as suggested by Lowther)
sold to Robinson 14 February 1616/17 (P.R.O., Wards 9/205, f10; Wards 9/204,
f201.). Dalston sold the wardship to John Fleming of Rydal; Lowther took over
the Salkeld mortgage (C.R.O.K., WD/Ry, Barwise papers).

secretarie denied, but[53] the ordinarie proces were stayed[54]; whitch course   351r *cont.*
I directed bycause he did sew all men and none durst sew him and I towlde
Mr Salkeld if he did reward his blowes and never strike he might still
be hurt but the other was never in daunger, whitch was the Lord William's
pollicie ever to be plaintif and to sew and eyther out of the substance of
the cause or by some trick in law for some forme in proceding he ever gotte
advantage, saving of the Lord Hunsden whome he sewed for Strangneys
lands as heir to Dacres by whome he was overmatched but with all others
he was like the brasse potte whitch Solomon speaketh of that dasheth the
earthen potte to peaces and the law whitch showlde be the buckler and
the defence of the innocent he made his swoord to oppresse theim haveing
a superfluitie in his estate whitch he yearly spent in law to[55]
whitch useing the force of his powerfull Kinred, he allawyes prevayled or   351v
deleyd his adversarie though he and his cause was never soe just yea and
some times trifles were aggravated and made fatall to his adversaries as
Mr Dacres killing a Hinde in Martindale upon the day he made it be soe
pursewed that he was cast into the Flete above a year and it cost him above
£500[56] in fines for himself and his servants by decree in the Starre Chamber,
as likewise he gotte Mr Salkeld to be fined their for meintenance in
incourageing his tenants of Gilsland to defend theimsleves in his
oppresions,[57] and brought Sir H. Curwen Sir James Bellingham their
ladies, Mr Rigge Mr Thwaytes and manie other into a lingring costly sewet
in the Starre Chamber for tearing out a lefe of the Coutcher booke of the
Abbey of Shappe whitch concerned his lands of Thornethwayte whitch he
purchased of Sir H Curwen, whitch booke cowlde noewayes belong to him,[58]
these few perticulers of manie I repeat that thow may be advised in thy
course and consider with whome thow dealest, and that thow be not allwayes
to confident to Justefie a good cause unlesse thow stand upon equall termes;
and knowe thy adversarie and thy Judge well, wherein it is not fitte with
all men to be soe easie nyther for though the poyets say
    In court men best doe live and kepe their Rankes
    that cantake Injuries and (*interlined*: yet) give men thanks
Yet in the (*interlined*: court) and cuntrie it is not allwayes soe, though some
time it be soe, for nulla regula quin fallit, though generally they be good
directions, but be thou wise and use thy Rules according unto times and
occasions, otherwise they will befoole thee, and thus haveing made a great
digression in this great exemple of this great man out of whitch thow
mayest observe mutch, I leave him for the present and stand as yett without
the supporte of anie by my selfe, not without the love of my frinds in
whose occasions I am dayly imployed, but without anie great help from
theim in that I governe mine oune soe that I never trouble theim in it, for

---

53. Smudged.
54. For the complaint see Surtees Soc. LXVIII, pp. 423, 427, 430.
55. f351v has *unto* instead of *to*.
56. Altered from £300.
57. See Surtees Soc., LXVIII, p. 425.
58. Lord William Howard had such a chartulary, or a copy, *c.* 1639, see p. 18, n. 69,
    above.

351v *cont.* whitch I thank God, for wee hathe he that nedeth, and though he getteth pittie yet but litle help

352r whitch made me woorke out my fortune with my oune peins, whitch I was the rather constreined to doe for that my Grandfather and my Father did disagree and theirin I being yoong forsaw my daunger, whitch I Indevored to prevent as well as I cowld upon all occasions but I being maried and my father haveing had and spent all my portion and I to supply his present means haveing ingaged myself in a statute of £1000 for a Jointure of £180 to ⟨his⟩ Mrs Burdett his second wife,[59] after my grandfather showld die, yet did soe fall foorth that I being not then secured of the possibilitie of my Grandfathers lands, my Grandfather was drawent to sell Wethoppe to Richard Fletcher for £1600 woorth above £2000 whitch I impeatched and questioned uponn the estates I had founde, and upon a parley having a litle displeased my grandfather in that oppositionn, I drew it to this conclusion that my father and I Releasing Wethope the money to be received theirupon was to be satisfaction to my Uncle Willyam for his leas he had in Hackthroppe Helton and Lowther Milne,[60] and then my Grandfather being displeased with my father offered to estate all his lands upon me whitch I refused, and desired and prevayled with him to estate theim to himself for lief the remeinder to my father for lief the remeinder to me for lief, thenc to my sonne John intayle and soe further[61] with a charge onely of £50 by year to my Uncles Heugh and Lancelot[62] and Penrith lands to my Uncle Gerard for lief[63] and Sewborwens or £100 to be given to John Threlkeld whome my grandfather did take as his chylde though he was borne after the womans mariage with Threlkeld,[64] at the doeing whereof It was agreed my Grandfather showlde goe to the parsonage house of Lowther and my father to Lowther Hall at a rent (*interlined*: of £200) whitch he would not undergoe untill my uncle Gerard let it (*interlined*: to) ferme for £240, with whitch overplus of £40 my father was content and did undergoe the same with condition for non payment to reenter by whitch condition he was like to have lost the benefit theirof and had soe done if my Grandfather had lived but in my Grandfathers sicknesse, I being at London and then soe mutch beloved of him that he purposed to have lived with me or I with him, my father and he did differ in that ⟨he⟩ my father wowld not lett him have the house whither he did desier to remove, whither neverthelesse after some letters passed betwixt theim he did goe as appears by the letters whitch my Granndfather

59. P.II.3. Marriage settlement, 6 February 1605/6, Lowther B.II.5.
60. William and his brothers released their interests in Hackthorpe for £900 and a short lease of the demesne, deeds: [*blank*] April and 15 April 5 Jas I [1607] Lowther B.II.5.
61. Deed: Lowther B.II.5, 16 April 5 Jas I [1607].
62. Deed: Lowther B.IV.17, 14 April 5 Jas I [1607], for £30 p.a. to Elizabeth, wife of Lancelot. This annuity was purchased by Sir J.L.(1) for £180 30 November 11 Jas I [1613]; deed: *eadem*. See above p. 26.
63. Deed: Lowther B.II.5, 14 January 41 Eliz I [1599].
64. Below, p. 222. For other comments on grants to relatives see pp. 7, 16, 22-3, above.

APPENDIX I—AUTOBIOGRAPHY 221

caused to be written in this booke,[65] shortly after whitch my Granndfather 352v
died, and then some difference did grow betwixt my uncles and my father
whitch we did soone attone, and (*interlined*: my grandfather) his second
wife being incowraged by theim and some others to demaund dower of my
father I did so prevayle with hir and insist of former estates that I
compounded with hir for £50, and got hir Release,[66] and shortly after an
office being to be found for my father after my Granndfathers death and
I offering and desireing to finde the estate whitch my Granndfather and
father did last make Henrie Fetherstone whoe served my great uncle and
maried my uncle Wiberghs daughter then his servant, and gott all his estate
by my uncle being turned one of the Lord Willyam's Instruments moved
my father to oppose those estates and to get the office found that my
granndfather died seysed in fee whitch I opposed and before divers Juries
at divers metings pressed the estate as the law was clere, yet was their noe
office found for a long time, in all whitch time neverthelesse I came with
my father to the offices and did use him with all reverence as became a
sonne, and did as I aught to doe to him (and left it to him to doe to me
as he pleased) wherein I still stoode for the trewth and yet kept peace bycause
I did see and towld him it was but a devise by those that loved neyther
of us to sette us at difference, and soe to overthrow us but in time I soe
prevayled that with my fathers goodwill I founde all the estates last made
in office before my self then being escheator and have sewed liverie for my
father theirupon,[67] since whitch my father hathe bene well pleased with
me except sometimes when he wrote to me to lend him money when I did
not or cowlde not, and sometimes that my Brothers and others not thriveing
in their oune course wowld impeatch me in that I helped theim not, but
now in time he hathe sene their frowardnes in that my Brothers Gerard[68]
and Richard[69] maried ageinst his will and my sister now will allsoe to their
overthrow and the rest will not live soe soberly as becometh, it dothe please
him to say that I onely of theim all am advised by him and comfortable
(*interlined*: to[70]) him, and he now as often and generally useth me kindely
and taketh pleasure (as be it without vanitie or arrogancie he hathe cause)[71]
when in all assemblies he referreth all his busines to my care and manageing

---

65. A1/1, f17r.
66. P.I.3. Deed: 11 March 5 Jas I [1608], Lowther B.III.15.
67. A copy of the Inquisition, taken 26 September 9 Jas I [1611], endorsed by
    Sir J.L.(1): *The Office after Sir Richard Lowther taken before John his Grand-
    childe which Sir Christopher his father long opposed deseringe libertie to sell,* and
    the livery, are Lowther B.II.5.
68. Is this Gerard of Poland and not Gerard of Ireland? Gerard of Ireland married,
    n.d., Ann daughter of a Baron of the Irish Exchequer. Gerard was in Ireland
    by 1619 (*CW2*, II, pp. 12, 20). PP. III.5, III.18, III.19.
69. Married Ann, d. of Mr. John Williams of Flint (Sir William Lowther's notebook;
    A1/1, f283r); Richard was called to the Bar in 1614 from Grays Inn (J. Foster,
    Alumni Oxiensis, p. 945). PP.III.6, III.7.
70. Interlined in same ink as p. 200, n. 1.
71. Brackets are in the same ink as p. 200, n. 1.

353r whitch I have done without blame or Just fallt to be found for him ever since I was twentie yeres of age, and helped soe well as cowlde be sutch errors as through Inconsideration he fell unto, as his busines for Highead whither he went from Lowther ageinst all our mindes whitch cost him tow or thre hundred pounds, and now we bothe being in the Commission ⟨as⟩ Justices of peace in Westmerland, I doe discerne that he is pleased in me when I give the Charge and that my opinion is taken as a Rule in the Court and that I am not overruled by anie of my fellowes, but well reputed of in my cuntrie, wherein their is now a faction like to be nourished and an opposition to be sette up ageinst me by the Lord Willyam, whoe hathe this terme being Kandle 1616[72] got John Dudley a lawyer younger Brother to Tho Dudley of Yeanwath thrust into the comission of the peace who being backed with his Brother Thomas, and Sir Christopher Pickering his coosen and sillie Mr Crackenthroppe of Newbiggin, Sir John and Sir George Dallstone must all over rule my father and me, wherein I shall god willing be circumspect to doe as becometh me and to preserve my credit without toutch, and to take these times as they are, and if I must I will yeald and reserve myself for better times, but as yet I stand rectus in curia and my opinion hathe respect with Sir James Bellingham and the rest, whitch with good Indevors I hope to Increas. I came into the comission by the Judges nomination whoe did lodge in my house in Kendale thre or foure assises times not being furthered by the Lord of Cumberland, nor anie other great one and soe am tied to none in dependancie, but in the governement of the cuntrie I finde sutch weak and careles assistance that I am wearied and discouraged theirin for in oure taxations in provision for the poore for Bridges, sowldiers highwayes, houses of correction Reformation of Cottages alehouses, etc moste understand not how to procede legally soe as we may Justefie our proceding and none will take peins, soe that when the Lord William or anie other opposite pleseth to question oure procedings we cannot Justefie the same, yet shall, I with that temper and moderation soe carie my self as I may be excuseable

353v Considering well that sometimes a litle awfullnes in the publique cause maketh the private to rest in good peace, whitch peace on earth everie wiseman showld desier for it feedeth the poore mans labours and filleth the Richmans coffers it is a blessing in a familie and a glorie to a Kingdome they are blessed that kepe it and cursed that break it, whitch theirfore above all things though with some losse, studie to meintein in thine oune estate, ⟨and⟩ as hitherto I have done, yet am I now sewed with my father, and the widdowe of Sewborwens,[73] by the Bastard Jo Lowther[74] for Sewborwens, whoe is stirred up theirin by the Lord Willyam as I fear, yet I hope the cause it selfe in my time or some other time hereafter will defend it self,

---

72. i.e. Hilary 1616/17.
73. Presumably Margaret Lowther, wife of William Lowther of Sewborwens. It is not clear what, if any, relation he was of the Lowthers of Lowther. Mentioned in Newton Reigney B.24.
74. Known as John Lowther alias Threlkeld, bastard of Sir Richard, see p. 200, above.

for speaking now withoute view of my evidence I think the case stands thus. 353v *cont.*
My Grandfather did let the same to Will[75] for thre lives from a day to
come whitch was voyde, and he a disseisor, then my Grandfather being
tenant in tayle theirof he my father and I bargein and sell to the Bastard
never acknowledged[76] by my grandfather, whitch is voyd first for that we
had but a right (2) by not acknowledgeing by him, we haveing then noe
estate, it being made the 14th of Aprill[77] and my granndfathers estate of
the mannour the 16th[78] (3) if it were good and my graundfather tenant
in tayle it is voyde by his death. In equitie it is with a condition upon
payment of £100 to be voyd (2) he anothers sonne and noe consideration
(3) it was convenanted to my father bothe at his mariage and my grandfathers (4) he covenanted with me to take an estate for lief, and writte
divers letters to that end. In[79] whitch fear I resteing made peace with the
Lord Willyam in other occasions whoe interteined my familiaritie gladly
Imediately upon the decease of my father whoe died 2 augusti 1617 whitch
I fought by faire means knoweing how his opposition might brede me
trouble in draweing or Incourageing my tenants
to opposition in their fines especially Hilton (*interlined*: in halfe) whereof 354r
I had onely a leas, and haveing (*interlined*: him) in the opinion of men in
Kindenes, at least in faire tearmes I then opposed the Bastard for Sewborwens and soe did gein him from the bastard whome my pevish coosen
Thomas Carleton the lawyer used as a countenance ageinst me, indeavoring
to sell the Bastards tytle to him and soe I gotte the Bastard to order in
the absence of my coosen his mayster and to take bond and give bond to
be content with a leas for three lives of Sewborwens and to pay £50 for
it,[80] and to regrant to me the estate in fee bargeined and sowlde to him by
my Grandfather my father and me[81] and I haveing thus geined the Lord
Willyam proceded in my business without anie opposition and assessed
the fines upon chaunge of Lord upon all my tenants at one woord unto whitch
they submitted, and gave bill for fear of death as I used, but the Lord
of Cumberland and his sonne the Lord Clifford being joined in the
Lieuetenancie over these northern cuntries with the Lord of Walden, an

75. i.e. Wm Lowther of Sewborwens (p. 222, n. 73, above)?
76. L.h. margin, note: *que quaque* NON *suit Lowther alias Threlkeld.*
77. Deed: *eadem*, 14 April 5 Jas I [1607].
78. i.e. Sir Richard Lowther's settlement of all his estates, above, p. 220.
79. Change of ink, preceeding stop in new ink.
80. Bond, 22 Oct. 15 Jas I [1617], Newton Reigney B.24.
81. Deed: 22 October 16 Jas I [1618], *eadem*. Later Sir J.L.(1) bought in a lease
which Margaret Lowther (p. 200, n. 73, above) and her son Gerard had made to
Tom Harrison (which tenancy is referred to on p. 26). Harrison assigned the lease
to a Penrith mercer, Thomas Sledall, who had married Jane Smith, common
law wife of John Lowther alias Threlkeld (A1/4, f71r; D.C.C., Machell family
MSS, V, no. 97; will of Lowther alias Threlkeld, Newton Reigney B.24). Sledall
gave bond to Sir J.L.(1) as his tenant (*eadem*) on 29 December 1619 and thus
the reference to Sledall on p. 46, above.
As late as 1623, after arbitration, Lowether was still buying out interests. In
1663 Sir J.L.(2) added land to the demesne, above p. 174.

354r *cont.*   Howard, and being in great enmitie with the Lord Willyam the young Lord
Clifford in his fathers weakenes (yet under his fathers officers) managing
all, did take it verie unkindely of me that I showlde goe to the Lord
Willyam, and was informed by his officer whoe feared he would make
me of his counsell that I was made by the contrarie faction ageinst him,
and theirupon grew angrie whitch I neglecting at oure next meting did
interrogate with him the reasons of his distrust, and freed my self as I justly
might, yet then he feared I showlde be neuter, to whitch I replied That I
wowlde be free and those who had onely life and means by great ones must
enter into opposition for theim but I was not in sutch necessitie and
theirfore purposed to be free and to honor him and respect him as my
Kinsman, and to be his assured whyle he did soe thinke, yet he towlde me
that I had sayde that I wowlde be of counesell against him[82]

354v   whitch I acknowledged if soe that I was neglected by his officers and not
reteined for him for that I thought it was an Indignitie offered me in my
profession to be of noe side yet I Towlde him that hitherto I had forborne,
and I shewed him a letter[83] in token of my love to him that the countesse
of Dorsette wrote to me to be for hir all whitch might shew him that if
I had anie waivering Inclination from him I might have interteinment
and thankes all whitch notwithstanding I ⟨gotte soe mutch from him⟩
(*interlined*: gotte his kindenes but full of suspition and[84]) feintly haveing
before while he and his father neaded the favor of the countrie before
the Kings award for they had large promises, unto whitch I never trusted
findeing it comon in Lords still to use meaner men as their instruments
and seldome to requite but if the meritt be great at their hands rather to
hate, bycause they thinke theimselves further bounde to requite then they
will, and theirfore upon the least occasion are redie to, to [*sic*] reject their
inferiors if they be not followed and pleased in all things, whitch I resolve
to doe as litle as I can, or not at all but where it stands with my oune
pleasure or profitte as well as theirs, whitch pleasureable or profitable offices
if they committe to their servants, or to some other whome they like of,
lett theim committe the rest to theim allsoe or to some cuntrie fooles, whoe
is amazed with tytles and dumbeshewes, and the name of honor, and now
at this instant if I wowlde be crosse he is to have seven yeres valew of all
his tenants to alter their custome and they have bene with me and I have
deferred theim, the trewth is his estate at the best is but an intayle to the
males by the Kings award and he hathe noe issew male and soe can neyther
confirme sewerly, neyther dothe the law admitte anie alteration

---

82. *against him* added later.
83. The controversy between Anne, Countess of Dorset, d. of George Clifford 3rd
Earl of Cumberland, and Francis, his brother and heir, over the descent of
some titles and estates of the Clifford family (see above pp. 208–9) was
eventually settled by the King (below, and see G.E.C., *Complete Peerage, sub*
Clifford; G. C. Williamson, *Lady Anne Clifford* (Kendal, 1922), chap. VII). This
letter refers to disputes over property after the death in 1616 of Anne's mother,
the 3rd Earl's wife (H.M.C., *12th Report, Appendix VII*, pp. 13–15).
84. Interlineation perhaps in a different style and ink.

(*Blank*)   355

of custome without an act of parliament whitch howsoever he talkes of and   356r
is then to have a yeres value more, it is a thing the parliament will not
doe to the prejudice of a third person in remeinder, whitch if I showlde
advise the tenants to looke into they wowlde all goe back, whitch will be
£20000 losse to him, if ever they be able to performe their undertakeings,
for his owlde rent is £300 by year whitch is woorth by year near £3000,
and eight yeres valew showlde be payed and yet doe I forbear though mutch
provoked to doe theim sutch a fatall displeasure, ⟨well⟩ whereby I showlde
profitte notheing but purchase an irreconcileable hatred, yet will I not
betraye the tenants if I be trusted theirin nor theirby gein their pleasure
or displeasure but leave it to others with some honest cautions and hearein
may be observed that a man of understandeing may hinder or profitte mutch
theirfore if anie sutch be Interested in thy business displease theim not, but
make theim for thee soe mutch as thou canst.

* 24 Aprilis 1619[85]

Since whitch things have soe proceded by my cautelows[86] cariage that, I
(haveing gotten a good opinion of bothe the lords and the tenants was chosen
and feed by bothe to be Indifferent Betwixt theim and to Joine with Mr
Davenport the lawyer to draw their assewrance whitch we did and added
some small matters to satisfie the tenants but relied upon the decree in
Chauncerie and the Kings award since whitch I have bene gratious with theim
and of their private counesell, and they wholely directed, and led back and
forward in this busines by me, the tenants being a multitude and simple
and suspitious and waivering, and giveing theim dayly occasion to neede
me, whitch I nourished and abated as occasion required purpposeing to
setle my selfe

of counesell and in fee with theim, for whitch I have bothe their woords   356v
and earnest, and Mr John Taylors word upon some secret meeteing with
me, whome I finde to be naturally wise and sutle by practise, but short in
the Judgement of perticulers, wanteing learneing, and If I be not deceived
of him one that can submitte willingly to a better Judgement then his oune,
and in this directed by me and hungrie after my directions, yet fearfull
as yet to bring me in to my Lord least I might derogate from him, but
that I have satisfied or will satisfie, that I shall concurr with him in all things,
and soe have I made of him my enemie, or one that maligned me my frind,
and one that in sinceritie semes to promise to me all Imployement I desier
from his lord (vayle qi vayle purra) and as yett their is noe perfect peace
for though the assewrance be in a manner agreed, yet the valew and some
particular customes are not agreed and now this Easter terme 1619 the
Tenants of Kings Meaborne are served with subpenaes to goe forward with
the agremeint whitch bit I have by Importunitie directed, and another Bill
for the tenants of Stainemoore that doe agree ageinst the Earles by consent,[87]
and to make bothe stand togither, by magnifieing the custome to be con-

---

85. Date in l.h. margin.
86. Crafty, cautious (*O.E.D.*).
87. The Stainemoore case is P.R.O., C2 Jas I/C4/31.

356v *cont.* firmed in the one and derogating from the other that agreed not I was
troubled, and yet did soe consider that if they can agree they may meete,
and noe bleim upon record appear to discountenance the tenants tytle
hereafter, and soe it now stands, and I finde theim glad

357r of anie occasion whitch I (at their desier invent) that they may have
conference with me, whereof I make deiutie as is fitte that the tenants may
not be suspitious of me, whitch theirfore I never doe but at publique
meeteings, save once at his Importunitie I mett him privately in the Owlde
Parke at Lowther, and upon their letters sent by Mr Rigg I direct as they
desier, in all whitch I have an especiall care not to medle in anie matter
In difference betwixt theim and the Lord Willyam but privately hear bothe
their courses, and assent, but direct not for now I have him upon kinde
tearmes, and when we meete or that I goe to see him he useth me excedeing
kindely owtwardly, whitch let the Inward hart be what may be I make good
use of for the present (whitch use of the present time, without daunger or
Impediment to future is a principall consideration, in my opinion since manie
things may Intervein, and hinder things projected, though never soe
providently foresene, if they be to come or a farre of).
I have allsoe at this time a busines on foote betwixt the Prince and all his
tenants of the Baronie off Kendale, whose Steward I am of the Richmond
fee,[88] the effect whereof is to alter their customes, (whitch are allwayes
ageinst reason, and Increas dayly and especiall ageinst the King and great
Lords that live a farre of and have neglectfull officers) and to bring a
profitte to the prince, whitch Busines dothe wholely Relie upon me, the
whitch I undertake by coolor

357v and means whereof I fear the Lord of Cumberlands tenants, and my oune,
tenants, and I haveing newly purchased the Mannour of Crosbie [Ravens-
worth] and 100 tenants ther at least, have need of some fearbabes[89] to bring
theim to some reason,[90] whitch I doe by this means, for I fear the whole
cuntrie to overthrow the name of tenantright since the King and Prince
dislike it as a name of hostilitie, and their president will make way for meaner
Lords whoe are now overborne with their tenants, and soe I keep the tenants
in fear, but I see the fears of the Prince his counesell, whoe will be content
with Reason, and I kepes theim their, and yet I soe carrie the Busines as
the tenants see noe other means to help theim, nor shall finde none but
through me; for the effecteing of whitch my desiers I have a comission from
the prince everie woord of mine oune draweing, and sutch comissioners
named as I please, whome I use or not use as I list, and I have added the
Best to take the blame of me and to perswade the tenants, and the
Escheator and feodarie whoe are at my dispose have I made of the Quorum,
whoe are wittie and with help inforce the matters ageinst the tenants, whitch
I moderate, whereby what I shall effect I know not ([91]and what I intend
I will not shew before least if I prevayle not thou laugh my purpose to

88. Appointed 25 October 1617, Kendal Barony B.I.15.
89. *O.E.D.*: something to scare a baby with.
90. See pp. 13–14.
91. Parenthesis not completed.

scorne, but in the Interim I am sewer I gein, bothe opinion and means, 357v *cont.*
wherein my best adavantage is my patience, and consideratenes before
I speake;
first whether I showlde speake or answer directly secondly what I speak 358r
and that I know theim well to whome (*interlined*: and to offer a doubtfull
speatch as procedeing from another not my selfe though I mean it[92]), and
theirein I drawe from the comissioners their opinions and reserve myne oune,
for I onely propose the matters, and drawe the resolution from some of
theim whitch if I gette from none of theim I help theim with it, or father
it of some of theim (*interlined*: whome) I trust whoe will acknowledge it
though it be none of theirs, the tenor of whitch comission followeth, whitch
I confesse I was a litle to blame in for I Scribled it in haste upon the backe
of a letter, yet did it please the comissioners to allow it all addeing onely
a line in the conclusion whitch had in it more fear than woorth, and sutch
a fear, as not prevaileing they will rather Insult upon, I mean the discharge-
ing theim of their tenements and not being able to doe it
Charles Prince[93] of Wales Duke of Cornwall and of Yorke Earle of Chester
to trustie and wellbeloved, Sir James Bellingham 〈knight〉 Sir Frauncis
Duckett and Sir Christopher Pickering knights John Lowther esq. Steward
of oure Richmond fee John Fleming and Christopher Phillipson esquiers
Roger Otway (*interlined*: escheator) and Robert Curwen feodarie of the
county of Westmerland greeteing whereas it appeareth by auntient Records
that we have a great seyniorie and manie frehowlders that howlde of us
as of oure baronie of Kendale, and that we have likewise their mutch demein
Lands and divers forests and other profitts their whereupon divers
Neighboureing Lords as allsoe others cleymeing
a tenantright estate in a great part theirof through the neglect of officers 358v
have greatly Incrotched tendeing to oure disinheritance theirin, and whereas
we out of oure accustomed favor to our tenants, have offered to setle theim
good estates upon reasonable fines, whitch as yet they have not accepted
of, but moste Ignorantly and obstinately the moste part of theim stand oute,
and yet some of theim seemed to oure comissioners, that divers of theim
wowlde be willing to enter into composition with us and yet through the
Inconsiderate obstinacie of others, they cowld not undertake in generall,
we have theirfore for the great trust and confidence we have in you made
choyce of you or anie three of you whereof the Escheator and feodarie to
be tow to Inquier by all lawfull wayes and means what tenures we have
in that countie whitch are howlden by knight service or otherwise, and what
rents wardshipps or other profitts ariseing their upon be now dew, and
what concealed and what not and Likewise to Inquier what demein groundes
were auntiently belongeing to the Castle of Kendale and in whose hands
they now be, and what estate they have theirin, what Improvements or
Inclosiures are made within our forests or else where within oure wastes,
and what rents are payed for the same and the yearly valew theirof soe

---

92. Interlined in a different ink.
93. L.h. margin, note: *per president of notes but not formal, how to looke in to thine
    oune estate bycause I did it in haste.*

358v *cont.* near as you can and what woods are their that may be sowlde, and what other profits we have their unrented or unletten or whitch may [be] letten, and to assess what rents are fitte to be sette theirupon, and to inquier what fines our tenants cleymeing a tenantright estate have payed to the late Lord, or Ladie marques of Northampton, or to anie others, whether arbitrable or certein, and what composition they have made with anie Lord or lesse of that seyniorie, to have their fines setled, and to certefie the same

359r unto us (*MS damaged*) your selves and other neighbouring Lords doe take of your tenants their upon chaunge, and the difference in valew betwixt our lands and yours the rents and services dewly considered and to call for all bookes Rowles accompts and other evidence, whitch were the Lord or Ladie marquesses or their officers or whitch doe belong to us in whose hands soever they be, and after you have perticulerly informed your selves herein, then to treat and compounde with our tenants or soe manie of theim as you finde tractable, and to rate asses and accept sutch fines upon theim as you or anie three of you as aforesayde by the advise of our sayde Steward shall thinke fitte or otherwise to treat of some fitte composition to be generally concluded upon, respecting the goodnes of everie mans perticluer ferme, and soe allwayes to continew, and if you shall not agree of anie certein rates, to certefie your opinions theirin and we likewise authorish you to offer upon leas at reasonable rates sutch things as be unletten or unrented, and to offer sutch of oure wooddes upon sale as may be well spared, and to siese the court house now imployed and their or elsewhere to meete soe often as you thinke fitte, for the execution hereof of all your procedeing wherein we requier you to certefie us the fourth day of June next[94] and if they refuse to pay sutch fines as is directed to some of you, then not to admitt theim our tenants nor to suffer theim to Injoye anie of our lands dated the 19th of Februarie 1619. The event of whitch comissionn you shall know when it is executed whitch when myne oune ends are served I resolve, to finish with a peaceable agrement and whether dear or cheap soe it be agreed it is Indifferent but to Imbarke my selfe in the difference to loose love for notheing I will not

359v (*MS damaged*) theim tenants at will upon arbitrarie fines wherein all the Lords Joint Comissioners Joined, whitch the counsell of the prince all apprehended but Justice Hutton haveing a tenantright at Cawmyre soe prevayled with the Lord Chief Justice Hubbart the Chancellor, that they wowld not thinke of aniething but a faire composition, whitch seeing theim Inclined to I was made a partie to it and the tenants beholding me for it and soe they payed £3000 and odde hundered poundes for composition and had their estates confirmed by decree at a fine certein by the counsell whoe were lessees for yeres to the princes use.[95]

After whitch the Lord Willyam haveing a comission for the forest of Ingelwood and Sir Henrie Faine Joined, and haveing inquisited mutch his kinred being then of the hookes in favar[96] got nothing but disgrace for

---

94. L.h. margin, note: *additio in vanem terrorem*, marked for insertion here.
95. For the tenantright problem see Phillips, Thesis, pp. 127–139.
96. i.e. Off the hooks in favour; out of order or to excess in favour (*O.E.D.*).

his peins, and then was he allsoe foyled in his sewet ageinst Sir Thomas   359v *cont.*
Carleton in the Starre Chamber for (*interlined*: a) supposed practise to kill
him since whitch he hathe bene ever quiett. (*space*) But now agein 1635
he (*interlined*: and his sonne Sir Frauncis and Roger Witherington a recusant
convict) being made comissioners of Oyer and Terminer with Sir Rich
Graham to delivar the Goale, he Intermedles mutch presumeing upon a lettar
of thankes from the King whitch perhaps he may hear of, sitting secondly
without adjornement wherein I have avoyded to sitt though Joined in
comission[97] since whitch busines of the Baronie ended (*erasure*) I was knight
for the shire in parliament 21 Jacobi, and after chosen agein twice in King
Charles time and my sonne John with me, where in 21 Jacobi I did good
service and by Sir Edward Cookes help whome I drew being his dayly
companion dinner and suppa and I alone. And I then in the late parliaments
observed how few or none did labour In the generall good or generall favor
but for private bills factions aboute elections and labour to pull doune great
officers for the private splene of some leaders, the Multitude glorieing in
distruction and their had sutch passages as are cited in my parliament
bookes[98] as I shall never with my good will desier to be their agein,
though then I suffered noe disgrace from the house as manie did, but was   360r
beloved of theim, untill the Duke of Buckingham did take likeing to me,
and then by him brought to the King and unexspectedly knighted by the
King in his oune Bedchamber the Duke and Earle of Sunderland present
and Sir Rich Graham my kinde frind whoe commended me to the Duke
and then was I made of the counsell in fee for the north parts gratis without
one pennie given[99]; and soe brought in Mr Dyott yet the Duke payed of
his bonds arere to the Lord President soe noble he was to me promising
me I should not stay their but have what place I would after, whoe in his
hart beinge a moste noble nature (yet a courtier) loved me hartily and often
had me privat with him bothe day and night, yet in all these favors times
then soe stoode by the Interruption of the parliament as I durst not nor
was it safe to desier anie higher place.

And since my comeing to this place standing to right and reason and upon
Justice differing from the Lord President Wentwoorth in his recusant
comission I gott hard measure where he coulde though before he professed
himself my servant for the right I did him in parliament when he was put
out of the house. But since in compositions for knighthood I being knight
was sett by him to £100 whitch I payed els showld have drawen the state
upon me, and since had divers contrivements to have drawen me to forsake

---

97. For these activities see Penry Williams, "The Northern Borderland under the
    Early Stuarts", in *Historical Essays Presented to David Ogg*, ed. H. F. Bell and
    R. L. Ollard (1963), and Surtees Soc., LXVIII, p. 469.
98. With one exception these were printed in H.M.C., *Thirteenth Report, Appendix
    VII*. The exception is a diary for 1624.
99. Knighted 6 June 1626 (W. A. Shaw, *The Knights of England* (1906), p. 190).
    Graham was a Buckingham man (*Calendar of State Papers, Domestic, 1623–
    1625*, p. 462; H.M.C., *Mar and Kellie MSS*, II, index, *sub nomine*). For Mr.
    Dyot see p. 58, n. 3, above.

360r *cont.* the place, yet I houlde it, and with his outward love, and the same of most
men, by whitch I will now Indevor, for my peace sake, my oune comfort,
and my posterities foreseeing I have a sufficient foundation for an estate
like to Grow if things stand as now if God please of it selfe well husbanded
above my desiers and above that I can howlde without envie. And now
being by falls and slips fallen into a Rupture whitch by nature and kinred
of my mother I was partly Inclyned to, I doe think of all means to give my
self ease and to contemplate my end weighing seriously all I have done
and all I intend and to what end I have done it or showld doe

360v   yet will not be alltogither the Idle while I have abilitie to doe good, and
may doe it, and be without eminent daunger, for I have now soe setled
my Eldest sonne John as he hathe in certein revenew £450. And gets before
me by the Law upon £250 per annum, and my sonne Cristopher I intend
St Bees now woorth near £300 per annum and to give him the Stock he
hathe being aboute £1500, and to my sonne Willyam whoe is verie diligent
allsoe I intend Eglestone and £1500 stock, and to give Frances my younger
daughter £2000 whitch I prayse God I can doe and leave John my Eldest
above £1600 per annum with what he now hathe besides his fines and woods,
whitch are sufficient beginnings for their Industrie as I direct theim everie
of theim to excede me in estate with lesse toyle then I have had, soe that
If I could doe more I fear it wowld be more to their hurt, Increasing their
care and daunger as their estates Increas unlesse wisely by theim considered,
for I finde (mediocria firma) and lesse care, trouble envie and daunger and
grief of hart, and trouble of bodie is Incident to moderate fortunes then
greater if one Intend to governe theim well. Wherfore being now 54 yeres
of age and in good health but for the Infirmitie of Rupture with whitch
manie live to 80 that I know, I have moderated my desiers, and Resolve
to take a moderate comfort in that I posses whitch if I had more is better
for health then excesse, and to give furtherance to my childrens good
Indevors, not alltogither bycause they are my children but bycause I finde
theim carefull to follow my direction, Industrious and diligent to doe good
in the wordeld to theimselves and others, and I know none more carefull
and lesse vitious then they none of theim loveing nor useing anie ploy, drink,
venerie, nor other vice though younge (*erasure*) unlesse they be to carefull
of the world, yet neyther of my (*interlined*: younger) sonnes that I made
marchants and bought their fredomes but they now kepe

361r   50 or 60 men of woorke in their coleworkes sallt woorkes shipping, clothe
woorkeing and dressing to whome they pay dayly wages out of their
Industrie and my stock and pay (*interlined*: about) £500 per annum custome
to the King the one being under 24 yeres the other 25.[1]

Whose Industrie for the good of the comon wealth I thought good to
Incourage and for ther oune profitt and advancement in their youth, that
in their age (*interlined*: they) may take rest proper to that age and studie
how to doe good to their posteritie and others, and not be busied then with
necessitie to live whitch being the product of my care and peins and they

---

1. These comments seem to pre-date those of 20 February 1636/37 on p. 40, above;
the ages of his sons suggest a date between mid-April and mid-September 1636.

yet dayly directed by me I hope within tow years will be soe setled as they 361r *cont.*
will take the surplus of my revenew and use it to better purpose then I
can for theim and me wherein if it please God to make our Labours
succesfull and to direct us right whitch I doe desier of him that ruleth heaven
and earth, and to putt into all our mindes to doe what may be moste
for his honor and our good, I shall then live and Die happilie, and leave
theim in sutch estate one loveing another as I have desired theim and have
it under their hands upon serious consideration,[2] and in sutch sorte desiering
to perpetuate good counsells and directions to our posteritie one to another
as well as our lands, be pleased in my life soe to think, and to see theim
have like thoughts not for that after death it will be aniething to me or
theim but in our lief it giveth us comfort we have in us more of the goodnes
of that benificent god to take comfort in then others of whome he hathe
not bestowed like blessings whitch draweth us dayly more and more and
giveth us peace more and more to doe him service whitch agein beseetching
our Good God to grant I end at this time in contemplation of that
(*interlined*: Infinite and) everlasting goodnes whitch noe man nor finite
creature can comprehend nor perfectly understand as I think, haveing well
observed the doubtfullnes and vanitie of manie teatchers theirin in all
cuntries and religions, being now pleased in the reading of Erasmus booke
of the prayse of follie or foolishnes.

---

2. Perhaps a reference to the written criticisms of his sons, and their replies to
   him, which Sir J.L.(1) wrote in A1/1, ff362–372.

APPENDIX II

STATEMENT OF SIR J.L.(1)'S WEALTH, 1634

D/Lons/L, A1/3, (no foliation)

[*Hand of Sir J.L.(1)*]

A consideration of the personall estate of me Sir John Lowther
Knight 1 May 1634

	£
I have oweing in detts Morgages and leases, and in stock not chargeable whitch I call my setled estate	7110
Detts dew within a year	0690
Remote detts some after deaths	190
Whitson rents besides the rents assigned My Man Giles in the setled detts aboute	150
In my purse above	150
Totall is	8290
I owe for Marton, rents, and other trifles	1190
Soe resteth clear	7100

This accompt will appear treu by my dett booke and booke of rents
and stock.

And I have disbursed above twentie thousand pounds in money for
lands as may appear by my great booke besides this stock and
building.

My Revenew in land of Inheritance being now as I esteme it £1800
by year with that my sonne hathe in Jointure made by me at his
mariage.

232

APPENDIX III

D/Lons/L, A1/1, ff270–285

[Hand of Sir J.L.(2). Changes in ink and style are indicated by an asterisk at the beginning of a paragraph. Cross references in the text to the long white book *or* the other booke *are to the "diary" entries in A1/4, ff104v–110r* (above, pp. 58–74) *and A1/4a, ff227r–242r* (above, pp. 152–198), *and are not here cross-referenced; neither are textual differences between these "diaries" noted. Cross references to other manuscripts are noted. A1/2 is a late eighteenth century transcript of this "diary".]*

Memorable observations and rememberances of the House ⟨and⟩ Grounds, at Lowther, and the qualitie and conditions thereof, soe farr as I know, or have beene certainely informed, a satisfaction to posteritie what alterations and changes happen according to the severall opinions and pleasures of the succeedinge owners.   270r

Taken per me J. Lowther, Kt. Bt. 1640

The owlde towre Eastwards is not knowne which of our auncestors builte, ther beeinge noe mention thereof.

The Buildinge betwixt the tow Towres was new built by my father 1630, beeinge aunciently manie several low owlde roomes, viz. a Halle, a greate Chamber, and several other rooms accordinge to antiquitie with owlde Houses of Office, as Brewhouse, Backehouse and Nursery, all where the new Backehouse now is placed, and new built likewise by my father.

The Roufe of the said buildinge betwixt the two Towres I bought by my father's appoyntment (viz. both leade and wood,) of the Lord William Howard, beeinge then the rooufe of the Greate Hall at Kirkeoswald Castle, which then was, before it was pulled downe by the said Lord William, a most magnificent and princely House, Cost about £140.[1]

The New Towre westwards was built likewise in memorie by my greate Grand father Sir Richard Lowther and his wife, (a carefull woman of Midleton Hall,)[2] when he was in the Towre at London for intertayneing the Queene of Scotts, in Queene Elizabeth tyme; from whence he was happely delivered with much honour after he had beene twise there imprisoned, to his greate cost, as appeareth by his bookes of expence, in goeing and remayneinge there; remayning in the evidences in Lowther Box.[3]

My Grandfather, Sir Christopher Lowther, builte Hackthropp Hall, beeinge

---

1. *Cost about £140* a later addition in another ink.
2. P.I.2.
3. These accounts are in A1/3.

270r *cont.*   formerly tenants houses and claymed a kinde of customarie lease which was bought out and cleared and by him intended for a joynture for his Wife he married out of Warwickshire, the Ladie Burditt.[4]

  6. He likewise builte Meaburne House the Walles; which my father finished and perfected and bought all the demesne belongeinge unto it, except about £8 per annum beeinge the severall possessions of divers tenants, beeinge caled the Hall Fawld. And after he bought and added unto (*interlined*: it) that part of Regill Grainge which is tyth free, beeinge part of the Abbey of Bylands which is of the Cestertian Order and thereby freed from tythes.

270v 7. It is not knowne who brought the water to the house (*interlined*: at Lowther) which had beene worthie of memorie, a thinge soe convenient and usefull; as greate care is to be had to preserve the same from hurt ⟨and⟩ at the springe heade that it (*interlined*: stopp not in the way, and to stake it what way it goeth to finde the defaulte).[5]

  8. My greate Grandfather Sir Rich. Low*ther* walled the low Orchard aboute, and my father and I the High Orchard; (*interlined*: which was auncientlie) there used as was said to be much more plentie of frewte then is in these later tymes.

  9. My Grandfather (*interlined*: Sir C. Lowther) repaired the Wale about the New Parke, and was a great lover of the deare, and made the Parke stanch; he was a good husband at hombe, And an orderly housekeeper, but noe getter, not haveinge the way, and manie children, and indebted when he came unto the Estate; lived not longe, viz. but about 10 years, and his estate but about £700 p. ann.; soe not much to be expected from him.

10. My father repaired and new walled (*erasure*) most part of the Owld Parke he walled Burtribanke, the High Feild, bought in the Heade Close which was the tenants on it; and new walled Rowlandfeild, which was all formerly stick and (*erasure*) dry hedge, and was in continuall repairinge, and spent much wood.

11. He walled the furside of Greeneriggs, and laid Brackenber to Lowther demayne, which was formerly parte of Hackthropp; and laid Thrimby Inge likewise, which was part of Thrimby, and bought of Jo. Salkeld in my tyme, before which tyme there was noe water belongeinge to Greeneriggs, the water formerly runninge through the midle of the Inge, and never came in Greenriggs.

12. Rowlandfeild was bought in by my Great Grandfather Sir Rd. Low*ther* of one Salkeld of Whale, beinge a freehold ⟨there⟩ anciently, yet was but a lease ended when he compounded them out of it.

13. Wale Inge was new waled by my father; the tenants of Whale haveinge the fogge and Springeage formerly for makeinge the hedge about it, for which I give £5. per annum to look unto it, and orderinge the water, to make it wett and dry at pleasure, by which meanes it may be much helped with as litle care as cost, which it is worthie of, meadow being pretious in these parts, and the nature of the Grasse is cleare altered by this meanes, beeinge formerly generally stronge seaves and rushes.

---

4. P.II.3.
5. Interlined in a different ink.

My Father walled Jackcrofte aboute, and felled the Wood; you may perceve   271r
by an owld Deede that one of our Anncestors tooke the (*erasure*) same
for one cropp, and sew ackorons upon it in the tyme of Edward the first,
beeinge (*space*) years since; which cropp was not taken of untill my father
cutt the same. There was manie goodly ockes the wood beeinge worth near
£400 at that tyme, and the ground but about 4 acres: beeinge good discretion
to cutt it, for the okes were decayeinge; and there was 20 okes left unfelled,
which I cutt when I built the new Oxhouse and kilne upon the Halebanke.
And lett posterite plant and sett such wood as will grow againe as my father
and I have done for use and orniment, beeinge the greatest grace belongeinge
to the house. And to sett or sow sume okes, if manie faile yet sume will
take, as we have had experience of;
My father in his tyme cutt and sprunge all Buckhoulme except the Horse
Houlme; and all the Owlde Parke except the Birkes adjoyninge to Winerigge,
which Rigg was all a greate wood of Birkes and cutt by my Greate Grandfather, and came not againe, but those others below them in there places
where none was formerly. And soe upon cutinge of Jackcroft manie Seales
came upp where there was never anie before that tyme, Soe in the low end
of Buckhoulme manie younge birkes came where never anie was formerly;
Soe that oftentymes the ground produceth a new kinde, as beeinge desirous
of cainge, as liveinge creatures are;
My father waled Esklaymooreside, and tooke a part of Skellan by the
parsons agreement which he had in lew of part of the composition for
the tyth of the demesne.
The Parsons of Lowther have had most of the gleabe out of the demesne
(*erasure*) as a composition for the tyth, as (*erasure*) there was the Parson
Houlme and the Lords Houlme, the Lords Mill feild and Parson Millfeild
taken out of it. The Lord's Flatt and Parson's Flatt, which appear to be
taken out of the demeyne; And he hath 6 Catle gates grassed from
Whisunday untill Michelmas beside in lew of all mannour of tythes.
Only my father bought the Low Crofts and High Crofts (*erasure*) of the
tenants for which wee pay tyth in kinde for (*interlined*: corne,) and soe
for Atkinsons tenement, which I bought my selfe for the nearnesse unto
the house; which I new walled.
My father Inclosed the Farr Heades which layd formerly to the comon,   271v
purposeing therby after to make more use of the Comon above by Inclosure,
haveinge debarred Lowther thereby who had only Intercomon therein.
I entered unto Lowther upon my father's death (*interlined*: at Mich) anno.
1637; shortly after which I paid £5000, in dets and legaces, and stand yet
charged to pay £3500 in legaces. In 1640, & [16]41 I built the Gatehouse
and Clostered walke; the stables and Garners etc all de novo; the new
Oxhouse and barne over it on the Hale banke. I translated the garden,
which was in 2 parts, made the garden at the Pidgen Cote, and that
Adjoyninge to the High Croft, which was nothing but netles and quarie.
I built the Smithie, repaired and new waled Buckhoulme house, Rowlandfeild house, Dearehouse, Hayclosehouse, all which were in great decay and
rewines. I cast all the hedges about Buckhoulme, Esklamoore, Skellan, and
Flatts, which had not beene cast in memorie, and cast the gutter on the

271v *cont.*   farr side of Esklamoore to gaine the Okes in the hedge which were doubtfull, and claymed to belonge to Clifton feild.

I lymed Rowland feild and made it thereby much more frewtfull. I made the halfmoone fawld, out of that which was all a greate quarie of stones above ground, which made it frewtfull by reason of the goods that draw unto it for bealed and shelter. I lymed and mended the Haycloses and had greate increase of corne which I fallowed for the ease of plowinge though the distance was further and imployed the boones in the easie ground.

I walled that side of the Owlde Parke towards Brackenbure and made the stack garth adjoyneinge to Thrimby Inge, the high one beeinge to Cowld; yet may be used for a chainge, for mendinge the ground;

I devided the High Feild by the cross wall de novo; and repared and new cast and quick sett the severall hedges in the other part of it.

I bought in Jacksons tenement and Runraven part of Thrimby, and have a mortgage of Pawles, intendinge to inclose that part of the Comon adjoyninge with lesse clamour because they joyne on everie side.

I bought the water into the low side of the High Feild (*erasure*) by byeinge a parcell in Thrimby feild, and adinge unto it and drawinge a Springe unto that place the ground formerly wholey wantinge water a greate defect, which now it may have plentifully, with care to keepe the water in the course, which may be done with a sodd or turfe at the well heade.

I made the 2 Stackgarths convenient for both sides of the feild, for Sheepe or Catle, which is dry though cowld.

For Hackthropp, while I lived there after my mariage in my fathers tyme, I built the out Stable and Workehouse; I bought the new Close next the feild, which was a tenement and waled the same, and inclosed a peece of waste in the high end, out of the towne gate;

272r   I bought the Low Houlmes of Walker, I cast all the hedges about it I (*erasure*) new walled the roove aboute, and burne the topp of it, which was a wett ground, and had wheat and bigg 3 years together on it.

I walled the wall at the end of Winers and cast that hedge anew, and walled the wall downe the edge loneinge which leade down unto the high way before; I waled the wale betwixt the edge and Parke, and that at the end of the litle Bottome.

I inclosed a peece at Thrimby Poole which belonged formerly to Thrimby for to gett water to all that ground, which formerly it wanted;

I bough the Close on the farr side on the Gill which is part of Thrimby and then I tooke upp and laid the Gill unto it, (*erasure*) which was formerly wast ground and belonged to Thrimby and Hackthropp; though sume though*t* much yet they durst not disturbe mee in it.

That I thought would be fitt to cherish for the deare to lye that way, which they much desired, and would be a good shelter for them;

I lymed and much improved Graystans, the Edge and the Parkes by lymeinge, which bore exceedinge Corne for manie yeares thereby and a litle helpe of manure; which in former tymes was full of Catt Whins; and when it was come formerly in my tyme had scarcely the seede for want of good husbandry and a little cost which was 3ble recompenced. But my profession in the Law hindered my endevours, and tooke my care of it, though I

272r *cont.*

naturally loved much the improvement and meliorateinge of grounds, howldinge it noe lesse good husbandry to improve the wast and baren ground, as to purchas new;

I allwayes left my ground in greate hart, and lett it lye ether upon bigg stuble well manuered, or very rich, whereby I found, contrary to the comon opinion, that the grasse was much richer, fatter, fedd much better, came as soune toe and was reddie and ripe for corne againe much souner then otherways, and then answerd the losse of an ote cropp with double use;

Yet in Corne I never found much profitt, but only it was a pleasure (*erasure*) to see thinges mended, the poore sett on worke; and the ground thereby amended, which was the principall thinge I still aymed at in plowinge anie more than was necessarie for my house.

For a Cuntry house, especially in these parts, cannot be without one draught to leade ones fewell, both Wood Peates and Coles all which are carefully to be preserved; and wee have to serve ourselves with good husbandry viz. to cutt one Springe every other yeare, and springe it carefully for 6 or 7 yeares at least, for the better it is saved in the 2 or 3 first years the souner it will be for use againe.

And for peates, if they be looked and mynded that the mosse be not runn over in disorder, but well beded and taken before them, and not to suffer anie others to get in it; It will serve forever plentifully.

272v

Yet I howld it fitt and better that, Askham and wee devide, for they gett much more peates in it than wee, and doe more harme; for as yet it is not devided betwixt us, and wee ought to have the greater part, for that our rent (*interlined*: in Helton) is greater;

For Coles there is at Slegill in James Willans ground, a tenant of my owne, which I forbeare as longe as others cann be gotten; And when those faile there will be found about Meaburne ether adjoyneinge to Regill, or about Skitterrigg; where there was got in my father's tyme, though the seame was but about 7 or 8 inches; Yet a better seame might be expected there or about.

Litle Strickland, though much monie was spent there, and noe good done, which may be a Caviat.

Likewise a draught is necessarie to gett your hay, and for sume Straw for horse litter and other uses, which cannot be bought, soe that the boones aded thereunto well followed would be convenient, and asmuch as I could wish to be used except necessitie inforce that you cannot lett nor farme your ground.

Yet I was forced to keepe 2 or 3 draughts while I was in buildinge and waleinge and fencinge my grounds, and lymeinge and leadinge of coles for that use principally; for which I paid 21s. for 80 lode of Coles, and had a Cowp that contayned about 12 lode, yet I had filled 10 lode in regard of the greate quantitie I used in regard of others.

I felled the doled okes in Ravenrash and have begun a wale at the head of it, to springe it safely, which must be carefully preserved, that beeinge the principall support of this house for oke tymber, which will be the greatest want of anie thinge in this Countrie; therefore I could wish a speciall care and diligence be had to preserve it in all places. For I brought wood

272v *cont.*   from Threlkeld which I had with my Wife, to preserve this neare home, and will not sell anie, for anie monie but preserve it for our owne use and soe it may serve as longe as the house shall endeure; except sume ungracious unthrift happen to be, which God prevent;

273r   1642. I inclosed the new Close at Beareslack in a quarter of a yeares tyme; which I did upon these reasons; first, because it was a roff ground, and spoyled all our flock and others that went adjoyneinge (*erasure*) 2ly I offerred the tenants that they should have it at a reasonable rent which they refused not willinge to be at that cost. 3ly It was a ground which soe joyned upon the demesne, that it in a mannour only belongeinge to me. 4. I bought the 3 tenements adjoyneinge which had the nearest interest therein, viz. Jacksons and Powleyes in Lowther Lordshipp, and Heydales in Thrimby; And if there were noe other reasons, yet beeinge Lords of Quale in whome I only clayme it, and Lord of Thrimby, Bampton, and Knipe, the Adjoyneinge Lordshipp I might doe it, leaveinge compitent for the tenants which there is. Besides, Inclosures are noe new thinges though now it seemeth strainge; for I have the deede from the Abbott of Shap for the inclosure of Trantran, and Rosgill Scarr Sweetehoulme and Fristenrigg were all inclosures, and soe all the improvements about Shapp wherein they have much incroched upon Thrimby and Meaburne.

Yet for all these reasons of Justice and equitie, sume were soe malivolent as in the night to pull downe gapps and stones out of the Walle though divers both Knipe and Thrimby served to give me thankes for it, as a saftie for there sheepe.

I have likewise this year first the buildinge of a new house for Corne and Catle at Skellan heade, which will be very usefull both for Skellan and Flatts, the greate distance formerly eateinge upp the profitt, and takeinge away the pleasure, Besides (*erasure*) when it is farmed as I have now lett Skellans and Esklamoore for 7 years the fother is thereby eaten upon the ground, and thereby kept in hart and manure which otherways is cleare, spoyled except it bee grasseinge.

I butified the Hall Porch with Pilosters and other cutt woork, which was only playne formerly, I gott the stone in Clifton demayne, in the banke under the Hall, which is a fine white Stone, but very difficult to woorke, but that I happened of expert and skillfull Maysons and Carvers, one Alexander Pogmire;

There must care be taken if I live not to doe it, on the west side of the new towre that sume (*interlined*: rough) wale be brought upp about halfe a yard from the towre, and covered over at the topp to prevent beateinge of the Wether, which wee finde by experience to beate through the wall, and hath rotten the tymber, soe wee have beene forced to putt in Corbells; but especially in at the Middletowre Chimney which is soe thinne that it beateth through it; And to leade the south side betwixt the windowes with thinn webes of leade, to be nayled to the Wall;

273v *   1642. In the latter end of this yeare, in regard of the great troubles and civill Warr by the participants betwixt the Kinge and the Parlement, wee could doe nothinge for matter of profitt, or management of our private affaires, beeinge

wholy taken upp in publicque imployment for the Cuntry (*erasure*)[6] who 273v *cont.*
were then up in armes in Yorkshire the Lord Fairefax, Sir John Hotham, and
his sonne Sir Henry Annderson, Sir Mathew Bayenton, Sir Edward
Loftehouse.

1643. 1644, 1645, & 1646 were all tymes of Warr and trouble which cost
me much in compositions, taxes, plunder, and losses: the particulers may
bee seene in the Longe white booke of rents amongest other thinges the
perticulers.

1647. I paid legacies given my Sister Kirkby £500, and bought land in Bishopricke, called Stayton, for £930, which I exchanged next year for land at
Marton with Mr. Fultropp of like value, much more convenient.
⟨And that yeare I maried my Daughter Wandesford and gave her £2000
portion as to⟩

1648. The Scots came in with Duck Hambleton,[7] wherein wee had greate losse,
as by an estimate appeareth in the aforesaid booke appeareth [*sic*].

1649. I added to Lowther demesne two tenements which were Threlkeld's and
Barney Lowther's caled Thwaitlands and Sherflatt, which were neare and
convenient and thereby, and by incloseing a peece betwixt the Church yeard
and Esklamore gate, all the ground from Buckholme to the Low Orchard
may be layd together to milke the kine when you please at your doore;
which could never be before: and is neare the house for tyallage.
And there was 2 Crofts adjoyneinge to the Low Orchard heade, which
hedges I grubed upp, and turned the plowinge of part of Thwaitlands
towards the Orchard, which is more levell, lesse washinge, and soe keepeth
the manure the better.

1650 I bought likewise about that tyme in the Bancke Croft adjoyneinge   274r
to Ravenrash, (*erasure*) and aded it to the demesne for conveniencie of
puttinge to horse in; which one Tho Clarke had before and under couller
thereof distroyed and lopped all the wood in Ravenrash; and I new quicksett
the hedge at the farr end of Ravenrash, and new fenced and repaired the
wale all about it towards Dowlands, for it laid downe to Dowlands before.
And I waled the owt side of Bankecroft towards the Scarr, all a new.
In that yeare and the yeare before I and my Unkle Robt the Alderman
purchassed Maske in Yorkshire, which was Sir Will. Peniman's cheefe seate,
for ⟨1350⟩ £13500.

* I bought likewise a part of Marton of Mr. Goodyear, that cost £600.
In that yeare I sowld Barnard Castle Brigg end Mills for £450[8] for the
reasons in the other booke.

1651. I maried my daughter Wandesford, and gave hir £2000.

1652. In April [16]52 I maried my seacond Wife; the reason, grounds proceedings, and other particulers may see in the other booke; by whome I
had £700 per annum for her life; but was covenanted at her former mariage
to have beene £800; but £100 or neare is abated in Sesses, as it is now,
that Cuntry beeinge much deeper then this.

---

6. The erasure extends over six lines of text.
7. i.e. The Duke of Hamilton.
8. Remainder of paragraph a later insertion.

274r *cont.*   And ⟨in⟩ about Whisuntyd after I agreed for the saile of Maske to my
Uncle Rob. as most convenient for him that wanted a Seate and I had but
to manie and it to greate a house not to be used; and I held it to cowld
a Seate for mee, growinge now more infirme then formerly, beeinge now
in my 47th yeare of my age.

   1653. You may see in the other booke the monies bestowed againe in
Anuities, that cost me above £8000; and besides I bought part of Mr. Fosters
at Tollsby, cost me above £500.

274v * 1653. In this yeare and the yeare before I plowed and lymed that part of the
New Parke next Cragg's, and fenced with a great cast earthen hedge, and
brushed above, and a rayle above that, soe that never anie Deare troubled
it. It cost me in 2 greate lymekilns, which I burnt in the 2 years, above
£40, besides 2 years manure I had at Hayclose House, and Rowlandfeild
House; and after the first yeare plowinge I plowed it twice for the next year
once after Michelmas and in seede tyme and had halfe of it Otes, and half
Bigge, which was the goodliest and strongest that ever I see grow; It was
but formerly a light brackeny ground, and full of great stones which I digged
upp and made the Wale with at the heade of it, and led to other places.

   There was above 500 Stookes of Oates, and neare 400 of Bigge, and about
12 stookes was a futher.

   That yeare I made the new way to the Parke, slopeinge the scarre which
went in formerly at Crag house; but was a myry dirtie way;

   But I ledd all the low end of it trough the low end of Cragg close, and
soe by the hen house; Soe that I accompt that years crop would quitt all
Charges, and hope to have 5 or 6 cropps as good, and then leave it rich.

   But meane if please God I live and enjoye peace to beald a house in the
midle of it to serve for the tyme I intend to plow it and soe to improve
the rest of the playne, findeinge it a fitt ground for Corne, and earely ripe,
and easie and dry to plow after it be brooken to land; but fir the first yeare
wee had 8 strongest oxen wee could gett, and all could scarce plow it the
bracken roots were soe stronge and it rise soe thicke; but after limeinge
and twice plowinge anie 6 oxen would plow it with greate ease.

   And I have begun to wale Rowland Feild to keepe in Deare, and to ley
it to the Parke while I

275r   make use of this for tyllage haveinge brought that to the best perfection
that could be;

   For I finde by experience that in husbandry there is noe profitt like to fresh
ground, and not to plow it to longe; for it will have a double cropp with
half the manure, after once brought into good husbandrie;

   1653. This yeare and the former I gott all the earthfast stones I could out
of the Millfeild, which it was full of and led all the other small stones off
which was about 100 futher fir it was a very stonie ground; haveinge but
layd it to grasse 2 yeares before the most of [it] haveinge never layd in
memorie of man before; I bestowed the best of the stones in waleinge about
it, and makeinge a Stack yard and the rest threw into the River and (*erasure*)
in wast places;

   It was one yeare grasse, and one yeare medow before, but had but very
smale cropps upon it.

And my Wife towld mee jestingly that I made Stackyards, but where would 275r *cont.*
the hay cume from; And this yeare beeinge but the 3rd yeare (*erasure*) after
lyeinge lea; there was more then could well stand in the Stackgarth and
above 12 load brought hombe; which was principally by drawinge, trench-
inge, and conveyinge the water carefully over all places to overflow it and
not to suffer anie water to be lost in vayne which was the reason I turned
it from an arable to a Medow close, haveinge observed the advantage thereof
in the South that ground hath beene brought from 4s. to 40s an acer. The
low end of the Flatts, Brodegards, part of Dowlands, Whale Inge, and
Thrimby Inge may be improved thereby and part of Sherflatt bottom, if
carefully ordered. And it is the cheapest and profitablest husbandry can be
used; Halegarth was and still may be much bettered by it.

1654. At Martinmas this yeare I walled Rowlandfeild, from Crage close at 275v
Whale, unto the crosse wall in the heades that goeth unto the corner of
the Hay Closes accordinge as I had formerly intended about tenn quarters
high on the innside, which I finished before May Day followinge; haveinge
intended to add that part of the heades to the Parke and Rowlandfeild,
but findeinge the way to be inconvenient to ley through it, I intend to follow
the owld wall about unto the heade of Rowlandfeild, and soe joyne it to
the Parke and soe to exclude the heades and keepe it for fatt sheepe or
the like, as most convenient; and to add more of the heades to that I have
which I am to take upp in lew of the right to 3 tenements I have lately
bought from the tenants, viz. Atkinson tenement, Barney tenement and
Threlkeld tenement and part of Clarke tenement.

And this winter I plowed the rest of the New Parke unto the Frith which
was in part growne over with bushes, and much Brackeney and mossie;
I had one draught, and in it 12 Oxen it was soe stronge with Brakes, and
rootes of thornes. It tooke 80 bushells of otes, and had about 800 stookes
of greate sheafe increase, at 10 sheaves in a stooke, beeinge most of very
goodly corne, except the bancke towards Quale, which I intended to improve
by lymeinge and manueringe.

I likewise new cast and cutt the old hedge betwixt the Frith and the playne
and sett the old thorne I grubed upp in it with younge quickewood, and
made ⟨it⟩ a double ditch which I Brushed well with greate thornes, and
Rayled it above to turne deare, which it did sufficiently, and after the corne
inned, I made a gapp or tow and sett open the gate for the deare to have
libertie to runne in the Winter tyme into it.

And in the Springe I new builte the House or Barne in the midle of the
Parke playne, to sett the corne in, and to breede manuere for improveinge
the ground findeinge the cariage of corne hombe, and recariage of the
Dunge to be longesume and chargeable, and often to misse oppertunitie
by such lenght of tyme in inninge the Corne, which I did Inn this yeare
in lesse then tow days, with 2 draughts and three carts.

In the Lower Close next Crages this yeare there was 480 stookes of Bigge,
and 240 of Mashelden very good and proud Corne; the Mashelden was
all sowne on Bigg stuble.

* In this yeare I bought the reversion of Yeanwith with the Wood in
possession which cost mee £2200, to Add to Lowther for use and ornament

242

LOWTHER FAMILY ESTATE BOOKS

275v *cont.* soe longe as please God.

      * 1655. And likewise the Manor of Rosgill, which cost £440.

276r * 1655. This yeare I contracted with Alexand. Pogmire for the new Buildinge the Gallery and Romes under and above it on the east side of the court, beeinge formerly an old useless house, intended for a Cowhouse and Stables which I transposed to other places more decent. I was to give him by Artickles for Ash/er woorke, gettinge, settinge, and woorkeinge 2s. a yard square; for window woorke 5d per foot longe for ground table 9d per yard; for Doores, playne without mould, 10s a peece; for Rigginge 9d a yard; flagginge 10d a yard square.

For raw wall against the Ashler 6d a yard; for other rowgh Wall, a yard at bottom, and 2 fott at topp; the height of the Gallery, 1s 3d a yard; for Stayres 9d a yard, and flagginge woorke 10d a yard.

I was to bringe all materiall as stone lyme and sand to the ground I computed the owte woorke would stand mee in about £150 but the extraordinarie woorke about the Cante Window with Pillers the Chapell windowes intended to be tracery woorke with the Chimney peeces intended to be inlayed with marble will cost above £50 more at least. And the wood woorke, which was done by doytaile woorke with the wood slate, and workemanshipp will cost above £100 more; besides wainscott and inside furniture will be nearely £200 more. Soe I suppose aboute £500 will but finish the Gallery and Chapell; but this will add much to the bewtie and ornament of the house and make it much more uniforme; and, this beeinge done I have built three parts of the house, viz. the tow sides and the (*erasure*) front where the Wallke (*erasure*) besides the new Barne and Oxhouse.

I proceeded only this yeare unto the Window sole in the Gallery, by reason the woorkemen failed much in number to make good the undertakeinge and the sumer proved extreame wett and unseasonable for Leadinge stones which wee gott all in Ravenrash and made wayes to the Quaries with much lawboure.

The wood for buldinge was most cutt in Ravenrash such as was decayinge only about 8 trees in the Short Wood (*erasure*) and about (*erasure*) 10 trees in Buckholme hedge, betwixt Mr Wiberg ground and mee, which I had then in mortgage and yet have, unto which they made noe clayme though sumetymes formerly they would with little coulor clayme part of them though it be a double ditch, and wee make the fence; I cutt only one tree in Yeanewith Wood for that use, but must cutt more there for boordes; I spare that Wood for the prospect from the house, beeinge a greate ornament.

    * This yeare I bought the Towne and Lordshipp of Rosgill, which cost me above £440, and the last part of the Short Wood.[9]

276v * 1656. In this yeare wee only gott the out walls of the Gallery and Chapell finished, and slated; I ledd 34 further of Slate from Penreth Fell, which cost but 2s a futher and 4d dressinge besides leadinge with my owne draughts; there was old Slate besides that came of the old House and old Chapell which slated the backeside of the Chapell, and I gave 8s 6d a roode for slatinge without meate and drinke only I found latts, nayles, and slate pines of sheepe bones wee bought for 2½d a hundreth which are of more last

9. This reference to Rosgill, and that at the foot of f275v, are later additions.

then wood which is apt to rott and soe sett downe the slate; There was
about 11 roode of slate in all.
I (*erasure*) agreed for the tarras on the foreside of the Court, except that
over the Cant window, for aleven pounds;
Upon computation of the charge of the mayson woorke and wallinge of
the new woorke there it cost mee in monie upon the former agreements
£150 and I had over paid them above £40 more then the woorke amounted
unto upon measure which I am like to loose beeinge but poore through
imprudence. And I accompt the leadinge of stone lyme sand and my owne
servants lawbour about the same, though I did it at spare tymes, and at
the most advantage; haveinge draughts and Coach Horses I imployed, which
did likewise other service (*erasure*) as ther was occasion for plowinge leadinge
of fewell London journeys and the like; My Wife and I haveinge this Springe
caried upp our foure daughters to London, where wee left 2 of myne, viz.
Mary and Frances, and one of hers, viz. Jane,[10] and brought Barbara, my
eldest not maried, downe into the Cuntry. And beeinge then at London,
my brother Will and I bought Greate Preston and Astley near Swillington
of the Lord Darcies son; the moitie cost me £3050—and will be, after a
life or 2, worth per annum above £200.[11] There is in it rich Cole mynes,
and Lyme quaries, which is of good value there; and that part called Astley
is very rich ground, lyinge upon the River, and rich medow; and good pasture
and Arable; and the house at Preston though rewenous might be made a
good seate, haveinge a goodly prospect as most in Yorkshire.
656. In 9br this yeare I bought the moitie of the tyth of Ashegarth[12] with
Mr. Clapeham, beeinge a Trenitie Colledge lease of Cambridge; which Sir
Wingfeild Bodenham former had; it cost us both parts £1570. I had sume
end in aboute my owne tythes of Wensladale, to preserve them if I parted
with it; or else, if tymes prove well, to ⟨sell⟩ buy the other moitie. But as
now it is I forbeare makeinge use of him as an assistant; it payeth about
£200 rent to the Colledge and Minister, but have heard it accompted worth
above £500 per annum.
This yeare all that had beene delinquents on the (*interlined*: late) Kinges
partie, notwithstandinge the General Pardon and act of oblivion were as
they called it decimated; viz. to pay the teneth ⟨of the⟩ part of the revenew
of there reall estate; and to pay £10 per annum for every £1500 in personall
estate, without respect of debts or other charges upon the estate; assessed
by Commissioners as they pleased, without anie appeale. I was assessed
for Westmerland, and Cumberland in land and goods at £75 per annum
though I made it appeare I had noe estate in most of the lands I was assessed
for and in Yorkshire at £120 per annum without giveinge in anie particuler
though I had the like reason for mitigation (*erasure*) and £5 for the rent
charge of Preston upon Tease; beeinge in all £200 per annum. A hard
Chapter, but the generalitie of it; made it more tollerable; in hopes of future
ease; but fiat voluntas Domini; and nota we paid 3 halfe years payment

---

10. P.IV.9. She married Sir John Lowther of Whitehaven, P.IV.8.
11. Altered from £400 at time of writing.
12. i.e. Aysgarth, in Yorkshire.

277r *cont.* in one yeare; power beeinge prevalent to doe aniethinge.

Notwithstandinge all this, and (*interlined*: manie) other of like nature, payinge in sessments and the like above £300 per annum more I was not discuraged, but went on with honest endevors (soe longe as it was but generall;) and though it was more necessare to use all honest industrie to recompence those charges extraordinarie; and besides imployment and businesse did in part lessen the other crosse attendents which dayly hapend. This Tearme haveinge losst a suit in Chancerie for £2500, lymitted to my daughter in law for want of issue mayle by hir father, wherein ⟨was⟩ it was thought there

277v had not beene faire cariage, but hard to judge; but in that wee lost not that wee never had only the charge that was above £100.

And wee recovered in a bill, wherein he was plaintiff, for Bampton Tyth, which was dismissed; soe that the reputation was equall; and it was not convenient to give the hopes of such a some without a tryall[13]

In this 9br I walled in that part of Thrimby feild that adjoyneth to Greenrigges which was purchased of several persons, and exchanged and soe laide together; which may be used severall for medow, pasture or keepeinge (*erasure*) lambes or Hoges in and sett a stacke in them;

In this moneth I setled the Parsonage of Lowther upon one Mr. Smith, upon resignation of Mr. Teasdell, the then parson or Incumbent who had beene Parson above 40 years and was 84 years of age; this I got him to doe, and I did confirme him, and present him, and made such conditions for our enjoyment of all our tyths as was accustomed, (*erasure*) declareinge the old composition, or prescription; and further agreed to have the Parson Millfeild and the High Holme and winterage of the Low Holme, that all our goods might freely goe from the Brodegards and Dowlands unto Buckholme and soe round about unto the High Orchard as one pleased; which was a great convenience, and I had the libertie of the water for goods out of Dowlands & Thwaitelands with crossinge only the Towregate; and the kine might cume from Skelan and be milked in Low or High Dowlands and soe have the libertie of water, which was wantinge befor.

*In this yeare I bought the rent charge of £100 per annum out of Stranton and other places in Bishoprique, which cost mee £1475 beeinge an inheritance free from all sesses or other charges which was considerable in the (*erasure*) tymes of great charges and sessments.

278r 1656. ⟨In August (*erasure*) in this yeare my Brother Will and I joyntly purchased the Lordshipp of Great Preston and Astley neare Swillington, it will be worth per annum my part £200 per annum though now but about £170; and it cost my part with charges above £3100 beeinge goodly Coleymynes and Lyme Quaries⟩[14]

In 9br[15] this yeare I bought Andersons tenement neare the Langelands at Marton which cost £200, and is better than £13 6 8 per annum (*erasure*) haveinge a convenient house upon it for to add other ground to, which

---

13. i.e. The suits with Allan Bellingham of Levens, see above, pp. 64, 170.
14. This paragraph struck through, and noted [by Sir J.L.(2)]: *This putt in befor.*
15. *9br.* smudged.

was Mr. Goodyears adjoyneinge to it; that one may make it A £50 farme at least;

I walled the heade of Thwaitelands, which was an old coble rewenus wall, and gott stones most in the Slacke (*erasure*) neare the Gate that goeth downe to the church; haveinge opened a very goodly quarie never sought for before, from whence I ledd most part of the rough stones for wallinge the Chapell and Gallery.

I likewise burnt 2 greate lyme kills in the New Parke, for lymeinge that part towards the Frith; the lower ends of which, and of all the Parke playne before I bestowed such husbandry upon it was very poore Brakenie ground; with sume shrubbs, and aboundance of Greate Earthfast stones, which I had 4 Men most part of 6 monethes to gett upp, and bestowed them in walles, and about the house; and the Walle at Lynebanke Foot, to make a part severall for 4 or 5 horses beeinge well watered and there wantinge such a conveniencie neare the house; the Parke beeinge to large for such an[16] use.

In 9bre this yeare I new built the Millne at Helton, caled Winewath Millne, which was burnt downe by Edmond Noble who was tenant of it at £16 owld rent, for which he paid a fine, but was formerly let to him by lease for yeares; and soe beeinge not able to build the same, was willinge that I should doe it and have the benefitt, and rebate him the rent, which I did in 6 weekes tyme. It cost mee about £50, and will be worth about £10 per annum; as I thinke at leaste.[17]

656. I found out Slate in Bampton Lordshipp which was never found before and soe gott the tenants to lead it; and slated the same, and made a chimney in it to prevent the like dainger. And advise never to have anie kilne in the Mills, haveinge known manie lost upon that accompt; and they distroy a greate boundance of wood to build, as I found by experience in that at Egleston, Marton, Sledale, and now this, all which I new built; aslikewise that of Newton, and brought most wood from Threlkeld for that Mill. And this yeare wee altered it, and made a Wheate Mill in it, haveinge found an Injenious Man that tooke it for 21 years, and added that unto it, for which I gave him in hand £20 besides wood from Yeanewith Wood; And he improved the rent £2 per annum, beeinge now £12 and was before but £10; and would not then give so much.

656. Upon the Nativitie of our Lord God oure late parson, Mr. John Teasdell dyed, haveinge beene parson above 44[18] years at Lowther, a very sober and good Man, though noe exact preacher; who formerly resigned upon my motion; though, in these pearceinge tymes, this day I heare it is intended to be questioned, and sume (*interlined*: other) intended to be obtruded upon us. [19]But since I presented one Mr. Smith, who was admitted upon my presentation.

---

16. Ampersand struck out and *an* interlined.
17. See above, p. 13.
18. Cf. above, p. 74; he was parson from 10 Sept. 1613 to Nov. 1656.
19. This sentence in a different ink.

278v *cont.* * 1657. In the end of last yeare, and begininge of this I new scoured and quicke
 sett in all places which wanted round about the Millnefeild, which had not
 beene done in probabilitie 100 years before, beeinge most dryed and decayed
 hedge, and walled severall parts of it towards Welterans and sett quicke
 wood before the wale, becase the wall was but low and not good stones.
 That part adjoyneing to the Parson Holme I did scoure and cast at the
 Parson Mr. Smith his charge because I farmed the Gleabe of him the first
 yeare of his entrance beeinge unprovided himself, to doe it.

279r 1657.   The fence belongeinge to the Parson to make, soe I had allowance
 for it from him; I gave him for the £5 I agreed to pay him yearely, and
 the six Catle Gates, and the Gleable in all £24 for this yeare; and I sprunge
 and cutt; [20]the Underwood then in Welterand, and made and cast a new
 hedge about (*interlined*: it).
 In the end of the former yeare, and begininge of this year I perfected the
 purchas of the other moitie of Shapp tyth together with the advowson of
 the Vickerage which cost mee about £600; soe have the whole now, which
 was formerly devided, and occasioned trouble about collecteinge; and the
 like; and is worth about £55 per annum.
 In this moneth I finished the new Wall about the low side of the Faulds,
 or Whale cragge Little Close Adjoyneinge to Quale, which was troublesome
 for the hight of it on the low side, soe most of it was waled overhand; save
 one that stood upon a ladder to order the stones on the farrside which was
 Rowland Stephenson that lived 〈at the〉 against the Low Orchard and,
 (*erasure*) who, when he was waleinge 〈upon〉 the lader sliped from him,
 and (*erasure*) with the Capestone struck out one of his fore teeth in my
 presence, which I remembered to his advantage otherwayes;
 * In the end of this yeare I bought a smale parcell adjoyneinge to Whale Inge
 of Jo. Pruddey; 〈 both to save the fence which I formerly made, and is
 now belongeinge to Knipe〉 aslikewise for a Shelter and beald towards the
 West Winde, which was formerly wantinge.
 In this Winter I tooke upp and new walled, and inclosed that parcell of
 ground at the slacke end betwixt Esklamoore heade and Barney feild
 intended for a Calfegarth ether for Skellans or Barney feild when the kine
 went in ether place.
 In this yeare I built the Towfall to the Old Towre, beeinge for my Wives
 clossett, and a Rome above and below for maydes; and did likewise finish
 the owteside of the Gallery, and slated it and laid the leade gutters; and
 new laid and cast the leade gutters on the other side, viz. the garner side.

279v 1657. In January this yeare I new hightened and repaired the 2 sides of the
 Old Parke towards Murreys and Hackthropp grassinge.
 In february I burnt a Greate Lymekilne in the New Parke and lymed that
 above the lymekilne and severall other parts, but it will take yet two more
 to finish all that is wantinge, it cost mee a good some in makeinge it fitt
 Arable; viz. in strubinge old trees bushes, and greate stones: yet I had constant
 croppes that did answer the cost: haveinge had in the yeare [16]56 above 300

---

20. The remainder of the paragraph a contemporary addition.

bushells of Otes, and about 200 of bigge, and I thinke noe lesse, if not more this yeare 1657.

658. In Aprill this year I partly walled the the [*sic*] Orchard under the Pidgen Cote neare 3 yards high; and finished the winter after. Cost above £50.

In May after I bought out the tenement at the Towne heade, from Lycock, the heire that claymed it, though there was neare as much dew to mee as it was worth upon mortgage fines arre and rents. Soe it stood me in all above £140, but it was neare and convenient. And repaired the house, and new built upp the barne.

I bought a Cottage at Marton called Semur Cott, which ley convenient, and let it to Will. Airsume.

The 11th of November I maried my daughter Mary beeinge that day 17 yeares old, to Mr. Trotter of Skelton Castle in Yorkeshire, his estate better then £800 per annum; Shee to have £300 per annum joynture. And paid £1000 in hand, and to pay £1000 more at Lam. after, viz. 1659; if shee be then liveinge or have issue.

The 29th dyed my daughter Elizabeth, the eldest daughter (*erasure*) then liveinge by my now wife Elizabeth, soe as one entered upon the Worlde the other went out; God grant us to make right use of it.

658. In the begininge of March [16]58, it beeinge a backward (*erasure*) Springe that yeare, I planted the Pidgen Cote Garden, and the high end of the Brodegards with frewte trees, which I had from one Peter Hardcastle at Burow Briggs, a Gardener that planted with most Gentlemen in the North parts, beinge of the best sort of frewt the North afforded; which cost mee 2s. a tree besides his waiges of cuminge and goeinge out of Yorkeshire and plantinge them; for which he and his sone had ether 1s. per diem for plantinge and dressinge the other Orchard. They were but graftes of 2 or 3 yeares growth, by which may bee knowne the tyme and age of the trees, and how longe they may last and continew. They bore the seacon yeare; sume of them had 40 Apples a peece: and those in the bottom (*erasure*) better then those above;

In this month I opened the water pipes from the well heade unto the high Orchard Wall, and new layde about 70 yards at the Well heade where it was decayed, and mended the rest, which cost neare £20; I prepared pipes for at least 100 yards more, but there was noe neede of them, but soe much as was taken up was very much decayed, beeinge neare 100 hooles in a yard, and yet the water did run, though but weeakely by reason of the waste; I sett stones to direct, and to guide by a lyne from one to another, if anie default appeare to finde it out the better. And if you keepe a grayte upon the pipe at the well heade, there will not be anie defect for longe tyme; else you will have constant trouble by sumethinge gettinge in and stayinge which occasioneth stopinge; and that causeth often openinge, and by consequence spoyleinge the Pipes.

About that tyme I laide the pipes out of the Brewhouse into the Buttery for caringe the Beare thereby through the gardinge; wherein was formerly both losse, and inconvenience; and this done with more ease and better if well myned.

I heightened the outer walle of the high Orchard, and planted those Ash

280r *cont.*   (*erasure*) trees on the outside of the Wale, and all about the new Barne, and befor the Stables about 3 or foure years before this tyme, for shelter of the houses, rise and orniment;

280v * 1659. For the severall purchases, and monies disbursed this yeare see the longe Vellum white Booke, there beeinge nothinge else memorable, haveinge bought Millby that yeare in Yorkeshire, cost about £3700 and paid my daughter Trotter last part of hir portion.

The 16th of 9br dyed my Mother at Meaburne, as appeareth more at large in the booke of Memorandums.

I bought great Ayton, cost me in all upon £1900, as appeareth in that booke. The 1st of 9br this yeare beeinge All Saints day wee were robbed by 6 or 7 men who came in the habit of Souldiers (*erasure*) at none day, beeinge above 30 persons in the house which was a wounder, but that it was in the very Conjunction when the tow Armies of Lamberts and Mounkes were supposed to meete lyeinge one neare another about Newcastle and the forces of Horse dispersed about the Country soe came under that notion and pretended the whole regiment was cuminge to them, and that they came before, untill they had locked all upp, and then they discovered there intention and tooke what monie, plate, and what else they pleased; and used crewell threates to mee to discover with Sword Pistoll and butcherly knives, yet God delivered us from there crewueltie without further harme then the losse of our goods. And since wee heare that severall of them are executed upon other accompts, for the act of oblivion upon the Kinges cumeinge in and restoration quited that fact, We heare that there is 3 Hillereges, that lived at Maricke, one was husband to my son Ralphes nurse as is said that was there leader, that is yet liveinge, whome God will punish in dew tyme, haveinge been accused for manie fellonies since; for the more particuler naration see the other booke.

1660. In this yeare I added a smale tenement, called Sadamanhow, to Bampton Demesne, fitt for the Comon.

I bought a tenement at Quale of Christopher Wilkinson; which I intended for the Keeper of the Parke to live at, though not yet made use of, the old man beeinge yet liveinge.

I bought several tenements in Wensladale, on the farr side the River, adjoyneinge upon my other lands, which doth much fashon the Lordshipp, lyeinge soe fittly.

281r 1660. The 12th of this moneth I was ellected Knight of the Shire for this Countie, ⟨not⟩ beeinge only desired by Sir Tho. Wharton to beare him companie, who intended to stand but had opposition by others, but goeinge without anie purpose myself of standinge I was chosen against other 4; viz. Burton, Tho. Wharton of London, Tho. Brathwaite, and Sir Tho. Wharton (*interlined*: who) with my assistance was the other which he tooke kindly, the others beeinge persons of meaner qualitie. This Parlement though called by the Councell or Comittee of saftie (*interlined*: as then called)[21] proved fortunate and happie; and ⟨by⟩ beeinge tyred out (*erasure*) after tryall of all other Governments and Governors agreed to invite the Kinge to his

---

21. These two interlineations by Sir J.L.(2) are in a different ink.

Regall charge and his full power and prerogative; who after in May by God's 281r *cont.* blessinge, and his wounderfull assistance, was received in London the 29th of May withall joye and acclymations; Soe that I caried upp my Wife and familie that yeare to London, and continewed there unto the end of the Parlement, which was not till neare March after when wee returned well satisfied to see the Kingdome setled againe in peace, after neare 20 yeares warr and troubles, in most of which tyme I was a sufferer but beeinge for my loyaltie to the Kinge, and beeinge soe generall, I was better satisfied; and the more to see such a turne as could not be the act of anie man, but only the omnipotent powre to bend the harts of all good men to that end; and to devide the Armie, which seemed to be wrought sudenly, and not by ordinarie and outeward causes; Soe that this yeare noethinge was done at hombe.

661. In 9br I was chosen High Sheriff of Cumberland, not at all expectinge anie such thinge, not haveinge beene in the light or paper before, and soe was forced to accept it; which the Kinge did as he said that he might have such as he might trust after the tymes of trouble not setled. There is an ill Gaole which is the greatest hazard; the rest of businesse my Servant and Clarke, Will. Atkinson who had served me above 16 yeares, was able, with one Ri. Tubman, a good Countie Clarke, to doe the businesse: and for the profitt and losse, it shall be declared in bookes kept for that purpose. My Cos., Dan. Fleminge, was my predecessor. It cost me after about 5 or £600, and the profitt was about £250 soe losse about £400. All diners, which were confined to 40 by the act of Parlement, and all other thinges at my proper charge; which others used not, but to accept of such as were sent, which I excused, beeinge soe confined, else I might have displeased sume.

661. The severall purchasses this yeare, and monie paid out is to be seene 281v in the longe Vellum booke.

This yeare I maried my daughter Barbara to Mr. Beilby, as may be seene in that booke, and gave £2000 portion with hir, which was well bestowed to a sober good husband, a good scholler, and good parts; in whome shee is happie. His estate towards £900 per annum, and well wooded.

662. This yeare I maried my daughter Frances to Sir James Peniman's Son of Ormesby, his only child. I gave with hir £2300 portion, and had £350 Joynture. He had neare £1000 per annum, and a growinge man in the worlde, and like much to improve his estate; who was but about 17 yeares, and had a son within a yeare and $\frac{1}{2}$ after. And what I did for my other sons and daughters that yeare is to bee seene in that booke.

663. I bought the lease of Ringefeild, and gave it to my son John, adjoyneinge to Bemont Hill, which he hopeth to have halfe of for his sone and heire to his mother after the Ladie Bellinghams death.

I bought Marton Tyth.

I gave my son Christo. to sett upp with, beinge then out of his apprenticeshipp £740 which hath made £1500, besides £300 cost byndinge apprentice, in all £1800: and intend him about £500 in full of his portion.

This yeare I builte the Coach house.

I bought my Son Rich. a fott Companie in Ireland of Sir Tho. Wharton, for which I paid £500 which besides his other employment, gives him a noble

281v *cont.*   report in the Kingdome, beeinge most Noblemen that have the like commands in the standinge armie;

I walled in the horse Close in this corner of the New Parke, for to putt 3 or 4 horses for present use; wantinge such a place near. I cutt and sprunge the banke of wood in the Farr holme, which the Parson would have pretended to be part of the gleabe, soe it may be knowne in tymes to cume how longe since it was cutt, and setled my tytle to it beinge all the water wee have for Dowlands, which is now a Cowpasture.

* 1664. This yeare I added the Butteres to the Chapp end which shurck and new topped the low old Towre Chimney our owne Chamber which tottered and smoked; which is much mended thereby.

In this year my Son John taken with an affection to one Miss Withens at London, by me disliked for severall reasons; he went to travill into France and Italy, beeinge now at Rome, to divert that intention as pretended, whether reall or not tyme will manifest;

282r * 1664. In the end of the former yeare I sowld the Manor of Thwaites to Sir Willya. Hudleston for £1700 which cost my father about £1000 beeinge remote out of my way, and soe much profitt was considerable, if well paid; of which I have received about £900; And am now upon the purchas of the Fearage at Yarm,[22] with other lands at Eysciff, Ayselayby, and Preston upon Tease, which is to cost mee about £6550 and to lend Mr. Sayer more £1500, which will (*erasure*) if perfected cost and make to bee disbursed then £8000; in which have had a greate deale of trouble, beeinge uncertaine men to deale with; of which more when perfected in the longe Vellum booke.

* 1665. This last proceeded not only I lent £3100 upon the estate. And afterwards I purchased that part of the Manor of Skelton that belonged to Mr Markeham, intended for my Son Trotter, if he be ever to pay mee as it cost mee, which was £1800 besides costs and charges which was about £40; it should yeild me £120 per annum cleare rent, as it was lett when I bought it.

* 1666. In Aprill this yeare I new built the high end of Hayclose House for the Keper to live at, haveinge lett him the 4 Haycloses, and the Heades for £17 per annum and lett him have Thwaitlands at the heade of Quale Inge for his service in keepinge the Parke makeinge and mendinge the fences in and about it, and gettinge the faules; and 4 dayes mowinge in the Parke for the deare; and dressinge the grounds and fotheringe to the Catle, Sheepe, and Deare; and lookinge to the Old Parke: and intend him a horse-grasse in Somer in the Old Parke, or elsewhere if he please mee.

Nota. This yeare the Chimney harthes were, as was given in to mee, was asfolloweth, viz.

The number in the Baronie of Kendall	2627
The number added and found out upon the last revew	0536
The number of harthes in the Bottom of Westmorland	2800
The number upon the last revew there	0548
The total of all is	6511

22. A house and property formerly a friary, *V.C.H., Yorks N.R.*, II, p. 321.

The number stopped upp in the Baronie...................... 0053
In the bottom stopped upp.................................. 0053

This was enquired after in regard my son Chris, was upon tearmes to disburse some monies beforehand upon that securitie.

*In July this yeare I made the wateringe Troughs in Greenerigges both the higher and lower; which if regared, and the water looked unto that it be not stopped in the way, it will never faile; I new repaired the walle betwixt Greenerigges and Thrimby feild, and brought stones from Booneby;

666. In this yeare about 10br and the yeare before I cutt and sprunge the 282v owld Hasle wood, and the old Ashes on the backe of the Old Parke Tarne unto the end of the Birkes towards Brackenberge; and sowld the Hasle wood for £35 payable at Cand. [16]66, and Cand. [16]67; and the Ashe Trees that were old and decayed, for about £24. Soe one halfe of the Wood cutt next Lowther is a yeare elder then the further part; Soe that by this may be knowne, how longe since it was cutt, and in what tyme it will be fitt to cutt it againe; it beeinge the best husbandrie to cutt often, provided you springe it well and let nothinge come in it for 4 yeares at least; and then only sheepe, but not to manie, for other 3 yeares before you lay downe the hedge about it: and lett noe great Catle at all cropp it in the Winter for 2 or 3 years after, if you will have it good wood; for one yeare eateinge will put it 4 backe. [23] A hedge will but last 3 yeares, soe you must have it twice made before you ley it downe.

667. In May this yeare I maried my Grand Child Mary Lowther to Mr. Preston Son of Holker, and gave her £2000 portion, and was to have £400 for joynture and present mayntenance, though it proved not soe much. And I lent the old Man, to redeem the Estate that was mortgaged £3150 for which I was to have £400 per annum declaro for 14 yeares, the first payment to beginn at Mart. 1667; for which see more in the longe booke. In 9bre this yeare I begun to take in part of Greenerigges, which wee cale Mathew Cloasse, for medow, there beeinge a want of Medow in Winter for those Groundes; and its like to have a good load of course hay for younge Catle. It will cost £20 or £30 to inclose it, though 2 sides was done before.

668. In March this yeare [16]68, I cutt the underwood in Ravenrash, and pruned the oakes in Aprill, beeinge the best season when the Wether is warme and temperate. And in (*erasure*) 8bre in that yeare I planted above 100 younge Ashes in all the vacant and emptie places; and intend that never anie goods whatsoever should cume in at anie time as a place fittest for wood and soe I fenced it accordingely; beeinge formerly neglected, and the banke in the Parson Holme was before I cutt it, and planted younge Ashes in it. I likewise planted above 200 Ashes in this end of the New Parke, the old ones which was in the Frith above the Troughs beeinge all decayed when that banke of wood was cutt, which was about the yeare 1645, in the tyme of the warr betwixt the Kinge and Parlement, and soe beinge forced from hombe, the hedges were broken down and the springe much spoyled by the Deare and other goods; especially the Ashes.

---

23. This sentence an addition [by Sir J.L.(2)].

282v *cont.*   In 9br in this yeare wee had a mortall disease in horses, havinge lost 3 younge horses at Meaburne. But the sickness begun with them at Cleyburne, where manie were lost, and the Countesse[24] lost above 20 at Whinfell Browham and Appleby and soe manie others. And ours now beginn to dye heare; And in 1658 I lost 16 prime horses of the same disease, which is a stupified disease without anie remedie.

283r–283v   [*Change of hand; unknown hand*[25]] *Copy letter: Anne Lowther*[26] *to Sir J.L.(1), about their children's progress, and a servant of Mr. Allden. Shoreditch, 20 June n.d.*

283v   *Wm. Howard to Sir J.L.(2), 2 August n.d.*

284r [*Change of Hand; hand of Sir J.L.(2)*]

1669. In May and there about my wife had the longe settworke Carpett made at Bradford, haveinge in the 2 yeares last before had a skilfull woman with her 2 daughters or Cousins in the house, who made all the Settworke Quishons, and the Chaires and Stooles with the Cotes of armes; and Couch Chaires and Window Quishons; which were all wrought in the house by day: and the Wool our owne; and bought dyeinge stuffe, I believe they all cost above £50. The Carpett standinge to about £18.00.0.

8bre [16]69, My brother, Sir William, came to visit us with my Sister Kirkeby and seven daughters, (*interlined*: and 4 of there husbands) all then (*interlined*: well) maried, viz. (*erasure*) one to Mr. Crowle at Hull, 2d to Mr. Dickinson of Wrightington, 3rd to Mr. Blenherhasset of Flimby, 4th to Mr. Willson of Dallen Towre, 5th to Mr. Doding of Furnesse, 6th to Mr. Spencer at Leeds, 7th to Mr West in Lanckashire.

This somer I ledd and walled part of Mathew Close about in Greenrigges This springe, and in Winter before was the first tyme the high end of Barney feild was riven out of lea, and well lymed, beeinge a course most wettish soyle which bore little grasse; and thinke it may come unto tollerable Wheate ground, beeinge clay; but beeinge drawne upp into ridges will dry, it lyeinge soe upon the fall: and is reasonable neare the house; That feild I purchased (*erasure*) of one Barnard Lowther, who had sometymes beene a servant at the house, soe called it Barney feild. The owld tyllage feild haveinge formerly beene the 2 Skellands, the Narr Flatt, Millfeild, and Dowlands, most of which were remote ⟨and not⟩ and ill leadinge of manure unto; which are all now much improved, especially the Mill feild, which was butt formerly lett for £10 or £11 per annum and now is worth double as much, with that little Millfeild added to it which the Parson had; and I pay him £2 per annum for it, beeinge part of the composition, or prescription monie of £8 per annum that I pay him; I think that Thwaitelands Barney feild, Dowlands and Lantie Croft Cotdikes, with the bottom about it will be sufficient to plow as nearest the house, and to lett one lye bye turnes, and plow some fresh ground in lew of it. ⟨as if⟩ Wee lett Dowlands Dowland lye to grasse beeinge so well watered with the River, and fitt for about 14 or 15 Cowes, and now

---

24. i.e. Anne Clifford, Countess of Pembroke.
25. Both letters noted by Sir J.L.(2): *This was my daughter Beilbyes coppinge.*
26. Anne wife of Richard Lowther, Sir J.L.(1)'s brother, P.III.7.

plow and medow this low part of the New Parke; but when that laid, then 284r *cont.*
may plow Dowlands.

* This yeare in 8br was the low end of Barne feild fallowed and sowne with
Wheate, which showes very faire, beeinge but about 4 bushels and ½, which,
well done is sufficient since wee ⟨by⟩ buy all our white bread; but when
our estate was lesse, in my greate Grandfathers tyme, they used to sow
20 or 24 bushells to make monie of, which I neede not trouble myselfe with;
but for pleasure and diversion.

1669. In February this yeare I new walled in a Kitchinge Gardinge in the low 284v
end of the Smithie Crofts; all other places proper for that use beeinge converted in Orchards, and Plantation of Trees for shelter and ornament, since
the house stands soe exposed to winde and wether; and that beeinge low,
and the soyle most of it deepe is fitt for rootes, and for the Kitchinge; and
freest from shade, and best for the sun, and neare for manureinge.

In this and the next moneth I new walled that part of Cotdikes or Lantie
Croft next the Scarr, which was an ill Coble Wale, and the sheepe of the
comon could not be kept out; and intend, or those that succede may add
that at the end of called Salkeld Close to it, to inlarge it, haveinge beene
formerly an inclosure; and since I have bought in soe manie parcells and
tenements, and not makeinge use of the Heades for my Sheepe, it may with
good reason and conscience be taken upp; and may be in tyme the whole
Heades. Only Dick Wilkinson (*erasure*) and Jo. Ritson haveinge hindered
my intentions formerly when I ⟨was⟩ thought to have done it.

1670. In June I bought the Collery of Staynemoore, with the Toll of Bowes,
and land at Gilmanby of Capt. Hanby, which I redevised for 999 yeares
at the rent of £45 per annum, ⟨in⟩ and Coles for my house, and toll free
of my goods; ⟨and⟩ as a comodious appurtinant to the house of Lowther.
In August followinge I fell sicke of a kinde of Rumatisme, and distemper
in all the parte of my bodie, and after all Docters from Yorke and the
1671 Country I went to London in May followinge 1671, and stayed there untill
May followinge, and had there divers fitts of the Stone, which was a great
cause of my distemper, and voyed severall stones, some as bigg as a beane,
and sharpe at the endes. And was at Tunbrigge Wells for a moneth, and
druncke the Waters of Barnett Hempson, as prescribed by the Docters; and
in May went unto the Bath with my wife, and stayed there 3 weekes, and
soe returned hombe, beeinge but still weake in bodie, but at this tyme,
praysed be God, am much better then I have only a Tumor, the effect
of the sicknes falinge downe into a swellinge on one side, caused my beeinge
twice cutt at London by Mr. Molines out of which issued at each tyme,
more than halfe a pinte of Water as cleare as Sacke, and doth still gather
againe, which though it was thought did preserve me at that tyme, yett
if it continue, may occasion an other journey; or may prove of bad consequence for though when rightly prepared and ripe, its noe payne, not
soemuch and as blood lettinge, yet is dangerous if not from a skilfull hand;
In that yeare, beeinge at London ⟨1671⟩ in 10bre 1671, my Son Christopher,
who had cost me in his profession of A Turkie Merchant about £5000,
dyed of a consumpson of about a monethes sicknesse, though he had not
bene well above 12 monethes before.

285r * 1671. In October this yeare dyed my shee Cousin Dudley, soe that the Manor of Yeanewith came to mee in possession, after her husband and her death; which stood mee above £6000 consideringe it cost mee £2200 after 2 lives, who lived 18 yeares after my purchas;

I new repaired all the houses at Wood House, and walled them all anew, and added that open house at this end of the dwellinge house; And intend to repaire the houses at the Hall at Yeanewith which was left very Ruinous; And in this moneth, viz. in 10bre 1672, I have gotten men from Carlisle to burne Brick at Crakeabanke, and am to give 4s a thousand, and provide all materialls, as Cole, Straw Sand; and intend the like at Yeanewith, the ground beeinge approved as very good in both places for that purpose, beeinge very usefull for Ovens, backs of Chimneys, ⟨and the⟩ paveinge, and the inside of walles, and Pidgon Cotes beeinge dry, and not subject to cast a swett as stones are; And when stones are not neare may be allmost as cheape; but experience will instruct us more;

1672. In 8bre this yeare I made a new wood bridge over into Yeanewith Wood, for the better accommodation and management of that estate, which cost me above £30, and cutt the wood in Clifton fitts. And this day, beeinge the 22nd of December after a Snow, and a sudden thaw, the water was soe greate as I see it goe over the bridge neare a yard deepe; sow it was thought it could not have stood, which if there had beene anie iyce it could not have done; yett it suffered litle, but must be rayesed in Somer, if it stand untill then, neare a yard hyer, to save it from Iyce or trees, or the like cominge downe in greate flodds.

* But in 3 or 4 dayes after it was taken away by the flood which was the highest that ever was knowne; at which tyme the greate bridge at Lanthwateby was totally caried away, which coste the Cuntry neare £800, and the greate bridge at Midleham, and 5 or 6 other Greate bridges in Craven in Yorkeshire Yett I gott all, or most of my bridge, though some of the planckes were caried as farr as Langonby holmes and below Lowther brigg, and about Buckholme Islands; and is prepared to be sett againe though all the yeare 1673 was soe continewed a rayne, that the water was soe greate it could not be sett againe though it stand redie, but will be next somer before it can be sett.

1673. Note, that in May [16]73 the Bricke was brunt at Crakabanke, beeinge 60,000, and at Yeanewith 20,000, but (erasure) the Season was soe wett as they could never be gotten well dryed, soe they proved worth noethinge. Soe lost about 200 load of Coles; and £15 in monie paid the workemen, who should have had 4s a 1000.

285v * 1673. In this yeare, about April, I sowld the Tenants of Clifton, all but 2 or 3, to pay only the old rent, and reserveinge all Royalties, for which they were and are to pay after 52 years purchas, after the proportion of there old rents, and I to have a 3rd part of the Comons, and a proportion more for the tenements I purchased at Howcarl and Hartley tenement; upon which I built a new Barne, good Tymber, and lett the same to Baynebrigg, my Cooke for £11 per annum pro ut. And intend ether I or who shall succeed to improve my part of the Comon, and ley it adjoyneinge as neare as may

be, which may be usefull in severall respects, as the boundes betwixt Lowther,
Hackthropp, and Clifton.
* In 9br I sowld all the underwood in Buckholme, from the topp of the Hill
towards Clifton, untill the waterside, beeinge, as I compute it about 10 Acres,
to the tenants of Lowther and Hackthropp and Clifton for £26 halfe to
ether, to be paid in 2 years. It was cutt when my father came to the estate
which is about 56 yeares since; and I might have had as much for it neare
20 yeares since: soe have lost the use of soe much ever since. And, but
(*interlined*: that) this was soe wett a Somer, that noe earth fewell could be
gott, it would not have sowld at all. There is now soe greate a scarcitie
of monie, by reason of Warres with Holland, Greate taxes, and noe vent
of anie comodities Bigg beeinge but about 3s 4d the bushell, 20 gallons; and
Woll but at that rate for a stone, and all thinges answerable, and all foraine
comodities deare, which must needes impoverish a Country when importa-
tion is more then is exported; And thats the present condicon of the
Kingedom at this tyme. What greate sumes I disbursed in these 2 yeares,
viz. in 1672, and 1673, you may see the perticulers in the longe vellume
rent booke, beeinge each yeare neare or above 8 or £9000. But its trew I
sowld some land in Wenslade, that was not well rented, for about £600;
and Clifton to a fine certaine about 7 or £800; but much of this yett arrere;

APPENDIX IV

ILLUSTRATIVE PEDIGREE OF THE LOWTHER FAMILY
IN THE SEVENTEENTH CENTURY

This is not, for reasons of space, a complete pedigree. It omits children who died young, and excludes daughters, unless mentioned in the text. It lists only those members of collateral branches who are named in the text.

Apart from the text, the main contemporary genealogical sources for this pedigree are the notes of baptisms of the children of Sir Richard Lowther, in A1/6 and A1/7; A1/7 also gives information on the children of William Lowther of Ingleton. Pedigrees recorded at Sir William Dugdale's visitation of Cumberland and Westmorland in 1664/5 are printed by J. Foster, *Pedigrees Recorded at the Heralds' Visitations of the Counties of Cumberland and Westmorland*, [1891]. A later source, not always accurate, is the note book of Sir William Lowther of Swillington, Earl of Lonsdale from 1807. Family events are recorded, mainly, in the parish registers of Lowther and Crosby Ravensworth (Maulds Meaburn).

Among modern genealogies the work of J. Foster, *Pedigrees of the County Families of England: Yorkshire*, (1888) is useful. Canon C. M. Lowther Bouch's genealogies of the collateral branches of the family, published in *CW2* between 1939 and 1944, are valuable for the Lowther of Swillington, Lowther of Marske and Holker, and Lowther of Colby-Lathes branches. Sir E. T. Bewley deals with the Lowthers in Ireland in *CW2*, II, 1902. G.E.C., *Complete Peerage*, and *Complete Baronetage*, are invaluable.

Abbreviations used in the pedigree:

    d—died, da—daughter, m—married, fl—living

    (C) Cumberland, (L) Lancaster, (W) Westmorland, (Yo) Yorkshire

    = (1) (2) 1st and 2nd marriages.

Notes to the pedigree

(a) In Burke's *Peerage*, and Foster's *Pedigree of County Families*, Sir Christopher's first marriage is said to be with an unnamed da of Middleton. The Musgrave and Burdet marriages then follow. There is no evidence for the Middleton marriage of an earlier date than 1665; no marriage settlement, no mention in the Middleton pedigree—which does mention the marriage with Sir Richard Lowther. Sir J.L.(1) explicitly refers to Mrs Burdet as his father's second wife (above, p. 220) The origin of this mistake is the 1665 visitation pedigree of Lowther of Colby-Lathes, where Sir Christopher's grandson, who had forgotten his grandmother's name, confused her with his great-grandmother Frances Middleton, wife of Sir Richard Lowther, Sir William of Swillington incorporated this error into his note-book, whence it passed to Burke and Foster, and so on.

(b) Date of marriage unknown; their first child baptised August 1637, cf. above, pp. 40, 230–1.

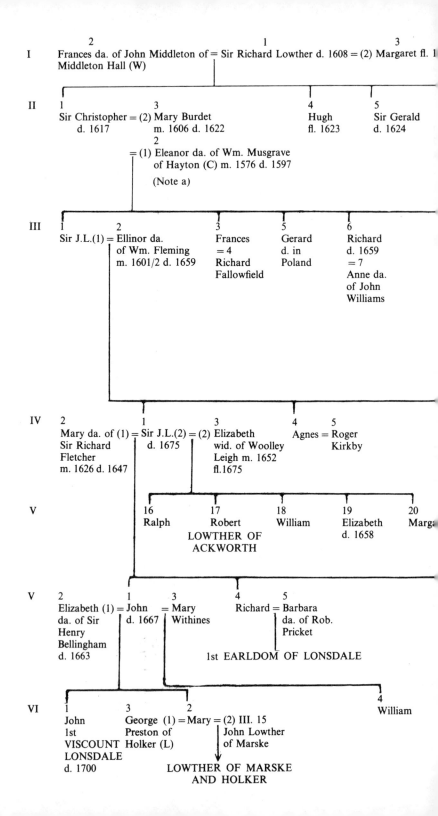

I   2   Frances da. of John Middleton of = Sir Richard Lowther d. 1608 = (2) Margaret fl. 1
Middleton Hall (W)   1   3

II   1   Sir Christopher = (2) Mary Burdet
d. 1617   3   m. 1606 d. 1622
            2
= (1) Eleanor da. of Wm. Musgrave
of Hayton (C) m. 1576 d. 1597
(Note a)

           4   Hugh
fl. 1623

           5   Sir Gerald
d. 1624

III   1   Sir J.L.(1) = Ellinor da.
        2   of Wm. Fleming
m. 1601/2 d. 1659

3   Frances
= 4
Richard
Fallowfield

5   Gerard
d. in
Poland

6   Richard
d. 1659
= 7
Anne da.
of John
Williams

IV   2   Mary da. of (1) = Sir J.L.(2) = (2) Elizabeth
Sir Richard   1   d. 1675   3   wid. of Woolley
Fletcher   Leigh m. 1652
m. 1626 d. 1647   fl.1675

4   5
Agnes = Roger
Kirkby

V   16   Ralph

17   Robert
LOWTHER OF
ACKWORTH

18   William

19   Elizabeth
d. 1658

20   Marga

V   2   Elizabeth (1) = John
da. of Sir   1   d. 1667
Henry
Bellingham
d. 1663

3   = Mary
Withines

4   5
Richard = Barbara
da. of Rob.
Pricket

1st EARLDOM OF LONSDALE

VI   1   John
1st   3
VISCOUNT
LONSDALE
d. 1700

George   (1) = Mary = (2) III. 15
Preston of   2   John Lowther
Holker (L)   of Marske

LOWTHER OF MARSKE
AND HOLKER

4   William

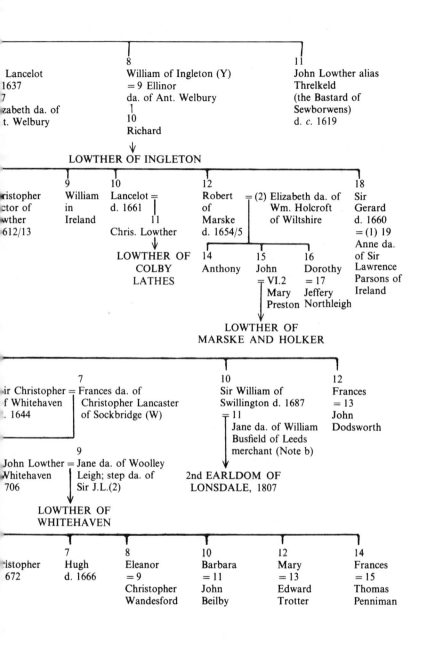

Lancelot
1637
7
zabeth da. of
t. Welbury

8
William of Ingleton (Y)
= 9 Ellinor
da. of Ant. Welbury
1
10
Richard

↓
LOWTHER OF INGLETON

11
John Lowther alias
Threlkeld
(the Bastard of
Sewborwens)
d. c. 1619

9
ristopher
ctor of
wther
612/13

10
William
in
Ireland

12
Robert
of
Marske
d. 1654/5

18
Sir
Gerard
d. 1660
= (1) **19**
Anne da.
of Sir
Lawrence
Parsons of
Ireland

Lancelot =
d. 1661
11
Chris. Lowther
↓
LOWTHER OF
COLBY
LATHES

= (2) Elizabeth da. of
Wm. Holcroft
of Wiltshire

14
Anthony

15
John
= VI.2
Mary
Preston

16
Dorothy
= **17**
Jeffery
Northleigh

↓
LOWTHER OF
MARSKE AND HOLKER

7
ir Christopher = Frances da. of
f Whitehaven   Christopher Lancaster
. 1644   of Sockbridge (W)

10
Sir William of
Swillington d. 1687
= **11**
Jane da. of William
Busfield of Leeds
merchant (Note b)

12
Frances
= **13**
John
Dodsworth

9
John Lowther = Jane da. of Woolley
Vhitehaven   Leigh; step da. of
706   Sir J.L.(2)

2nd EARLDOM OF
LONSDALE, 1807

↓
LOWTHER OF
WHITEHAVEN

7
Hugh
d. 1666

8
Eleanor
= 9
Christopher
Wandesford

10
Barbara
= 11
John
Beilby

12
Mary
= 13
Edward
Trotter

14
Frances
= 15
Thomas
Penniman

lstopher
672

MAP I

GROWTH OF THE LOWTHER ESTATES:

MAIN PURCHASES 1617–75 IN THE LOWTHER AREA

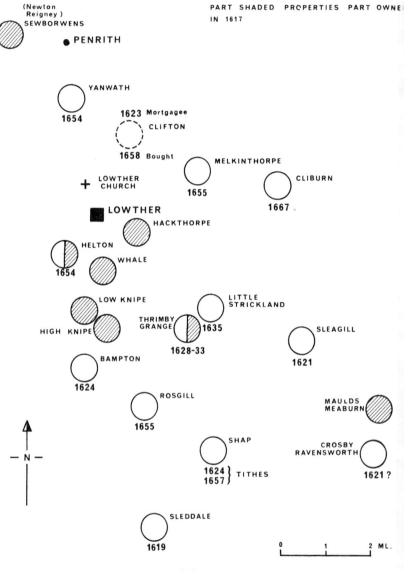

SHADED PROPERTIES OWNED IN 1617
PART SHADED PROPERTIES PART OWNE
IN 1617

(Newton Reigney)
SEWBORWENS

● PENRITH

YANWATH
1654

1623 Mortgagee
CLIFTON
1658 Bought

MELKINTHORPE
1655

CLIBURN
1667

✛ LOWTHER
CHURCH

■ LOWTHER
HACKTHORPE

HELTON
1654

WHALE

LOW KNIPE

HIGH KNIPE

THRIMBY
GRANGE
1628-33

LITTLE
STRICKLAND
1635

SLEAGILL
1621

BAMPTON
1624

ROSGILL
1655

MAULDS
MEABURN

N

SHAP
1624 }
1657 } TITHES

CROSBY
RAVENSWORTH
1621 ?

SLEDDALE
1619

0   1   2 ML.

260

MAP II

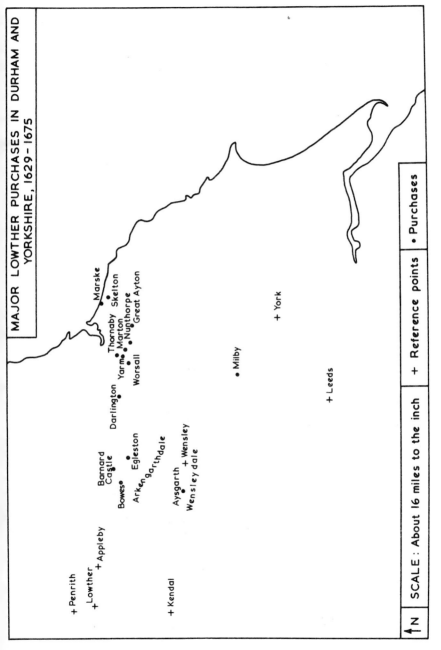

MAJOR LOWTHER PURCHASES IN DURHAM AND YORKSHIRE, 1629-1675

Marske
Skelton
Thornaby
Marton
Yarm
Nunthorpe
Great Ayton
Worsall
Darlington
Barnard Castle
Bowes
Egleston
Arkengarthdale
Aysgarth
Wensley
Wensleydale
Milby
+ York
+ Leeds
+ Penrith
+ Lowther
+ Appleby
+ Kendal

↑N | SCALE: About 16 miles to the inch | + Reference points | • Purchases

261

INDEX

** indicates more than one reference on a given page, including footnotes.
Italics are used for persons and places not identified with certainty.
Significant variations in spelling found in the texts are given in ( ).
[ ] enclose information supplied for purposes of identification.

Metcalfe (Medcalfe), Abraham, 53;
Alex, 148; Augustine, 177;
Edmond, 148; James, 92, 184;
Jo, 93; John, 148; Richard, 54
Meynell (Menell), Mr, of Thornaby,
110, 166, 172; the three Mey-
nells, 156
Michells, Hugh, 196
Micklethwaite Grange, [Collingham,
Yorks], 167
Midleton, Sir Wm, of Belsay,
Northumb, [1st Bt], 92, 100,
104, 110, 114, 124, 151, 154; as
High Sheriff of Northumb, 178;
Wm, of Stockeld, Yorks,
Cousin of J.L.(2), 68, 92, 100,
110, 188, da of, married, 188;
Will, 129
Midleton, [?Durh, or Westm], 80;
animals bought/sold at, 23
Middleham, [Yorks], bridge, 254
Milburne, Bartholomew, 172
Milburn, [Westm], 197; Howgill, 197
Milby, (Millby), Yorks, manor, 151;
stinted common, 108; and
Lowther, Wm, 151; Ellinthorp
and Thornton Ings, 108; pur-
chase of, 157**, 158**, 248;
rental, 108; rents, 114, 124–5,
132, 142, (arrears), 148, (free
rents), 114, 132, 151, 158;
survey, 108
Mill, —, 120
Miller, Will, 160, (wife of), 160
Millbrowes, see sub Hackthorpe
Millne, Tho, 160
Millom, Cumb, see Thwaites; resi-
dent of, see Hudleston, Sir Wm
mills, 5, 6**, 81; and see, Amble-
side, Ayton, Barnard Castle,
Cliburn, Crosby Ravensworth,
Egleston, Helton, Kentmere,
Kirkby Lonsdale, Lowther,
Lowther Cragg, Marton, Mea-
burne, Newby, Newton, St
Bees, Scout Green (sub Crosby
Ravensworth), Sleddale, Little
Strickland, Threlkeld, Thrimby,
Thwaites, Widewath (sub Hel-

ton), Yanwath; types: corn, see
Ayton, paper, see Ambleside,
peck or poak, see St Bees, Yanwath, walkmill, see Little Strickland, [Thwaites], Yanwath; and
see kilns
Mills Close, see sub Thrimby
Millfield (Milnfield), see sub Lowther demesne
Milnthorpe, [Heversham, Westm],
animals bought/sold at, 17, 23
Mirkmire, Michelmire, [?Bampton,
Westm], 2, 9, 17
Molines, see Mullins
money and money lending, bankers,
180, and see scriveners; bills of
exchange, 152, 178; debts and
stock of Sir J.L.(1), and Sir
J.L.(2), 9, 10, 16, 19, 21–3, 26,
35, 37–8, 41, 52, 54, 58, 60, 111,
148, 149**, 150–2, 232, and see
appendix III; interest, 79, 90,
102, 116**, 143, 144, 149–50;
interest rates, 40**, 90, [149–
150]; money on account, 111,
148, 152; money returned to
London, 188, 191; monies payable, (at Egleston), 69, 178,
(Leeds), 69**, (London), 69,
178, 183, (Marton), 178; mortgages, xi, xiv, xvi, xxii–xxiv, 10,
16**, 18, 19, 22, 26, 42, 53, 58–
74 passim, 76, 85, 108, 148–98
passim, 232, 247, 251, and see
rentals; rent charges; scriveners,
152n, 192n
Moore, Mr, of Lerpoole, [Liver-
poole], 195; Mrs, of London,
166; Giles, steward of Sir
J.L.(1), 4, 21–2, 24**, 29**, 30,
31**, 32–3, 34**, 38, 45, 50,
232; Mr Roger, of Wensleydale,
Yorks, 4, 42, 54**, 59
Moors, Wilfrid, 54
Morland, Westm, see Newby, Sleagill, Great Strickland, Little
Strickland, Thrimby
mortar pits, 82, 84
mortgages, see sub money and

Thrimby manor, Thrimby Grange and Thrimby town—*cont.*
let with stock, 90; rents, 45, 78, 81, 90, 96, 114, 120, 134, 138; mill, 17, 30, 31, 45, (purchased), 37; purchases of, 26, 28**, 36, 37**, rent, free, 79, 90, 114, 134; tenements, (Heydale's), 238, (Powley's), *see sub* Lowther manor, (Webster's), 36, (Westgarth's), 118, 120, 144, 175, 176, 180; tithe, 28**, 31; value of, 38

Thwaites, John, of Ewanrigg, 26, [219]

Thwaites (Hall Thwaits), [Millom, Cumb], animals bought/sold at, 24

Thwaites manor, xvii, 58, 84n, 185; Bailiff, [Jo Wrenington, *q.v.*], 97, 103, (account book), xxii; customary tenants (admittances), 15, (fines, running fines), 44, 55, 79, 90, 130, (rents, including forest meal, green-hew, swinetake, and walkmill silver), 29, 31–2, 43, 46, 49, 55–57, 77, 83, 88, 100, 112, 126, 130, 144, (services, including hens), 29, 44, 46**, 55, 78–9, 90, 126; demesne, called Rayslack (Rayslace, Reaslack, Reslacke), rent, 32, 34, 49, 50, 84, 102, 116, 128, 134; mill, 26, 29, 31, 43–4, 46**, 49, 50, 81, 84, 96, 102, 134; purchase of, 26; sale and mortgage, 149, 150, 175, 182, 250; value of, 3, 37

Thwaitlands, *see sub* Lowther demesne

Thynne, Sir Henry-Frederick, [1st Bt], 198; Katherine, da of, wife of 1st Viscount Lonsdale, 198; Sir Thomas, [2nd Bt], 198

timber, *see* wood

Tinckler, —, 121, 148

tithes, 234; Mr Howard's tithe, 125; Mr Layton's tithe, 31, [32]; Mr Washington's tithe, 31–2, 47–9;

and see sub Bampton, Catterlen, Egleston, Hackthorpe, Helton, Lowther, Marton, Meaburne, Newton Reigny, Newton and Allonby, Nunthorpe, Plumpton, Rosgill, *Rutford*, St Bees, Shap

Todd, [Chris], 116, 126, 178

Todhunter, Thomas, of Threlkeld, 16

Tollesby (Tolsby), Marton, Yorks, xvi, 188n; mortgage at, 184; purchase of, 37–9, 68, 240; rental, 42; rents, 43, 46, 48–9, 55

tolls, *see sub* Appleby, Bowes, Penrith

Tompson, —, 94, 119; Chris, 83; Richard, 80

town term, *see* customary tenants

trade, xiv, xvi, 40, 61, 148, 154, 170, 230, 255; with Africa, 148, 176; Levant, 152; Italy, 148

Trantran, ancient enclosure at, *see sub* Shap

Trawton, Andrew, 135

Trinity College, Cambridge, 74, 243

Trotter, [Edward], of Skelton, Yorks, m Mary da of Sir J.L.(2), 136, 142, 147–8, 155, 157**, 158**, 168, 171, 177, 189**, 247, 250

Trussels, —, 185

Tubman, Richard, 249

Tunbridge Wells (Tunbrigge Wells), [Kent], 253

Tunstall, Mr, 188

Turbary, at Helton, 70; *see also sub* commons

Tynedale, Mr, 86

Underbank, 18

Vane (Fane), Sir Henry [the elder], 64, 228

Verstigan, [Richard, antiquarian], 208

Villiers, George, Duke of Buckingham, ix, 229